MW01057088

CHRONOLOGY
OF THE
COLD WAR AT SEA
1945–1991

CHRONOLOGY
OF THE
COLD WAR AT SEA
1945–1991

NORMAN POLMAR

Eric Wertheim

Andrew Bahjat

Bruce Watson

NAVAL INSTITUTE PRESS

ANNAPOLIS, MARYLAND

Chronology of the Cold War at sea, 1945–1991 / Norman Polmar . . . [et al.].
    p.   cm.
Includes bibliographical references (p.) and index.
ISBN 1-55750-685-X (alk. paper)
    1. Naval history—20th century—Chronology.   2. Cold War—Chronology.
3. United States. Navy—History—20th century—Chronology.   4. Soviet Union.
Voenno-Morskoĭ Flot—History—20th century—Chronology.   5. Navies—
History—20th century—Chronology.   6. World politics—1945-   —Chronology.
I. Polmar, Norman.
D842.3.C48   1997
359'.009'045—dc21   97-35957

Printed in the United States of America on acid-free paper   ∞

05 04 03 02 01 00 99 98   9 8 7 6 5 4 3 2

First printing

Dedicated to the Memory of
Bruce W. Watson and Susan M. Watson

CONTENTS

PREFACE

The Cold War dominated world political, economic, and military activities for almost half of the 20th century. In many respects the Cold War was "fought" at sea.

The Cold War was a conflict fought in many arenas and in many ways, mainly between the United States and the Soviet Union—the world's two superpowers. Many stages of the Cold War also involved allies of the two superpowers; for the United States, from 1949 onward, the principal allies were the other members of the North Atlantic Treaty Organization (NATO). The Soviet Union in 1955 established a similar "defensive" alliance, the Warsaw Pact. From time to time, each superpower was aided in its endeavors against the other by members of its alliance and by nonmembers and even Third World nations as the superpowers sought to increase their respective "spheres of influence."

From the outset, the United States employed its massive naval and merchant forces to undertake campaigns to halt Soviet-inspired or -supported aggressions and to advance its own agenda. Indeed, the first major move in the Cold War occurred early in 1946 when the US battleship *Missouri* was dispatched to Turkey to demonstrate American support for nationalist forces fighting communist-led insurrections in the area. A year later the US Marshall Plan—the economic rehabilitation of Western Europe—was carried out through massive US shipping efforts, while the so-called Berlin Airlift of 1948 employed large numbers of Navy transport aircraft. The importance of naval forces to the West was fully recognized in the establishment of NATO, an effort to link allies across a broad ocean; indeed, two of the three principal commands established within the NATO structure were primarily naval organizations, the Supreme Allied Commander Atlantic and Commander in Chief Channel, with the third command being the Supreme Allied Command Europe. The last—SACEUR—

included major naval contingents in the eastern Atlantic and European waters, including the US Sixth Fleet in the Mediterranean.

While the Soviet Union emerged from World War II with virtually no oceangoing Navy, the overrunning of German shipyards, research institutes, and manufacturers of naval equipment by Soviet armies raised the specter of a massive Soviet undersea force being built. Soviet planners envisioned a force of more than 1,000 submarines, ostensibly to help defend the coastal regions of the Soviet Empire.

The Red submarine force, however, was to be just one component of a large ocean fleet conceived by Soviet dictator Josef Stalin. He envisioned a force of battle cruisers, aircraft carriers, and other surface warships as well as submarines and supporting ships that could wrest control of major sea areas from the West. Further, by the early 1950s, the Soviet Union was developing torpedoes with nuclear warheads as well as sea-launched missiles—cruise and ballistic types—to attack Western coastal ports and cities. But Stalin's massive naval buildup was aborted immediately after his death in March 1953.

By the late 1950s, however, under the direction of the indefatigable Adm. Sergei G. Gorshkov, the Soviet Union was again embarked on a naval buildup. This time the naval buildup stressed more innovative weapons and operational concepts. The Red Navy and the increasing Soviet merchant, research, and fishing fleets became major factors in the Cold War during the 1970s and 1980s.

While the Red Navy was used primarily in a political context, the Western allies did employ their fleets regularly in crises and conflicts (undoubtedly reinforcing Admiral Gorshkov's entreaties to the ruling Politburo for more funding for his fleet). The US Navy saw extensive action in the Korean War (1950–1953), the Cuban Missile Crisis (1962), and the Vietnam War (1964–1975) as well as in numerous crises and confrontations, mostly in the Third World. Other Western nations, mainly Britain and France, used warships and naval aircraft in their respective conflicts in Indochina (1946–1954) and the Falklands (1982), and together in the ill-fated Suez Campaign (1956).

While most of these conflicts involved Soviet surrogates and Soviet weapons were employed extensively, often carried to the conflict area in Soviet or Warsaw Pact merchant ships. In the Korean and Vietnam conflicts, however, there was direct Soviet participation—MiG-15 pilots in Korea and air defense personnel in Vietnam—resulting in direct fighting between US naval forces and Soviets. And, of course, in the Cuban military buildup of 1962, Soviet and Warsaw Pact merchant ships transported almost 42,000 troops and advisors to Cuba, plus massive amounts of military equipment, aircraft, and missiles; also 134 nuclear warheads—unknown to American intelligence at the time—were landed in Cuba. (Another 24 warheads reached a Cuban port but were not landed.)

Still another aspect of the Cold War was the insatiable quest for intelligence by the opposing superpowers. For the US Navy this meant submarines operating in Soviet waters, and naval aircraft flying along the periphery of Eurasia, resulting in numerous attacks against Navy reconnaissance aircraft by Soviet, Chinese, and North Korean forces; for the Soviet Navy reconnaissance against the West was carried out by submarines and by spy ships—mostly converted fishing ship designs (but *not* disguised as fishing craft). The brief US effort to employ passive intelligence collection ships led to two disasters—the *Pueblo* and *Liberty*.

And, from the early 1960s, overlaying the Cold War environment, the Soviet Union and United States (and subsequently Britain and France) employed nuclear-propelled submarines armed with strategic missiles. The sea-based missiles provided the most survivable and hence most stable element of the strategic nuclear balance.

Thus, at all levels of the lengthy Cold War, from political confrontation, to economic assistance, to countering crises and actual conflict, naval and maritime forces had vital roles.

In addition, the US Navy and Marine Corps were active participants throughout the Cold War in a vast number of research and development programs. Four naval aviators were among the first seven American astronauts, with a Navy officer being the first American in space and a Marine officer the first to orbit the earth. (Mercury, Gemini, Apollo, and Skylab spacecraft were recovered at sea by Navy and Coast Guard ships.) The Navy led in the exploration of the Arctic and Antarctic regions and provided support for nonmilitary activities in those areas. And, the Navy's bathyscaph *Trieste I* reached the deepest-known ocean depths to date.

The *Chronology of the Cold War at Sea, 1945–1991* details the numerous maritime operations of the superpowers and their allies.

This book is a product of the United States Naval Institute's summer intern program. This effort could not have been undertaken without the early, strong, and continued support of Fred Rainbow, Editor in Chief of the Naval Institute *Proceedings*, Barbara Broadhurst, Naval Institute personnel officer, and during its formative period, Jim Sutton, Director of Marketing for the Naval Institute Press.

Others who assisted the authors include John C. Reilly, Bernard F. Cavalcante, Ella Nargele, Kathy Lloyd, Jeffrey Barlow, and Richard Russell of the Naval Historical Center; Capt. Ken Crandall of Navy Fighter Squadron 32; Master Chief Quartermaster Michael Harrison and Chief Journalist David Rourk of the USS *Enterprise*; Rear Adm. Alfred G. Harms, Jr., US Central Command; Comdr. Frans Kuipers, Office of Naval Intelligence; Vice Adm. Joseph T. Metcalf; Rear Adm. Harry T. Rittenour, Director, Carriers and Programs Branch, Office of the Chief of Naval Operations; researcher Samuel Loring Morison; and Jacquelyn Day and Mark Gatlin of the U.S. Naval Institute.

The authors are in debt to the staff of the Naval Institute Press for their efforts in publishing this book, especially J. Randall Baldini, Paul Wilderson, Linda O'Doughda, and Susan Artigiani, and freelance editor Deborah Patton.

Norman Polmar
Eric Wertheim
Andrew Bahjat
Bruce Watson

GLOSSARY

AFB	Air Force Base		MSTS	Military Sea Transportation Service (later MSC)
ANZUS	Australia-New Zealand-United States (treaty)		NAF	Naval Air Facility
ASROC	Anti-Submarine Rocket		NAS	Naval Air Station
ASW	Anti-Submarine Warfare		NASA	National Aeronautics and Space Administration
CIA	Central Intelligence Agency		NATO	North Atlantic Treaty Organization
CO	Commanding Officer		NROTC	Naval Reserve Officer Training Corps
COD	Carrier On-board Delivery		NS	Nuclear Ship
COIN	Counter-Insurgency		RAF	Royal Air Force
DARPA	Defense Advanced Research Projects Agency		RN	Royal Navy
DMZ	Demilitarized Zone (Vietnam)		ROTC	Reserve Officer Training Corps
DOD	Department of Defense		RPV	Remotely Piloted Vehicle
DSRV	Deep Submergence Rescue Vehicle		SEAL	Sea-Air-Land (team)
FY	Fiscal Year		SEATO	Southeast Asia Treaty Organization
GLCM	Ground-Launched Cruise Missile		SES	Surface Effect Ship
ICBM	Intercontinental Ballistic Missile		SLBM	Submarine-Launched Ballistic Missile
INF	Intermediate-range Nuclear Force		STOL	Short Take-Off and Landing
IRBM	Intermediate-Range Ballistic Missile		SU	Soviet Union
JATO	Jet Assisted Take-Off		SUBROC	Submarine Rocket
MAB	Marine Amphibious Brigade (later MEB)		ULMS	Underwater Long-range Missile System (later named Trident)
MAC	Military Airlift Command (formerly MATS)		UN	United Nations
MACV	Military Advisory Command Vietnam		USA	US Army
			USAAF	US Army Air Forces
MATS	Military Air Transport Service (later MAC)		USAF	US Air Force
			USCG	US Coast Guard
MAU	Marine Amphibious Unit (later MEU)		USMC	US Marine Corps
MEB	Marine Expeditionary Brigade (formerly MAB)		USN	US Navy
			USNR	US Naval Reserve
MEU	Marine Expeditionary Unit (formerly MAU)		USS	US Ship
			VSTOL	Vertical/Short Take-Off and Landing
MSC	Military Sealift Command (formerly MSTS)		VTOL	Vertical Take-Off and Landing
			WAVE	Women Accepted for Volunteer Emergency Service (U.S. Navy)

GLOSSARY OF
SHIP DESIGNATIONS

Note: The prefix "T-" was assigned to ships of the Military Sea Transportation Service (later Military Sealift Command).

AF	store ship	CB	large (battle) cruiser
AFS	combat store ship	CC	national command ship
AG	miscellaneous auxiliary	CG	guided missile cruiser
AGB	icebreaker	CGN	guided missile cruiser (nuclear propulsion)
AGC	amphibious command ship (later LCC)	CL	light cruiser
AGM	missile range instrumentation ship	CLAA	anti-aircraft cruiser
AGMR	communications relay ship	CLC	tactical command ship
AGOS	ocean surveillance ship	CLG	guided missile light cruiser
AGS	surveying ship	CV	aircraft carrier
AH	hospital ship	CVA	attack aircraft carrier
AK	cargo ship	CVA	heavy aircraft carrier (only *United States*/CVA 58)
AKA	attack cargo ship (later LKA)		
AKS	stores-issue ship	CVAN	attack aircraft carrier (nuclear propulsion)
AKV	cargo ship and aircraft ferry		
AM	minesweeper	CVB	large (battle) aircraft carrier
AMS	auxiliary motor minesweeper	CVE	escort aircraft carrier
AO	oiler	CVHE	helicopter escort aircraft carrier
AOE	fast combat support ship	CVL	small (light) aircraft carrier
AOG	gasoline tanker	CVN	multipurpose aircraft carrier (nuclear propulsion)
AOR	replenishment oiler		
AOT	transport oiler	CVS	anti-submarine aircraft carrier
AP	transport	CVT	training aircraft carrier
APA	amphibious transport (later LPA)	CVU	utility aircraft carrier
APD	amphibious transport (small)	DD	destroyer
APD	high-speed transport	DDG	guided missile destroyer
ARVH	helicopter repair ship	DE	escort ship
AS	submarine tender	DEG	guided missile escort ship
ASR	submarine rescue vessel	DER	radar picket escort ship
AV	seaplane tender	DL	frigate
AVG	aircraft escort vessel (later CVE)	DLG	guided missile frigate
AVM	guided missile (test) ship	DLGN	guided missile frigate (nuclear propulsion)
AVS	aviation supply ship		
AVT	auxiliary aircraft transport	DMS	destroyer-minesweeper
AVT	auxiliary aircraft landing/training ship	FFG	guided missile frigate
BB	battleship	IFS	inshore fire support ship
CA	heavy cruiser	IX	miscellaneous unclassified
CAG	guided missile heavy cruiser		

LCAC	landing craft air cushioned		PBR	river patrol boat
LCC	amphibious command ship		PCF	fast patrol craft (Swift)
LCU	utility landing craft		SS	submarine
LHA	amphibious assault ship (general purpose)		SSBN	ballistic missile submarine (nuclear propulsion)
LHD	amphibious assault ship (multipurpose)		SSG	guided missile submarine
LPA	amphibious transport		SSGN	guided missile submarine (nuclear propulsion)
LPD	amphibious transport dock			
LPH	amphibious assault ship (helicopter carrier)		SSK	hunter-killer submarine
			SSN	attack submarine (nuclear propulsion)
LSD	dock landing ship		SSR	radar picket submarine
LST	tank landing ship		SSRN	radar picket submarine (nuclear propulsion)
LSV*	vehicle cargo ship (later AKR)			
MSB	minesweeping boat		WAGB	Coast Guard icebreaker
MSC	coastal minesweeper		WHEC	Coast Guard high-endurance cutter
MSO	ocean minesweeper		WPB	Coast Guard patrol boat
PACV	patrol air-cushion vehicle		WPG	Coast Guard cutter

* Formerly vehicle landing ship; from 1956 assigned to vehicle cargo ships (later AKR).

MILITARY LEADERSHIP

Union of Soviet Socialist Republics

Minister of Defense

After World War II, in 1946, the Soviet Army and Navy were unified in the Commissariat for the Armed Forces. The Navy again had a brief period of independence, but immediately following Stalin's death in March 1953 the current, unified Ministry of Defense was established.

Mar 1953–Feb 1955	Marshal of the Soviet Union Nikolai Bulganin
Feb 1955–Oct 1957	Marshal of the Soviet Union Georgi Zhukov
Oct 1957–Mar 1967	Marshal of the Soviet Union Rodion Ya. Malinovsky
Apr 1967–Apr 1976	Marshal of the Soviet Union Andrei A. Grechko
Apr 1976–Dec 1984	Marshal of the Soviet Union Dmitri F. Ustinov
Dec 1984–May 1987	Marshal of the Soviet Union Sergey L. Sokolov
May 1987–Aug 1991	Marshal of the Soviet Union Dmitri T. Yazov*
Aug 1991	Army Gen. Mikhail Moiseyev†
Aug 1991–May 1992	Marshal of Aviation Yevgeni I. Shaposhnikov

Commander in Chief, Naval Forces and Deputy Minister of Defense

Apr 1939–Jan 1947	Adm. Nikolai G. Kuznetsov
Jan 1947–July 1951	Adm. I. S. Yumashev
July 1951–Jan 1956	Adm. of the Fleet of the Soviet Union Nikolai G. Kuznetsov
Jan 1956–Dec 1985	Adm. of the Fleet of the Soviet Union Sergei G. Gorshkov
Dec 1985–Dec 1991	Adm. of the Fleet Vladimir N. Chernavin

United States

Secretary of Defense

Sep 1947–Mar 1949	James V. Forrestal
Mar 1949–Sep 1950	Louis Johnson
Sep 1950–Sep 1951	Gen. of the Army George C. Marshall, USA
Sep 1951–Jan 1953	Robert A. Lovett
Jan 1953–Oct 1957	Charles E. Wilson
Oct 1957–Dec 1959	Neil H. McElroy

* Promoted from General of the Army to Marshal of the Soviet Union on 29 Apr 1990.
† Moiseyev served as Minister of Defense for less than 24 hours following the Aug 1991 attempted coup against Mikhail Gorbachev.

Dec 1959–Jan 1961	Thomas S. Gates, Jr.
Jan 1961–Feb 1968	Robert S. McNamara
Mar 1968–Jan 1969	Clark M. Clifford
Jan 1969–Jan 1973	Melvin R. Laird
Jan 1973–May 1973	Elliot L. Richardson
July 1973–Nov 1975	James R. Schlesinger
Nov 1975–Jan 1977	Donald H. Rumsfeld
Jan 1977–Jan 1981	Harold Brown
Jan 1981–Nov 1987	Caspar W. Weinberger
Nov 1987–Jan 1989	Frank C. Carlucci
Mar 1989–Jan 1993	Dick Cheney

Chairman of the Joint Chiefs of Staff

July 1942–Mar 1949	Fleet Adm. William D. Leahy, USN*
Aug 1949–Aug 1953	Gen. of the Army Omar N. Bradley, USA†
Aug 1953–Aug 1957	Adm. Arthur W. Radford, USN
Aug 1957–Sep 1960	Gen. Nathan F. Twining, USAF
Oct 1960–Sep 1962	Gen. Lyman L. Lemnitzer, USA
Oct 1962–July 1964	Gen. Maxwell D. Taylor, USA
July 1964–July 1970	Gen. Earle G. Wheeler, USA
July 1970–June 1974	Adm. Thomas H. Moorer, USN
Julu 1974–June 1978	Gen. George S. Brown, USAF
June 1978–June 1982	Gen. David C. Jones, USAF
June 1982–Sep 1985	Gen. John W. Vessey, Jr., USA
Oct 1985–Sep 1989	Adm. William J. Crowe, Jr., USN
Oct 1989–Oct 1993	Gen. Colin L. Powell, USA

Secretary of the Navy

May 1944–Sep 1947	James V. Forrestal
Sep 1947–May 1949	John L. Sullivan
May 1949–July 1951	Francis P. Matthews
July 1951–Jan 1953	Dan A. Kimball
Feb 1953–May 1954	Robert B. Anderson
May 1954–Mar 1957	Charles S. Thomas
Apr 1957–June 1959	Thomas S. Gates, Jr.
June 1959–Jan 1961	William B. Franke
Jan 1961–Dec 1961	John B. Connally
Jan 1962–Nov 1963	Fred H. Korth
Nov 1963–June 1967	Paul H. Nitze
Sep 1967–Jan 1969	Paul R. Ignatius
Jan 1969–May 1972	John H. Chafee
May 1972–Apr 1974	John W. Warner

* Chief of Staff to the President from 1942 to 1949, he was *de facto* Chairman of the Joint Chiefs of Staff in that period; promoted to Fleet Admiral on 15 Dec 1944.
† Promoted to General of the Army on 22 Sep 1950.

June 1974–Feb 1977	J. William Middendorf
Feb 1977–Oct 1979	W. Graham Claytor, Jr.
Oct 1979–Jan 1981	Edward Hidalgo
Feb 1981–Apr 1987	John F. Lehman, Jr.
Apr 1987–Feb 1988	James H. Webb, Jr.
Mar 1988–May 1989	William L. Ball III
May 1989–June 1992	H. Lawrence Garrett III

Chief of Naval Operations

Mar 1942–Dec 1945	Fleet Adm. Ernest J. King, USN*
Dec 1945–Dec 1947	Fleet Adm. Chester W. Nimitz, USN
Dec 1947–Nov 1949	Adm. Louis E. Denfeld, USN
Nov 1949–July 1951	Adm. Forrest P. Sherman, USN
Aug 1951–Aug 1953	Adm. William M. Fechteler, USN
Aug 1953–Aug 1955	Adm. Robert B. Carney, USN
Aug 1955–Aug 1961	Adm. Arleigh A. Burke, USN
Aug 1961–July 1963	Adm. George W. Anderson, Jr., USN
Aug 1963–July 1967	Adm. David L. McDonald, USN
Aug 1967–July 1970	Adm. Thomas H. Moorer, USN
July 1970–June 1974	Adm. Elmo R. Zumwalt, Jr., USN
June 1974–July 1978	Adm. James L. Holloway III, USN
July 1978–June 1982	Adm. Thomas B. Hayward, USN
June 1982–June 1986	Adm. James D. Watkins, USN
June 1986–June 1990	Adm. Carlisle A. H. Trost, USN
June 1990–Apr 1994	Adm. Frank B. Kelso II, USN

Commandant of the Marine Corps

Jan 1944–Dec 1947	Gen. Alexander A. Vandegrift, USMC†
Jan 1948–Dec 1951	Gen. Clifton B. Cates, USMC
Jan 1952–Dec 1955	Gen. Lemuel C. Shepherd, Jr., USMC
Jan 1956–Dec 1959	Gen. Randolph McC. Pate, USMC
Jan 1960–Dec 1963	Gen. David M. Shoup, USMC
Jan 1964–Dec 1967	Gen. Wallace M. Greene, Jr., USMC
Jan 1968–Dec 1971	Gen. Leonard F. Chapman, Jr., USMC
Jan 1972–June 1975	Gen. Robert E. Cushman, Jr., USMC
July 1975–June 1979	Gen. Louis H. Wilson, Jr., USMC
July 1979–June 1983	Gen. Robert H. Barrow, USMC
June 1983–June 1987	Gen. Paul X. Kelley, USMC
July 1987–June 1991	Gen. Alfred M. Gray, Jr., USMC
July 1991–June 1995	Gen. Carl E. Mundy, Jr., USMC

* King became Commander in Chief US Fleet (COMINCH) on 30 Dec 1941; by Executive Order that position and Chief of Naval Operations were combined on 18 Mar 1942. In 1945 the position of COMINCH ceased to exist. King was promoted to Fleet Admiral on 17 Dec 1944.

† Promoted to general in Mar 1945.

Commandant of the Coast Guard

June 1936–Dec 1945	Adm. Russell R. Waesche, USCG*
Jan 1946–Dec 1949	Adm. Joseph F. Farley, USCG
Jan 1950–May 1954	Vice Adm. Merlin O'Neill, USCG
June 1954–May 1962	Adm. Alfred C. Richmond, USCG†
June 1962–May 1966	Adm. Edwin J. Roland, USCG
May 1966–May 1970	Adm. Willard J. Smith, USCG
June 1970–May 1974	Adm. Chester R. Bender, USCG
June 1974–May 1978	Adm. Owen W. Siler, USCG
June 1978–May 1982	Adm. John B. Hayes, USCG
May 1982–May 1986	Adm. James S. Gracey, USCG
May 1986–May 1990	Adm. Paul A. Yost, Jr., USCG
May 1990–May 1994	Adm. J. William Kime, USCG

* Appointed commandant with the rank of rear admiral; promoted to vice admiral on 10 Mar 1942 and to admiral on 4 Apr 1945.

† Promoted to admiral on 1 June 1960.

CHRONOLOGY
OF THE
COLD WAR AT SEA
1945–1991

1945

2 SEP

World War II ends with the Japanese surrender on board the US battleship *Missouri* (BB 63) at anchor in Tokyo Bay. Gen. of the Army Douglas MacArthur, USA, the Supreme Commander for Allied Powers, accepts the Japanese surrender. Fleet Adm. Chester W. Nimitz, USN, signs on behalf of the United States.

7 SEP

The American flag is raised on Wake Island after the surrender of the approximately 1,200 Japanese troops on the bypassed atoll by Rear Adm. Sakaibara Shigematsu. Resistance to the Japanese assault by US Navy and Marine personnel in Dec 1941 had been a brief, tragic—but inspiring—event in the war.

8 SEP

US troops land at Jintsen near Seoul, the capital of Korea.

9 SEP

All Japanese forces in China, northern Indochina, and Formosa are surrendered in ceremonies at Nanking, China.

10 SEP

The large carrier *Midway* (CVB 41) is placed in commission at Norfolk, Va. At the time the *Midway* is the largest aircraft carrier in the world and at 45,000 tons standard displacement is the largest warship yet built except for the three ships of the Japanese *Yamato* class. Two additional carriers of this class are under construction, the *Franklin D. Roosevelt* (CVB 42) and *Coral Sea* (CVB 43). The *Midway*'s first CO is Capt. Joseph F. Bolger, USN.

12 SEP

All Japanese forces in Southeast Asia surrender in ceremonies at Singapore.

20 SEP

British Field Marshal Sir Henry (Jumbo) Wilson, Chief of the British Joint Mission to Washington, issues a statement to the press predicting that the Soviets will have atomic weapons within the next five years. Wilson asserts that the atomic bomb "will make Russia the most powerful nation on Earth. With the United States curtailing its military forces in Europe and by limiting the size of its future draft,

there is nothing to prevent Russia from becoming master of that area."

The world's first turboprop aircraft flies in Britain. The turbojet Gloster Meteor was refitted with Rolls-Royce Trent prop-jet engines for the flight.

21 SEP

President Harry S. Truman directs that the Office of Strategic Services (OSS) be disbanded. Its activities will be taken over by the State and War Departments. The OSS was the nation's wartime intelligence agency, established in June 1942 under the Joint Chiefs of Staff.

22 SEP

President Truman signs the Federal Register giving approval to the term *World War II* as the official government designation for the recently ended conflict.

23 SEP

General Order 223 reorganizes the Office of the Chief of Naval Operations (OPNAV). The Office of Naval Material (NAVMAT) is created as well as five Deputy Chiefs of Naval Operations (DCNO): Personnel (OP-01), Administration (OP-02), Naval Operations (OP-03), Logistics (OP-04), and Naval Aviation (OP-05). This basic structure, albeit with many changes, will survive until July 1992. The order is implemented on 10 Oct 1945.

25 SEP

Vice Adm. Louis E. Denfield, USN, Chief of Naval Personnel, informs Congress that the postwar Navy requires 58,000 officers and 500,000 enlisted men.

Adm. Thomas Kinkaid, USN, announces that the Seventh Fleet will take over the responsibilities of the old Asiatic Fleet as the US naval presence in the Far East.

27 SEP

Rep. Carl Vinson (D-Ga.), Chairman of the House Naval Affairs Committee, addresses the military unification question by stating "There is no chance of merging the Army and Navy. The two services should remain both separate and distinct."

28 SEP

Gen. Alexander A. Vandegrift, USMC, Commandant of the Marine Corps, in testimony before Congress, calls for a peacetime Marine Corps of 9,200 officers and 100,000 enlisted men. Vandegrift further states that the Marines should be used as "a modern-day Minuteman, held in readiness to strike hard at any attempt to disrupt the peace of the world."

29 SEP
President Truman issues Executive Order 9635, decreeing that the Chief of Naval Operations (CNO) is the senior uniformed officer of the Navy and tasks him as principal naval advisor to the President and the Secretary of the Navy. The order eliminates the post of Commander in Chief US Fleet (COMINCH), combining the COMINCH fleet operational functions with the planning responsibilities of CNO. The positions of COMINCH and CNO had been combined in 1942; Fleet Adm. Ernest J. King, USN, had held these posts since Apr 1942.

2 OCT
Vice Adm. Marc A. Mitscher, USN, Deputy Chief of Naval Operations (Air), announces Navy plans to train 3,000 naval aviators a year in addition to 2,000 air crewmen.

3 OCT
The Navy's Bureau of Aeronautics forms a special committee to study the feasibility of placing a satellite in orbit around the Earth.

5 OCT
The final tally of US Navy warship losses in World War II is made public. The list includes 696 ships of all types, including two battleships (BB), five fleet aircraft carriers (CV-CVL), six escort carriers (CVE), seven heavy cruisers (CA), three light cruisers (CL-CLAA), 71 destroyers (DD), and 52 submarines (SS).

10 OCT
The post of Commander in Chief US Fleet (COMINCH) is officially abolished and command of naval operating forces is transferred to the Chief of Naval Operations (CNO). The positions of COMINCH and CNO had been combined in March 1942.

15 OCT
A Soviet fighter aircraft fires on a US Navy PBM Mariner flying boat on a reconnaissance flight near Soviet-occupied Port Arthur. The aircraft was monitoring Japanese ships evacuating troops from North China. The Soviet plane "buzzed" the Mariner when

it was approximately two miles (three km) off the China coast and opened fire when the PBM was 40 n.miles (74 km) south of Port Arthur.

17 OCT
The prefix symbol K for pilotless aircraft (drones) is added to the US Navy's basic aircraft designation system.

22 OCT
The US government asserts that the Soviet Union is in violation of the Yalta Accords by signing an economic trade treaty with Hungary without Allied consultation. (President Franklin D. Roosevelt, Prime Minister Winston S. Churchill, and Marshal Joseph Stalin reached agreements on the future of Europe at Yalta in the Soviet Crimea in Feb 1945.)

27 OCT
President Truman is present at the Navy Day commissioning of the aircraft carrier *Franklin D. Roosevelt* at the New York Navy Yard in Brooklyn, N.Y. He then reviews the fleet at anchor in a seven-mile (11-km) line in New York harbor from the destroyer *Renshaw* (DD 499) and, in a speech given in Central Park, Truman pays tribute to the Navy and states US foreign policy objectives. The first commanding officer of the "FDR" is Capt. Apollo Soucek, USN.

28 OCT
Communist Chinese troops fire on the barge of Vice Adm. Daniel E. Barbey, USN, Commander Amphibious Forces, Seventh Fleet, as he attempts to land at the port of Hulutalo in Manchuria. This is the first indication that Chinese troops and not Soviet Army units are garrisoning Manchuria.

29 OCT
Rep. Vinson proposes a peacetime Navy of 297 active ships including five battleships, ten fleet carriers, and ten escort carriers.

30 OCT
The initial War Department proposal for defense unification is submitted to Congress. The proposal, written by Lt. Gen. J. Lawton Collins, USA, does not absorb naval aviation into a separate air force and the Marine Corps is not folded into the Army.

5 NOV
Rear Adm. James L. Holloway II, USN, proposes a doubling of Naval Academy enrollment from 3,000 midshipmen to 6,000 and increasing NROTC/college

training to 20,000 men. The goal is for an officer corps with an equal split between Annapolis and civilian trained officers to allow for "flexibility of thought in this atomic age."

First landing by a jet-propelled aircraft on an aircraft carrier takes place aboard the US escort carrier *Wake Island* (CVE 65) by a Ryan FR-1 Fireball piloted by Ens. Jake C. West, USN. The Fireball, a combination piston-turbojet aircraft, suffers a reciprocating engine failure as it is about to land and West starts his jet engine to come aboard the ship.

The USS *Williamsburg* (AGC 369, former PG 56) is designated as the presidential yacht. The *Williamsburg*, built in 1930 as the private yacht *Aras*, served as a convoy escort in World War II. She replaces the ex–Coast Guard cutter *Potomac* (AG 25).

7 NOV

World speed record of 606.25 mph (975.5 kmh) is set by Group Capt. H. J. Wilson, RAF, in a Gloster Meteor. (The previous record was 469.142 mph/754.85 kmh flown by German pilot Fritz Wendel in an Me 109R on 26 Apr 1939.)

9 NOV

Lt. Gen. James H. Doolittle, USA, testifies to Congress that "Aircraft Carriers are going into obsolescence having reached their peak of usefulness. Carriers have two attributes; they can move around and they can be sunk." As an aside, Doolittle also adds that the B-29, not naval aviation, was the prime cause of Japanese capitulation.

13 NOV

In order to counter pro-unification testimony before Congress by Gens. Doolittle and Dwight D. Eisenhower, Secretary of the Navy James V. Forrestal recalls Fleet Adm. Nimitz from Hawaii to state the Navy's views before Congress.

14 NOV

The New York Times reports that President Truman and British Prime Minister Clement Atlee would agree to turn over the secrets of the atomic bomb to the United Nations, providing the Soviets also "throw all of her military secrets into the pool."

15 NOV

Gen. Henry (Hap) Arnold, USA, Chief of the Army Air Forces, demands that the Navy let the AAF have a role in the forthcoming atomic bomb tests at Bikini Atoll. The AAF, as the sole military service with expe-

rience in atomic warfare, he contends, desires to set the conditions under which the tests will be conducted ". . . so as to leave no questions unanswered as to the effect of the atomic bomb on ships."

A joint congressional committee in Washington opens the major postwar investigation of the Pearl Harbor attack.

16 NOV

Fleet Adm. King testifies before Congress that the rapid demobilization of the Navy is causing a major disintegration of capability. According to King "the Navy currently could not fight a major battle."

17 NOV

Appearing before Congress, Fleet Adm. Nimitz addresses the defense unification issue by stating that "Unification would hinder the Navy and reduce the role of sea power in the nation's defense." Nimitz also states that "A separate Air Force is no more needed than a special agency to control submarines."

20 NOV

During a press conference at the White House, President Truman announces that he will be sending a message to Congress urging unification of the land, sea, and air forces. No commissions will be appointed to study the issue, the President says, because Congress is the organization to decide such matters. Truman adds that he is irritated with "The scrambled military set-up which is an open invitation to catastrophe."

An unrefueled, nonstop distance record flight of 8,198 miles (13,190 km) is achieved by a B-29 Superfortress flying from Guam to Washington, D.C., in 35 hours, 5 minutes.

23 NOV

The rationing of meat and butter ends in the United States.

30 NOV

All US Navy Yards are redesignated as Naval Shipyards except for the Navy Yard in Washington, D.C.

3 DEC

A British Vampire I fighter piloted by Lt. Comdr. Eric M. Brown, RN, traps aboard the light fleet carrier *Ocean,* the first landing of a "pure" jet-propelled aircraft on a carrier. (*See* 5 Nov 1945.)

4 DEC

Secretary of the Navy Forrestal announces that henceforth at least one-half of all staff positions in the

Office of the Chief of Naval Operations are to be filled by naval aviators. Additionally, naval aviators would be considered to be as eligible for fleet commands as are other line officers. In effect, this ends the prewar dominance of the surface warfare or "gun club" admirals.

5 DEC
Five US Navy TBM Avenger torpedo planes, on a training flight from Fort Lauderdale, Fla., with 14 on board, are lost just off the Florida coast. The duration of the careful search for the wreckage led the press to contend that the planes were lost in the infamous Bermuda Triangle.

10 DEC
The Navy and War Departments announce that they will conduct joint tests of atomic bombs against warships. *The New York Times* editorial page states that the results will "determine the fate of seapower in an atomic era."

12 DEC
Secretary of the Navy Forrestal submits the "Navy Plan for National Security." Highlights include formation of a National Security Council comprised of the Secretaries of War, Navy, and State to which the JCS will report. As is typical of Navy thinking at the time, the service secretaries would remain at the cabinet level, with no unified single military department or department head.

19 DEC
Capt. Charles B. McVay III, USN, late CO of the US cruiser *Indianapolis* (CA 35), is acquitted by a Navy court martial of charges that he failed to give prompt orders to abandon the warship after being torpedoed by a Japanese submarine. He is found guilty of failing to zig-zag during the ship's transit from Tinian to the Philippines.

First flight of the Grumman XTB3F-1, prototype for the AF Guardian aircraft, a specialized carrier-based anti-submarine aircraft (which will be produced in radar detection and attack variants).

28 DEC
The US Coast Guard is transferred from the Navy and returned to the jurisdiction of the Treasury Department. The Coast Guard had been transferred to the Navy on 1 Nov 1941.

1946

24 JAN

The newly completed British light fleet carrier *Warrior* is transferred to the Canadian Navy. This is the first of several British aircraft carrier transfers to the Argentine, Australian, Brazilian, Canadian, Dutch, and Indian navies.

23 FEB

Chief of Naval Operations Adm. Chester W. Nimitz, USN, announces the final disposition of the *Indianapolis* (CA 35) affair. Secretary of the Navy James V. Forrestal "has remitted the sentence of Captain [Charles B.] McVay [III, USN,] in its entirety, releasing him from arrest and restoring him to duty." Asked by the press if there had ever been an officer in Navy history who had been court-martialed and later promoted to flag rank, Nimitz pointed to himself. (He had been court-martialed for running a destroyer aground in 1908.)

25 FEB

The Soviet government changes the People's Commissariat for Defense to the People's Commissariat for the Armed Forces, absorbing the previously independent Commissariat for the Navy.

The Main Political Directorate for the Soviet Armed Forces is established with subordinate political directorates formed for the Ground Forces, Air Forces, Navy, and Long-Range Aviation. This organization provides a separate chain-of-command from the Communist Party down to all levels of the military structure.

28 FEB

French troops in Saigon embark in the aircraft carrier *Bearn* and several naval transports for movement north to occupy Haiphong in Indochina. Chinese troops entered north Indochina in late 1945 as occupying Japanese troops were disarmed and surrendered.

1 MAR

The US Eighth Fleet is established as the carrier strike force of the Atlantic Fleet. Adm. Marc A. Mitscher, USN, assumes command of the force at Norfolk, Va., on board the USS *Lake Champlain* (CV 39).

The large carrier *Midway* (CVB 41) with portions of Air Group 74 on board departs Norfolk with three destroyers, under the command of Rear Adm. John H. Cassady, USN, to conduct cold-weather tests in the Davis Strait. Operating off the coast of Labrador and above the Arctic Circle from 7–22 Mar 1946, this evaluation of carrier operations in Arctic waters is called Operation Frostbite.

5 MAR

The conversion of two submarines to launch the Loon, American version of the German V-1 missile, is approved by Secretary of the Navy Forrestal. The diesel-electric submarines *Tunny* (SS 282) and *Cusk* (SS 348) will be selected for conversion to this role.

6 MAR

The French naval force approaching Haiphong is taken under fire by Chinese artillery. The light cruiser *Le Triomphant* is hit as is the carrier *Bearn*.

7 MAR

Operation Frostbite commences off the coast of Labrador with air operations from the carrier *Midway*. The exercise demonstrates that cold-weather carrier operations are feasible, although the inclement weather reduced the operational tempo. The task force will return to Norfolk on 22 Mar.

8 MAR

Some 4,000 French troops move ashore in Haiphong, Indochina. Another 8,500 disembark during the next two days. The French landing in northern Indochina forces the withdrawal of the majority of Chinese troops by the summer.

11 MAR

The symbols B for Bomber and T for Torpedo for US naval aircraft are dropped from the designation scheme in favor of the all inclusive A for Attack aircraft (e.g., the Douglas BTD-1 will become the AD Skyraider). However, the B is retained in existing patrol aircraft designations, as PBM Mariner and PB4Y-2 Privateer. (The PB designation aircraft will be changed to P in 1951; *also see* 15 May 1946.)

14 MAR

Secretary of the Navy Forrestal sends a letter to Secretary of War Robert Patterson stating that the Navy desires to undertake the engineering development of atomic power plants for ship propulsion. At that time all US nuclear activities are under the aegis of the Army's Manhattan Project.

15 MAR

The Soviet People's Commissariat for the Armed Forces is changed to the Ministry of the Armed Forces as the Soviet government adopts Western titles for its ministries.

16 MAR

Former British Prime Minister Winston S. Churchill, speaking at Westminster College in Fulton, Mo., declares that "From Stettin in the Baltic to Trieste in the Adriatic, an Iron Curtain has descended across the continent [of Europe]." President Harry S. Truman is in attendance.

21 MAR

The US Army Air Forces establishes the Strategic Air Command (SAC) under Gen. George C. Kenney, USA. SAC will subsequently become a US specified command (*see* 1 Jan 1959).

22 MAR

The US battleship *Missouri* (BB 63) departs New York with the remains of Melmet Munir Ertegun, the Turkish ambassador who died in Washington, D.C., in 1944, and was temporarily buried at Arlington National Cemetery. The warship sets course for the Strait of Gibraltar en route for Istanbul.

25 MAR

The first US twin-engine helicopter, the McDonnell XHJD-1, makes its first hovering flight. The Navy-developed helicopter is intended for experimental use as a prototype for use in utility and air-sea rescue.

29 MAR

Dr. Phillip Abelson, working for the US Naval Research Laboratory, submits a report to the Atomic Energy Commission entitled "Atomic Energy Submarine" that describes the feasibility of constructing an undersea craft capable of up to 30 knots underwater for years without refueling. Given sufficient financial support, Dr. Abelson predicts that such a craft could be operational in two years.

5 APR

The battleship *Missouri* anchors in the Bosphorus off Istanbul, Turkey. The *Missouri,* accompanied by the light cruiser *Providence* (CL 82) and the destroyer *Power* (DD 839), flies the flag of Adm. H. Kent Hewitt, USN, Commander, US Naval Forces Europe. The backdrop of the voyage is the increasing Communist activity in Greece and Turkey; American

newspaper columnist Walter Lippman writes: "With the *Missouri* treated as a symbol of our power in the Mediterranean, we can make it unmistakably clear in Moscow just what we believe the outer limits of their expansion are."

11 APR

The Joint Planning Staff presents a report to the US Joint Chiefs of Staff describing their estimates of the possibility of a major conflict with the Soviet Union. They conclude that the Soviets would overrun most of Europe, the Middle East, Korea, Manchuria, and China in a major war. In this scenario, the first US task would be to get as many US troops out of the way of the initial Soviet onslaught as quickly as possible (in effect, a global "Dunkirk"). Afterward, the Navy would secure bases on the periphery of the Eurasian land mass (i.e., Iceland, Britain, Japan, Greenland, the Aleutians) from which a massive strategic bombing campaign would be waged against the Soviets.

18 APR

The US Navy's Blue Angels flight demonstration team is established at Pensacola, Fla. Grumman F6F-5 Hellcat fighters are the initial plane flown by the team.

25 APR

The *Vanguard,* with a standard displacement of 44,500 tons and 51,450 tons full load, the last battleship and the largest warship to be built by Great Britain, is completed at the John Brown shipyard. Her main armament of eight 15-inch (380-mm) guns came from storage, having been previously fitted in the World War I battle cruisers *Courageous* and *Glorious.*

15 MAY

US Navy patrol squadrons revert to the prewar designation VP in place of VPB (patrol bomber squadron).

22 MAY

The first operational tests of the XCF "dipping" sonar are conducted off Key West, Fla., by a US Navy HO2S helicopter. The sonar provides a high degree of bearing accuracy against submarines.

24 JUNE

North American Aviation receives a contract from the US Navy for the design and construction of three XAJ-1 aircraft, beginning the active development of nuclear-capable aircraft for the Navy. The aircraft will later be named Savage.

30 JUNE

Ten months after the end of World War II, the US nuclear arsenal consists of nine nuclear components and assemblies for Fat Man–type weapons designated Mk 3. (The original Fat Man and Little Boy designs had the first two numerical places, although they were not given numerical designations.)

1 JULY

At Bikini Atoll in the Marshall Islands, a B-29 named *Dave's Dream*, piloted by Maj. Woodrow P. Swancutt, USA, drops a Mk 3 atomic bomb that detonates 520 feet (158 m) above the target ships in Test Able. The abandoned battleship *Nevada* (BB 36) is the aim point at the center of a target array of 78 ships; the bomb misses the aim point by 2,130 feet (649 m). The 40-year-old *Nevada* is burnt and battered by the 23-kiloton blast, but not sunk; several other ships sink and others are wrecked or damaged. The tests—given the code-name Operation Crossroads—involve some 42,000 Army, Navy, and civilian scientific and press personnel.

Navy Experimental Squadron (VX) 3 is commissioned at NAS New York to evaluate the adaptability of helicopters for naval purposes.

14 JULY

The light carrier *Saipan* (CVL 48) is commissioned with Capt. John G. Crommelin, USN, in command. The 683½-foot (208-m) carrier, with a standard displacement of 14,500 tons, is one of only two purpose-built US light carriers, her sister ship being the *Wright* (CVL 49), to be completed in 1947. Nine earlier CVLs were converted during construction in World War II from cruisers of the *Cleveland* (CL 55) class. The *Wright* and *Saipan* will be employed primarily for training during their brief service careers.

21 JULY

Lt. Comdr. James J. Davidson, USN, becomes the first US pilot to land an all-jet aircraft on a carrier as he tests the XFD-1 Phantom aboard the *Franklin D. Roosevelt* (CVB 42). The XFD-1 is able to take off with a deck run of 460 feet (140 m); Davidson makes five landings and take-offs on the ship.

25 JULY

In Test Baker at Bikini Atoll, a Mk 3 atomic bomb suspended 90 feet (27 m) below the landing ship *LSM 60* is detonated. The bomb—of approximately 20 kilotons of explosive power—pushes up a column of wa-

ter nearly a half-mile (0.8 km) across that rises almost 6,000 feet (1,830 m) into the air, tossing warships around like toys. Many of the 75 moored target ships are sunk or damaged.

30 JULY

The escort carrier *Tinian* (CVE 123) is "accepted" by the Navy but not placed in commission. She is the last of 86 "jeep" carriers built or converted from merchant ships and naval oilers for US Navy service since 1941. The ultimate in CVE design, the *Tinian*, a unit of the *Commencement Bay* (CVE 105) class, is 557 feet (169 m) long, has a standard displacement of 10,900 tons, and can carry some 30 aircraft.

8 AUG

The carrier *Franklin D. Roosevelt* departs for the Mediterranean as a follow-up to the visit of the battleship *Missouri* earlier in the year. With her 123-plane air group the FDR has a greater striking power than the entire air force of any Mediterranean nation. The FDR's deployment includes a port visit to Athens to bolster the government of Greece against communist incursion. (The *Roosevelt* will depart the Mediterranean on 4 Oct 1946.)

The prototype Convair XB-36 long-range bomber makes its first flight, almost six years after contract award. The B-36, a swept-wing aircraft powered by six piston engines, was developed as a trans-Atlantic bomber, intended to bomb targets in Europe from bases in the United States in the event Germany defeated Britain in World War II.

21 AUG

The US Office of Naval Research (ONR) is established by the redesignation of the Office of Research and Inventions, which had been set up in May 1945. ONR—established by an act of Congress —is to plan, foster, and encourage scientific research. The first head of ONR is the Chief of Naval Research, Rear Adm. Harold G. Bowen, USN, who was appointed the research chief in July 1945.

11 SEP

First flight of the North American XFJ-1 Fury, a straight-wing fighter similar to the later P-86/F-86 Sabre. The later Navy FJ-2 variant is a swept-wing aircraft. The FJ series (later redesignated F-1) will be employed mainly in the attack role carrying air-to-surface missiles.

20 SEP

First flight of the Martin XP4M-1 Mercator maritime patrol aircraft. The aircraft will be employed primarily in the electronic surveillance role.

29 SEP

An XP2V-1 Neptune prototype named *Truculent Turtle* completes a flight of 11,235.6 n.miles (20,819.6 km) from Perth, Australia, to Columbus, Ohio, in 55 hours, 17 minutes. The world-record flight was piloted by Comdr. Thomas D. Davies, USN. The aircraft had planned to land at NAS Anacostia, in Washington, D.C., but bad weather caused the flight to end at Columbus. (Neptunes were not configured for in-flight refueling.)

1 OCT

Naval Air Missile Test Center established at Point Mugu, Calif., under the command of Capt. A. N. Perkins, USN.

2 OCT

The Vought XF6U-1 Pirate makes its first flight. The turbojet-propelled aircraft will be flown in small numbers and not assigned to fleet squadrons.

31 OCT

Maj. Marion Carl becomes the first US Marine Corps pilot to land a jet aircraft aboard a carrier when he flight tests a modified P-80 Shooting Star on the *Franklin D. Roosevelt*.

1 NOV

The carrier *Randolph* (CV 15) enters the Mediterranean, beginning a postwar pattern of regular US carrier deployments to the Mediterranean.

3 NOV

The US Navy airship XM-1 lands at NAF Glynco, Ga., completing a flight of 7 days, 2 hours, 20 minutes, a world record for duration in unrefueled flight by any type of aircraft. Lt. H. R. Walton, USNR, was in command.

15 NOV

The US Navy reorganizes carrier air groups and squadron assignments. Carrier squadrons are limited to fighter (VF) and attack (VA) units, thus abolishing VB, VBF, and VT squadrons.

Other naval aviation designation changes include indicating aircraft class for patrol squadrons (VP), with MA indicating medium seaplane and HL for long-range, as VP(HL)-22; utility squadrons (VJ) are changed to VU; photographic squadrons (VD) became VPP; and meteorological squadrons (VPW) became VPM.

6 DEC

The Douglas AD-1 Skyraider enters fleet service with Attack Squadron (VA) 19 at NAS North Island, Calif. The Skyraider will be one of the most successful naval aircraft ever built and will remain in active fleet service until 1968. Designed by Ed Heinemann, the AD-1 has an unmatched carrying capability for a single-engine piston aircraft and will fly in a variety of specialized configurations.

14 DEC

President Truman approves the first US unified command plan, which establishes a comprehensive, worldwide system for establishing command of US forces under the Joint Chiefs of Staff. Seven unified commands are immediately set up on an interim basis: Alaskan, Atlantic Fleet, Caribbean, European, Far East, Northeast (Newfoundland, Labrador, Greenland), and Pacific.

1947

1 JAN

The Commander in Chief US Pacific Command is established with Adm. John H. Towers, USN, as the first CINCPAC. Until 14 Jan 1958, the CINCPAC will also serve as CINC Pacific Fleet.

The newly established Atomic Energy Commission (AEC) takes control of all US atomic efforts and resources, both military and civilian. (The AEC will be abolished in 1974 with its functions transferred mainly to the Energy Research and Development Administration [later Department of Energy] and the Nuclear Regulatory Commission.)

2 JAN

The carrier *Philippine Sea* (CV 47) departs Norfolk for Antarctica as part of the Operation Highjump task force commanded by Rear Adm. Richard E. Byrd, USNR.

9 JAN

The Submarine Officers Conference—a periodic conclave of senior submarine officers in the Washington, D.C., area—presents a report to Chief of Naval Operations Adm. Chester W. Nimitz, USN, addressing nuclear propulsion for submarines. The report supports development of nuclear-propelled submarines, noting "The development of a true submarine capable of operating submerged for unlimited periods, appears to be probable within the next ten years. . . ."

11 JAN

The XF2H-1 Banshee carrier-based fighter makes its first flight. Developed by McDonnell, the aircraft will be used in large numbers as a fighter and photo-reconnaissance aircraft. (Later redesignated F-2.)

14 JAN

A horizontal red stripe is added to the blue-and-white side panels of US military aircraft insignia.

29 JAN

The carrier *Philippine Sea,* from a position 600 n.miles (1,112 km) off the Antarctic continent, launches eight ski-equipped R4D Skytrain transports (the Navy version of the commercial DC-3). The aircraft are fitted with Jet Assisted Take-Off (JATO) auxiliary rockets for the deck-run take-off. This is the largest aircraft to take off from an aircraft carrier to this time with an average take-off weight of 26,000 pounds (11,794 kg). (In 1939 the Navy flew carrier landings and take-offs with the twin-engine XJO-1, and in 1944 with the PBJ-1H Mitchell, a modified version of the B-25H. The B-25B bombers launched from the carrier *Hornet* [CV 8], led by then-Lt. Col. James H. Doolittle, USA, on 18 April 1942, did not land back aboard the carrier.)

17 FEB

The US large cruisers *Alaska* (CB 1) and *Guam* (CB 2), the only battle cruiser–type ships ever completed by the US Navy, are decommissioned and laid up in reserve. The *Alaska*s were the result of an inaccurate prewar intelligence estimate that reported the Japanese were constructing extremely fast "large cruisers" as commerce raiders. This threat proved to be false. The ships carried a main battery of nine 12-inch (304-mm) guns.

18 FEB

The US submarine *Cusk* (SS 348) launches a Loon missile, becoming the first submarine to launch a guided missile. The missile, surface-launched from a ramp fitted to the submarine's after deck, crashes after travelling 6,000 yards (5.5 km). The Loon is an "Americanized" version of the German V-1 "buzz bomb."

12 MAR

President Harry S. Truman addresses a joint session of Congress to request direct financial aid to help the Greek and Turkish governments deal with Communist incursions. He urges the United States to "support free peoples who are resisting attempted subjugation by armed minorities or by outside pressure." This policy becomes known as the Truman Doctrine.

2 APR

The French escort carrier *Dixmude* begins air strikes against Viet Minh (communist) targets in Indochina. The American-built *Dixmude* was operated by the Royal Navy during World War II (as HMS *Biter*). Her French air group consists of SBD Dauntless dive bombers. These are the first combat strikes ever flown from a French aircraft carrier.

11 APR

Rear Adm. John Wilkes, USN, Commander, Submarine Force Atlantic Fleet, in a speech at the submarine base in New London, Conn., prophesies that "Atomic energy will revolutionize submarine operations. These craft will be armed with rockets and guided missiles equipped with nuclear warheads, nuclear energy will supply the necessary power for high submerged speeds and eliminate the problem of exhaust gases. Thus, the submarine will maintain its place as a most powerful offensive weapon."

15 APR

A US congressional study to determine whether or not the atomic bomb has made universal military training unnecessary, concludes that "a conscript army is the best guarantee for peace for the next five years." The study is the final chapter in a congressional survey on the implications of the atomic bomb, which Congress will consider in revising national defense policy in the postwar era.

30 APR

The US military services establish a standard designation system for missiles. These are three-letter combinations, the first letter indicating the launch mode (A = Air, S = Surface, U= Underwater); the second the target; the third the letter M for Missile. These are followed by a letter to indicate service and a sequential number in a single series, odd for Army (and Army Air Forces) and N for Navy (e.g., the Terrier missile becomes the SAM-N-7).

16 MAY

Secretary of the Navy James V. Forrestal and Chief of Naval Operations Fleet Adm. Nimitz call for the development of an Arctic defense in testimony before a Senate committee. Forrestal states that "these regions have attained new significance as the great circle routes over which attacks by missiles and aircraft will be made." The Navy request for Arctic equipment includes a dock landing ship with icebreaking capability, an icebreaking cargo ship, and an "attack type streamlined, submarine picket." Additionally, Forrestal and Nimitz emphasize the role of the Navy as the "guardian of peace" until "the UN takes over." According to Nimitz, "Our peace and stability depend on a balance of power where American and British seapower are arrayed on one side."

The House Appropriations Committee cuts the Navy's FY 1948 budget request by $377 million, a ten percent reduction. The Navy will now face a force reduction of 40,000 men. According to Forrestal, the cuts "will have a crippling effect on active fleet operations."

19 MAY

In a speech to the American-Russian Institute in New York City, Soviet Deputy Foreign Minister Andrei Gromyko warns that "the US monopoly on atomic weapons is an illusion." Gromyko urges the UN to outlaw nuclear weapons and states that if there is no agreement on atomic energy, the US might be threatened by "other weapons of mass destruction."

4 JUNE

Chief of Naval Operations Fleet Adm. Nimitz approves Project 27A for the conversion of *Essex* (CV 9)–class carriers to meet requirements for operating advanced aircraft. The modifications include strengthening the flight deck and elevators to operate aircraft up to 40,000 pounds (18,144 kg), installation of two H-8 hydraulic catapults, removal of flight-deck 5-inch (127-mm) twin gun mounts, and the installation of jet blast deflectors. The unfinished carrier *Oriskany* (CV 34) will be the first to have the 27A configuration.

5 JUNE

Gen. of the Army George C. Marshall, USA, the Secretary of State, speaking at Harvard University in Boston, announces a plan for the economic rehabilitation of Europe. This effort becomes known as the Marshall Plan.

26 JULY

President Truman signs the National Security Act directing the unification of the US armed services into a National Military Establishment to which the Navy and War Departments are subordinate. A separate Air Force is created with a service secretary of equal stature to the Navy and Army. The War Department is renamed Department of the Army. Due to the fervent anti-unification feelings of the Navy, President Truman nominates Secretary of the Navy Forrestal to be the first Secretary of Defense to try and mend some fences within a very disgruntled Navy.

The diesel-electric submarine *Pomodon* (SS 486), commissioned in 1945, completes a nine-month conversion to the GUPPY configuration (Greater Underwater Propulsive Power). In this first GUPPY conversion the *Pomodon*'s outer hull and conning tower have been streamlined; more powerful batteries provided to give improved underwater performance; and all deck guns and certain projections were removed. (Later GUPPIES will have a snorkel fitted.) A total of 52 US submarines will be converted to various GUPPY configurations through 1962.

20 AUG

A Navy D-558-1 Skystreak turbojet research aircraft flown by Comdr. Turner Caldwell, USN, reaches 640 mph (1,030 kmh), setting a world speed record. This beat the USAAF speed record for the first time since 1923—by 17 mph (27.4 kmh).

6 SEP

The US carrier *Midway* (CVB 41) successfully launches a German V-2 ballistic missile from her flight deck, the test known as Operation Sandy. This was the only launch of a German-built V-2 from a moving platform.

17 SEP

James Forrestal is sworn in as the first Secretary of Defense. He previously served as Secretary of the Navy. On the following day the National Military Establishment will come into being; it will be renamed the Department of Defense two years later.

18 SEP

John L. Sullivan is sworn in as the 49th Secretary of the Navy; he is the first Navy secretary not to hold cabinet rank.

The Department of the Air Force is created as a military department coequal with the Departments of the Army and Navy. Former Sen. Stuart Symington is named first Secretary of the Air Force and Gen. Carl A. Spaatz, USAF, becomes the first Chief of Staff.

1 OCT

The New York Naval Shipyard begins the conversion of the unfinished carrier *Oriskany*, which was 65 percent complete, to the Project 27A specifications. The construction of the ship, a carrier of the *Essex* class, had been halted at the end of World War II.

First flight of the North American XP-86 (later F-86 Sabre). F-86 production will total 6,233 aircraft in the United States, more than any other US aircraft in the post–World War II era. (Another 2,448 would be built in Australia, Canada, Italy, and Japan.) The aircraft is also produced as the US Navy FJ Fury series,

with the straight-wing FJ-1 Fury having flown before the swept-wing XP-86 variant. The Navy will procure 1,148 FJ series aircraft.

14 OCT

Capt. Charles (Chuck) Yeager, USAF, becomes the first American to intentionally break the sound barrier, at Edwards AFB, Muroc, Calif., flying the Bell X-1 rocket plane. Released in flight from a B-29 Superfortress, the aircraft, named *Glamorous Glennis,* reaches Mach 1.015 (670 mph / 1,078 kmh) at an altitude of 42,000 feet (12,801 m).

(The Mach number, used to express aircraft speed, is the ratio of the velocity of a moving body to the local velocity of sound. Thus Mach 1 equals 760.98 mph [1,224.4 kmh] at sea level at 59° F [15° C]. Named for Dr. Ernest Mach.)

18 OCT

The first successful launch of a Soviet ballistic missile takes place; this is the R-1 missile (R for Raket), a modification of the German V-2.

1 NOV

Commander in Chief US Caribbean Command is established for US forces in that area. Lt. Gen. Willis D. Crittenberger, USA, is the first CINCARIB. (On 6 June 1963, the command will be renamed US Southern Command.)

2 NOV

The largest aircraft built in World War II, the "Spruce Goose" flying boat built by Howard Hughes, flies for the first and only time, being airborne for one minute and reaching an altitude of some 85 feet (25.9 m). It was to be the prototype for a "flying cargo ship" that could move troops and weapons overseas without the risk of loss to enemy submarines. The aircraft—designated HK-1 for Hughes-Kaiser as well as H-4 Hercules—was to carry 120,000 pounds of cargo or 750 troops or 350 litter patients plus a medical crew. The aircraft has a wingspan of 320 feet (97.5 m), a length of 218½ feet (66.6 m), with an estimated gross weight of 300,000 pounds.

21 NOV

First flight of the Grumman XF9F-2 Panther; this will be the first US Navy carrier-based turbojet fighter produced in large numbers. The Panther will be used extensively in the Korean War.

28 NOV

The seaplane tender *Norton Sound* (AV 11) is assigned to the Operational Development Force as a rocket/missile test ship. Modifications will be performed at the Philadelphia Naval Shipyard beginning in Mar 1948.

29 NOV

The United Nations votes to partition Palestine when the British withdraw from supervising the Mandate in May 1948; the Soviet Union sides with the United States in favor of the establishment of separate Jewish and Arab states.

1 DEC

Commander in Chief Atlantic is established as the US unified command in the Atlantic area with Adm. William H. P. Blandy, USN, as the first incumbent. The CINCLANT additionally serves as CINC Atlantic Fleet until 4 Oct 1985. From 30 Jan 1952, CINCLANT will also serve as the NATO Supreme Allied Commander Atlantic (SACLANT).

Marine Helicopter Experimental Squadron (HMX) 1 is established at the Marine Corps Air Station Quantico, Va.; later changed to Marine Helicopter Squadron (HMX) 1.

5 DEC

Chief of Naval Operations Fleet Adm. Nimitz formally endorses Navy plans for a nuclear propulsion program.

17 DEC

Rear Adm. Daniel V. Gallery, USN, the Assistant Chief of Naval Operations (Guided Missiles), submits a report urging the Navy to "start an aggressive campaign aimed at proving the Navy can deliver the atomic bomb more effectively than the Air Force can." The Gallery report explains why the need for overseas bases and fighter escorts to support Air Force bombers makes carriers the best means for launching such strikes.

30 DEC

First flight of the Soviet MiG-15, an advanced swept-wing turbojet. Developed by the MiG design bureau —named for A. I. Mikoyan and M. I. Guryevich—the aircraft was intended to intercept US strategic bombers attacking the Soviet Union. The aircraft's appearance takes Western intelligence analysts by surprise. At least 15,000 MiG-15s will be built (more than twice the number of F-86 Sabres produced, which was the largest production Western jet fighter).

1948

1 JAN

Gen. Clifton B. Cates, USMC, becomes the 19th Commandant of the Marine Corps. He is the first commandant to become a full general upon assuming the position. (His predecessor, Alexander A. Vandegrift, was promoted to four-star rank in Mar 1945, having become commandant in Jan 1944.)

20 JAN

The diesel-electric submarine *Cusk* (SS 348) is redesignated the US Navy's first guided missile submarine (SSG). She is used primarily to launch Loon test missiles.

4 FEB

First flight of the Douglas D-558-2 Skyrocket research aircraft. The Navy-sponsored aircraft, developed from the D-558-1 Skystreak, has a combination turbojet and rocket propulsion system (later changed to an all-rocket system). Two D-558-2 aircraft are built. A D-558-2 will exceed Mach 1 for the first time on 24 June 1949. It is normally launched from an airborne Navy P2B-1 aircraft (modified B-29).

10 MAR

In a demonstration to the press of the practicality of jet aircraft operations from a carrier, Comdr. Evan P. Aurand, USN, of Fighter Squadron (VF) 5, conducts 15 launches and landings in an FJ-1 Fury from the carrier *Boxer* (CV 21) off the coast of southern California. A Navy spokesman explains that the "introduction of the FJ-1 into the fleet, is a major step in keeping the Navy at top efficiency as the nation's first line of defense. With aircraft like the FJ-1, which can operate on even or better terms with land based aircraft, the Navy can stop transoceanic bombers long before they reach our shores."

11 MAR

In an effort to quell interservice fighting over roles and missions, Secretary of Defense James V. Forrestal assembles the Joint Chiefs of Staff for a series of meetings at the naval base in Key West, Fla. Following the conference, Forrestal issues a statement which spells out the specific functions of the JCS, Army, Navy, Marines, and Air Force. The Navy agrees that strategic bombing is an Air Force prerogative and that the Marines would never deploy units larger then a division or "have a field unit headquarters larger than a corps." In this spirit of reconciliation, the Air Force agrees not to oppose Navy plans for a new aircraft carrier (i.e., the CVA 58).

17 MAR

Foreign ministers of Great Britain, France, Belgium, Luxembourg, and the Netherlands sign the Treaty of Western European Union in Brussels. The treaty is a mutual defense pact embodying political conceptions, plans for coordinated military action in the event of an emergency, closer economic cooperation, and cultural clauses designed to encourage better understanding between the signatories. At the request of the French, Germany is specifically mentioned as a potential aggressor.

In a speech to a joint session of Congress, President Harry S. Truman bluntly accuses the Soviet Union of plotting the subjugation of Europe. Truman calls for universal military training supported by a temporary draft to "forestall threatened communist control and police state rule of the remaining free nations on the European continent." Truman emphasizes that "the Soviet Union and its agents have destroyed the independence and democratic character of a slew of nations in Eastern Europe, and they now propose to extend this ruthless course to the remaining free nations of Europe."

26 MAR

By Executive Order of President Truman, the Key West Accords are officially adopted as a part of US defense policy.

1 APR

US Navy Helicopter Utility Squadron (HU) 1 is commissioned at NAS Lakehurst, N.J., the Navy's first helicopter squadron.

US Navy Patrol Warning Squadron (VPW) 1 is established to operate land-based radar picket aircraft.

27 APR

Two P2V-2 Neptune aircraft are launched from the carrier *Coral Sea* (CVB 43) steaming off Norfolk, Va., to test the suitability of these planes for an interim nuclear strike aircraft (pending availability of the AJ Savage). This is the largest aircraft to take off from an aircraft carrier up to this time. Comdr.

Thomas D. Davies, USN, and Lt. Comdr. J. P. Wheatley, USN, pilot the aircraft, which are too large to land aboard a carrier.

30 APR

First flight of the Martin XP5M-1 Marlin flying boat. Developed from the wartime PBM Mariner, the aircraft will be the last flying boat in US Navy squadron service. (Later redesignated P-5.)

5 MAY

Fighter Squadron (VF) 17-A becomes the US Navy's first operational jet squadron, beginning three days of carrier qualifications on board the USS *Saipan* (CVL 48) with the FH-1 Phantom.

14 MAY

The Jewish state of Israel is established in Palestine. However, no Arab state is established as the armed forces of Egypt, Transjordan, Iraq, Lebanon, Saudi Arabia, and Syria immediately attack Israel.

1 JUNE

The Sixth Task Fleet is established as the forward deployed US naval force in the Mediterranean. Commander, Sixth Task Fleet replaces the position of Commander, Naval Forces, Mediterranean. Vice Adm. Forrest P. Sherman, USN, is the first Sixth Task Fleet commander.

The Naval Air Transport Service (NATS) and the USAF Air Transport Service (ATS) are consolidated into the Military Air Transport Service (MATS), a unified command of the National Military Establishment under the direction of the US Air Force.

11 JUNE

The US Air Force revises its aircraft designation scheme: the most significant change is the letter F for Fighter type being adopted in place of P for Pursuit; the P series had reached XP-92 (e.g., the P-80 Shooting Star becomes the F-80).

24 JUNE

The Soviet forces blockade all road, rail, and waterborne traffic in and out of the western sectors of Berlin, initiating the Berlin Blockade.

25 JUNE

The first planeload of Western supplies for Berlin arrives in the blockaded city.

1 JULY

The Naval Air Transport Service is officially disestablished. NATS had been established on 12 December

1941, directly under the CNO, for worldwide air delivery of critical equipment, parts, and personnel.

The Soviet Air Defense Forces (PVO-*Strany*) is established as an independent service, ranking with the Ground Forces, Air Forces, and Navy.

3 JULY

Marshal of the SU Vasily Sokolovsky, the commander of the Soviet Zone of Germany, informs the Western Zone military governors, including Gen. Lucius D. Clay, USA, that he will lift the blockade only when plans for establishing a West German government are abandoned. The Soviets insist that access to Berlin depends upon continuation of quadripartite rule there and any attempt to create a separate West German state violates those rules.

First flight of the North American XAJ-1 Savage, prototype of the first carrier-based aircraft designed to carry a nuclear weapon. The aircraft has twin piston engines with a turbojet booster fitted in the after fuselage. (The aircraft will later be designated A-2.)

6 JULY

Talks on North Atlantic defense begin in Washington, D.C., between the United States, Canada, and the Brussels Treaty Powers.

US Navy Carrier Airborne Early Warning Squadrons (VAW) 1 and 2 are established, the first such units in the Navy. The units will fly modified AD-series Skyraider aircraft from carriers deployed in forward areas.

15 JULY

As a response to the Soviet blockade of Berlin, the US National Security Council decides to deploy 60 B-29 Superfortress bombers to Great Britain. However, these are not nuclear-capable aircraft. (Some of the B-29s that could carry nuclear weapons are deployed to Britain in mid-1949; all B-29 atomic strike capability at the time rests with the 509th Bomb Wing in New Mexico.)

17 JULY

The first of 60 B-29 Superfortress bombers arrives in Great Britain.

22 JULY

Three B-29 Superfortress bombers depart Davis-Monthan AFB in Arizona on the first postwar, around-the-world flight. One B-29 crashes in the Arabian Sea with the others returning to Davis-Monthan on 6 Aug 1948 after the 20,000-mile (32,186-

km) flight. The aircraft made eight en route stops and had an actual flight time of 103 hours, 50 minutes.

29 JULY

President Truman approves the construction of a flush-deck, 65,000-ton standard displacement aircraft carrier, subsequently named the *United States* (CVA 58). Funding was provided for the ship in the Naval Appropriations Act of 1949.

4 AUG

Vice Adm. Earle Mills, USN, Chief of the Bureau of Ships, establishes a nuclear power branch and names Capt. H. G. Rickover, USN, as head of the branch.

10 AUG

The Navy orders the "heavy" aircraft carrier *United States* from Newport News Shipbuilding and Dry Dock Co. in Virginia.

20 AUG

In another effort to end inter-service disputes, Secretary of Defense Forrestal takes the service chiefs to the Naval War College in Newport, R.I., for a three-day, closed-door session in an effort to straighten out the roles and missions issue. In his diary, Forrestal will note that as a result of the conference, total cooperation had been reached on strategic air warfare. The control of the atomic bomb would be temporarily given to the Air Force until a decision on the control of atomic operations was reached by the Military Liaison Committee to the Atomic Energy Commission.

28 AUG

The US Navy JRM-2 flying boat *Caroline Mars* lands on Lake Michigan at Chicago after a record nonstop flight from Honolulu of 4,748 n.miles (8,798 km) in 24 hours, 12 minutes.

9 SEP

Composite Squadron (VC) 5 is commissioned to evaluate heavy attack aircraft and to develop the tactics and procedures for delivering nuclear weapons from aircraft carriers. Capt. John T. Hayward, USN, is the first CO. (During World War II VC squadrons were mostly composite units assigned to escort carriers.)

13 SEP

As the Berlin Blockade continues and the crisis mounts, President Truman discusses the possible use of atomic bombs with Secretary of Defense Forrestal. In his diary Forrestal notes that Truman said "he prayed that he would never have to make such a deci-

sion, but that if it became necessary, no one need have a misgiving but what he would do so. . . ."

16 SEP

National Security Council (NSC) Directive 30 is adopted. This rather simplistic statement is the only nuclear warfare policy directive to win presidential approval until 1959. NSC 30 states that in the event of war, the military "must be ready to utilize promptly and effectively all appropriate means available, including atomic weapons." This would, however, be contingent on presidential approval.

27 SEP

The defense ministers of the Brussels Treaty Powers begin a two-day meeting that leads to the decision to create a Western Union Defense Organization.

1 OCT

Modification of the large seaplane tender *Norton Sound* (AV 11) to a guided missile test ship is completed at the Philadelphia Naval Shipyard. In coming years the *Norton Sound* will be a testbed for advanced gun, missile, and electronic systems, among them the Sea Sparrow, Terrier, Typhon, and Aegis.

27 OCT

Navy Transport Squadrons (VR) 6 and 8 are ordered to Germany from the Pacific to participate in the Berlin Airlift.

3 NOV

Lt. Comdr. Eric M. Brown, RN, lands a Vampire aircraft without wheels aboard HMS *Warrior*. The *Warrior* had been fitted with a flexible rubber deck to absorb the shock of the landing. After landing, a crane hoists the Vampire onto a trolley for catapult launch. The flexible deck permits aircraft to reduce weight by five percent (due to no landing gear) and also allows the plane to land in a relatively small area (after the tailhook engages the arresting wires, the Vampire had a run out of only a few feet). Unfortunately, an aircraft equipped for a flexible deck could not land anywhere else. Tests continue ashore and on the modified *Warrior*.

10 NOV

As the Berlin Blockade continues, Soviet Gen. G. S. Lukyanchenko, Chief of Staff of the Soviet military administration, declares that the Soviet Union will force down all US and British aircraft flying outside of the air corridors to Berlin. Brig. Gen. Charles Gailey, USAF, replies that the Soviets will be held responsible for any loss of life. Gen. Clay, USA, Military Governor of Germany, vows "we intend to keep the airlift planes flying."

16 NOV

The heavy cruiser *Des Moines* (CA 134) is commissioned at the Boston Naval Shipyard, the first ship in the world's ultimate class of heavy cruisers. The *Des Moines* is armed with the first fully automatic 8-inch (203-mm) guns, permitting a fire rate of 20 rounds per barrel per minute. Carrying nine 8-inch guns, the warship displaces 16,000 tons standard and is 716½ feet (218.4 m) long; except for battle cruisers, she is the largest cruiser built by any nation. Her first CO is Capt. A. D. Chandler, USN.

29 NOV

The French light fleet carrier *Arromanches* arrives off Indochina as a replacement for the departed *Dixmude*. The *Arromanches'* air wing is immediately flown onto airfields near Saigon, while the ship herself moves up the Saigon River to the city. The French carrier is the largest warship to ever transit the river to Saigon.

10 DEC

Negotiations begin in Washington, D.C., between representatives of the Brussels Treaty Powers, Canada, and the United States to draft the North Atlantic Treaty.

18 MAY
House Armed Services Committee Chairman Vinson proposes an aerial duel between the Air Force's B-36 strategic bomber and Navy's F9F Panther and FJ-1 Fury fighters. The Navy asserts that it could win the mock battle using propeller-driven F8F Bearcats and F4U Corsairs. Vinson "strongly suggests" that the Air Force accept the Navy dare to duel at 40,000 feet (12,192 m). Secretary of Defense Johnson replies that he will take the matter under consideration. No mock duel is fought.

1 AUG
The Seventh Task Fleet is reestablished as the forward deployed US naval force in the Western Pacific. Commander, Seventh Task Fleet, replaces the position of Commander, Naval Forces, Western Pacific.

9 AUG
In the first test in the United States of a pilot-ejection seat for emergency escape from an aircraft, Lt. J. L. Fruin, USN, of Fighter Squadron (VF) 171 ejects from an F2H-1 Banshee fighter at a speed of more than 575 mph (925 kmh) near Walterboro, S.C.

10 AUG
The National Security Act of 1947 is amended to increase the authority of the Secretary of Defense and to replace the National Military Establishment with a Department of Defense. The amendment also creates a Chairman of the Joint Chiefs, who will serve as the senior ranking officer for the nation's armed forces. Gen. Omar N. Bradley, USA, is selected as the first Chairman. The act further provides that naval aviation would be "integrated with the naval service, within the Department of the Navy." Additional provisos increased the Joint Staff to 210 military officers and removes the individual service secretaries from the National Security Council.

24 AUG
NATO is formally established.

25 AUG
The first Soviet atomic bomb is detonated atop a tower at a test site is in the Kazakh desert, between the Caspian and Aral Seas. Like the US Trinity test of a "Fat Man" bomb four years earlier, this was a plutonium bomb.

The US submarine *Cochino* (SS 345) sinks in the Greenland Sea approximately 100 n.miles (185 km) north of Hammerfest, Norway. The *Cochino,* on a sur-

veillance operation with the submarine *Tusk* (SS 426), suffers a battery explosion while submerged. Able to surface, her crew transfers to the *Tusk* despite high seas; many of her crew are badly burned, but the only fatality is a civilian technician. The *Tusk* loses six sailors in the rescue.

3 SEP
A US Air Force WB-29 Superfortress weather reconnaissance aircraft flying from Japan to Alaska detects the first signs of a Soviet nuclear test from upper-atmosphere sampling.

10 SEP
Capt. John G. Crommelin, USN, a combat-experienced naval aviator and carrier commander, releases a statement to the press alleging to a "potential dictatorship" in the Pentagon. Crommelin asserts that the Navy is "being nibbled to death" by a pro–Air Force administration that has a "landlocked concept of national defense." As a result of his press release, Crommelin is suspended from duty by Secretary of the Navy Francis B. Matthews.

26 SEP
First flight of the North American T-28 Trojan. Originally developed for the USAF, the T-28 will be adopted by the Navy following a 1952 decision to standardize training techniques and equipment between the two services.

27 SEP
First session of the North Atlantic Council convenes in Washington, D.C.

1 OCT
The Military Sea Transportation Service (MSTS) is established within the Navy; the basis for the new service are the ships of the Naval Ocean Transport Service (NOTS). The following year oceangoing cargo ships and transports of the Army Transportation Corps will be transferred to MSTS. Ships assigned to the MSTS—with either civilian or Navy crews—have the prefix "T-" in their hull designations.

5 OCT
In another demonstration of potential carrier strike capabilities, a P2V-3 Neptune piloted by Comdr. Frederick L. Ashworth, USN, takes off from the carrier *Midway* (CVB 41) at sea off Norfolk, Va., flies to the Panama Canal, and then northward, overflying Corpus Christi, Texas, and flying on to land at San Diego,

Calif. The 4,800-n.mile (8,894-km) flight is completed in 25 hours, 40 minutes.

6 OCT
The US Congress passes the mutual defense bill. The law specifically authorized that military equipment, technical assistance, machine tools, and industrial equipment could be sent to allied areas. The law resulted from the many mutual assistance treaties the US was signing at this time, all of which provided for the extension of US credits, supplies of weapons, and modernization of old allied weapons. In effect, the Lend-Lease Act of 1940 is modernized for the postwar era.

The US Congress begins hearings on defense "Unification and Strategy."

7 OCT
Adm. Arthur W. Radford, USN, Commander in Chief Pacific Fleet, testifies that while "national air power is the dominant factor in National Security, the B-36 is a symbol of the unsound theory of atomic blitz warfare." Radford adds that the B-36 is a "billion dollar blunder that has undermined unification and prevented mutual trust, understanding and planning amongst the armed services." When asked by Rep. Vinson how many other high-ranking naval officers support his views, Radford offers the names of Fleet Adms. William D. Leahy, Ernest J. King, Chester W. Nimitz, and William Halsey as well as the Chief of Naval Operations, Adm. Louis E. Denfield, "among others."

15 OCT
As the congressional hearings on unification and strategy continue, Chief of Naval Operations Adm. Denfield testifies that the Navy ". . . has real misgivings over the reductions taking place today. Arbitrary reductions that impair or even eliminate naval functions. Limitations are imposed without consultation and without understanding of the Navy's role in defense of our maritime nation." Denfield describes himself as an "advocate of air power" but also adds that "it is illogical, damaging, and dangerous to proceed directly to mass procurement of an uncertain weapon [the B-36 bomber] while the Army and Navy are starved for funds and our strategic concept of war frozen." This testimony will cause Adm. Denfield to be removed from office.

17 OCT
Gen. Carl A. Spaatz, USAF (Ret.), writing in *Newsweek* magazine, adds fuel to the Navy's concerns regarding Air Force intentions to absorb Navy and Marine Corps aviation as he reiterates the Air Force position on the supremacy of strategic bombing. Spaatz writes, "The Navy now spends more than half its total appropriations in support of naval aviation. The result is that the nation is wasting aviation talent in support of two air forces." Spaatz sees the existence of both naval aviation and an Air Force as "dangerous." In his summary, Spaatz states that "Nothing less than United States air supremacy is at stake. This leadership cannot be maintained unless the country's military air resources are pooled and placed under the control of one organization."

19 OCT
Chairman of the Joint Chiefs of Staff Gen. Bradley, addressing the question of conventional-versus-strategic operations, tells the House Armed Services Committee: ". . . by appraising the power of the atomic bomb, I am wondering whether we shall ever have another large-scale amphibious operation. Frankly, the atomic bomb, properly delivered, almost precludes such a possibility."

30 OCT
A world helicopter record is set by a US Navy HO3S piloted by Lt. G. A. Rullo, USN, which flies from NAS Seattle, Wash., to NAS Alameda, Calif., a flight of 10 hours, 50 minutes covering a distance of 755 miles (1,215 km).

31 OCT
With Chief of Naval Operations Adm. Denfield about to be relieved from duty for his statements before Congress, President Truman contacts Fleet Adm. Nimitz about his returning to active service as CNO. Nimitz declines, believing that it would be a mistake to return a retired officer to duty during peacetime. Nimitz recommends Adm. Forrest P. Sherman, USN, to replace Denfield, citing Sherman's lack of involvement with the defense unification battles.

The first meeting of the North Atlantic Regional Planning Group takes place with the chiefs of naval staff of Canada, Denmark, Iceland, France, Belgium, the Netherlands, Norway, Portugal, Britain, and the United States. This group is tasked with planning the unified defense of the North Atlantic, including offensive operations, convoys, and protecting the sea lines of communication.

1 NOV
Adm. Denfield is relieved of his duties as Chief of Naval Operations by Secretary of the Navy Matthews.

10 NOV
First flight of the Piasecki HRP-2 Rescuer helicopter. Although not procured by the Navy, which developed the aircraft, the H-21 version—given the names Shawnee and Workhorse—will be extensively flown by the US Army and Air Force as well as foreign services. It will be flown in combat in Vietnam by US forces and in Algeria by the French Army.

21 NOV
First flight of the Sikorsky YH-19 helicopter. Named Chickasaw by the US Army and designated HO4S and HRS by the US Navy and Marine Corps, the heli-

copter is also widely used by other nations for troop transport and anti-submarine operations.

30 NOV
The member nations of NATO agree to pool merchant shipping in the event of a major war. These individual ships would come under NATO authority in a wartime situation. Additionally, the nations agree to produce a combined allied shipping control manual. Britain, Canada, and the United States agree to combine the *Routing and Reporting Instructions* book of the US Navy with the Royal Navy's *Naval Control of Shipping in War* into a single publication.

8 DEC
Chiang Kai-shek moves his Nationalist government from China to the island of Formosa (later renamed Taiwan). Communist forces rapidly complete the conquest of mainland China.

1950

6 JAN

US Navy Composite Squadron (VC) 5 is declared ready to launch atomic strikes from carriers of the *Midway* (CVB 41) class. The effectiveness and practicality of this as a deterrent is questionable as the AJ-1 Savage has yet to operate aboard a carrier. In the event a nuclear strike was ordered, the carrier would have to return to port to load the existing P2V-3C Neptune nuclear strike aircraft for a subsequent carrier launch; after a strike the surviving Neptunes would either rendezvous with an Allied ship or submarine, or divert to a friendly airfield.

12 JAN

Secretary of State Dean Acheson, speaking at the National Press Club in Washington, D.C., defines a US defensive perimeter in the Far East that does not include either South Korea or Formosa (now Taiwan). According to Acheson, the US defensive perimeter "runs along the Aleutians to Japan and then goes to the Ryukyus and from the Ryukyus to the Philippine islands."

17 JAN

The battleship *Missouri* (BB 63), under the command of Capt. William D. Brown, USN, runs aground in Thimble Shoals channel in Hampton Roads, Va. The *Missouri* had been preparing to make a calibration run on the Norfolk acoustical range. Her CO mistook two spar buoys marking a shallow fishing channel for the two marker buoys of the acoustical range. The *Missouri* grounded just in front of Fort Monroe, in full public view. The ensuing uproar results in the courts martial of Brown and the *Missouri*'s navigator, operations officer, and combat information officer, all of whom are buried far down in their respective promotion lists. The battleship will be refloated on 1 Feb 1950.

21 JAN

The Politburo of the Central Committee of the Soviet Union introduces deputy commanders for political matters at the company, battery, and squadron level.

31 JAN

President Harry S. Truman decides that the United States will proceed with development of the hydrogen bomb.

7 FEB

In another demonstration of long-range carrier attack abilities, a P2V-3C Neptune launches from the carrier *Franklin D. Roosevelt* (CVB 42) off the Atlantic coast of Florida and lands at San Francisco 25 hours, 59 minutes later, ending the longest flight ever to be made from a carrier deck—5,060 n.miles (9,376 km). The plane is piloted by Comdr. Thomas Robinson, USN.

9 FEB

Senator Joseph McCarthy (R-Wisc.) launches his campaign against "subversives" and communists in the State Department in a speech in Wheeling, W. Va. His tirade will lead to congressional hearings and extend to the Department of Defense. However, his theatrical charges will reveal no spying or other communist-inspired efforts to bring about the downfall of the US government.

12 FEB

The US Sixth Task Fleet in the Mediterranean is renamed Sixth Fleet; the Seventh Task Fleet in the Far East is renamed Seventh Fleet.

13 FEB

First flight of the Douglas XF3D-1 Skynight, a specialized night fighter intended for carrier use. Rarely deployed on board carriers, the F3D is flown mainly by the Marine Corps and sees combat in small numbers in the Korean War as a night fighter and in the Vietnam War as an electronic surveillance aircraft.

1 MAR

First flight of the Vought XF7U-1 Cutlass carrier-based fighter. The F7U has a swept wing with no horizontal tail surfaces. Despite difficulties in landing the aircraft, it is one of the US Navy's first successful missile-armed aircraft.

8 MAR

Operation Portex—the largest peacetime amphibious maneuvers yet held—reach a climax with a combined amphibious and airborne landing at Vieques Island off Puerto Rico. The exercise runs from 20 Feb to 14 Mar 1950.

10 MAR

President Truman gives development of the hydrogen bomb additional emphasis by declaring it to be "of the highest urgency" and directing the Atomic Energy Commission to begin planning immediately for quantity production.

Secretary of Defense Louis Johnson announces that the Navy has developed a lightweight titanium alloy for use in jet aircraft engines. The alloy is described as being "as strong as steel and only half as heavy."

5 APR

The US GUPPY II–type submarine *Pickerel* (SS 524) completes a record underwater transit on snorkel, having left Hong Kong on 16 March and surfaced off the entrance to Pearl Harbor. Under the command of Lt. Comdr. Paul R. Schwartz, USN, the *Pickerel* snorkeled ("snorted") continuously for 21 days, 1 hour while traveling 5,194 n.miles (9,624 km). The submarine suffered superficial damage to her deck structure, the loss of both emergency buoys, and other minor damage during the underwater transit.

8 APR

An unarmed US Navy PB4Y-2 Privateer electronic reconnaissance aircraft from Patrol Squadron (VP) 26 is shot down by Soviet fighters over the Baltic Sea; it carried a crew of ten, none of whom survive, although there are reports of some being captured by the Soviets.

18 APR

First flight of the XP5Y-1 patrol flying boat; the aircraft, powered by four turboprop engines with contra-rotating propellers, will not enter production because of engine problems.

21 APR

First carrier take-off by an AJ-1 Savage, marking a milestone in the US Navy's development of a carrier-based nuclear strike capability. Capt. John T. Hayward, USN, pilots the aircraft from the *Coral Sea* (CVB 43).

Subsequently, Lt. Comdr. R. C. Starkey, USN, takes off a P2V-3C Neptune from the *Coral Sea* with a gross weight of 74,668 pounds (33,869 kg), the heaviest aircraft yet launched from a carrier deck.

25 APR

President Truman approves National Security Council policy paper No. 68 (NSC 68). This will be the basis for American defense policy for more than 40 years; it specifies that up to 20 percent of US Gross National Product (GNP) will be devoted to defense. Additionally, the paper states that it would be US policy to resist any communist threat to non-communist nations "wherever they may be."

4 MAY

First flight test of a ramjet-powered Rigel test vehicle, intended as a high-speed successor to the Regulus land-attack missiles. On the flight the Rigel vehicle travels only 21 miles (34 km) but achieves a speed of Mach 1.9; a later Rigel firing reaches Mach 2 and travels 74 miles (119 km) before the weapon is canceled because of problems with the ramjet engine.

14 JUNE

President Truman releases 90 non-nuclear bomb assemblies from the Atomic Energy Commission (AEC) to permanent military control; some are to be placed aboard aircraft carriers of the *Midway* class as they depart from Norfolk, Va., for operations in the North Atlantic and Mediterranean.

25 JUNE

Six North Korean infantry divisions, supported by armor and artillery, cross the 38th parallel into South Korea, initiating the Korean War. The same day the UN Security Council adopts a resolution condemning the North Korean action and demanding immediate withdrawal.

27 JUNE

President Truman authorizes Gen. of the Army Douglas MacArthur, USA, to use American naval and air forces to support South Korea. The public communiqué reads "At the direction of the President, the Commander in Chief, Far East, is authorized to utilize Navy and Air Force elements of the Far East command to attack all North Korean military targets south of the 38th parallel in order to clear South Korea of enemy forces."

The carrier *Valley Forge* (CV 45) departs the Subic Bay naval base in the Philippines for Buckner Bay, Okinawa. The United States is concerned over possible communist military action against Formosa. With the *Valley Forge* at Okinawa, she is in a position to support operations against either North Korea or in defense of Formosa.

28 JUNE

North Korean forces occupy the city of Seoul, the capital of South Korea.

The commander of British naval forces in the Far East, Rear Adm. Sir Patrick Brind, RN, places his forces under the command of the senior US naval commander, Vice Adm. C. Turner Joy, USN. Rear Adm. Brind's forces include the light aircraft carrier *Triumph*, the cruisers *Jamaica* and *Belfast*, two destroyers, and three frigates.

29 JUNE

The US anti-aircraft cruiser *Juneau* (CLAA 119) engages a North Korean troop concentration at Okkye with her 5-inch (127-mm) guns, delivering the first naval shore bombardment of the conflict.

The British carrier *Triumph*, cruiser *Belfast*, and the destroyers *Cossack* and *Consort* arrive at Buckner Bay, Okinawa. Rear Adm. J. M. Hoskins, USN, on the *Valley Forge*, immediately integrates the British ships into his own carrier group in preparation for joint offensive operations against North Korea.

The Seventh Fleet is placed under the operational control of Gen. MacArthur by order of the Joint Chiefs of Staff. During World War II both Adm. Ernest J. King (Commander in Chief US Fleet and Chief of Naval Operations) and Adm. Chester W. Nimitz (Commander in Chief Pacific Ocean Areas) had refused to place major US carrier forces under MacArthur's direct operational control. In the view of Nimitz and King, MacArthur's headquarters viewed aircraft carriers as "expendable."

Gen. MacArthur flies from Japan to South Korea to assess the tactical situation in South Korea. While his plane is coming in to land at Suwon airport, 20 miles (32 km) south of Seoul, it is attacked by North Korean Yak-3 fighters. A combat air patrol of US Air Force F-51 Mustang fighters is able to intercept the North Korean planes.

I JULY

The combined American-British carrier strike force departs Okinawa, on course for the west coast of Korea.

2 JULY

Four North Korean torpedo boats attack the US cruiser *Juneau*, the British cruiser *Jamaica,* and the British frigate *Black Swan*. Three of the North Korean craft are destroyed with no Allied casualties.

3 JULY

The US carrier *Valley Forge* and the British carrier *Triumph* launch the first Allied carrier air strikes against Korea. During this baptism of fire, two North Korean Yak-9 fighters are shot down by F9F-2 Panther fighters from Fighter Squadron (VF) 51 F9F-2 Panthers flown by Lt. (jg) Leonard Plog, USN, and Ens. E. W. Brown, USN, while flying with a strike over Pyongyang, northwest of Seoul.

The US cruiser *Juneau* destroys seven North Korean trawlers that had been under the escort of the torpedo boats sunk on 2 July. The trawlers had slipped away during the fog of battle and had taken refuge in the harbor of Chumunjin when the *Juneau* took them under fire.

4 JULY

President Truman orders a naval blockade of North Korea.

7 JULY

The UN Security Council adopts a resolution calling on North Korea to withdraw from South Korea and calls for all member nations to render military assistance to South Korea under a unified command led by the United States. The Soviet Union is absent from this UN meeting, having been in the midst of a boycott because of the UN's refusal to recognize the Communist government of China.

Gen. MacArthur is appointed Supreme Commander of UN forces in Korea.

8 JULY

An agreement is worked out between the commanders of the US air and naval forces in the Korean theater. Naval aircraft will be under Navy control when on specifically naval missions. On all other missions naval aircraft will be under US Air Force control, primarily for coordination with land-based strikes. The assignment of targets is placed under the control of a Joint Service Target Analysis Group.

13 JULY

In the first heavy bomber strike of the Korean War, 50 USAF B-29 Superfortress bombers strike targets in Wonsan, North Korea. The B-29s fly from bases in Japan and on Okinawa.

18 JULY

AD Skyraider attack planes from the carrier *Valley Forge* destroy the North Korean oil refinery at Wonsan.

20 JULY

Fourteen US Naval Reserve aviation squadrons are ordered to active duty: eight fighter, two attack, one anti-submarine, two patrol, and one fleet aircraft service.

Due to the US view that the invasion of South Korea is the first step in a worldwide Communist attack, the reinforcement of the Sixth Fleet begins to help defend Western Europe against a possible Soviet incursion. The carrier *Midway,* dispatched from Norfolk in mid-July, enters the Mediterranean on this date.

23 JULY

The carrier *Boxer* (CV 21) arrives in Japan with 145 USAF F-51 Mustang aircraft for close air support in Korea; also on board are six USAF L-5 liaison aircraft, 19 naval aircraft, and 1,021 passengers. There is no immediately available air group to enable her to perform her attack carrier role and the *Boxer* departs for the United States after unloading her aircraft cargo. On the voyage from NAS Alameda, Calif., to Yokosuka the *Boxer* set a trans-Pacific record of 8 days, 16 hours.

24 JULY

A reconnaissance flight from the *Valley Forge* reports large numbers of North Korean troops staging in southwest Korea. With North Korea's attempting to encircle the US Eighth Army, the Seventh Fleet is tasked to perform close air support for ground forces.

An Army WAC-Corporal is the first missile launched from Cape Canaveral, Fla. Later renamed Cape Kennedy, the facility will be the premier US satellite and spacecraft launch center.

25 JULY

The mothballed carrier *Princeton* (CV 37) is ordered to be pulled from the Reserve Fleet for reactivation and service in the Korean War.

1 AUG

The carrier *Philippine Sea* (CV 47) arrives in the Far East from San Diego for duty with Task Force 77, bringing to three the number of US carriers in the area, including the escort carrier *Sicily* (CVE 118). The *Philippine Sea* is an Atlantic Fleet unit that had been scheduled to relieve the *Valley Forge* in Oct 1950. After the Korean War began she was ordered to the Far East with hastily assembled and partially trained Carrier Air Group (CAG) 11, which had only recently been equipped with jet-propelled fighters.

3 AUG

Marine Observation Squadron (VMO) 6 with HO3S helicopters begins Korean operations supporting the 1st Marine Brigade near Changwon. This is the first deployment of Marine helicopters into a war zone.

Marine Fighter Squadron (VMF) 214, flying from the escort carrier *Sicily,* initiates combat operations of the 1st Marine Aircraft Wing in the Korean theater, launching a strike against Chinju.

5 AUG

The US carriers *Valley Forge* and *Philippine Sea* begin what will become nearly three years of unabated carrier air operations to support UN troops in Korea. The *Valley Forge* planes fly close air support missions and the *Philippine Sea* flies strikes against communist-held rail and highway bridges in southwestern Korea.

12 AUG

The North Korean port city of Wojin, a key rail, road, and sea supply center, is attacked by USAF B-29s. Because Wojin is only 17 miles (27.4 km) from Soviet territory, the B-29s bomb by radar; the result is that every single bomb dropped misses the city and explodes in the surrounding countryside. Due to State Department fears about strikes so close to the Soviet Union, Wojin is, for the moment, declared off limits.

14 AUG

The US submarine *Pickerel* departs Yokosuka, Japan, for a photo-reconnaissance mission off the eastern coast of Korea, north of Wonsan. The photography will be used to select a point for submarine-landed commandos to attack North Korean rail lines. These will be the only US submarine operations against North Korea during the conflict.

16 AUG

With so few tactical aircraft in-theater, the Air Force employs B-29 Superfortress strategic bombers in the tactical role. A group of 98 B-29s carpet bomb a North Korean troop concentration of some 40,000 men northwest of Waegwan.

The US Navy rescues the South Korean Army's 3rd Division at Yonghae. A surface action group consisting of the heavy cruiser *Helena* (CA 75) and three destroyers provides gunfire support while four landing ships evacuate the Korean division under heavy fire. During this daring nighttime rescue, over 6,000 men and 100 vehicles are saved without any loss. The 3rd Division is landed at Kuryongpo-ri on 17 August and immediately re-engages North Korean forces.

18 AUG

The USS *Missouri,* the only operational US battleship, departs Norfolk, Va., for Korea. Immediately upon clearing Norfolk, the *Missouri* runs into a hurricane that sweeps both of her helicopters overboard, damages a 40-mm gun mount, and causes minor flooding. This is the third hurricane/typhoon the *Missouri* has gone through since she was commissioned in 1944.

23 AUG

Gen. MacArthur conducts a final briefing prior to the planned invasion at Inchon. The goal of the landing is to sever the North Korean supply lines which, in the opinion of MacArthur, have become overextended during the drive south. MacArthur believes that "the amphibious landing is the most powerful tool we have." The Army expressed objections to Inchon based on the potential for failure. The Navy based its reservations on the severe tidal hazards at Inchon. According to Vice Adm. C. Turner Joy, USN, "At no time did I hear any naval officer tell MacArthur that Inchon was impossible." Despite objections from Chairman of the Joint Chiefs of Staff Gen. Omar N. Bradley and Army Chief of Staff Gen. J. Lawton Collins, USA, the Inchon landing will be made. In addition to MacArthur as supreme commander, Inchon would be planned and executed by Vice Adm. Arthur Struble, USN, Commander, Seventh Fleet; Rear Adm. James Doyle, USN, Commander Amphibious Group 1; and Maj. Gen. Oliver Smith, USMC, Commanding General, 1st Marine Division. For the Inchon assault, Vice Adm. Struble would also have the position of Commander, Joint Task Force 7. Struble, Doyle, and Smith are all veterans of major World War II amphibious assaults.

24 AUG

A Terrier surface-to-air guided missile successfully intercepts an F6F drone aircraft at a range of 11 n.miles (20.4 km) at the Naval Ordnance Test Station in China Lake, Calif.

Secretary of the Navy Francis P. Matthews, in a speech in Boston, openly advocates a "preventative war" with the Soviet Union. President Truman immediately rebukes Matthews' statement and reaffirms US peaceful intentions toward Moscow.

26 AUG

Final authorization for the Inchon invasion is given by the Joint Chiefs of Staff. The objectives of the assault are to neutralize Wolmi-do Island, invade and capture Inchon, capture Kimpo airfield, and liberate Seoul.

4 SEP

While launching air strikes against targets in the Pyongyang-Chinnampo region of North Korea, Task Force 77 is approached by a Soviet bomber flying out of Port Arthur. Carrier-based F4U Corsair fighters from the *Valley Forge* intercept the Soviet plane 30 miles (48 km) from the task force; upon sighting the American planes, the Soviet bomber turns east toward Korea and then opens fire on the Corsairs. The F4Us return fire and shoot down the Soviet twin-engine plane. A US destroyer picks up the body of a Soviet flier.

9 SEP

The aircraft carrier *Coral Sea* joins the *Midway* in the Sixth Fleet as replacement for the carrier *Leyte* (CV 32), which departs the Mediterranean for Korea.

10 SEP

Pre-invasion action for Inchon begins. Marine Fighter Squadrons (VMF) 212 and 323 drop 95 tanks of napalm on Wolmi-do Island in Inchon harbor.

13 SEP

A bombardment force consisting of the US cruisers *Toledo* (CA 133) and *Rochester* (CA 124), and the British cruisers *Kenya* and *Jamaica,* supported by six destroyers, begin bombarding Wolmi-do Island at 0700. As the bombardment continues throughout the day, mines are spotted in Flying Fish Channel. However, low tide in the harbor uncovers the mines and they are easily destroyed by gunfire.

14 SEP

The battleship *Missouri* arrives off Korea and immediately fires 50 rounds with her 16-inch (406-mm) guns against a bridge near Samchok. With gunfire spotting from a helicopter, the bridge is destroyed. The *Missouri*'s presence on the east coast of Korea is also a diversionary maneuver to draw enemy attention away from the Inchon invasion site on the west coast. This is the first combat involving a US battleship since July 1945.

15 SEP

The Inchon assault begins at 0633 with Marines landing on Wolmi-do Island where they encounter 500 communist troops, who are dazed and shocked from three days of bombardment and air attack. In only 42 minutes Wolmi-do is secure; 20 Marines are injured, none killed. At 1730, the main assault against Inchon itself begins in the first Marine Corps amphibious assault into a heavily fortified city. A fleet of 230 ships participates in the Inchon assault. In evaluating the landing, Gen. of the Army MacArthur declares "the Navy and Marine Corps never shone brighter."

(This is the only US amphibious assault against opposition to be carried out since the Okinawa landings of 1945.)

16 SEP

The battleship *Missouri* engages two North Korean divisions entrenched on the north bank of the Hyong-San River with the 16-inch (406-mm) guns. She fires a total of 300 16-inch rounds at the enemy troops, permitting the South Korean 3rd Division to easily move ashore and subdue the North Korean forces.

17 SEP

Two North Korean Yak-3s attack the heavy cruiser *Rochester*. Four bombs are dropped on the ship, three of which miss while the fourth strikes and bounces off the aircraft crane at the cruiser's stern. The two North Korean aircraft are destroyed by anti-aircraft fire from the nearby British cruiser *Jamaica*.

Kimpo airfield between Inchon and Seoul is captured by US Marines.

20 SEP

The 1st Marine Aircraft Wing begins operations out of Kimpo airfield.

21 SEP

Gen. of the Army George C. Marshall, USA, is sworn in as Secretary of Defense. He is the only career military officer to ever hold that office. The Army Chief of Staff during World War II, Marshall had served as Secretary of State from 1947 to 1949.

22 SEP

Gen. Bradley, the Chairman of the Joint Chiefs of Staff since Aug 1949, is promoted to the rank of General of the Army. He is the only US officer promoted to five-star rank since the promotion of four Army and four Navy officers in 1944–1945.

25 SEP

The British light carrier *Theseus* arrives off Korea to relieve her sister ship *Triumph*. The *Triumph* is the first aircraft carrier to complete a Korean combat tour.

27 SEP

The South Korean capital of Seoul is liberated by US and South Korean troops.

28 SEP

Gen. MacArthur informs the Joint Chiefs of Staff that he intends to send the Eighth Army northward to seize the North Korean capital of Pyongyang during the last half of Oct 1950. MacArthur's plan includes an amphibious landing at the port city of Wonsan. MacArthur declares that there is no indication of Chinese troops in North Korea.

29 SEP

The US minesweeper *Magpie* (AMS 25) strikes a mine and sinks while sweeping off Chuksan; 21 of her crew are killed. This is the first US warship to be sunk by enemy action since World War II.

10 OCT

A massive minefield consisting of more than 3,000 magnetic and contact mines is discovered in Wonsan harbor by US ships. The planned invasion of Wonsan is delayed until the field is swept (by which time US troops have entered the port city from the land side).

12 OCT

In an effort to expedite the minesweeping in Wonsan harbor, F4U Corsairs and AD Skyraiders from the carriers *Philippine Sea* and *Leyte* attack the minefields with hydrostatically fused bombs. Each bomb is fused to detonate at a depth of 25 feet (7.6 m). The strike aircraft drop two five-mile (eight-km) lanes of bombs 600 feet (183 m) apart. While many mines are destroyed, this method of minesweeping is generally seen as impractical.

President Truman orders four National Guard divisions and two National Guard regimental combat teams to be called into active service. These are the first reserve ground force units brought to active duty status in the Korean War.

13 OCT

The US minesweepers *Pirate* (AM 275) and *Pledge* (AM 277) are sunk by magnetic mines in Wonsan harbor while attempting to clear a channel.

Rear Adm. Allan Smith, USN, commander of the Wonsan minesweeping operation, sends a message to the Chief of Naval Operations reporting the destruction of the *Pirate* and *Pledge* and stating that "The US Navy has lost command of the sea in Korean waters . . . ." Chief of Naval Operations Adm. Forrest P. Sherman, USN, reluctantly agrees, commenting that "When you can't go where you want to, when you want to, you haven't got command of the sea. We've been plenty submarine and air conscious, now we're going to start getting mine conscious—beginning last week."

15 OCT

President Truman meets with Gen. MacArthur on Wake Island to confer on the Korean conflict. During the meeting MacArthur assures the President that any Chinese intervention into Korea could be easily and quickly dealt with due to the superiority of UN air power. MacArthur further states that UN troops could be withdrawn from Korea as early as Christmas.

19 OCT

US forces capture the North Korean capital of Pyongyang.

24 OCT

French Premier René Pleven outlines his plan for a European unified army, including West German contingents, within the framework of NATO.

25 OCT

Wonsan harbor is declared safe for Allied warships. A single clear channel exists although more than 2,000 unexploded mines remain in the area. An examination of unexploded mines indicates that they are of Soviet manufacture. US Navy frogmen also find Soviet 21-inch (533-mm) torpedoes and depth charges in the Wonsan area.

29 OCT

Task Force 77 retires to Saesbo, Japan. With UN troops rapidly approaching the Yalu River, the air strike areas within range of carrier-based aircraft are limited.

1 NOV

Chinese-flown MiG-15 fighters appear over the Yalu River area and attack a flight of USAF F-51 Mustang fighters. This is the first appearance by the jet-propelled MiG-15 in the war. The MiG-15 is generally considered the most advanced fighter aircraft in the world with a top speed of 680 mph (1,094 kmh) and a ceiling of 51,000 feet (15,544 m).

5 NOV

Gen. MacArthur formally informs the UN of the presence of Chinese communist troops in North Korea. However, the Korean battlefield becomes unusually quiet, with little action being reported by US forces.

6 NOV

In response to a Chinese incursion, Task Force 77 steams out of Japanese waters to return to operating areas off Korea. A primary mission assigned to the carriers is the bombing of bridges across the Yalu River to prevent additional Chinese troop movements. The request to bomb the Yalu River bridges comes directly from the Fifth Air Force, which lacks the precision strike aircraft to perform the delivery of large bombs at low level. Unfortunately, the bombing orders come with restrictions: The Navy aircraft are to bomb the Korean side of the bridges only. At no time are US aircraft to violate Chinese airspace, even to bomb anti-aircraft guns or to pursue attacking MiGs. Despite these restrictions, the Navy attacks are effective against the bridges.

8 NOV

The first all-jet air battle in history occurs over the Yalu River as four MiG-15s engage four USAF F-80 Shooting Stars. One MiG is destroyed and the other three quickly retreat across the border into Manchuria. Under US rules of engagement, "hot pursuit" of enemy aircraft over the border is forbidden.

9 NOV

Lt. Comdr. W. T. Amen, USN, flying an F9F Panther from Fighter Squadron (VF) 111 on the carrier *Philippine Sea,* shoots down a Chinese MiG-15 fighter, becoming the first US naval aviator to shoot down a jet aircraft.

A USAF RB-29 Superfortress on a reconnaissance mission near the Manchurian border is attacked and shot down by MiG fighters.

21 NOV

The US Army's 17th Regimental Combat Team reaches the Manchurian village of Hyesanjin. This is the northernmost penetration by Allied troops during the Korean War.

The US battleship *New Jersey* (BB 62) is recommissioned after being laid up in reserve since 1948, bringing to two the number of US dreadnoughts in active service. The two other ships of this class, the *Iowa* (BB 61) and *Wisconsin* (BB 64), are undergoing reactivation and will return to the fleet in 1951.

25 NOV

Two Chinese communist army corps containing six divisions attack the Eighth Army northeast of Tokchon. This successful attack allows the Chinese to split the US Eighth and Tenth Armies and enables thousands of troops to pour through the gap.

27 NOV

Nearly 100,000 Chinese troops attack the 1st Marine Division near the Chosin Reservoir. The Marines begin a slow withdrawal south, maintaining a steady rate of fire on the Chinese the entire way.

29 NOV
Task Force 77 shifts primary air tasking from bridge destruction to close air support due to the deep penetrations made in UN lines by Chinese forces.

1 DEC
The carrier *Valley Forge* arrives at her home port of San Diego, Calif., from the Korean conflict.

4 DEC
Ens. Jesse L. Brown, USN, the Navy's first black pilot, is shot down while flying a strike near the Chosin Reservoir. Lt. (jg) Thomas Hudner, USN, crash-lands his F9F Panther near the injured Brown and attempts to put out the fire in Brown's aircraft. Brown dies before the rescue helicopter arrives. For his heroic actions, Hudner is awarded the Medal of Honor.

6 DEC
With UN forces reeling from the large Chinese onslaught, the carrier *Valley Forge* is ordered to immediately return to the Korean theater to support UN forces.

President Truman issues a directive to his senior military commanders—and primarily to Gen. MacArthur—forbidding direct communication to the press. All military press statements must be coordinated and approved by the administration to ensure that they conform with stated policy.

18 DEC
Patrol Squadron (VP) 892, the first all-reserve squadron to operate in the Korean war zone, begins operations from Iwakuni, Japan. The squadron flies PBM-5 Mariner flying boats.

19 DEC
Due to the Chinese intervention in the Korean conflict, and the subsequent losses to UN forces, President Truman declares a state of national emergency. The North Atlantic Council appoints Gen. of the Army Dwight D. Eisenhower, USA, to be the first Supreme Allied Commander Europe (SACEUR). British Field Marshal Bernard L. Montgomery is appointed Deputy SACEUR. Ike's high reputation and presence will have a strong influence on the shape of the embryonic NATO. When asked what it would take for the Soviet Army to reach the English Channel, Montgomery gives a one word reply, "Shoes."

20 DEC
The Brussels Treaty Powers decide to merge the military organization of the Western Union into NATO.

1951

2 JAN

The South Korean capital of Seoul is occupied by advancing Chinese troops.

25 JAN

First flight of the Douglas XF4D-1 Skyray, a delta-wing, tailless turbojet fighter designed for carrier operation.

29 JAN

The aircraft carriers of Task Force 77 begin a campaign to interdict the east coast railroads in North Korea.

2 FEB

The USS *Partridge* (AMS 31) is sunk by a floating mine while conducting sweep operations southeast of Wonsan. Eight men are killed and six wounded. She is the fourth and last US minesweeper sunk in the war.

5 FEB

A force of six AJ-1 Savage and three P2V-3C Neptune bombers of Composite Squadron (VC) 5 depart Norfolk, Va., for a trans-Atlantic flight (with stops) to Port Lyautey, French Morocco. All but one AJ, grounded in the Azores, arrive on 8 Feb. This marks the first time the Navy has deployed nuclear strike aircraft overseas and the first flight across the Atlantic by carrier-type aircraft. The Savages will be assigned to *Midway* (CVB 41)–class carriers during their deployments into the Mediterranean. The carriers will have the atomic bombs, which will not be based ashore.

10 FEB

The USS *Grenadier* (SS 525) is commissioned, the last submarine of the Navy's World War II building program to be completed. From 7 Dec 1941 through 15 Aug 1945 a total of 202 submarines were completed to the generally similar *Gato* (SS 212), *Balao* (SS 285), and *Tench* (SS 417) classes; nine additional submarines of the *Balao* class and 13 of the *Tench* class were completed after the war. The *Grenadier*'s first CO is Comdr. Henry G. Reaves, Jr., USN.

18 MAR

As the see-saw Korean conflict continues, Seoul is again liberated by the Eighth Army.

20 MAR

The battleship *Missouri* (BB 63) departs the Korean war zone to return to the United States. During her tour she fired 2,895 rounds of 16-inch (406-mm) ammunition as well as considerable 5-inch (127-mm) ammunition in support of Allied operations. The *Missouri*'s departure leaves UN troops without battleship gunfire support. Due to the impressive performance of the *Missouri*, her three sisters ships, *Iowa* (BB 61), *New Jersey* (BB 62), and *Wisconsin* (BB 64), are being prepared for action off Korea.

29 MAR

Carrier Air Group (CAG) 101, comprised almost entirely of naval reservists, carries out its first air strikes from the carrier *Boxer* (CV 21).

First flight of a Regulus missile test vehicle is successful.

31 MAR

The US Navy initiates development of Vertical Take-Off and Landing (VTOL) aircraft with a contract award to Convair for the XFY-1 Pogo fighter. The similar XFO-1 (later redesignated XFV-1) will be ordered from Lockheed three weeks later. The two planes, both powered by a turboprop engine, are competitive designs.

2 APR

In the first use of Navy jet aircraft as fighter-bombers, two F9F-2B Panthers of Fighter Squadron (VF) 191 from the carrier *Princeton* (CV 37) bomb a railroad bridge near Songin, North Korea.

Task Force 77 steams southeast from Korean waters to attain a position to protect Formosa from possible Chinese incursions as US intelligence indicates the possibility of a major Chinese attack on Formosa. During the ensuing 13 days no Navy air support will be available in the North Korean battle area.

Allied Command Europe becomes operational as Gen. of the Army Dwight D. Eisenhower, USA, sets up Supreme Headquarters Allied Powers Europe (SHAPE) at Roquencourt, outside of Paris, France.

7 APR

President Harry S. Truman relieves Gen. of the Army Douglas MacArthur from the position of Supreme Commander Allied Powers and Commander of UN forces in Korea. MacArthur's relief was caused by insubordination in his statements advocating an expansion of the Korean conflict and insinuating that the Truman Administration was following incorrect policies and hampering his direction of the war.

11 APR

Gen. Matthew B. Ridgeway, USA, commander of the Eighth Army, succeeds Gen. MacArthur, as Commander in Chief UN Command. MacArthur leaves the Far East for the United States, which he has not seen for more than 14 years.

22 APR

The Chinese spring offensive in Korea begins with attacks on the South Korean 6th Division and the US 1st Marine Division in an attempt to turn the left flank of Allied forces. The 1st Marine Division is able to stem the Chinese assault, but the 6th Korean Division is severely hurt in the attack.

1 MAY

Eight AD-4 Skyraiders from Attack Squadron (VA) 195 on the carrier *Princeton* launch an attack against the Hwachon Dam using Mk 13 aerial torpedoes. The only use of aerial torpedoes in combat since World War II, the attack is successful and causes flooding of the Han and Pukhan River valleys, denying North Korea use of the rivers for transportation of troops and supplies.

4 MAY

The Douglas bill—named for Sen. Paul Douglas—is unanimously passed by the US Senate, authorizing a Marine Corps of 400,000 men and women with four divisions and four aircraft wings. The bill makes the Commandant of the Marine Corps a member of the Joint Chiefs of Staff.

15 MAY

The US Army begins the prosecution of the case against a North Korean/Japanese spy ring. The ringleader of this group, Yoshimatsu Iwamura, was captured by Army intelligence in Japan one week before Inchon. Upon searching his apartment, the top secret plans of the Inchon invasion are discovered.

17 MAY

The USS *New Jersey* arrives off Korea and opens fire on enemy emplacements around Wonsan. The battleship's guns destroy an ammunition dump and a truck convoy, and score a direct hit on a bridge, dropping the span and destroying the supports.

20 MAY

Capt. James Jabara, USAF, flying an F-86 Sabre fighter, becomes the first US jet ace when he shoots down his fifth and sixth MiG-15 fighters over North Korea. Jabara will down 15 MiGs during the war to become the second highest-scoring US jet ace.

21 MAY

The USS *New Jersey* is fired on by a North Korean 5-inch (127-mm) shore battery off Wonsan while performing a shore bombardment. One man is killed and several wounded before the enemy artillery is destroyed.

25 MAY

Three AJ-1 Savages land aboard the recently completed USS *Oriskany* (CV 34), beginning a program to provide nuclear strike aircraft to Pacific Fleet aircraft carriers.

1 JUNE

The 1st Marine Aircraft Wing begins basing one squadron of aircraft to the immediate rear of the 1st Marine Division in order to provide close air support with a faster response time.

5 JUNE

The aircraft carriers of Task Force 77 begin a series of intense air strikes known collectively as Operation Strangle. The strikes are designed to interdict the battlefield by attacking supply roads behind enemy lines. A one-degree strip of latitude across North Korea just above the front lines is selected. Eight air routes within this area are parceled out with the Fifth Air Force attacking the three westernmost routes, Task Force 77 the two central routes, and the 1st Marine Air Wing the three easternmost routes.

6 JUNE

The USS *Langley* (CVL 27) is transferred to France under the Mutual Defense Assistance Program. The carrier is renamed *La Fayette*. Previously the only US aircraft carriers transferred to other nations were escort carriers (AVG-CVE).

12 JUNE

The US destroyer *Walke* (DD 723) strikes a mine while on patrol off Hungnam, North Korea. Twenty-six of the ship's crew are killed in the incident.

18 JUNE

The Allied Command Southern Europe becomes operational. Adm. Robert B. Carney, USN, the first CINCSOUTH, sets up his headquarters in Naples, Italy. The new command is responsible for US naval forces in the Mediterranean as well as NATO forces in Southern Europe.

The Navy-built airship ZPN-1 makes its first flight.

1 JULY

Lt. Comdr. J. M. Glaser, RN, in a Firefly piston-engine fighter, makes history's first steam-catapult launch from the carrier *Perseus*. The steam catapult provides the solution to the problems posed by the heavier aircraft being developed that could not be safely launched by hydraulic catapult. The steam catapult along with the angled flight deck and mirror landing system is one of the three major British contributions to postwar carrier design.

8 JULY

UN military representatives led by Vice Adm. C. Turner Joy, USN, and Rear Adm. Arleigh A. Burke, USN, arrive at Kaesong to begin armistice talks with North Korean and Chinese representatives.

10 JULY

The first actual truce meeting over a military demarcation line, between allied and enemy representatives begins at Kaesong. Sitting down with Rear Adms. Joy and Burke are Gen. Nam Il, Chief of Staff of the North Korean Army, and Lt. Gen. Tung Hua, deputy commander of Chinese forces in Korea. As truce talks begin, the battlefield front lines stabilize along the general lines between Munsan and Kosong. The ground war enters a new phase, where the goal is position and neither Allies nor enemy will expend major resources to change the situation.

12 JULY

Congress approves funds for the construction of the first supercarrier, the *Forrestal* (CVB 59).

22 JULY

Chief of Naval Operations Adm. Forrest P. Sherman dies in Naples, Italy, following a heart attack.

26 JULY

During truce discussions, North Korea representatives assert that it controls the 200 square miles (518 km²) of South Korea that are west of the Imjin River and south of the 38th parallel. Rear Adms. Joy and Burke dispute the claim, declaring that UN guerrillas control the area. Joy sends a message to Gen. Ridgeway stating that it was of the utmost urgency that UN control be visibly demonstrated in and around the Ongjin Peninsula.

28 JULY

In order to demonstrate that the disputed Ongjin Peninsula area of Korea is under UN control, the heavy cruiser *Los Angeles* (CA 135) enters the swept channel of Haeju-man and engages enemy shore positions with her 8-inch (203-mm) guns. The North Koreans are caught by surprise not realizing that such a large ship could steam into the shallow waters around the peninsula.

7 AUG

The Douglas XF3H-1N Demon carrier-based fighter makes its first flight. The Demon program will be plagued by numerous problems, including an underpowered engine. Eleven test flight accidents kill four pilots. (The Demon will enter fleet service in 1956 with a more powerful, but still underpowered engine, and will be quickly superseded by the superior F4H Phantom; the F3H is later redesignated F-3.)

A US Navy D-558-2 Skyrocket research aircraft, piloted by test pilot William B. Bridgeman, sets an unofficial world speed record of Mach 1.88—1,238 mph (1,992 kmh)—at 66,000 feet (20,165 m) over Muroc, Calif. Again piloted by Bridgeman, the D-558-2 reaches 74,494 feet (22,705 m) on 15 Aug 1951, the highest altitude yet reached by man.

8 AUG

The missile test ship *Norton Sound* (AV 11) is redesignated AVM 1.

9 AUG

During a conference at the Royal Aircraft Establishment in Bedford, England, Capt. Dennis Campbell, RN, proposes a novel flight deck idea arrangement—a 10.5° offset (angled) landing area. With the angled deck, an aircraft missing the arresting wires could accelerate and become airborne, to come around for another landing attempt as opposed to crashing into a barrier or aircraft parked forward.

22 AUG

The Royal Navy forms its first operational squadron flying jet-propelled aircraft: No. 800 Squadron is equipped with eight Supermarine Attacker F.1 fighters, which will operate from the carrier *Eagle*, to be commissioned later in the year.

23 AUG

The aircraft carrier *Essex* (CV 9), newly recommissioned and modernized, arrives off Korea for combat operations. The *Essex* deploys to Korea following her

Project 27A conversion that enables her to better operate jet aircraft. The *Essex* was also the first carrier to bring the McDonnell F2H Banshee fighter to action in the Korean War.

25 AUG

For the first time in the Korean conflict, F2H Banshees and F9F Panthers (from the *Essex*) provide escort to USAF B-29s on a mission against the previously off-limits port and railroad facilities at Wojin. The B-29s, bombing visually, drop 97 percent of their bombs on target, wiping out the railroad marshaling yards.

1 SEP

Australia, New Zealand, and the United States sign the Pacific Defense Pact (ANZUS). Unlike NATO, ANZUS will not endure the duration of the Cold War, but will dissolve in the mid-1980s due to New Zealand's militant anti–nuclear weapons posture.

7 SEP

In the first shipboard launching of a Terrier missile, a missile is fired from the test ship *Norton Sound* and simulates a successful interception of an F6F target drone.

16 SEP

An F2H Banshee returning to the *Essex* from a strike misses the arresting wires and slams into the deck park. The ensuing fire kills eight and injures 27. Four planes are destroyed. The *Essex* is forced to retire to Japan for repairs.

20 SEP

Operation Strangle is halted. The damage done to the North Korean road network is considered minimal. Task Force 77 and the other Allied air units shift back to attacking the enemy railroad lines.

First flight of the Grumman F9F-6 Cougar, a swept-wing variant of the F9F Panther. Large numbers of the carrier aircraft will be flown in the training and photo-reconnaissance roles (later designated F-9).

1 OCT

HMS *Eagle* is placed in commission after being under construction for nine years. With a displacement of 45,720 tons full load, she is the largest aircraft carrier ever to serve with the Royal Navy; the *Ark Royal* is a near sister ship. The *Eagle* has the largest aircraft capacity of any British carrier, with the ability to operate 80 aircraft.

3 OCT

Helicopter Anti-Submarine Squadron (HS) 1 is commissioned at Key West, Fla., under Comdr. J. T. Watson, USN. HS-1 is the Navy's first specialized ASW helicopter squadron and flies the Sikorsky HO4S-1 helicopter.

7 OCT

The US destroyer *Small* (DD 838) strikes a mine near Hungnam in almost the exact location the destroyer *Walke* (DD 723) had been mined four months earlier. Nine men aboard the *Small* are killed.

29 OCT

Navy Fighter Squadron (VF) 54 from the US carrier *Essex,* flying AD Skyraiders, strikes the headquarters of the North Korean Communist Party in Kapsan. This raid is based on intelligence received from guerrillas operating inside North Korea. The precisely timed raid results in the first bomb falling exactly 13 minutes after North Korean and Chinese sit down to begin their meeting. More than 500 senior party members are killed in the attack, which damages no other part of the city of Kapsan except the Communist Party compound itself.

3 NOV

Allied minesweeping operations get under way at Chongjin on the east coast of North Korea, 75 n.miles (139 km) south of the Soviet naval base at Vladivostok. No amphibious landing is planned for the Chongjin area, the purpose of the operation being to clear mines inside the 50-fathom curve in order to allow for closer inshore bombardments.

6 NOV

A US Navy P2V-3 Neptune patrol aircraft on a weather reconnaissance mission disappears off the coast of Siberia after being fired on by Soviet fighters. All ten crewmen are lost.

8 NOV

North Korean radio offers a large reward for the heads of the pilots who flew the 29 Oct raid on Communist Party headquarters. The raiders are labeled the "Butchers of Kapsan" by Communist media.

10 NOV

The first US submarine of post–World War II design and construction, the *K-1* (SSK 1), is placed in commission at the Electric Boat yard in Groton, Conn. She is a small (765-ton) hunter-killer submarine, intended to ambush Soviet submarines transiting straits and narrow seas. Her first CO is Lt. Comdr. Frank A. Andrews, USN.

21 NOV

The USS *Los Angeles* rescues the 1st Republic of Korea Corps from almost certain destruction. Enemy troops had broken through 1st Corps lines at Kojo and seized a large cache of ammunition, cutting 1st Corps off from any supplies. The *Los Angeles* was detached from Task Force 77 and immediately opened fire upon arriving off Kojo. She drove the enemy back to their previous positions with 91 rounds of 8-inch (203-mm) gunfire.

1 DEC

The US Naval Aviation Safety Activity is established at Norfolk, Va., to promote aviation safety; its name will be changed to the Naval Aviation Safety Center in April 1955. (*See* 3 May 1968.)

12 DEC

First flight of the Kaman K-225 demonstration helicopter fitted with a YB-502 turbine (jet) engine. This flight at Windsor Locks, Conn., is part of a Navy program and the first US demonstration flight of a turbine-powered helicopter.

19 DEC

The carrier *Philippine Sea* (CV 47) at San Diego carries out drills for the assembly of nuclear weapons, marking the introduction of nuclear weapons into the Pacific Fleet.

1952

4 JAN

The US Navy ship designations CAG and CLG are established for heavy and light cruisers armed with guided missiles.

7 JAN

The 3rd Marine Division is activated at Camp Pendleton, Calif. The division was created by increasing the size of the existing 3rd Marine Brigade.

30 JAN

Vice Adm. Lynde D. McCormick, USN, the Commander in Chief US Atlantic Fleet, is appointed the first Supreme Allied Commander Atlantic (SACLANT) within the NATO structure.

1 FEB

The 3rd Marine Aircraft Wing is activated to provide air support for the 3rd Marine Division.

8 FEB

Trials begin on the British carrier *Triumph* to test the feasibility of the angled flight deck. The *Triumph* has an angled layout painted onto her axial deck and various obstructions are removed. The touch-and-go landings are all flown successfully.

21 FEB

The NATO Channel Command is established with Adm. Sir Arthur John Power, RN, as the first Commander in Chief Channel (CINCHAN). This is the last of three major NATO military commands to be set up, the others being Supreme Allied Commander Europe (SACEUR) and Supreme Allied Commander Atlantic (SACLANT).

15 MAR

While performing a fire suppression mission off Songjiin, the battleship *Wisconsin* (BB 64) closes the shoreline to engage a train with her 40-mm gun mounts. After destroying the train, the *Wisconsin* is taken under fire by a North Korean 155-mm artillery battery, which scores a direct hit on the battleship, tearing a 24 × 30-foot (7.3 × 9.1-m) hole at the 02 deck level. Three men are wounded. The *Wisconsin* is able to destroy the artillery with her main guns. Most battleship shore bombardments are generally carried out

at the 50- to 100-fathom curve off both Korean coasts, that distance having been determined as the optimum to avoid enemy mines.

10 APR

Supreme Allied Command Atlantic (SACLANT) becomes operational with headquarters at Norfolk, Va. The NATO command has responsibility for the area from the North Pole to the Tropic of Cancer and from the coastal waters of North America to those of Europe and North Africa.

15 APR

First flight of the Boeing YB-52 Stratofortress strategic bomber. The six-jet, swept-wing aircraft will enter USAF service in 1955 with 744 aircraft produced through 1962. The planes will see combat in the Vietnam War and Persian Gulf conflict. Extensively modified, B-52s will serve into the 21st century.

16 APR

NATO opens its provisional headquarters at Palais de Chaaillot, Paris.

21 APR

During gunfire support operations off the Korean coast, the heavy cruiser *St. Paul* (CA 73) suffers a magazine fire in her No. 1 8-inch (203-mm) gun turret. Thirty crewman die and others are injured.

26 APR

While conducting night flight operations in the North Atlantic, en route to Gibraltar and a Sixth Fleet deployment, the carrier *Wasp* (CV 18) collides with the destroyer-minesweeper *Hobson* (DMS 26). The *Hobson* is split in two and quickly sinks with 176 crewmen lost, including her commanding officer. The *Wasp* returns to the New York Naval Shipyard for repairs.

28 APR

The US Navy announces that British-designed steam catapults will be adopted for use in US aircraft carriers. The first two catapults will be installed in the USS *Hancock* (CV 19).

First meeting of the North Atlantic Council in permanent session convenes in Paris.

15 MAY

The Soviet cruiser *Sverdlov* is commissioned, the first major warship of Stalin's postwar shipbuilding program. Displacing 17,200 tons full load and 688⅝ feet (210 m) long, the *Sverdlov*s carry 12 6-inch (152-mm) guns and lighter weapons, torpedo tubes, and mines. The 14 *Sverdlov*s completed through 1955 will symbolize the Soviet fleet of the 1950s and 1960s. (After the death of Stalin in Mar 1953 additional *Sverdlov*s will be canceled, some scrapped on the building ways.)

19 MAY

First flight of the Grumman XF10F-1 Jaguar, the first aircraft fitted with a variable-sweep (swing) wings. The Jaguar will not enter fleet service primarily because of its underpowered J40 engine.

26 MAY

The outline of an angled landing area is painted on the flight deck of US carrier *Midway* (CVB 41) for evaluation. Several aviators from the Naval Air Test Center Patuxent River, Md., conduct trial landings and enthusiastically recommend its adoption.

13 JUNE

A US Air Force RB-29 Superfortress on a reconnaissance mission over the Sea of Japan disappears. There is no trace of the aircraft or of its 12 crewmen; a Soviet fighter attack is reported by some sources.

14 JUNE

The keel for the nuclear-propelled submarine *Nautilus* (SSN 571) is laid down at the Electric Boat yard in Groton, Conn., her keel being initialed by President Harry S. Truman. The *Nautilus* will be the world's first vehicle to be propelled by atomic energy.

23 JUNE

US forces begin a two-day aerial campaign to destroy the electric power of North Korea. Previously, these power plants were off limits to Allied air attack. Navy aircraft join land-based planes from the Air Force and Marines in knocking out electrical plants at Suiho, Chosen, Fusen, and Kyosen. Due to the proximity of the North Korean power plants to Chinese airfields, 84 USAF F-86 Sabre fighters provide a continuous combat air patrol for the attacking naval forces. The two-day effort involves more than 1,200 sorties in the largest American air effort since World War II.

For the first time in 18 months a four-carrier task force is available to UN forces off Korea, consisting of the *Boxer* (CV 21), *Bon Homme Richard* (CV 31), *Princeton* (CV 37), and *Philippine Sea* (CV 47).

28 JUNE

President Truman signs Public Law 416 providing for the Commandant of the Marine Corps to sit with the Joint Chiefs of Staff and vote on all issues of direct interest to the Marine Corps with the Commandant determining those issues. The compromise legislation also mandates a Marine Corps of three divisions and three aircraft wings (as opposed to the four divisions and air wings in the bill passed by the Senate; *see* 4 May 1951). The Marine Corps is the only service that has force levels mandated by law.

1 JULY

The US Naval Guided Missile School is established at Dam Neck, Va.

6 JULY

The US-flag liner *United States* attains 35.59 knots in crossing the Atlantic to capture the coveted Blue Ribbon, previously held by the British-flag liner *Queen Mary*. The *United States*—operated by the United States Lines—was built for wartime use as a troop transport. On secret speed trials in May 1952 she reached 38.52 knots.

11 JULY

US Navy, Marine, and Air Force, and Australian and British aircraft begin a 24-hour attack on the railroad yards and surrounding industrial areas of Pyongyang, North Korea. During this raid 1,400 tons of bombs and 23,000 gallons of napalm are dropped on Pyongyang, destroying 1,500 buildings and damaging 900 others.

14 JULY

The keel for the carrier *Forrestal* (CVB 59) is laid down at Newport News Shipbuilding and Dry Dock Co. in Virginia. At this stage in her development the *Forrestal* is planned as a straight (axial) deck carrier with hydraulic catapults. The *Forrestal*'s basic design is similar to the aborted *United States* (CVA 58) with the later ship having a fixed island structure.

31 JULY

A US Navy PBM-5S Mariner patrol plane is attacked by Chinese MiG-15 fighters off Formosa. The Mariner is damaged and two crewman are killed and two wounded in the attack.

1 AUG

The Commander in Chief US European Command (CINCEUR) is established as the US unified command in Europe with Gen. Matthew B. Ridgeway, USA, as the first CINCEUR. Ridgeway also assumes concurrent duties as Supreme Allied Commander Europe (SACEUR), relieving Gen. of the Army Dwight D. Eisenhower of this post. From 15 Mar 1947 to 1 Aug 1952, CINCEUR was essentially an Army command.

6 AUG

A hangar deck fire on the carrier *Boxer* kills eight. The fire is caused by an exploding fuel tank from a parked aircraft which also cooks off a 500-pound (227-kg) bomb. The *Boxer* had 58 armed and fueled aircraft on her flight deck, preparing to launch against Korea, but the conflagration is extinguished before those planes are involved.

9 AUG

Four piston-engine Sea Furies from the British light carrier *Ocean* are attacked by eight MiG-15 fighters north of Chinnampo on the northwest coast of Korea. In the ensuing air-to-air battle, one MiG is destroyed; none of the British planes are damaged.

25 AUG

The US Joint Chiefs of Staff forward their convoy and resupply requirements to the Supreme Allied Commander Atlantic. The report states a requirement for resupply operations to begin as soon as possible from the commencement of hostilities due to the American commitment to the forward defense of Europe. The first convoy must leave the United States for Britain within 15 days of the start of hostilities.

28 AUG

The US carrier *Boxer* launches an explosive-filled F6F-5K drone aircraft against a railroad bridge in North Korea. The drone is radio controlled by two AD Skyraiders that steer the F6F-5K to the target. This is the first of six such drone attacks launched by the carrier.

29 AUG

A second massed UN around-the-clock air attack begins on the Pyongyang area as all Task Force 77 air groups combine with the Fifth Air Force, 1st Marine Aircraft Wing, and British and South Korean planes to strike North Korean supply dumps in and around the city.

1 SEP

The North Atlantic Treaty Organization (NATO) begins its first major naval exercise, code-named Mainbrace. This operation is conducted in the eastern Atlantic under the joint command of the Supreme Allied Commander Atlantic and the Supreme Allied Commander Europe. The Mainbrace exercise involves more than 160 ships, including the US carriers *Midway* and *Franklin D. Roosevelt* (CVB 42), and the battleship *Wisconsin;* the Royal Navy contributes the carriers *Eagle, Illustrious,* and *Theseus,* and the battleship *Vanguard.* The exercise scenario is that West Germany has been overrun by Soviet forces and they are advancing into Norway and Denmark. Mainbrace tests SACLANT's ability to provide support to the European northern flank during a major land battle.

The North Korean oil refinery at Aoji is destroyed by aircraft from the carriers *Essex* (CV 9), *Boxer,* and *Princeton.* Aoji's proximity to the Chinese and Soviet borders prohibited its attack by USAF B-29 bombers, which would have had to fly over the borders to strike Aoji.

3 SEP

The Naval Ordnance Test Station at China Lake, Calif., begins testing the Sidewinder air-to-air missile.

8 SEP

The carrier *Antietam* (CV 36) enters the New York Naval Shipyard for installation of an angled flight deck. When completed in Dec 1952, the deck will be angled to port 10.5° off the centerline of the ship; the landing area will be 525 feet (160 m) long and 70 feet (21.3 m) wide.

16 SEP

The USS *Barton* (DD 722) strikes a mine about 90 n.miles (167 km) east of Wonsan. The *Barton* was serving as a plane guard for Task Force 77 at the time and was thought to be in safe waters. The mine is believed to have broken loose from the Wonsan minefield when a typhoon swept the area on the 18th. Over the next several weeks, the Commander, Seventh Fleet, Vice Adm. Joseph (Jocko) Clark, USN, would report 40 mines around his ships. Five on the *Barton* were lost in the mine detonation.

22 SEP

The Canadian Tribal-class destroyer *Nookta* captures a North Korean minelayer south of Cho-do Island. The enemy craft had been laying magnetic mines in the area for the past 72 hours. This is the only seizure of an enemy vessel at sea during the conflict.

26 SEP

The US destroyer *Timmerman* (DD 828) is placed in commission as an experimental destroyer. She has lightweight machinery with three types of boilers providing steam to two turbines rated at 100,000 horsepower. Begun as a *Gearing* (DD 710)–class ship in 1945, she was the last ship of the World War II destroyer program to be completed. (She will be reclassified EAG 152 in 1953.) The ship's first CO is Comdr. Edward E. Hoffman, USN.

1 OCT

All US aircraft carriers designated CV and CVB are reclassified as attack carriers (CVA). This change is made to reflect the ships' mission rather than size. CVB had indicated "large" aircraft carriers since 1943. The aborted *United States* was a "heavy" carrier (CVA 58).

At a press conference in Paris, Secretary of the Navy Dan A. Kimball reveals that the Soviet Union has more than 300 deployable submarines, more than four times the number that Germany had in 1939. Kimball adds that "the Russians generally train their crews well, but not as good as the Germans did."

3 OCT

Great Britain explodes its first atomic bomb at a test site in the Monte Bello Islands, 50 miles (80 km) northwest of Australia. This event expands the nuclear club to three nations—the United States, Soviet Union, and Great Britain.

7 OCT

A US Air Force RB-29A Superfortress on a routine flight off the coast of Japan disappears; it is believed to have been shot down by Soviet fighters. Eight crewmen are lost.

22 OCT

The Douglas XA3D-1 Skywarrior makes its first flight. The Skywarrior will be the largest aircraft to enter carrier service with a maximum weight of 70,000 pounds (31,752 kg) and a wingspan of 72 feet (22 m). Despite its size, the Skywarrior can operate from *Essex*-class carriers. The Skywarrior—nicknamed "Whale"—will remain in naval service for more than 30 years, flying in the nuclear and conventional attack, reconnaissance, tanker, and electronic

countermeasures roles. (The aircraft will be designated A-3 in 1962.)

1 NOV

The United States detonates the first thermonuclear or hydrogen device at Eniwetok Atoll in the central Pacific. President Truman calls the test ". . . a dramatic success. So powerful was the explosion that an entire island was blown away and a huge crater left in the coral. It was an awesome demonstration of the new power. . . ." The test—code-name Mike shot in the Ivy test series—is a 10.4-megaton thermonuclear "device." It is not a weapon, but a device that weighs almost 70 tons (63,504 kg). The island that was "erased" from the map was Elugelab.

3 NOV

In the first shipboard launch of the Regulus land-attack missile, the USS *Norton Sound* (AVM 1) launches a Regulus while steaming off the California coast. The missile is then landed by radio control on San Nicholas Island.

12 NOV

The US and Japanese governments sign an agreement for the loan of 18 PF-type frigates and 50 landing craft as the first step toward Japanese rearmament.

18 NOV

While operating in northern Korean waters near the Soviet naval base complex at Vladivostok, Task Force 77—consisting of the carriers *Essex, Kearsarge* (CVA 33), and *Oriskany* (CVA 34), and screening ships—is approached by seven Soviet MiG-type fighter aircraft. The MiGs are intercepted by F9F-5 Panthers of Navy Fighter Squadron (VF) 781 from the *Oriskany*. In the ensuing aerial combat, two MiGs are shot down and one damaged. The MiGs attempted to box in the Panthers in an aerial pincer movement when the F9F-5s break away. No US aircraft are lost.

The feasibility of employing a helicopter as an aerial minesweeper is demonstrated by a Navy HRP-1 Rescuer in a series of tests off Panama City, Fla.

23 NOV

A US Navy P4Y-2S Privateer patrol plane is attacked by two Chinese MiG-15 fighters over the China Sea off Shanghai. No damage is incurred and the American plane returns safely to Okinawa.

3 DEC

Fulfilling his campaign promise, President-elect Eisenhower arrives in South Korea to assess the situation. Despite his reputation for sound military thinking, Eisenhower stresses that he "has no trick solution" to the Korean situation.

4 DEC

First flight of the S2F Tracker, the US Navy's first aircraft designed specifically for both anti-submarine search and attack. The carrier-based aircraft will be produced in large numbers for US and foreign use. (The S2F is redesignated S-2 in 1962.)

16 DEC

The aircraft carrier *Princeton* becomes the first warship to launch a Regulus land-attack missile.

1953

12 JAN

Capt. S. G. Mitchell, USN, CO of the carrier *Antietam* (CVA 36), traps aboard his ship in an SNJ Texan training aircraft, initiating four days of test operations with *Antietam*'s canted or angled fight deck. Rear Adm. Thomas Combs, USN, the Chief of the Bureau of Aeronautics, says that the *Antietam* trials will determine whether or not the angled deck design is incorporated into the new *Forrestal* (CVA 59) class.

18 JAN

A US Navy P2V-5 Neptune patrol aircraft is forced down at sea in the Formosa Strait off Swatow, China, after being fired on by Chinese anti-aircraft guns. Seven crewman are missing, two of whom may have been taken prisoner by the Chinese; the three other fliers are rescued. A US Coast Guard flying boat crashes during take-off to rescue the crew raising the total fatalities in the incident to 11.

13 FEB

First test flight of the Sparrow air-to-air missile with full radar guidance.

15 FEB

Two Soviet MiG-15 fighters from Vladivostok violate northern Japanese airspace and are intercepted by two USAF F-86 Sabres. One Soviet plane is fired upon and damaged when it ignores directions to leave Japanese airspace. Both Soviet planes return to Vladivostok.

1 MAR

Task Force 77 planes destroy the North Korean hydroelectric plant at Chosen.

4 MAR

The frigate *Norfolk* (DL 1) is commissioned at the Philadelphia Naval Shipyard. Begun as a hunter-killer cruiser (CLK 1), she is a large destroyer-type warship fitted with advanced ASW weapons. She is unusual in having 3-inch (76-mm) rapid-fire guns in lieu of the traditional 5-inch (127-mm) guns of destroyer-type ships. Additional ships of this type will not be built because of the high cost (a planned CLK 2 was to have been named *New Haven*). The *Norfolk* is commanded by Capt. Clarence M. Bowley, USN.

A Polish Air Force pilot defects to the West in a MiG-15 fighter. The pilot departed a Polish air base

on the Baltic and flew to the Danish island of Bornholm. This is the first completely intact MiG-15 acquired by the West.

5 MAR

Josef Stalin dies following a stroke. The dictator of the Soviet Union since 1924, he leaves no named successor. Leadership of the Soviet state is vested in a troika of Lavrenti Beria, Nikolai Bulganin, and Annastav Mikoyan.

6 MAR

The USS *Tunny* (SSG 282), the first US submarine fitted to launch the Regulus surface-to-surface attack missile, is commissioned at Mare Island, Calif., following her missile conversion. She can carry two of the surface-launched weapons.

A major fire occurs on the carrier *Oriskany* (CVA 34) when a returning strike aircraft releases a bomb onto the flight deck. Two are killed and 15 wounded before the fire is extinguished several hours later. The *Oriskany* is able to resume flight operations the next day.

7 MAR

The USS *Northampton* (CLC 1), the Navy's first specifically designed tactical command ship, is commissioned at the Boston Naval Shipyard. The *Northampton* was begun in World War II as the heavy cruiser CA 125 of the *Oregon City* (CA 122) class; the ship's construction was canceled in 1945 when she was 56.2 percent complete. Subsequently the *Northampton* was completed as a command ship to operate with carrier task forces. She will be redesignated as a national command ship (CC 1) in 1962. Her first CO is Capt. William D. Irvin, USN.

15 MAR

The NATO Allied Command Mediterranean (AFMED) becomes operational with headquarters in Malta. The Mediterranean area has been a source of contention between American and British leaders for over a year. Adm. Robert B. Carney, USN, Commander, Allied Forces Southern Europe, had refused to place the Sixth Fleet under the command of a non-American. The British contended that a unified supreme commander meant nothing without complete and total allied support, especially from its most powerful member. In the event, the command area was left divided. The Sixth Fleet would still operate as an independent force, although CINCAFMED did have certain poorly defined responsibilities for coordinating Sixth Fleet movements with local NATO air forces. Under CINCAFMED are the navies of Italy, Greece, and Turkey in addition the French and British Mediterranean fleets. Each member is assigned an operating patrol zone that they are responsible for in the event of war. The prime wartime mission of CINCAFMED is to prevent Soviet submarines from exiting the Black Sea. The first Commander in Chief Allied Forces Mediterranean is Adm. Lord Louis Mountbatten, RN.

The Soviet government issues an edict merging the Military Ministry and the Ministry of the Navy to form the Ministry of Defense. This in effect ends the independent status of the Soviet Navy.

20 MAR

The US Navy airship ZP2N-1 (later redesignated ZPG-2) makes its first flight. This craft will be the only series-produced airship of the post–World War II era, with 17 procured in anti-submarine and radar surveillance variants.

30 APR

President Dwight D. Eisenhower issues his plan for an "Efficient and Prepared Defense Establishment." The proposal will place more control in the hands of civilian Department of Defense officials and will limit the activities engaged in by military leaders. The Eisenhower plan's highlights include: (1) Revamping the Joint Chiefs of Staff to reduce administrative workloads; (2) Elimination of the Munitions Board, Research and Development Board, and Defense Supply Management; (3) Create six additional Assistant Secretaries of Defense to handle the functions now scattered amongst boards, committees, and advisors; (4) Increasing the role of the service secretaries in relations with the Joint Chiefs of Staff and making them "truly responsible" officials; (5) Reorganization of procurement and supply to prevent, among other things, equipment shortages for field troops. An additional proviso removes the Joint Chiefs from directing the unified commands and places them strictly in the roles of planners and advisors. Finally, the President insists that a professional military stay clear of political matters, saying that the JCS has "frequently exceeded their authority as military advisors as prescribed by law."

The Eisenhower policy is based upon the following premises: (1) The struggle with Russia and China would continue for the immediate future; (2) The US economy cannot support an infinite-sized defense budget, limits exist that have to be understood; (3) At present, the United States has an overwhelming superiority in the numbers of nuclear weapons and delivery systems.

1 MAY

The F-80 Shooting Star, the first operational US jet fighter, is withdrawn from the Korean theater. An adequate number of F-86 Sabres now are operational in the war zone. The F-80 had been criticized for its short range and minimal strike capability. The US Navy flew a small number of these aircraft with the designations TO and later TV.

15 MAY

The frigate *Mitscher* (DL 2), a large destroyer-type ship, is placed in commission. The first of four such ships configured primarily for anti-submarine warfare and intended to operate with large carriers, the *Mitscher* had been ordered as a destroyer (DD 927), but changed to DL 2 while under construction. The ship's first CO is Comdr. Terrell H. W. Connor, USN.

20 MAY

Due to the buildup of Soviet naval and air forces in the Murmansk/Kola Peninsula area, the government of Norway agrees to allow some foreign military personnel to serve at its NATO bases. NATO plans for the defense of Arctic Norway revolve around the Andya Island air base in the Norwegian Sea.

21 MAY

Aircraft from the carriers *Boxer* (CVA 21) and *Philippine Sea* (CVA 47) destroy 200 buildings and shatter enemy transport lines in the North Korean port cities of Pukchon and Songjin.

Based on the *Antietam* trials, the Navy announces a revision to the design of the aircraft carrier *Forrestal* to include an angled flight deck. Thirteen carriers of the *Essex* (CVA 9) class and all three carriers of the *Midway* (CVA 41) class will be rebuilt with angled flight decks.

An AD-4 Skyraider takes off from NAS Dallas, Texas, with a bomb load of 10,500 pounds (4,763 kg); combined with the weight of its guns, ammunition, fuel, and pilot, the aircraft has a useful load of 14,491 pounds (6,573 kg), which is 3,143 pounds (1,426 kg) more than the weight of the aircraft.

23 MAY

The French government urgently requests the loan of a second US light carrier for use in the Indochina conflict. The French have been operating the USS *Langley* (CVL 27), on loan since 1951.

Operation Skyhook begins in Korea during a lull in the fighting. This two-day experiment is an attempt to supply a division entirely by helicopter. Each helicopter will carry 800 pounds (363 kg) of supplies in nets slung under the aircraft.

24 MAY

The New York Times reports Soviet defector Zanis Nicis indicating that the "Soviet Navy has excellent morale and its sailors have little fear of US atomic weapons." Nicis worked at a Soviet naval base in Latvia.

25 MAY

South Korean President Syngman Rhee announces that his government will not accept any armistice that leaves Korea divided. Additionally, Rhee threatens to withdraw his forces from the UN command and use them to continue the war if a truce is signed against South Korean desires.

30 MAY

The US Navy begins an experimental hydrofoil project to test and evaluate the military applications of this type of craft. Hydrofoils are expected to be applicable to various small craft, the Navy goal is to design a foil with less water friction and more speed.

25 JUNE

The STR Mark I, the prototype for the nuclear reactor for the submarine *Nautilus* (SSN 571), achieves full power at the Navy's test facility at Arco, Idaho. The reactor had reached sustained criticality on 30 Mar 1953. The first full-power run lasts 96 hours and is equivalent to the submarine making a submerged transit of 2,500 n.miles (4,633 km), i.e., across the Atlantic Ocean.

Task Force 77 deploys four F4U-5N Corsair night fighters to Kimpo airfield in Korea for an indefinite period to deter night attacks on the field by North Korean aircraft that are too slow to be intercepted by jet fighters.

1 JULY

After a veracious debate in the press as well as within the Navy and Department of Defense, Capt. H. G. Rickover, USN, is selected for promotion to rear admiral.

8 JULY

The classification anti-submarine support aircraft carrier (CVS) is established and assigned to the carrier *Antietam* (formerly CV 36). Additional carriers of the *Essex* class will be redesignated and embark ASW air groups. CVS is later changed to ASW aircraft carrier.

11 JULY

Maj. John Bolt, USMC, becomes a jet fighter ace as he shoots down two MiGs over Korea (for a total of six). At the time Maj. Bolt is serving as an exchange pilot with the Fifth Air Force and flying an F-86 Sabre. He will be the only naval jet ace of the Korean War.

While performing gunfire support operations off the coast of Korea, the US heavy cruiser *St. Paul* (CA 73) is fired on by North Korean coastal artillery. Before the *St. Paul* can destroy the battery, she suffers several hits but suffers no casualties. The North Korean gun emplacement is destroyed.

15 JULY

The USS *Tunny* successfully launches the first Regulus missile to be launched from a submarine.

25 JULY

Carrier pilots of Task Force 77 set a new record for the Korean War by flying 600 sorties in a 24-hour period.

27 JULY

The Korean conflict ends at 2200 with the signing of an armistice at Panmunjom. In the 24 hours leading up to the ceasefire the US Navy continues to wage war against North Korea: 250 sorties are flown by the carrier air groups of Task Force 77 and the heavy cruiser *St. Paul* fires the last naval gunfire support of the conflict at 2159.

29 JULY

A US Air Force RB-50 Superfortress is shot down by Soviet fighters over the Sea of Japan. The copilot is recovered; the other 16 crewmen are lost.

4 AUG

The New York Times reports that Swiss intelligence shows that the Soviets have rebuilt the Nazi missile base of Peenemünde on the Baltic. Photos and sketches smuggled out of East Germany show the Soviets testing improved versions of the German Wasserfall radio-guided anti-aircraft missile.

8 AUG

Soviet Premier Georgi Malenkov announces that the Soviet Union has successfully exploded a hydrogen bomb. The Atomic Energy Commission replies that even though no hard evidence exists to prove the Soviet claim, British atomic spy Klaus Fuchs is known to have passed hydrogen weapon information to the Soviets during the 1940s.

12 AUG

The Soviet Union detonates a thermonuclear (hydrogen) "device" atop a tower at a Siberian test range. This is not a "true" hydrogen bomb, but an enhanced fission device with a yield on the order of 200 to 300 kilotons. It was only the fourth known Soviet nuclear detonation. (*Also see* 22 Nov 1955.)

In the first shipboard launching of a Terrier surface-to-air missile, the missile from the USS *Mississippi* (EAG 128), collides with an approaching F6F target drone.

15 AUG

Adm. Arthur W. Radford, USN, becomes Chairman of the Joint Chiefs of Staff, the second naval officer to hold that position. (Fleet Adm. William D. Leahy, USN, Chief of Staff to the President, was *de facto* chairman from 20 July 1942 to 21 Mar 1949.) A naval aviator, Radford has not commanded a ship. (He will serve until 15 Aug 1957.)

21 AUG

A Navy D-558-2 Skyrocket research aircraft flown by Lt. Col. Marion E. Carl, USMC, sets an altitude mark of 83,235 feet (25,370 m) over Edwards AFB, Calif.

10 SEP

US Navy minesweeping operations in Korean waters are concluded. The minesweepers remain, however, to function as patrol and surveillance ships.

11 SEP

In the first successful intercept, a Sidewinder air-to-air missile destroys an F6F target drone over the Naval Ordnance Test Station, China Lake, Calif.

16 SEP

NATO's Allied Command Atlantic, Allied Command Channel, and Allied Command Europe begin a month-long maritime exercise code-named Mariner. More than 300 ships participate in the exercise, designed to test a wide range of naval capabilities. Operation Mariner will end on 4 Oct 1953, having identified problems in communications and logistics.

3 OCT

A US Navy F4D Skyray fighter piloted by Lt. Comdr. James F. Verdin, USN, sets a world speed record of

752.943 mph (1,211.5 kmh) over a three-kilometer course.

12 OCT

In a speech at the commissioning of the frigate *John S. McCain* (DL 3), Chief of Naval Operations Adm. Carney, USN, reports that "numerically at least, Russia has become the world's second naval power. It is obvious that the Soviet Union is determined to emerge from its landlocked position and assume a place in the maritime world." The *McCain,* second ship of the *Mitscher* (DL 2) class, is commanded by Comdr. R. E. King, USN.

13 OCT

The Joint Chiefs of Staff completes planning on the military requirements of the "New Look" and presents it to the National Security Council. The plan calls for a minimum active force of 20 Army divisions, a 400-ship Navy, and 127 Air Force wings.

16 OCT

While undergoing an overhaul at the Boston Naval Shipyard, the carrier *Leyte* (CVS 32) is shaken by an explosion that destroys the portside catapult control room. The ship's company has the blaze under control within an hour, but 32 crewmen and five yard workers die in the fire. The damage to the ship will cost $600,000 to repair.

20 OCT

The NATO naval base at Iskenderun in Turkey is completed. This base, designed by the United States and built with US funds, will serve as the main eastern base for the Allied Mediterranean fleets. The base was constructed because of doubts about the long-term availability of British installations in Egypt.

30 OCT

The US National Security Council (NSC) directive No. 162 is adopted as a result of the growing US reliance on strategic air power and also was the one of the first indications of President Eisenhower's "New Look" military policy. NSC 162 codifies the United States maintaining a strong standing military force "with emphasis on the capability of inflicting massive retaliatory damage by offensive striking power." Additionally, NSC 162 states "the US will consider nuclear weapons to be as available for use as other munitions." In effect, any combat arena could become a nuclear battlefield.

20 NOV

In order to cut off a Viet Minh incursion into Laos and Thailand, the French parachute troops into the Dien Bien Phu valley. This classic airborne operation also sees vehicles, artillery, munitions, and building supplies parachuted into the valley. Dien Bien Phu is to provide an advanced base for troops to seek out and destroy Viet Minh forces.

A Navy D-558-2 rocket-powered research aircraft flown by A. Scott Crossfield reaches a speed of Mach 2.005—1,291 mph (2,078 kmh)—at 62,000 feet (18,900 m), the first manned aircraft to fly twice the speed of sound.

6 DEC

The US research submarine *Albacore* (AGSS 569) is commissioned. The 1,242-ton, diesel-electric craft is the first modern submarine with the "tear drop" hull design. She will serve as a high-speed underwater test platform, achieving a speed in excess of 35 knots on several occasions in her later configurations. This speed will be unsurpassed by any US submarine at the time of publication of this volume. (She will be decommissioned on 9 Dec 1972.) Lt. Comdr. Kenneth C. Gummerson, USN, is the *Albacore's* first CO.

18 DEC

The Sikorsky twin-engine XHR2S-1 heavy-lift helicopter flies for the first time. The helicopter, to be used by the US Army as the H-37 Mojave, was developed to carry Marine vehicles and artillery internally (being fitted with large clamshell nose doors). The Navy experiments with an HR2S-1W variant fitted with a large airborne early warning radar.

1954

3 JAN

The New York Times quotes an unnamed Navy official as saying that the nuclear-propelled submarine *Nautilus* (SSN 571), currently fitting out at Electric Boat, is "strictly a test vehicle, I doubt if she ever will fire a shot in anger." Navy planners say that the *Nautilus* is "too big" and "too unmaneuverable" to perform effectively as a first-line combatant.

4 JAN

The US carrier *Leyte* (CVS 32) departs the Boston Naval Shipyard as the first carrier of the *Essex* (CVA 9) class configured for anti-submarine operations. According to *Leyte*'s CO, Capt. Thomas Ahroon, USN, "the submarine is the greatest threat to our national security, the best way to get 'em is to hunt 'em and kill 'em." The CVS concept involves what essentially is the tactic of "wolfpack turned backwards." The *Leyte* will form the core of a Hunter-Killer (HUK) group that will include destroyers and, at times, submarines serving in the ASW role.

5 JAN

President Eisenhower approves a target goal of a 137-wing Air Force by 1957. This is a key provision of the "New Look" defense program that emphasizes air power and will cut sea and ground strength. The force is planned to provide 54 wings for the Strategic Air Command, 34 wings for the Aerospace Defense Command, 38 wings for the Tactical Air Command, and 11 troop carrier wings.

While addressing the National Academy of Scientists, Dr. Charles Bates, head of the Oceanographic Division of the US Navy's Hydrographic office, warns that the Soviet Union has a substantial lead over the United States in Arctic operations. Dr. Bates emphasizes that the Soviets are at least two years ahead in understanding how to carry out military operations in the extreme northern weather conditions.

7 JAN

In his State of the Union address to Congress, President Dwight D. Eisenhower explains the six fundamental premises of his "New Look" defense policy. In order they are: (1) An increase in the number of atomic weapons for both the United States and NATO allies; (2) Fewer ground troops and an increased emphasis on air power; (3) Greater strategic flexibility, including a "disengagement as far as possible" from Asia, small troop reductions in Europe, and an increase in the readiness of a continental US-based strategic reserve; (4) An increase in the benefits (medical care for dependents, improved living quarters) given to the average soldier, sailor, airman, and Marine to increase morale; (5) An up-to-date industrial mobilization base with more realistic plant expansion and stockpiling goals; (6) The strengthening of continental defenses against the "Soviet hydrogen threat." Eisenhower pledges $1 billion for defense against the threat of atomic war.

The US Navy announces a six-month delay in the planned launching of the aircraft carrier *Forrestal* (CVA 59). The blame is placed on a contractor's late delivery of major equipment, including propulsion machinery, for the supercarrier.

10 JAN

The UN command in Korea goes to full alert over North Korean threats to interfere with the release of 22,500 anti-communist POWs taken by the UN during the Korean War. The UN insists that the men go free as civilians, but North Korea wants them to remain in captivity pending further discussions on their disposition. Gen. Maxwell D. Taylor, USA, Commander, Eighth Army, warns that any attempt by North Korea to halt the POW release would "most likely start the Korean war over again."

12 JAN

In a speech before the Council of Foreign Relations, Secretary of State John Foster Dulles elaborates on the Eisenhower policy of massive retaliation. Dulles says that "local defense must be reinforced by the further deterrent of massive retaliatory power. The way to deter aggression is for the free community to be willing and able to respond vigorously at places and with means of its own choosing."

21 JAN

The nuclear-propelled submarine *Nautilus* is christened by Mrs. Mamie Dowd Eisenhower, wife of the President, at the Electric Boat yard in Groton, Conn.

22 JAN

A USAF RB-45 Tornado reconnaissance aircraft is attacked by unidentified MiG-15 fighters while flying northwest of Sokto Island off Korea's west coast. An escorting flight of F-86 Sabres intercepts the MiGs and shoots one down before the MiGs disengage. There are no US casualties.

6 FEB

The Department of Defense announces that 40 B-26 Marauder medium bombers and 200 American technicians are being sent to Indochina. This is the first time that American personnel are sent to Indochina to assist the French forces.

8 MAR

First flight of the Sikorsky XHSS-1 Seabat helicopter, developed specifically for anti-submarine operations. It also will be produced in large numbers for the cargo/troop-carrying role and flown by the US Marine Corps as the HUS Seahorse and by the US Army and Air Force as the H-34 Choctaw. Several foreign forces also use the helicopter in large numbers.

13 MAR

The 56-day siege of French forces at Dien Bien Phu begins as Viet Minh troops surround the valley. The garrison—numbering some 20,000 men and a few women (nurses and prostitutes)—will be supplied entirely by air during the siege.

14 MAR

The Royal Navy displays the mirror landing system developed by Comdr. H. C. Goodhart, RN. The mirror landing system is a response to the faster landing speeds of jet aircraft which precludes the usual visual communications between an incoming pilot and a gesturing flight deck Landing Signal Officer (LSO). The landing pilot aligns his aircraft with a series of gyro-stabilized lights that reflect his attitude—either too high, too low, or in the groove—and follows the signals down onto the deck.

16 MAR

At a press conference, President Eisenhower is asked to comment on the statement by Secretary of State Dulles that in the event of war in the Far East, "we would probably make use of some small tactical atomic weapons." Eisenhower responds that he would use atomic weapons "just exactly as you'd use a bullet or anything else." In his memoirs, Eisenhower explained: "I hoped this answer would have some effect in persuading the Chinese Communists of the strength of our determination."

20 MAR

Five days of meetings between the French high command and US military leaders begin in Washington, D.C. Adm. Arthur W. Radford, USN, Chairman of the Joint Chiefs of Staff, is advised of the gravity of the situation at Dien Bien Phu. The French estimate the outcome of the "battle" at 50–50.

28 MAR

The Navy announces the planned decommissioning and mothballing of the battleship *Missouri* (BB 63). The *Missouri* has been in continuous service since her original commissioning on 11 June 1944, having served in the Pacific in World War II and was twice deployed to Korea. *The New York Times* reports that the increased firepower of the new aircraft carriers of the *Forrestal* (CVA 59) class will replace the battleships.

24 APR

US planning for Operation *Vautour* (Vulture)—the intervention of US air forces in the Indochina War—is essentially complete. There are many variations of the plan, with one providing for all 98 B-29 Superfortress bombers in the Far East to use conventional bombs to destroy the Viet Minh forces around Dien Bien Phu.

26 APR

The US light carrier *Saipan* (CVL 48) arrives at Tourane (now Da Nang) and delivers 25 F4U Corsairs to the French Navy.

30 APR

The US light carrier *Belleau Wood* (CVL 24) is commissioned into the French Navy as the *Bois Belleau* at Philadelphia. This is the second US aircraft carrier other than escort ships (AVG/CVE) to be transferred to other navies.

MAY

The Regulus missile becomes operational on board the submarine *Tunny* (SSG 282) in the Atlantic Fleet.

3 MAY

The surviving French positions at Dien Bien Phu capitulate to Viet Minh forces led by Gen. Vo Nguyen Giap. More than 2,200 French, North African, Foreign Legion, and loyal Vietnamese troops have been killed at Dien Bien Phu; almost 10,000 are taken prisoner.

25 MAY

A US Navy ZPG-2 airship, commanded by Comdr. M. H. Eppes, USN, lands at NAS Key West, Fla., establishing a record by remaining airborne for eight days, eight hours over the western Atlantic, Caribbean, and Gulf of Mexico. Eppes is awarded the 1955 Harmon International Trophy for Aeronauts.

26 MAY
While conducting air operations in the North Atlantic, the US carrier *Bennington* (CVA 20) is shaken by an explosion as the port catapult accumulator bursts and releases huge amounts of heavily pressurized hydraulic fluid throughout the ship; 103 officers and enlisted men are killed and another 201 are injured. The carrier is able to return to her home port of Quonset Point, R.I., under her own power.

27 MAY
Carrier Modernization Project 125 is approved by the Chief of Naval Operations for the *Essex* class. Project 125 includes the addition of an angled flight deck and an enclosed ("hurricane") bow to improve seaworthiness. The enclosed bow will prevent a repetition of the damage experienced by the *Hornet* (CVA 12) and USS *Bennington* during the 1945 typhoons that buckled their flight decks.

1 JUNE
An S2F-1 Tracker flown by Comdr. H. J. Jackson, USN, is launched from the carrier *Hancock* (CVA 19) in the initial trials of the C-11 steam catapult.

3 JUNE
The USS *Dealey* (DE 1006), is commissioned, the Navy's first postwar escort vessel. The 1,950-ton, 315-foot (96-m) warship, slightly larger and faster than World War II destroyer escorts, will be the prototype for a large number of DEs built in US and foreign shipyards. The *Dealey*'s first CO is Lt. Comdr. R. H. Rossell, USN.

7 JUNE
The four *Iowa* (BB 61)–class battleships perform maneuvers off the coast of Virginia. This is the first and only time that the four dreadnoughts will operate together as a unit.

22 JUNE
First flight of the Douglas XA4D-1 Skyhawk carrier-based attack aircraft. The Skyhawk is the smallest aircraft ever designed to carry a nuclear weapon. Production of the A4D (later designated A-4) will total 2,960 aircraft for US and foreign use.

The US Navy XZS2G-1 (formerly XZP5K-1) airship makes its first flight.

Chinese fighter aircraft shoot down a British Cathay Airlines DC-4 aircraft 20 n.miles (37 km) south of Hainan Island.

20 JULY
The Geneva accords are signed by the French and Viet Minh. The treaty divides Vietnam at the 17th parallel into northern and southern halves. The accords permit civilians on either side of the parallel to migrate to the other. For the US Navy, this will result in the operation known as Passage to Freedom, where the US Navy ships ferry some 311,000 men, women, and children into South Vietnam.

25 JULY
Two F9F Panther fighters from the US carrier *Hornet* (CVA 12) are attacked by two Chinese fighters while searching for survivors from the downed Cathay Airlines DC-4. Both Red aircraft are shot down with the F9Fs returning to the *Hornet* unharmed.

26 JULY
Two AD Skyraider attack aircraft from the carrier *Philippine Sea* (CVA 47) are attacked off Hainan Island by two Chinese La-7 fighters. The Skyraiders return fire and destroy both Chinese aircraft. The Skyraiders were engaged in search-and-rescue operations for the survivors of the Cathay Airlines DC-4.

30 JULY
First flight of the Grumman F11F Tiger, a high-altitude fighter aircraft that will be produced in only small numbers. (Later designated F-11.)

4 SEP
After receiving word of Chinese bombardment of the Quemoy Islands, the US Seventh Fleet, including three carriers, sorties from Manila. A pledge made by President Harry S. Truman in 1950 and subsequently endorsed by President Eisenhower commits the Seventh Fleet to the defense of Formosa.

A US Navy P2V-5 Neptune patrol aircraft is shot down by Soviet fighters some 40 n.miles (74 km) off the Siberian coast; one crewman is killed with nine survivors being rescued the following day.

The US Navy Office of Information releases details of Soviet naval strength: 350 submarines, 13 cruisers, and 125 destroyers. According to the Navy, "the USSR could supplant the US as the preeminent naval power in 10 years, at the present rate of expansion." A Soviet spokesman declares that the US claims are exaggerated and says that "this is simply an attempt to get bigger appropriations for the US Navy."

6 SEP

Australia, France, Great Britain, New Zealand, Pakistan, the Philippines, Thailand, and the United States establish the Southeast Asia Treaty Organization (SEATO) with the signing of the Manila accord.

12 SEP

Vice Adm. Robert Briscoe, USN, Deputy Chief of Naval Operations (Fleet Operations and Readiness), in testimony to Congress, says that the US Navy faces block obsolescence of fleet units between 1958 and 1961. According to Briscoe, unless $2.8 billion is authorized for new ships, "the Soviet Union will surpass the US as a naval power within four years." The most recent congressional shipbuilding appropriation was for $1.1 billion for FY 1955.

30 SEP

The world's first nuclear-propelled submarine, the *Nautilus* (SSN 571), is placed in commission at New London, Conn. She will not be ready for sea for another three months. Her first CO is Comdr. Eugene P. Wilkinson, USN. (*See* 3 Jan 1955.)

16 OCT

Secretary of State Dulles warns China that "the US has a powerful Pacific military force and will use it to defend Formosa." Four aircraft carriers currently patrol the Formosa Straits, enforcing an uneasy lull in Chinese artillery bombardments. Pacific Fleet assets at this time include 15 carriers, 25 cruisers, and 125 destroyers.

Chief of Naval Operations Adm. Robert B. Carney, USN, announces an expansion in the number of nuclear-capable shipyards. The Mare Island Naval Shipyard in Vallejo, Calif., will become the West Coast yard with nuclear submarine construction and support capability. Carney says the yard should prepare for "a significant role in the atomic age program."

22 OCT

A new NATO defense plan to integrate West German troops with the Allied Command is approved by the NATO council. The exact composition of forces will be left up to the discretion of the Supreme Allied Commander Europe. The proposed West German contribution to NATO is 400,000 men.

23 OCT

The Paris Agreement ending Allied occupation of West Germany is signed by British, French, West German, and US representatives. Despite Soviet protests, West Germany is invited to join NATO.

7 NOV

A USAF RB-29 Superfortress photo-reconnaissance aircraft is shot down near Hokkaido, Japan, by Soviet fighters; the 11 crewmen bail out, one of whom dies, the others are rescued.

2 DEC

The United States signs a Mutual Defense Treaty with Nationalist China (Taiwan).

30 DEC

The nuclear power plant of the submarine *Nautilus* is activated for the first time during her fitting out at the Electric Boat yard.

1955

3 JAN

The nuclear-propelled submarine *Nautilus* (SSN 571) departs New London, Conn., for sea trials. After a minor problem in her starboard reduction gear is quickly corrected, the *Nautilus* signals "Underway on nuclear power" in Long Island Sound en route to the Atlantic. Rear Adm. H. G. Rickover, USN, is on board.

10 JAN

A force of 100 Chinese aircraft attack the Nationalist-held Tachen Islands, 200 miles (321 km) north of Taiwan (Formosa).

17 JAN

US Navy Air Development Squadron (VX) 6 is commissioned at NAS Patuxtent River, Md., to provide aerial support for Task Force 43 and Operation Deepfreeze, the US scientific operations in the Antarctic. (The squadron will be redesignated Antarctic Development Squadron [VXE] 6 on 1 Jan 1969.)

27 JAN

A US Navy FJ-3 Fury piloted by Lt. Comr. W. J. Manby, USN, sets an unofficial climb record by reaching 10,000 feet (3,048 m) from a standing start in 73.2 seconds.

2 FEB

At a press conference President Dwight D. Eisenhower states that the Korean conflict started because the United States failed to make clear to the Soviet Union that South Korea would be defended by American forces.

6 FEB

The carrier *Midway* (CVA 41) becomes the first of her class to operate in the Pacific, arriving in the South China Sea via the Horn of Africa, for duty with Task Force 77.

The US Navy begins the evacuation of Nationalist Chinese from the Tachen Islands, 15 miles (24 km) from mainland China. Air cover for the operation is provided by the carriers *Yorktown* (CVA 10), *Kearsarge* (CVA 33), and *Princeton* (CVS 37). US amphibious ships evacuate 18,000 civilians and 20,000 military personnel in the operation that lasts until 12 Feb.

13 FEB

A US Navy F3H-1N Demon piloted by McDonnell test pilot C. V. Braun sets an unofficial record for climb, reaching 10,000 feet (3,048 m) in 71 seconds.

22 FEB

The last British conventional (non-VSTOL) aircraft carrier, HMS *Ark Royal,* is commissioned. The 808¼-foot (246-m) ship with a standard displacement of 43,340 tons was laid down in 1943, but not launched until 1950. She can operate up to 80 contemporary aircraft.

23 FEB

A US Navy F4D Skyray piloted by Douglas test pilot R. O. Rahn sets still another climb-to-10,000-feet (3,048-m) record by reaching that altitude in 56 seconds.

24 FEB

Chief of Naval Operations Adm. Robert B. Carney, USN, directs that the term "angled" be used in lieu of "canted" and other terms in describing carrier flight deck configuration.

26 FEB

The battleship *Missouri* (BB 63) is decommissioned for the first time and laid up at Bremerton, Wash. The three other dreadnoughts of the *Iowa* (BB 61) class will be deactivated in 1957–1958.

3 MAR

The rank of Admiral of the Fleet of the Soviet Union (*Admiral Flota Sovetskogo Soyuza*) is introduced in the Soviet Navy. Corresponding to the rank of Marshal of the Soviet Union, the new rank is awarded on this date to Adm. Ivan S. Isakov, the leading Soviet theorist of the 1930s and at the time a deputy Minister of Defense, and Adm. Nikolai G. Kuznetsov, who had directed Stalin's fleet buildups of the late 1930s and early 1950s. (Adm. Sergei G. Gorshkov will be the only other officer awarded this rank.) At the same time the rank of admiral of the fleet is abolished. (*See* 28 Apr 1962.)

25 MAR

First flight of the Chance-Vought F8U-1 fighter. Named Crusader and later designated F-8, this will be the US Navy's standard carrier-based day fighter through the 1960s. The F8U-1P (RF-8) variant will become the Navy's standard light photo-reconnaissance aircraft.

26 MAR

Chief of Naval Operations Adm. Carney makes an off-the-record statement to the press predicting a Chinese attack on the Nationalist-held Quemoy and Matsu Islands in Apr 1955. Carney also indicates that the Joint Chiefs of Staff advocate a full-scale attack on Chinese forces if they do so.

25 APR
President Eisenhower announces that a nuclear-propelled merchant ship will be built separate from the naval nuclear propulsion effort as part of his "atoms for peace" program. (*See* 15 Oct 1956.)

7 MAY
Following the admission of the Federal Republic of Germany into NATO—despite Soviet opposition—the Soviet Union renounces wartime treaties of friendship and alliance with Britain, France, and the United States.

14 MAY
The Warsaw Pact—a treaty providing for friendship, cooperation, and mutual aid between the European countries of the socialist community—is signed in Warsaw, Poland. The signatories of the treaty are Albania, Bulgaria, Czechoslovakia, East Germany, Hungary, Poland, Romania, and the Soviet Union.

25 MAY
The inshore fire support ship *Carronade* (IFS 1) is commissioned. She is the first US ship built specifically for the rocket fire support role, the previous rocket ships being modified landing ship designs (LSMR, LCIR, LCS). Only one ship of this type is built (later redesignated LFR 1). Her first CO is Lt. Comdr. D. O. Doran, USN.

29 MAY
The US Navy adds the suffix "(N)" to ship designations to indicate nuclear propulsion; e.g., nuclear-propelled guided missile submarines are SSG(N); subsequently the parentheses are dropped from designations.

1 JUNE
Navy Electronics Countermeasures Squadron (VQ) 1 is commissioned at NAS Iwakuni, Japan, to conduct electronic surveillance missions along the periphery of China and the Soviet Union. The squadron initially flies the P4M-1Q Mercator aircraft.

22 JUNE
A US Navy P2V-5 Neptune patrol aircraft is attacked by Soviet fighters near St. Lawrence Island in the Bering Sea. The plane crash lands on the island. Seven of the ten crewmen are wounded, but there are no fatalities.

14 JULY
First flight of the Martin XP6M-1 Seamaster flying boat. Powered by four turbojet engines, the aircraft is intended primarily for reconnaissance and minelaying, but is to have a nuclear strike capability.

22 AUG
US Navy operational evaluation of the mirror landing system for aircraft carriers begins on the USS *Bennington* (CVA 20). Comdr. R. G. Dose, USN, CO of the *Bennington*, makes the first landing in an FJ-3 Fury. Two days later the first night landing with the mirror landing system is made aboard the carrier by Comdr. H. C. MacKnight, USN, flying an F9F-8 Cougar.

12 SEP
The US Navy announces that all future production fighter aircraft will be equipped for in-flight refueling.

15 SEP
Due to lagging enlistments and the rapid departure of Korean War veterans, the Navy is forced to initiate a draft request of 56,000 men to the Selective Service Board. The Navy request will double the size of the national draft with 10,000 men a month going to the Army and 10,000 to the Navy.

16 SEP
The first launch of a ballistic missile from a (surfaced) submarine takes place when a modified Soviet Zulu IV-class submarine successfully fires an SS-1B ballistic missile. The SS-1B is a liquid-propellant, nuclear-capable missile with a range of about 80 miles (129 km). Each Zulu carries two missiles mounted in the sail structure, which are elevated prior to launching. (This test occurred 4½ years before the first submarine launching of a US Polaris missile.)

18 SEP
Soviet Defense Minister Marshal of the SU Georgi Zhukov announces the withdrawal of Soviet troops from the Porkkala naval base in Finland, which has been occupied by Soviet forces since 1947. Zhukov also suggests that the US "liquidate overseas bases in general." This is the last "foreign" base occupied by Soviet forces.

1 OCT
The aircraft carrier *Forrestal* (CVA 59) is placed in commission. The first "supercarrier," the *Forrestal* has the latest carrier features including angled flight deck, steam catapults, and mirror landing system; she will

initially embark more than 70 contemporary aircraft. Named for the late Secretary of Defense, the *Forrestal* will be the basis for future US aircraft carriers CV/CVN 60–76. Capt. Roy Johnson, USN, is the ship's first CO.

10 OCT

The only midget submarine built for the US Navy, the *X-1,* is placed in service. Weighing 29 tons, the diminutive craft was built by the Fairchild Engine and Aircraft Corp., to help develop harbor defense procedures. Her first officer-in-charge is Lt. Kevin Hanion, USN.

15 OCT

Lt. Gordon Gray, USN, pilots an A4D-1 Skyhawk to break the world record for a 500-kilometer course, reaching a speed of 695.163 mph (1,119 kmh) at Edwards AFB, Muroc, Calif.

17 OCT

Chief of Naval Operations Adm. Arleigh A. Burke orders creation of the Special Projects Office (SPO) for the development of a ship-based strategic missile with associated launch systems. A captain is named interim head of the office until 5 Dec 1955, when Rear Adm. William F. (Red) Raborn, USN, takes command.

1 NOV

The USS *Boston* (CAG 1), the world's first guided missile cruiser, is placed in commission at the Philadelphia Naval Shipyard. The *Boston* was originally the heavy cruiser CA 69 of the *Baltimore* (CA 68) class, commissioned in 1943. In her missile configuration she retains her two forward 8-inch (203-mm) gun turrets; the after main battery turret has been removed and replaced by two Mk 10 Terrier surface-to-air missile launchers. Capt. Charles B. Martell, USN, is her first CO.

The keel for the French aircraft carrier *Clemenceau* is laid down at the Brest Naval Shipyard. The *Clemenceau*, with a full-load displacement of 32,000 tons, will be the first carrier built from the keel up in France. (France's only previous home-built carrier, the *Bearn,* was converted during construction from a battleship.)

8 NOV

The National Ballistic Missile program is established by Secretary of Defense Charles E. Wilson as a joint Army-Navy program for an Intermediate-Range Ballistic Missile (IRBM). The Navy begins examining the Jupiter liquid-propellant missile for potential development as a Fleet Ballistic Missile (FBM).

9 NOV

Chief of Naval Operations Adm. Burke informs the Chief of the Bureau of Ships of his intention to equip all angled-deck carriers with mirror landing systems.

The destroyer *Forrest Sherman* (DD 931) is commissioned at Bath Iron Works, Bath, Maine, the first postwar US Navy ship to be completed with the "destroyer" designation. (The four large destroyers of the *Mitscher* class were built earlier, but completed with the frigate classification DL 2-5.) Comdr. R. S. Crenshaw, USN, is the *Sherman's* first CO.

17 NOV

Secretary of the Navy Charles S. Thomas creates the Special Projects Office (SPO) to handle problems associated with the ship-launched version of the Army's Jupiter IRBM. The target date for an operational ship-based Jupiter system is set as 1965.

22 NOV

The first Soviet hydrogen bomb is exploded. The weapon—carried to the target area by an aircraft and detonated at an altitude of several thousand feet—had a yield of some 1.6 megatons. (This event occurred exactly three years after the first US hydrogen bomb detonation; *also see* 12 Aug 1953.)

2 DEC

Chief of Naval Operations Adm. Burke states his approach to development of the Polaris missile in a memorandum to his staff; it is a remarkable document: "If Rear Admiral [William F.] Raborn runs into any difficulty with which I can help, I will want to know about it at once along with his recommended course of action for me to take. If more money is needed, we will get it. If he needs more people, those people will be ordered in. If there is anything that slows this project up beyond the capacity of the Navy Department we will immediately take to the highest level and not work our way up through several days. In taking this type of action we must be reasonably sure we are right and at least know the possible consequences of being wrong because we will be disrupting many other programs in order to make achievement in this one if we are not careful. That is all right if we really make an achievement."

5 DEC

Rear Adm. Raborn is formally appointed to head the Navy's Special Projects Office. A naval aviator and ordnance expert, he had previously commanded two aircraft carriers.

16 DEC

At a meeting of NATO foreign ministers the North Atlantic Council decides to equip alliance forces with nuclear weapons. Another proviso calls for closer cooperation between NATO members for strengthening air defenses. Eventually, this will result in the surface-to-air missile "Hawk Belt" throughout central and northern Europe.

20 DEC

Two US Navy P2V Neptune and two R5D Skymaster aircraft of Navy Air Development Squadron (VX) 6 forge the first "air link" with the continent of Antarctica with a flight from Christchurch, New Zealand, to McMurdo Sound.

30 DEC

The Soviet Union signs a treaty with the East German regime granting it the prerogatives of an independent country. This also is in response to West Germany joining NATO.

1956

3 JAN

US Navy Airship Airborne Early Warning Squadron (ZW) 1 is commissioned at NAS Lakehurst, N.J. The squadron is the first lighter-than-air unit of its type.

10 JAN

The US Navy's first nuclear power school is established at the submarine base at New London, Conn.

Navy Airborne Early Warning Wing Pacific is commissioned to operate radar aircraft flying a barrier in the North Pacific to provide early warning of hostile air attacks on the United States as part of the continental air defense system. Based at NAS Barbers Point, Hawaii, the wing is commanded by Capt. E. C. Renfro, USN; it will fly WV-series Warning Star aircraft (later designated EC-121).

1 MAR

HMS *Vanguard*, Britain's last active battleship, is decommissioned and placed in reserve. (She will be towed off for scrapping in 1960.)

12 MAR

The carrier *Intrepid* (CVA 11) departs Norfolk, Va., for service in the Mediterranean Sea in the first overseas deployment of a Navy aircraft squadron armed with missiles. On board the *Intrepid* is Attack Squadron (VA) 83 with F7U-3M Cutlass aircraft carrying the Sparrow I air-to-air missile.

20 MAR

The Ballistic Missile Committee of the Office of the Secretary of Defense approves a Navy program for development of solid-propellant motors for use in ship-based ballistic missiles. This decision will lead to the Polaris program.

3 APR

The Petrel air-to-surface guided missile intended for use against enemy shipping becomes operational with Navy Patrol Squadron (VP) 24 flying the P2V-6M Neptune aircraft. This is the US Navy's second operational air-to-surface missile. (The Bat air-to-surface missile was used in the latter stages of World War II.)

14 APR

The radar picket submarine *Sailfish* (SSR 572) is commissioned. She is the first new-construction SSR, pre-

vious submarines of this type were conversions of World War II–built fleet boats. Her first CO is Lt. Comdr. Stanley R. McCord, USN.

The attack aircraft carrier *Saratoga* (CVA 60) is commissioned, the second ship of the *Forrestal* (CVA 59) class. Her first CO is Capt. Robert J. Stroh, USN.

21 MAY

A USAF B-52 strategic bomber, flying at an altitude of 50,000 feet (15,240 m), drops the first airborne hydrogen bomb, which detonates over Bikini atoll.

29 MAY

First flight of the Navy's definitive Regulus II land-attack missile. With a planned 1960 operational date, the turbojet-powered Regulus II would have a speed of almost Mach 2 and a maximum range approaching 1,000 miles (1,609 km) at lesser speeds, carrying a nuclear warhead.

18 JUNE

In response to a request from Chief of Naval Operations Adm. Arleigh A. Burke, the Committee on Undersea Warfare of the National Academy of Sciences begins a three-month anti-submarine warfare study at Woods Hole, Mass. Organized by Columbus Iselin, the so-called Nobska conference proposed several submarine advances and contributed directly to Navy development of the Polaris fleet ballistic missile. Sixty men and women participated in the Nobska conference, one-third officers and civilians from Navy activities and two-thirds from the scientific community and industry.

31 JUNE

Lt. Comdr. P. Harwood, USN, pilots an A3D Skywarrior on a 3,200-n.mile (5,149-km) nonstop, unrefueled flight from Honolulu, Hawaii, to Albuquerque, N.M., in 5 hours and 40 minutes to demonstrate the aircraft's capabilities. The aircraft averages 570 mph (917 kmh). On 31 July Harwood will pilot the A3D back to Albuquerque at the same average speed.

4 JULY

The first US U-2 spyplane mission is flown over the Soviet Union. There will be 23 additional flights of the aircraft, operated by the Central Intelligence

Agency, the last, on 1 May 1960, shot down by a Soviet missile.

14 JULY
The first overseas deployment of the Sidewinder air-to-air missile begins with departure of the carrier *Randolph* (CVA 15) from Norfolk, Va., for operations with the Sixth Fleet in the Mediterranean. On board is Attack Squadron (VA) 46 with F9F-8 Cougar fighters armed with the infra-red (heat-seeking) Sidewinder. (The following month the carrier *Bon Homme Richard* [CVA 31] deploys to the Western Pacific with VF-211 equipped with Sidewinder-armed FJ-3 Fury aircraft.)

20 JULY
The helicopter assault carrier *Thetis Bay* (CVHA 1), the first US Navy ship of this type, is commissioned at San Francisco, Calif. Formerly the escort carrier CVE 90, the *Thetis Bay* was converted to operate helicopters and to carry 1,000 Marines to be flown ashore in an amphibious assault. (The ship later will be redesignated LPH 6.) Her first CO is Capt. T. W. South III, USN.

26 JULY
Egypt nationalizes the Suez Canal.

21 AUG
A Navy F8U-1 Crusader piloted by Comdr. R. W. Windsor, USN, captures the Thompson Trophy with a new national speed record of 1,015.4 mph (1,634 kmh) over the 15-kilometer course at the Naval Ordnance Test Station China Lake, Calif. The production model carrier fighter, equipped during its record performance with an armament of four 20-mm cannon and dummy ammunition, is the first operational aircraft to fly faster than 1,000 mph (1,609 kmh).

22 AUG
A US Navy P4M-1Q Mercator reconnaissance aircraft is shot down over the Shengszu Islands, 32 n.miles (59 km) off the coast of China, while on a night mission. Of the 16 men on board, all are killed with four bodies being found by US search aircraft.

The last passenger flight of a US Navy Mars-type flying boat is completed from Honolulu to NAS Alameda, Calif., by the JRM-1 *Marianas Mars*. Five of these giant, four-engine flying boats were operated by the Navy beginning in 1943.

1 SEP
During the National Air Show race for the North American Trophy, four Navy FJ-3 Furies of Fighter Squadron (VF) 24 take off from the carrier *Shangri-la* (CVA 38) at sea off the Pacific Coast of Mexico and fly nonstop 1,198 n.miles (2,220 km) to Oklahoma City without refueling. The winner is Lt. (jg) D. K. Grosshuesch, USN, with a time of 2 hours, 13 minutes, 39 seconds for an average speed of 537.848 mph (685 kmh).

The following day a Navy F3H-2N Demon fighter piloted by Lt. (jg) R. Carson, USN, captures the McDonnell Trophy for nonstop, unrefueled flight at the National Air Show by taking off from the carrier *Shangri-la* off San Francisco and racing to Oklahoma City in 2 hours, 32 minutes, 14 seconds for an average speed of 566 mph (911 kmh) over the 1,436-mile (2,310-km) distance.

3 SEP
Two A3D Skywarriors, piloted by Capt. J. T. Blackburn, USN, and Comdr. C. T. Frohne, USN, are launched from the carrier *Shangri-la* off the Oregon coast, fly across a finish line at the National Air Show in Oklahoma City, and continue on to Hacksonville, Fla., without refueling. Capt. Blackburn is awarded the Douglas Trophy after completing his 1,543.3-mile (2,483-km) leg in 2 hours, 32 minutes, 39.7 seconds for an average speed of 606.557 mph (976 kmh). After this flight, a three-day demonstration of carrier mobility is completed, in which the *Shangri-la* launches aircraft to Oklahoma City while steaming along the Pacific coast.

17 SEP
The USS *Mississippi* (EAG 128, formerly BB 41) is decommissioned. She was the last pre–World War II battleship in US naval service. Originally commissioned in 1917, the *Mississippi* had been employed as a missile and gunnery test ship since 1946.

21 SEP
An F11F-1 Tiger aircraft, piloted by Grumman test pilot Tom Attridge, shoots itself down while conducting test firings off eastern Long Island, N.Y., by running into 20-mm projectiles it fired seconds earlier.

15 OCT
President Dwight D. Eisenhower directs the Atomic Energy Commission and Department of Commerce to proceed as rapidly as possible with the design and con-

struction of a nuclear-propelled merchant ship as part of his "atoms for peace" program. This project will result in the NS *Savannah*.

22 OCT
First flight of the Bell XH-40 helicopter, the prototype for the Bell UH-1 Iroquois (commonly known as the "Huey"—derived from its later HU-1E designation). The Huey will be produced in greater numbers by US and foreign plants than any other Western helicopter.

23 OCT
Fighting between Soviet troops and Hungarian pro-democracy factions erupts in Budapest.

29 OCT
The Suez Crisis erupts into open warfare as Israel forces—with direct French military assistance—invade the Egyptian-held Sinai and drive toward the Suez Canal. The US Sixth Fleet in the Mediterranean is ordered to evacuate US nationals from the area. Carrier-based aircraft and warships provide cover for the evacuation of some 2,200 Americans by amphibious ships and Air Force transport aircraft from Alexandria, Haifa, Tel Aviv, Amman, and Damascus by 3 Nov. The Sixth Fleet also provides logistic support to the UN forces that arrive in the area in November.

31 OCT
British and French begin military operations against Egypt with RAF Canberra turbojet bombers from Cyprus striking targets in the Suez Canal Zone.

Seven US Navy personnel led by Rear Adm. G. J. Dufek, USN, land at the South Pole in an R4D Skytrain transport aircraft. The party remains at the pole for 49 minutes setting up navigational aids to assist the future delivery of materials and equipment for constructing a scientific observation station at the pole.

1 NOV
Cyprus-based RAF Canberra aircraft resume striking targets in Egypt, joined by aircraft from five carriers—the British *Eagle, Albion,* and *Bulwark,* and the French *Arromanches* and *La Fayette.*

2 NOV
With Egyptian forces routed, Israel controls the Sinai Peninsula up to the eastern banks of the Suez Canal.

4 NOV
Soviet troops begin suppression of the Hungarian people's rebellion.

5 NOV
British and French paratroopers drop on Port Said, Egypt.

6 NOV
The world's first helicopter assault landing is made by 16 Whirlwind and six Sycamore helicopters from the British light carriers *Ocean* and *Theseus*. The helicopters bring ashore 415 Royal Marines and 23 tons of ammunition and equipment at Port Said in 89 minutes.

British and French troops come ashore by landing craft at Point Said. After brief fighting, the British lose 22 dead and 97 wounded, the French 11 dead, 33 wounded. (One French pilot is also killed.) Egyptian losses are placed at 650 killed and 900 seriously wounded in the fighting around Port Said.

8 NOV
A US Navy Stratolab balloon, manned by Lt. Comdrs. Malcolm D. Ross, USN, and M. L. Lewis, USN, sets a new world altitude record by reaching 76,000 feet (23,165 m) over the Black Hills of South Dakota on a meteorological, cosmic ray, and scientific data gathering flight. As a result of the flight, the two officers will be awarded the 1957 Harmon International Trophy for Aeronauts.

9 NOV
A Sikorsky HR2S helicopter piloted by Maj. R. L. Anderson, USMC, at Windsor Locks, Conn., begins a three-day assault on world records and sets three new marks: On 9 Nov the helicopter carries a payload of 11,050 pounds (5,012 kg) to an altitude of more than 12,000 feet (3,657 m); on 10 Nov the helicopter carries 13,250 pounds (6,010 kg) to over 7,000 feet (2,134 m); and on 11 Nov the same helicopter sets a speed record of 162.7 mph (262 kmh) over a three-kilometer course.

29 NOV
The US Navy's ZSG-4 airship, the first craft of this type to be fitted with a Dacron envelope, makes its first flight at NAS Lakehurst, N.J.

3 DEC
The world's first destroyer armed with surface-to-air missiles, the USS *Gyatt* (DDG 712), is commissioned in Boston, Mass. Converted from a *Gearing* (DD 710)–class ship, the *Gyatt* was completed in 1945 as the DD 712; she will be redesignated DDG 1. The ship has a twin-arm Terrier missile launcher aft and retains two 5-inch (127-mm) twin gun mounts forward. Her first

CO in the missile configuration is Comdr. Charles F. Helme, Jr., USN.

8 DEC

Secretary of the Navy Charles S. Thomas authorizes the Navy to proceed with the development of the solid-propellant Polaris Fleet Ballistic Missile (FBM) and to terminate participation in the Army's liquid-propellant Jupiter missile program.

18 DEC

The Joint Army-Navy Missile Committee is dissolved.

19 DEC

The Special Projects Office, under Rear Adm. William F. (Red) Raborn, is assigned responsibility for developing the complete Polaris missile system, including the missile submarines.

1957

3 JAN

The US Navy's last operational Catalina flying boat, a PBY-6A of the Naval Air Reserve Training Unit Atlanta, is removed from service. The PBY Catalina was the most successful military flying boat ever developed by any nation; more Catalinas were produced than any other flying boat in history—2,398 built in the United States and Canada, plus some in the Soviet Union; they were flown by the air forces and navies of several nations.

10 JAN

First flight of the Hiller XROE-1 Rotorcycle, a one-man helicopter developed by the Navy and Marine Corps. Seven are built, but the vehicle is not produced for service use.

14 JAN

In a ten-day evaluation of their all-weather capability, Navy ZPG airships begin operating in relays from NAS South Weymouth, Mass., to maintain continuous radar patrol over the North Atlantic 200 n.miles (371 km) off the New England coast. They fly through some of the worst storms experienced in the area in years.

8 FEB

The Navy Department issues a requirement for a 1,500-n.mile (2,780-km), solid-propellant ballistic missile capable of being launched from a submerged submarine, to be operational by 1965. This will be the Polaris submarine-launched missile.

1 MAR

First flight of the aerodynamic prototype of the Grumman WF-2 Tracer (later E-1) carrier-based airborne early warning aircraft. The prototype is adapted from a TF-1 Trader, the cargo variant of the S2F Tracker anti-submarine aircraft. The WF-2/E-1B is the first aircraft produced specifically for the radar picket role.

4 MAR

A Navy ZPG-2 airship, commanded by Comdr J. R. Hunt, USN, takes off from NAS South Weymouth, Mass., and circles over the Atlantic Ocean toward Portugal, the African coast, and back for a new world record in distance and endurance, covering 9,448 statute miles (15,202 km) before landing at NAS Key West, Fla., on 15 March. The airship is airborne for

264 hours, 12 minutes without refueling. Hunt is later awarded the 1958 Harmon International Trophy for Aeronauts for this flight.

17 MAR

The US Navy's first satellite, *Vanguard I,* is launched from Cape Canaveral, Fla. It weighs 3.5 pounds (1.6 kg).

21 MAR

An A3D-1 Skywarrior piloted by Comdr. Dale Cox, Jr., USN, breaks two transcontinental speed records—the round-trip record from Los Angeles to New York and return, in 9 hours, 31 minutes, 35.4 seconds; and the record for the east-to-west flight in 5 hours, 12 minutes, 39.24 seconds.

30 MAR

The nuclear-propelled attack submarine *Seawolf* (SSN 575) is commissioned with Comdr. Richard B. Laning, USN, as her first CO. The second US nuclear submarine, the *Seawolf* uses liquid sodium as the heat exchange medium compared to pressurized water in the *Nautilus* (SSN 571); the *Seawolf*'s plant is not successful and will be replaced with a pressurized-water plant.

6 MAY

First flight of the ZPG-2W early warning airship, which has a large radar antenna mounted within the envelope. The flight takes place at Akron, Ohio.

17 MAY

The last escort aircraft carrier in active US Navy service, the *Badoeng Strait* (CVE 116), is decommissioned at Bremerton, Wash. Four older "jeep" carriers remain in service as cargo ships operated by the Military Sea Transportation Service (MSTS) with the designation T-CVU (utility carrier).

23 MAY

A radio-controlled HTK-1 drone helicopter (carrying a safety pilot) flies from the fantail of the frigate *Mitscher* (DL 2) near Narragansett Bay to begin tests of the feasibility of operating Drone Anti-Submarine Helicopters (DASH) from destroyer-type ships.

6 JUNE

In history's first carrier-to-carrier flight across the United States, two F8U Crusaders and two A3D Skywarriors fly nonstop from the carrier *Bon Homme*

Richard (CVA 31) off the California coast to the *Saratoga* (CVA 60) off the east coast of Florida. The F8Us complete the flight in 3 hours, 28 minutes, and the A3Ds in 4 hours, 1 minute.

12 JULY

President Dwight D. Eisenhower becomes the first US president to fly in a helicopter.

16 JULY

An F8U-1P Photo Crusader piloted by Maj. John H. Glenn, Jr., USMC, breaks the transcontinental speed record in a flight from Los Alamitos, Calif., to NAS Floyd Bennet Field, N.Y., in 3 hours, 22 minutes, 50 seconds for an average speed of 723.5 mph (1,164 kmh). This was the first upper-atmospheric supersonic flight from the west coast to the east coast.

30 JULY

The first US pilotless helicopter flight is made at Bloomfield, Conn., under a joint Army-Navy contract using a modified Navy HTK aircraft.

3 AUG

A Soviet SS-6 Sapwood intercontinental ballistic missile travels several thousand miles from its launch pad to impact in Soviet Siberia. In guarded words, the Soviet news agency Tass announced that a "super-long distance intercontinental multi-stage ballistic rocket flew at an . . . unprecedented altitude . . . and landed in the target area." Not for another 16 months will a US Atlas ICBM be tested over its full range. The SS-6 will become operational in 1960, with four single-warhead missiles being emplaced that year; however, that was the extent of SS-6 deployment as the missile fell far short of expectations and several, more capable ICBMs were in development.

10 AUG

The aircraft carrier *Ranger* (CVA 61) is commissioned, the third ship of the *Forrestal* (CVA 59) class. Her first CO is Capt. Charles T. Booth II, USN.

12 AUG

Lt. Comdr. Don Walker, USN, lands an F3D Skyknight "hands off" on the carrier *Antietam* (CVS 36) in the first test of an automatic carrier landing system. In the period 12–20 Aug more than 50 fully automatic landings are made on the ship.

30 SEP

The USS *Saipan* (CVL 48) is decommissioned. She is the Navy's last operational light carrier. Nine of these ships were converted while under construction from light cruisers during World War II and two additional ships were completed after the war with their hulls based on heavy cruiser designs. The *Saipan* will later begin conversion to a national command ship (CC 3) but will be completed instead as a major communications relay ship (AGMR 2).

1 OCT

Strategic bombers of the US Strategic Air Command (SAC) begin a 24-hour-per-day ground alert in the United States and at overseas bases, maintaining a specified number of aircraft ready for take-off within a few minutes of warning that the United States is under attack.

4 OCT

A Soviet SS-6 missile booster carries *Sputnik 1* into orbit, the earth's first artificial satellite. The satellite weighs 184 pounds (83.5 kg); this is 166 pounds (75.3 kg) heavier than the first US satellite, which will not be placed into orbit for another three months.

3 NOV

The Soviet satellite *Sputnik 2*, weighing a phenomenal 1,120 pounds (508 kg), is lifted into earth orbit. On board *Sputnik 2* is the live dog Layka, instrumented to relay psychological data back to earth on the animal's reaction to weightlessness, radiation, and other environmental conditions.

6 DEC

The first attempt by the United States to launch a satellite by the non-military Vanguard booster is a sensational failure as the rocket loses thrust and explodes while being launched.

9 DEC

Secretary of Defense Neil H. McElroy authorizes the acceleration of the Polaris submarine-launched missile program to achieve an operational weapon system in 1960—five years ahead of the original schedule for a surface-launched, sea-based missile system.

17 DEC

First successful launch and test flight of the Atlas ICBM. This is the first US ICBM, with the Atlas-D variant becoming operational on 15 July 1960 at Vandenberg AFB, Calif.

23 DEC

The nuclear-propelled submarine *Skate* (SSN 578), lead ship of the first class of production nuclear submarines, is commissioned. Comdr. James F. Calvert, USN, is her first CO.

1958

31 JAN

A US Army-developed Jupiter-C launch vehicle is used to orbit the first American satellite, *Explorer I.*

First flight of the North American T2J-1 Buckeye trainer (later redesignated T-2A). The turbojet aircraft is carrier capable; it will serve the Navy for more than four decades. (*See* 30 Aug 1962.)

14 FEB

The first definitive Sparrow III air-to-air missile is launched as the weapon begins operational evaluation.

7 MAR

The diesel-electric submarine *Grayback* (SSG 574), the first US submarine to be built to a guided missile configuration (Regulus), is commissioned. Her first CO is Lt. Comdr. Hugh G. Nott, USN.

8 MAR

The US battleship *Wisconsin* (BB 64) is decommissioned and laid up at Philadelphia, Pa., marking the first time in this century that the US Navy does not have a battleship in active service. No other country has an operational battleship. The Turkish battle cruiser *Yavuz* (ex-German *Goeben*) remains in service but is of dubious military value.

19 MAR

The first Bullpup air-to-surface missile is fired during the operational evaluation of the weapon.

1 APR

The USAF 576th Strategic Missile Squadron is activated at Cook AFB, Calif. (renamed Vandenberg AFB in Oct 1958). Part of the 704th Strategic Missile Wing, the squadron is the first operational US ICBM unit, operating the Atlas-D missile.

8 APR

The first Soviet nuclear-propelled submarine, the *K-3,* later named *Leninsky Komsomol,* is placed in commission. The NATO class name for this design is November. Capt. 1st Rank L. G. Osipenko is the first CO of the *K-3.*

18 APR

Lt. Comdr. G. C. Watkins, USN, pilots an F11F-1F Tiger fighter to a world altitude record of 76,939 feet (23,451 m). This is the second record set by Watkins in an F11F in a three-day period.

22 APR

First flight of the Boeing Vertol YHC-1A tandem-propeller helicopter, which will see extensive service with the US Navy and Marine Corps as the HRB-1 (later H-46 series). The H-47 Chinook series flown by the US Army and other nations is similar.

30 APR

First flight of the Hawker Siddeley Buccaneer S.1 naval strike aircraft. A high-subsonic aircraft with internal weapons bay, the Buccaneer was developed for carrier operation for the purpose of attacking Soviet *Sverdlov*-class cruisers. It will become an important strike aircraft for the Royal Navy and Air Force as well as the South African Air Force.

14 MAY

First flight of the Sikorsky HU2S Sea Guard helicopter (later designated HH-52A). In US service it will be used only by the Coast Guard; it is also flown by several other nations.

15 MAY

The satellite *Sputnik 3* is launched into orbit by the Soviet Union. Weighing 2,926 pounds (1,327 kg), the satellite payload is not matched by the United States for six years.

22 MAY

Flying an F4D-1 Skyray, Maj. E. N. Le Faivre, USMC, begins two days of record-breaking flights from the missile center at Point Mugu, Calif. He sets five records: 44.392 seconds to reach 9,144 feet (3,000 m), 66.095 seconds to 18,288 feet (6,000 m), 90.025 seconds to 27,432 feet (9,000 m), 111.224 seconds to 36,576 feet (12,000 m), and 156.233 seconds to 45,720 feet (15,000 m).

27 MAY

First flight of the McDonnell XF4H-1 Phantom fighter aircraft (later designated F-4). The carrier-based aircraft will become the principal fighter aircraft of the US Air Force, Navy, and Marine Corps as well as several foreign air forces. (*See* 20 May 1978.)

28 MAY

The US submarine *Stickleback* (SS 415) is severely damaged in a collision with the escort ship *Silverstein* (DE 534) during exercises off Pearl Harbor, Hawaii.

The submarine had broached during maneuvers and was struck between the forward battery room and control room. All crewmen are rescued from the submarine, which sinks late on 29 May despite attempts to keep her afloat.

The guided missile cruiser *Galveston* (CLG 3), converted from the light cruiser CL 93, is placed in commission. She is the first US warship fitted with the Talos surface-to-air missile.

26 JUNE
The designation for missile submarines to be armed with the Polaris missile is changed from SSG(N) to SSBN(N), the change indicating *ballistic* missiles.

A TF-1 Trader delivers a J34 jet engine from San Diego, Calif., to the carrier *Yorktown* (CVS 10) some 300 n.miles (556 km) at sea in the first delivery of an aircraft engine to a ship by Carrier On-board Delivery (COD) techniques.

27 JUNE
A US Air Force C-118 transport on a CIA courier mission with six crew and three CIA personnel is damaged by Soviet fighters and forced down 100 miles (161 km) inside of Soviet Armenia. Five men parachute from the aircraft before it lands, with two being injured; all are questioned and released after ten days. The flight had taken off from an airfield in Adana, Turkey, and was headed east toward Tehran when it crossed into Soviet airspace during bad weather and was attacked by fighters. The plane was not configured for a spy mission.

1 JULY
Submarine Squadron 14 is established in the Office of the Chief of Naval Operations to formulate plans for the operational logistics support, crew training and rotation, patrol doctrine, and refit procedures for Polaris missile submarines. (This first Polaris squadron will also be the last Polaris-Poseidon squadron, being disestablished on 1 June 1992.)

14 JULY
Arab nationalists seize the Iraqi government in a bloody coup, killing the pro-Western king and prime minister, and causing crises throughout the Middle East.

15 JULY
At the request of Lebanese President Camille Chamoun, US Navy and Marine forces under the command of Vice Adm. James L. Holloway II, USN,

land at Beirut to support his government, which is being threatened by both civil war and the prospect of foreign invasion. Two of the Sixth Fleet's three Marine battalion landing teams are brought ashore within 24 hours; the third follows shortly after. Within a few days the Marines are joined by a reinforced US Army airborne brigade flown from West Germany, and a US Air Force composite strike group subsequently flown in from the United States to support the Sixth Fleet carriers *Essex* (CVA 9), *Saratoga* (CVA 60), and *Wasp* (CVS 18). American negotiators bring the civil war to an end by arranging an election satisfactory to all parties involved. Simultaneous with the American landing in Lebanon, British troops are flown into Jordan which is also under threat of civil war.

25 JULY
The Department of Commerce names the States Marines Lines to operate the nuclear-propelled merchant ship *Savannah* for the government under a general agency contract. The firm was one of seven that replied to an invitation to operate the ship.

29 JULY
Comdr. Malcolm D. Ross, USN, and Lt. Comdr. M. L. Lewis, USN, make a balloon ascent to 82,000 feet (24,993 m), remaining aloft for 34 hours, 30 minutes to evaluate sealed cabin technology and to use an external telescope to observe Mars.

3 AUG
The nuclear-propelled submarine *Nautilus* (SSN 571), under the command of Comdr. William R. Anderson, USN, becomes the first ship to reach the North Pole, passing under the pole during a four-day, 1,830-n.mile (3,391-km) voyage under the polar ice from the Pacific to the Atlantic Oceans, where she surfaces on 7 Aug.

11 AUG
The US nuclear-propelled attack submarine *Skate* (SSN 578), under the command of Comdr. James F. Calvert, USN, becomes the first submarine to surface at the North Pole. She does so again on 17 Aug during an Arctic voyage of exploration that lasts from 30 July to 22 Sep 1958.

19 AUG
First flight of the aerodynamic airframe for the Lockheed YP3V-1 Orion maritime patrol aircraft, modified from an Electra airliner. (The P3V will later be designated P-3.)

23 AUG

China begins an intensive artillery bombardment of the Nationalist-held offshore islands of Matsu and Quemoy. President Dwight D. Eisenhower orders the US Seventh Fleet to assist the Nationalists in supplying the 100,000-man garrison of Quemoy, which it does by escorting their transports to the three-mile (4.8-km) territorial limit. Eisenhower also reminds China of a congressional resolution authorizing him to defend Formosa and deploys a six-carrier task force near the island. The crisis slowly wanes and is cooled by Dec 1958.

29 AUG

First flight of a Lockheed Electra airliner modified to the external configuration of the P3V-1 maritime patrol aircraft.

31 AUG

First flight of the North American YA3J-1 Vigilante carrier-based attack aircraft (later designated A-5). This is the first US supersonic carrier-based strike aircraft and the last carrier aircraft designed specifically for the nuclear strike role.

SEP

The Soviet government decides that the Navy will not have a long-range strategic strike role. Future strategic missile submarine construction is halted, with Hotel-class SSBNs components being shifted to the Echo II SSGN program and the planned Yankee SSBN design is put on "hold."

2 SEP

A USAF EC-130 Hercules on an electronic reconnaissance mission with 17 men on board is shot down by Soviet fighters and crashes in Soviet Armenia. Six bodies were returned by the Soviet government; no mention was made of the other 11 crewmen—they were listed by the US government as "presumed dead."

6 SEP

The missile test ship *Norton Sound* (AVM 1), operating midway between the extremities of South America and Africa, launches a rocket with a nuclear warhead to an altitude of 300 miles (483 m). Called Project Argus, the *Norton Sound* had launched research rockets on 27 and 30 Aug 1958. The nuclear detonation on 6 Sep produces a visible aurora and a radiation belt around the earth that extends 4,000 miles (6,436 km) into space and lasts for several weeks.

15 SEP

The Strategic Air Command (SAC) conducts an airborne alert test for B-52 strategic bombers from the 42nd Bomb Wing at Loring AFB in Maine from 15 Sep through 15 Dec. Code-named Head Start I, the test demonstrates the feasibility of keeping nuclear-armed B-52s airborne continuously and will be adopted as a standard practice the following year.

16 SEP

In the only launch of a Regulus II land-attack missile from a submarine, the USS *Grayback* (SSG 574) fires the missile off the California coast. The missile is flown under radio command in a simulated attack on Edwards AFB, Calif.

1 OCT

Project Vanguard is transferred from the US Navy to the National Aeronautics and Space Administration (NASA).

24 OCT

The US high-speed transport *Kleinsmith* (APD 134), supported by a task force including the carrier *Franklin D. Roosevelt* (CVA 42), evacuates 56 American citizens and three foreign nationals from Nicaragua, Cuba, as Castro's revolution nears its climax.

Rear Adm. H. G. Rickover, USN, head of the Navy's nuclear-propulsion program, is promoted to vice admiral.

25 OCT

The last US troops are withdrawn from Lebanon.

6 DEC

The guided missile frigates *Coontz* (DLG 9) and *King* (DLG 10) are launched in joint ceremonies at the Puget Sound Naval Shipyard in Bremerton, Wash. These are *Farragut* (DLG 6)–class ships. The *King* is the first of six US warships to be named in honor of five-star officers, the others will be the *Nimitz* (CVN 68), *Dwight D. Eisenhower* (CVN 69), *George C. Marshall* (SSBN 654), *Leahy* (DLG 16), and *Halsey* (DLG 23). The Air Force–sponsored conversion of the troop transport *Gen. R. E. Callan* (AP 139) is renamed *Gen. H. H. Arnold* (T-AGM 9), as a missile range instrumentation ship, honoring the only five-star USAAF/USAF officer.

12 DEC

Secretary of the Navy Thomas S. Gates, Jr., terminates the Regulus II surface-to-surface missile program. The decision to proceed with the Polaris submarine-launched ballistic missile forces the Navy to cut several other programs as well. The Regulus II had flown 48 test flights—30 successfully and 14 partially so; there were no manifest problems with the missile.

1959

1 JAN

The USAF Strategic Air Command is additionally designated as a US specified command, being made directly responsible to the Secretary of Defense and the Joint Chiefs of Staff. (A *specified* command differed from a *unified* command in having all forces assigned from the same military service.)

The Batista régime in Cuba is overthrown by Fidel Castro.

10 JAN

The US aircraft carrier *Independence* (CVA 62) is commissioned, the fourth ship of the *Forrestal* (CVA 59) class. She is commanded by Capt. R. Y. McElroy, USN.

17 JAN

The diesel-electric attack submarine *Barbel* (SS 580) is commissioned, the lead ship of the final US class of conventionally propelled combat submarines. She is commanded by Lt. Comdr. Ord Kimzey, Jr., USN.

24 JAN

In a demonstration of the capabilities of the diminutive A4D Skyhawk, Maj. J. P. Flynn, USMC, and Capt. C. D. Warfield, USMC, fly two "scooters" on a nonstop, unrefueled flight from El Toro, Calif., to Cherry Point, N.C., covering the 2,082 miles (3,350 km) in 4 hours, 25 minutes.

12 FEB

The last USAF B-36J long-range strategic aircraft is retired by the Strategic Air Command (SAC). With the aircraft's departure SAC becomes an all-jet bomber force. The B-36 was a key element in the carrier-versus-strategic bombing controversy of the late 1940s.

26 FEB

The Soviet fishing trawler *Novorossisk* is accused by the US government of cutting American trans-Atlantic cables off Newfoundland, Canada. The trawler is boarded by men from the US escort ship *Roy O. Hale* (DER 336) but no evidence of cable-cutting is found.

11 MAR

First flight of the Sikorsky XHSS-2 Sea King anti-submarine helicopter (later designated SH-3). It will become the standard ASW helicopter for the US and several foreign navies and will serve in other roles as well. Production in the United States, Great Britain,

Japan, and Italy will total 1,002 ASW, search-and-rescue, troop-carrying, cargo, and VIP variants.

27 MAR

A USAF C-130 Hercules transport is buzzed by Soviet fighters while flying in the Berlin Corridor at an altitude of more than 20,000 feet (6,096 m). A Soviet spokesman states that all Western flights must be below 10,000 feet (3,048 m).

9 APR

The National Aeronautics and Space Administration (NASA) announces the selection of the first American astronauts, all seven are military pilots: Lt. M. Scott Carpenter, USN; Capt. L. Gordon Cooper, USAF; Lt. Col. John H. Glenn, Jr., USMC; Capt. Virgil I. Grissom, USAF; Lt. Comdr. Walter M. Schirra., Jr., USN; Lt. Comdr. Alan B. Shepard, Jr., USN; and Capt. Donald K. Slayton, USAF.

15 APR

The US nuclear-propelled attack submarine *Skipjack* (SSN 585), lead ship of a class of high-speed submarines, is commissioned. The *Skipjack* combines nuclear propulsion with the advanced hull design of the USS *Albacore* (AGSS 569), producing a high-speed (33-knot) but relatively noisy submarine. Her first CO is Comdr. William Behrens, Jr., USN.

20 APR

First successful flight test of a Polaris test vehicle from Cape Canaveral, Fla.

25 APR

The Bullpup air-to-surface missile is deployed as the carrier *Lexington* (CVA 16) departs Alameda, Calif., for the western Pacific with Bullpup-armed FJ-4B Fury aircraft of Attack Squadron (VA) 212 on board.

7 MAY

The classification of 36 mothballed US Navy escort aircraft carriers previously designated CVE/CVHE/CVU is changed to cargo ship and aircraft ferry (AKV), ending the role of "jeep" carriers as combat ships in the US Navy.

15 MAY

The classification of four ASW support carriers (CVS) and seven light carriers (CVL) is changed to auxiliary aircraft transport (AVT) to remove them from the aircraft carrier (CV) roster.

16 JUNE

A US Navy P4M-1Q Mercator electronic surveillance aircraft is attacked by two MiG-type fighters over the Sea of Japan, 85 n.miles (157.5 km) east of Wonsan, North Korea. The damaged plane returns to Niho Air Base in Japan; the plane's tail gunner is seriously wounded in the attack.

19 JUNE

The first of four US Navy ZPG-3W airships is delivered to NAS Lakehurst, N.J. These radar-equipped airborne early warning craft are the largest non-rigid airships ever built.

2 JULY

First flight of the Kaman XHU2K-1 Seasprite utility helicopter. This helicopter (changed to UH-2 in 1962) will later be converted to the anti-submarine role as the SH-2 LAMPS I.

30 JULY

First flight of Northrop model N-156 Freedom Fighter. The aircraft, later designated F-5, was developed specifically for sales to Third World countries. It will be flown by the US Navy as an aggressor training aircraft.

7 AUG

The US *Explorer 6* satellite transmits the first television pictures to earth from space.

19 AUG

The Baghdad Pact, signed on 24 Feb 1955, becomes the Central Treaty Organization (CENTO). The full members of CENTO are Iran, Iraq, Pakistan, Turkey, and the United Kingdom; the United States is an associate member. Headquarters are established in Ankara, Turkey. (CENTO will be dissolved on 26 Sep 1979.)

24 AUG

The Navy's P6M Seamaster flying boat program is completely canceled. Earlier technical problems with the jet-propelled aircraft had been solved but its high costs and the need to fund the Polaris missile program led to successive reductions and final cancellation. Two test aircraft, six demonstration aircraft, and four production aircraft were built; the two test aircraft had crashed. This was the last aircraft produced by the Glenn L. Martin Co.

25 AUG

During carrier suitability trials aboard the carrier *Independence,* an A3D Skywarrior piloted by Lt. Comdr. Ed Decker, USN, takes off with a gross weight of 84,000 pounds (38,102 kg), the heaviest aircraft ever to take off from a carrier.

27 AUG

First flight of the Boeing Vertol CH-46A Sea Knight cargo helicopter.

First seaborne launch of a Polaris test missile from the USS *Observation Island* (EAG 154) at sea off Cape Canaveral, Fla.

10 SEP

The Bureau of Naval Weapons is established in the US Navy by merging the Bureau of Ordnance and the Bureau of Aeronautics. The first Chief of BUWEPS is Rear Adm. Paul D. Stroop, USN.

21 SEP

The submarine *Barbero* (SSG 317) begins the first Regulus I "deterrent" patrol in the North Pacific, carrying two of the surface-launched, land-attack missiles. From this time until Aug 1964, Regulus-armed submarines will be on continuous patrols in the North Pacific, their missiles targeted against targets in the Soviet Far East—one or two submarines carrying a total of four or five Regulus missiles. A total of 41 Regulus deterrent patrols will be conducted in that period. While the number of missiles on station is small, it does permit coverage of specific targets with nuclear weapons without requiring an aircraft carrier task force to be kept in the area or basing nuclear-armed aircraft in Japan or South Korea to strike the Soviet Union.

10 NOV

The nuclear-propelled radar picket submarine *Triton* (SSRN 586) is commissioned with Capt. Edward L. Beach, USN, former naval aide to President Dwight D. Eisenhower, in command. The *Triton* is 447½ feet (136.5 m) in length, the longest US submarine built to date and will be the only US submarine powered by two nuclear reactors.

25 NOV

First flight of the YP3V-1 Orion land-based patrol aircraft (later designated P-3). The aircraft will become the standard land-based patrol aircraft of many nations, with production in both the United States and Japan.

30 NOV

The US Navy decommissions the Airship Training Group at NAS Glynco, Ga., ending lighter-than-air training in the US Navy (and world-wide military airship training).

1 DEC

Twelve nations, including the United States and the Soviet Union, pledge that they will not undertake any kind of military activities in Antarctica.

6 DEC

Comdr. L. E. Flint, USN, pilots a Navy F4H-1 Phantom to a record altitude of 98,560 feet (30,041 m), taking off from Edwards AFB, Calif.

14 DEC

The Soviet Union establishes the Strategic Rocket Forces (SRF) as an independent military service to direct all intermediate- and long-range strategic missiles; this brings to five the number of separate services in

the Soviet armed forces. The first commander in chief of the SRF is Chief Marshal of Artillery Mitrofan Nedelin.

20 DEC

The Soviet icebreaker *Lenin,* the world's first nuclear-propelled surface ship, enters service at Leningrad. The 15,747-ton ship, fitted with three nuclear reactors, is the world's largest icebreaker.

22 DEC

The new NATO headquarters is established at the Porte Dauphine in Paris.

30 DEC

The US Navy's first ballistic missile submarine, the nuclear-propelled *George Washington* (SSBN 598), is commissioned at Groton, Conn. Comdr. James B. Osborn, USN, is the submarine's first Blue Crew CO and Comdr. John L. From, Jr., USN, is Gold Crew CO.

1960

1 JAN

The US Navy aviation designation VQ is changed from Electronics Countermeasures Squadron to Fleet Air Reconnaissance Squadron.

4 JAN

The US Navy's first guided missile submarine with nuclear propulsion, the USS *Halibut* (SSGN 587), is commissioned. She will be the only SSGN completed by the United States; the planned SSGNs of the *Permit* (SSGN 594) class will be completed as attack submarines. They were to carry the Regulus II strategic attack missile. Comdr. Walter Dedrick, USN, is the *Halibut's* first CO.

23 JAN

The US Navy bathyscaph *Trieste,* piloted by Lt. Don Walsh, USN, and Jacques Piccard (son of the craft's developer), reaches a depth of 35,800 feet (10,910 m) in the Challenger Deep off the Mariana Islands. This dive, to the deepest known spot in the oceans, is part of the Navy's Project Nekton. The craft remains on the bottom for 20 minutes before ascending to the surface.

24 FEB

The British Cabinet's Defence Committee makes the decision to cancel development of the Blue Streak Intermediate-Range Ballistic Missile (IRBM). In its place, Britain will first seek the Skybolt air-launched strategic missile, and when the United States cancels that project, the submarine-launched Polaris missile will be sought. (*See* 19 Dec 1962.)

1 MAR

A US Navy ZPG-3W airship returns to NAS Lakehurst, N.J., from a radar barrier patrol over the North Atlantic, having been on station for 2 days, 1 hour, 20 minutes with a total of 2 days, 10 hours in the air. The new record doubles the time spent on station by the smaller ZPG-2W airships.

16 MAR

The nuclear-propelled attack submarine *Shark* (SSN 591) is launched at the Newport News Shipbuilding and Dry Dock Co. in Virginia. She is the first nuclear submarine to be built at that shipyard. The yard had

previously built diesel-electric submarines, including some earlier in the century for Russia.

18 MAR

In the first test firing of Project Hydra, conducted at the Naval Missile Center Point Mugu, Calif., a 150-pound (68-kg) rocket is successfully ignited underwater and launched into the air. The test demonstrates the feasibility of launching missiles while they are floating upright in the water.

25 MAR

In the first launch of a guided missile from a US nuclear-propelled submarine, the USS *Halibut* (SSGN 587) fires a Regulus I missile during an exercise off Oahu, Hawaii.

29 MAR

The first atomic bomb detonation by France occurs in the Sahara Desert. France is the fourth nuclear power, after the United States, Soviet Union, and Britain.

30 MAR

The US Navy accepts its last airship, a ZPG-3W, from the Goodyear Corp., at Akron, Ohio.

1 APR

A US *Tiros 1* weather-reconnaissance satellite is launched, the first satellite to be orbited for that purpose.

Anti-Submarine Carrier Air Groups (CVSG) 53 and 59 are commissioned at NAS North Island, San Diego, Calif. The CVSG, with one helicopter and two fixed-wing ASW squadrons, will be assigned to ASW carriers (CVS); nine such groups will be established by the Navy.

13 APR

The US Navy *Transit 1B,* the first US navigational satellite, is orbited by a Thor-Able-Star rocket launched from Cape Canaveral, Fla.

19 APR

First flight of the Grumman YA2F-1 Intruder carrier-based attack aircraft (later designated A-6). This aircraft will be one of the most capable carrier aircraft to be built, able to fly day/night bombing missions with a heavy payload.

1 MAY

A CIA-operated U-2 reconnaissance aircraft overflying the Soviet Union is shot down by a surface-to-air missile near Sverdlovsk. The pilot, Francis Gary Powers, is captured and subsequently put on trial by the Soviet government.

Seventeen basic training groups of the US Naval Air Training Command are redesignated as training squadrons (VT).

6 MAY

The Cuban cutter *Oriente* fires on the US submarine *Sea Poacher* (SS 406) in San Nicholas Channel.

10 MAY

The nuclear-propelled submarine *Triton* (SSRN 586), commanded by Capt. Edward L. Beach, USN, completes a submerged circumnavigation of the world. The *Triton*'s historic voyage lasts for 84 days and covers 41,519 n.miles (76,935 km). The submarine's sail structure broached the surface off of Spain to allow a small boat to take off a sailor having a kidney stone attack.

24 MAY

The US *Midas II* early warning satellite, the first of its type intended to detect enemy ICBM launches, is placed in orbit by an Atlas-D/Agena-A booster.

25 MAY

A USAF C-47 Skytrain cargo aircraft flying from Copenhagen, Denmark, to Hamburg, West Germany, is forced down by Soviet fighters after the C-47 flies 22 miles (35 km) into East German airspace. The passengers and crew of the aircraft are taken into custody by the East Germans but are released after five days.

3 JUNE

A Marine Corps HUS-1 Seahorse helicopter completes a successful series of test launchings of the Bullpup air-to-surface missile at the Naval Air Test Center Patuxent River, Md.

1 JULY

A US Air Force RB-47 Stratojet electronic reconnaissance aircraft flying from a base in England is shot down by Soviet MiG-19 fighters over the Barents Sea. Of the six crewmen, four were reported killed when the plane crashed; the two survivors were released by the Soviet government on 25 Jan 1961 after incarceration in Moscow's Lubyanka Prison.

The US Navy's first specialized Carrier On-board Delivery (COD) squadron, Fleet Tactical Support Squadron (VRC) 40, is commissioned at NAS Norfolk, Va.

The frigate *Mitscher* (DL 2) demonstrates the feasibility of operating the DSN-1 (later QH-50) Drone Anti-Submarine Helicopter (DASH) from destroyer-type ships. Although the drone had a safety pilot on board during the trials, the helicopter was remote controlled from shore and maneuvered around the ship and into a landing position before the pilot took the controls for the actual landing.

9 JULY

The US carrier *Wasp* (CVS 18) sails from Guantanamo Bay, Cuba, for the western coast of Africa to support UN attempts to quiet disorders in the newly independent states of the Congo. By the time of her departure from the area in early August the carrier will have supplied a quarter of a million gallons of gasoline in support of the UN airlift.

19 JULY

The US destroyers *Ammen* (DD 527) and *Collett* (DD 730) collide off Long Beach, Calif. Eleven of the *Ammen*'s crewmen are killed and 20 are injured; the ship is damaged beyond repair.

20 JULY

The nuclear-propelled missile submarine *George Washington* (SSBN 598) successfully launches two Polaris A-1 ballistic missiles while submerged, marking the first time a missile is fired from a submerged US submarine. The missiles are fired at an interval of 2 hours, 53 minutes; they streak more than 1,000 n.miles (1,853 km) down the Atlantic test range.

11 AUG

In the first US recovery of an object after it had been in orbit, a Navy HRS-3 helicopter from the cargo ship *Haiti Victory* (T-AK 238) recovers the instrument capsule released by *Discoverer 13* on its 17th orbit. The capsule is located some 330 n.miles (611.5 km) northwest of Honolulu by USAF aircraft. The recovery was made less than three hours after the capsule struck the water. This test is part of the development of the Coronoa spy satellite.

25 AUG

While charting the Northwest Passage through the Canadian archipelago, the US nuclear-propelled submarine *Seadragon* (SSN 584) surfaces at the North Pole. Her crew romps on the polar ice and plays the first game of baseball at the North Pole.

5 SEP

An F4H-1 Phantom fighter piloted by Lt. Col. Thomas H. Miller, USMC, sets a new record for the 500-kilometer course at Edwards AFB, Calif., with a speed of 1,216.78 mph (1,958 kmh). On 24 Sep an F4H-1 Phantom flown by Comdr. John F. Davis, USN, sets a new record for the 100-kilometer course with a speed averaging 1,390.21 mph (2,237 kmh).

10 SEP

The US destroyer *Charles F. Adams* (DDG 2), the lead ship of a new class of missile-armed, general-purpose missile destroyers, is commissioned. Her first CO is Comdr. W. R. Monroe, Jr., USN. (The US Navy will take delivery of 23 destroyers of this class, with another three being built for Australia and three for West Germany.)

21 OCT

Great Britain's first nuclear-propelled submarine, the *Dreadnought*, is launched by the Vickers-Armstrongs yard at Barrow-in-Furness, christened by Queen Elizabeth II on the anniversary of the Battle of Trafalgar. The submarine has a modified US S5W reactor plant.

First flight of the Grumman W2F-1 Hawkeye carrier-based airborne early warning aircraft. (Later designated E-2.)

First flight of the British Hawker P.1127 Kestrel Vertical/Short Take-Off and Landing (VSTOL) aircraft. This is the progenitor of the Harrier VSTOL aircraft.

1 NOV

Prime Minister Harold Macmillan announces the British government's decision to allow US Polaris submarines to be based at Holy Loch, Scotland.

9 NOV

The nuclear-propelled attack submarine *Tullibee* (SSN 597) is placed in commission. Comdr. Richard E. Jortberg, USN, is her first CO. No additional submarines of this small, hunter-killer type will be built.

15 NOV

The US ballistic missile submarine *George Washington* (SSBN 598) sails from Charleston, S.C., on the Navy's first Polaris deterrent patrol. She carries 16 Polaris A-1 missiles.

13 DEC

A US Navy A3J-1 Vigilante aircraft piloted by Comdr. Leroy A. Heath climbs to 91,450.8 feet (27,874 m) over Edwards AFB, Calif., while carrying a payload of 454.5 pounds (1,000 kg), establishing a new world record.

19 DEC

The carrier *Constellation* (CVA 64) is swept by fire while under construction at the New York Naval Shipyard. Fifty workers are killed and another 150 injured. Damage to the ship is estimated at $75 million. Her completion will be delayed until late 1961.

1961

3 JAN

The United States breaks diplomatic relations with Cuba.

9 JAN

The US Department of State announces that the diplomatic break with Cuba will have no effect upon the legal status of the US naval base at Guantanamo Bay, Cuba.

20 JAN

John F. Kennedy is sworn in as the 35th President of the United States, the first chief executive with prior naval service. He commanded the motor torpedo boat *PT 109* in 1943 in the Solomons area. Kennedy had served in the House of Representatives from 1947 to 1952, and in the Senate from 1953 until his election as president in Nov 1960.

20 JAN

The ASROC (Anti-Submarine Rocket) is declared operational in US naval service when an ASROC is fired from the guided missile frigate *Mahan* (DLG 11). The rocket-propelled weapon can carry an anti-submarine torpedo with a conventional warhead or a nuclear depth bomb. From 1961 through 1980 ASROC is fitted to 251 existing and new-construction US Navy warships—35 cruisers, 151 destroyers, and 65 frigates.

21 JAN

US ballistic missile submarine *George Washington* (SSBN 598) completes the first Polaris deterrent patrol, returning to New London, Conn., after a submerged cruise of 66 days, 10 hours. The voyage marks the longest US submerged submarine operation made to date. (Previously the longest totally submerged operation was probably that of the German diesel-electric submarine *U-977*, which traveled submerged—using a snorkel—for 66 days from the coast of Norway to the mid-Atlantic, en route to Argentina after Germany's surrender in early May 1945.)

22 JAN

The Portuguese-flag cruise ship *Santa Maria* is seized in the Caribbean by armed Portuguese nationals opposed to the policies of Anton Salazar, the premier of Portugal. The United States and Great Britain are asked by the Portuguese government to help locate the cruise ship.

25 JAN

A US Navy P2V Neptune patrol aircraft locates the hijacked *Santa Maria*. She is subsequently tracked for 11 days until she is allowed to enter the Brazilian port of Recife where her 607 passengers are set free.

30 JAN

In his first State of the Union address, President Kennedy announces that he has instructed the Department of Defense to "reappraise our entire defense strategy." Kennedy also reveals that he had given orders to accelerate the Polaris missile and submarine programs.

31 JAN

A US Mercury capsule carrying a chimpanzee named Ham is launched into space by a Redstone rocket from Cape Canaveral, Fla., to test the feasibility of manned space flight. Following the 15-minute flight, which reaches an altitude of 155 miles (249 km), the capsule and Ham parachuted from the rocket and are recovered by a Marine Corps HUS-1 Seahorse helicopter.

6 FEB

Secretary of Defense Robert S. McNamara reports that studies done by the Kennedy administration indicate that no "missile gap" currently exists. Fear of the Soviet Union surpassing the United States in ICBM development was a major issue in the 1960 presidential election.

5 MAR

Four American warships are routed to the Congo region for possible action as a result of instability in that African nation. The task force, which resumes its original course to South Africa after four days, consists of the destroyers *Gearing* (DD 710) and *Vogelgesang* (DD 862), and the amphibious ships *Hermitage* (LSD 34) and *Graham County* (LST 1176).

8 MAR

The Polaris-armed submarine *Patrick Henry* (SSBN 599) arrives at Holy Loch, Scotland, completing her first deterrent patrol; she is serviced by the submarine tender *Proteus* (AS 19) in the first overseas replenishment and crew exchange of a ballistic missile submarine.

12 APR

Soviet cosmonaut Maj. Yuri Gagarin becomes the first man to orbit the earth. After his single, 108-minute orbit around the earth in his spacecraft *Vostok I*, Gagarin is brought back to earth near Saratov, 220 miles (354 km) north of Volgograd.

17 APR

A group of approximately 1,400 anti-Castro forces, consisting mostly of Cuban exiles, attempt an invasion of Cuba's Bay of Pigs on the island's southern coast. The invasion force, which is American organized and trained in Guatemala, encounters unexpected resistance from Cuban military forces and the invading force is defeated quickly. In one last attempt to aid survivors on the beach, President Kennedy reluctantly permitted six unmarked U.S. Navy jet fighters from the carrier *Essex* (CVS 9) to cover an attack by Cuban- and American-piloted B-26 bombers from Nicaragua. The jets were directed to fly for only one hour and not fire at ground targets, but could protect the B-26s by return fire if Cuban Air Force planes shot at the bombers. Due to a mixup over time zones, the B-26s arrived over the beach an hour before the Navy fighters. Two B-26s were shot down and four Americans —CIA pilots—were killed. (One pilot survived the crash of his plane but was killed by Castro's soldiers.)

Chief of Naval Operations Adm. Arleigh A. Burke, USN, testifies before the Senate Armed Services Committee that, "A Soviet version of our Polaris-firing submarine must be expected in the near future." (The Soviet Navy already operates primitive ballistic missile submarines; the Soviet Polaris-type system consisting of the Yankee-class submarines and SS-N-6 missile will become operational in 1967.)

29 APR

The USS *Kitty Hawk* (CVA 63), the first in a new class of aircraft carriers, is commissioned at Philadelphia. She is an improvement of the *Forrestal* (CVA 59) class, the most obvious difference between the two classes is the rearrangement of deck-edge aircraft elevators. Her first CO is Capt. William F. Bringle, USN.

4 MAY

A world balloon record of 113,740 feet (34,668 m) is reached by Comdr. Malcolm D. Ross, USN, and Lt. Comdr. Victor A. Prather (Medical Corps), USN. Launched from the deck of the carrier *Antietam* (CVS 36) off the mouth of the Mississippi River, the balloon is the largest ever employed in manned flight. It reaches the maximum altitude 2 hours, 36 minutes after take-off. Prather falls from the sling of the recovery helicopter and dies on the carrier an hour after being pulled from the water following the flight.

5 MAY

Lt. Comdr. Alan B. Shepard, Jr., USN, becomes the first American in space when he reaches an altitude of 116.5 miles (187 km) in the Mercury capsule *Freedom 7* in a suborbital flight from Cape Canaveral, Fla. The flight lasts 15 minutes. Shepard is picked up in the Atlantic Ocean, 302 n.miles (560 km) down range, by a helicopter from the carrier *Lake Champlain* (CVS 39).

17 MAY

An HSS-2 Sea King helicopter piloted by Comdr. Patrick L. Sullivan, USN, set a new world record of 192.9 mph (310.4 kmh) for three kilometers at Bradley Field, Windsor Locks, Conn. On 24 May he sets another helicopter record in an HSS-2 over a 100-kilometer course between Milford and Westbrook, Conn., with an average speed of 174.9 mph (281 kmh).

24 MAY

Three US Navy F4H-1 Phantom fighters competing for the Bendix Trophy beat the existing record for transcontinental flight from Los Angeles to New York. The winning aircraft, piloted by Lt. R. F. Gordon, USN, averages 870 mph (1,400 kmh) on the 2,421.4-mile (3,896-km) flight, setting a record of 2 hours, 47 minutes.

25 MAY

In a speech to Congress three weeks after the first American space flight, President Kennedy defines the goals for the United States in space: to land a man on the Moon and return him safely to earth by the end of the decade.

1 JUNE

US Second Fleet ships—including the carriers *Intrepid* (CVA 11), *Randolph* (CVS 15), and *Shangri-la* (CVA 38)—are ordered to stand off southern Hispaniola as a general uprising seems about to erupt following the assassination of President Rafael Trujillo of the Dominican Republic.

23 JUNE

A new US Navy radio station at Cutler, Maine, is commissioned. This will be the Navy's major low frequency transmitting station used to transmit signals to the Atlantic Fleet's ships and submarines.

26 JUNE

Former US Army Chief of Staff Gen. Maxwell D. Taylor, USA, is recalled to active service by President Kennedy to act as his advisor on military and intelligence matters.

29 JUNE

The first US space vehicle with a nuclear-powered generator, *Transit 4A,* is placed in orbit from Cape Canaveral, Fla. The navigation satellite is placed in a circular orbit of about 500 miles (804 km).

9 JULY

The Polaris-armed submarine *Robert E. Lee* (SSBN 601) completes her first deterrent patrol and arrives at Holy Loch, Scotland, after a record submerged operation of 68 days, 4 hours, 15 minutes.

16 JULY

The commander of the US Second Fleet, Vice Adm. Claude V. Ricketts, USN, announces that his flagship, the USS *Northampton* (CC 1, formerly CLC 1), has been equipped to serve as an emergency national command post for the President and military chiefs in the event the Pentagon and other command centers are destroyed.

21 JULY

The second American in space, Capt. Virgil I. Grissom, USAF, makes a 15-minute flight from Cape Canaveral, Fla., reaching an altitude of 118 miles (190 km). Premature blowoff of his hatch cover after the Mercury capsule comes down at sea causes its flooding and loss. Grissom is picked up from the water by a helicopter and delivered safely to the carrier *Randolph.*

25 JULY

Due to the ongoing crisis in Berlin and the increase in East-West tensions, President Kennedy speaks to the nation and announces a "call to arms" with a dramatic increase in the size of active US military forces. These include an increase in the size of the active Army by 133,000 personnel; a callup of 250,000 reservists (mostly from the Army Reserve) for one year; retention of several B-47 bombers that were to have been discarded; and an addition to the active fleet of an aircraft carrier, an anti-submarine carrier, 26 amphibious ships, 11 fleet support ships, 41 destroyer escorts, and five radar picket destroyers. (The majority of the ships will come from the Naval Reserve Fleet).

3 AUG

The USS *Thresher* (SSN 593), lead ship of a class of quiet, deep-diving attack submarines, is placed in commission. Her first CO is Comdr. Dean L. Axene, USN.

6 AUG

The first sustained, manned orbital space flight is made by Soviet cosmonaut Maj. Gherman Titov in the spacecraft *Vostok II.* Titov circles the earth 17 times in 25 hours, 18 minutes before coming down near Saratov.

8 AUG

The *Ethan Allen* (SSBN 608), the first of the second class of Polaris ballistic missile submarines, is commissioned. Her first COs are Comdr. Paul L. Lacy, Jr., USN (Blue), and Comdr. William W. Behrens, USN (Gold).

13 AUG

East German police close off East Berlin and begin erection of the Berlin Wall along the 30-mile (48-km) border of East and West Berlin. The barriers seek to halt the exodus of skilled German workers and engineers from East Germany to the West. (More than 4,000 fled East Berlin on the previous day.)

24 AUG

In a meeting of the UN General Assembly, Cuba challenges the validity of two treaties that allow the United States to retain a naval base at Guantanamo Bay, Cuba. The American ambassador to the United Nations, Adlai Stevenson, calls the Cuban charges "an extraordinarily new doctrine of international law—or rather international lawlessness."

26 AUG

The helicopter carrier *Iwo Jima* (LPH 2) is commissioned at the Puget Sound Naval Shipyard, Bremerton, Wash. The first of a class of purpose-built amphibious assault ships, she can accommodate some 25 troop-carrying helicopters and 1,900 Marines for vertical assault operations. Her first commanding officer is Capt. T. D. Harris, USN.

28 AUG

Setting another record, an F4H-1 Phantom piloted by Lt. Hunt Hardisty, USN, flies the three-kilometer course at Holloman AFB, N.M., averaging 902.769 mph (145.3 kmh) for a low-altitude speed record.

9 SEP

The cruiser *Long Beach* (CGN 9), the world's first nuclear-propelled surface warship, is commissioned. With a standard displacement of 14,200 tons, she is the world's first ship built with an all-missile weapons suite. (Later two 5-inch [127-mm] dual-purpose guns will be fitted.) Her first CO is Capt. Eugene P. Wilkinson, USN, previously the first commanding officer of the USS *Nautilus* (SSN 571).

1 OCT

The guided missile cruiser *Little Rock* (CLG 4) replaces the command ship *Northampton* (CC 1) as the flagship of the Second Fleet in the North Atlantic. The *Little Rock* completed her conversion to a missile cruiser-flagship in 1960, one of four such ships intended specifically to serve as flagships for numbered fleets.

23 OCT

The US ballistic missile submarine *Ethan Allen* (SSBN 608) launches the first Polaris A-2 missile fired from a submarine. The missile travels more than 1,400 n.miles (2,594 km) before the re-entry body falls into the sea.

27 OCT

The carrier *Constellation* (CVA 64), the second carrier of the *Kitty Hawk* (CVA 63) class is commissioned. Her first CO is Capt. T. J. Walker, USN.

First flight of the Saturn rocket booster that will carry the Apollo capsule in US space launches for the next 11 years.

30 OCT

A planned Soviet thermonuclear weapon test of 50 megatons at Novaya Zemlya in the Arctic produces an explosion of 58 megatons —the largest man-made explosion ever achieved. Soviet Premier Nikita S. Khrushchev would later write in his memoirs: "It was colossal, just incredible! Our experts later explained to me that if you took into account the shock wave and radioactive contamination of the air, then the bomb produced as much destruction as 100 million tons of TNT."

31 OCT

Great Britain is warned by Soviet Premier Nikita Khrushchev that their practice of allowing bases for US submarines will make them "among the first" nations to suffer a nuclear attack in the event of a war.

6 NOV

A fire occurs at sea aboard the newly commissioned carrier *Constellation*. Four men are killed and nine injured.

16 NOV

Acting upon a report by Gen. Taylor, USA, President Kennedy decides to increase the number of American military advisors in South Vietnam, which is being threatened by a communist insurgency sponsored by North Vietnam.

22 NOV

In still another record-breaking flight, an F4H-1 Phantom piloted by Lt. Col. Robert B. Robinson, USMC, averages 1,606.3 mph (2,585 kmh) on runs over the 15- and 25-kilometer courses at Edwards AFB, Calif.

25 NOV

The nuclear-propelled carrier *Enterprise* (CVAN 65), the largest warship yet built, is commissioned at Newport News, Va. Her first CO is Capt. Vincent P. DePoix, USN. The "Big E" is the third large carrier commissioned by the US Navy in 1961.

29 NOV

The US destroyer *Stormes* (DD 780) retrieves the chimpanzee Enos from waters off Bermuda after a two-orbit Mercury space flight.

30 NOV

The US Navy's lighter-than-air program is terminated. All but two airships are to be immediately deactivated and placed in reserve. The remaining two airships are scheduled to be decommissioned in 1962.

1 DEC

Three new helicopter climb records are set by an HSS-2 Sea King piloted by Capt. Bruce K. Lloyd, USN, over a course along the Long Island Sound, between Milford and Westbrook, Conn. The helicopter achieves 182.8 mph (294 kmh) on the 100-kilometer run, 179.5 mph (288.7 kmh) for 500 kilometers, and 175.3 mph (282 kmh) for 1,000 kilometers. On 30 Dec an HSS-2 piloted by Comdr. Sullivan will set a new three-kilometer record of 199 mph (320 kmh) at Windsor Locks, Conn.

5 DEC

Pushing the F4H-1 Phantom even harder, Comdr. George W. Ellis, USN, surpasses existing altitude records for sustained horizontal flight at 66,444 feet (20,252 m).

1962

1 JAN

The US Navy's first two SEAL (Sea-Air-Land) teams are established to operate primarily in the unconventional warfare role in restricted waters and river areas. This marks the Navy's entry into "special operations" with specially trained personnel and units.

27 JAN

Vice Adm. H. G. Rickover, head of the Navy's nuclear propulsion program, reaches the statutory age for retirement from the Navy (62); however, he will be retained on active duty until January 1982.

31 JAN

The nuclear merchant ship *Savannah* puts to sea from Camden, N.J., on her maiden voyage for a two-day trip to her home port of Yorktown, Va. She is commanded by Capt. Gaston R. DeGroote. The ship, which will enter commercial operation in May 1962, is immediately plagued by labor problems as deck officers object to wage increases for engineer officers. The 595½-foot (181.5-m) ship can carry 9,830 tons of cargo and 60 passengers at a speed of 20.25 knots.

5 FEB

An HSS-2 Sea King becomes the first helicopter to exceed 200 mph (322 kmh) in an officially sanctioned test flight. Piloted by Lt. R. W. Crafton, USN, the helicopter flies over the Milford to New Haven, Conn., course, reaching 210.65 mph (339 kmh) on both the 15- and 25-kilometer courses.

8 FEB

The US Military Assistance Advisory Group (MAAG) in South Vietnam, which was established in 1956, is reorganized as the US Military Assistance Command, Vietnam (MACV), under the command of Lt. Gen. Paul Harkins, USA.

20 FEB

Lt. Col. John H. Glenn, Jr., USMC, becomes the first American to orbit the earth, traveling 81,000 miles (130,353 km) at an average speed of 17,400 mph (28,000 kmh) in his Project Mercury space capsule *Friendship 7*. After three orbits around the earth in 4 hours, 55 minutes, Glenn's capsule descends into the Atlantic Ocean and is recovered by the destroyer *Noa* (DD 841), and subsequently transferred to the carrier *Randolph* (CVS 15).

21 FEB

An F4H-1 Phantom sets climb records, reaching 9,840 feet (3,000 m) and 19,680 feet (6,000 m) in 34.52 and 48.87 seconds, respectively. Lt. Comdr. John W. Young, USN, is pilot of the F4H flying from NAS Brunswick, Maine. More records fall to the F4H-1 on 1 Mar as the aircraft, flying from NAS Brunswick, Maine, reaches 27,432 feet (9,000 m) from a standing start in 61.62 seconds, and 36,576 feet (12,000 m) in 77.15 seconds; Lt. Col. W. C. McGraw, USMC, is the pilot. Two days later Lt. Comdr. Del W. Nordberg, USN, reaches 45,720 feet (15,000 m) in 114.54 seconds in an F4H-1. On 31 Mar an F4H-1 piloted by Lt. Comdr. F. Taylor Brown, USN, flying from NAS Point Mugu, Calif., sets a time-to-climb record of 178.5 seconds to 60,960 feet (20,000 m). Another record will fall to an F4H from Point Mugu on 3 Apr, this one piloted by Lt. Comdr. Young, reaching 60,960 feet (20,000 m) in 230.44 seconds. A clean sweep of the world climb records will be achieved by the F4H on 12 Apr when Lt. Comdr. Nordberg climbs to 91,440 feet (30,000 m) in 371.43 seconds.

11 MAR

US carrier *Constellation* (CVA 64) launches the first guided missiles to be fired by an aircraft carrier. The Terrier surface-to-air missiles are fired off Roosevelt Roads, Puerto Rico, and score four hits against aerial drones. (*See* 6 Sep 1947.)

17 MAR

The nuclear-propelled attack submarine *Pollack* (SSN 603) is launched at New York Shipbuilding Corp. at Camden, N.J. She is the first nuclear submarine to be built at that shipyard. Previously the yard had built one diesel-electric submarine.

21 MAR

The Center for Naval Analyses (CNA) is established to undertake studies for the Navy Department, initially under the sponsorship of the Franklin Institute. The organization is a not-for-profit federal contract research center that combined the Institute of Naval Studies (INS) in Cambridge, Mass., and the Operations Evaluation Group (OEG) in Washington, D.C.

12 APR

Three ships of the US Seventh Fleet's amphibious group—the *Navarro* (APA 215), *Point Defiance* (LSD

31), and *Valley Forge* (LPH 8)—land Marines in Thailand to help support the independence of that nation.

26 APR
First flight of the prototype Lockheed A-12 high-speed, high-altitude strategic reconnaissance aircraft; the follow-on production variant of the aircraft will be designated SR-71 Blackbird.

28 APR
The rank of Admiral of the Fleet *(Admiral Flota)* is reintroduced in the Soviet Navy. It corresponds to the military ranks of general of the army and marshal of an arm or service.

4 MAY
The US government commits five Polaris ballistic missile submarines to NATO during a three-day ministerial session of the Atlantic Council meeting in Athens, Greece. The submarines will remain under the operational control of the US Navy.

6 MAY
The ballistic missile submarine *Ethan Allen* (SSBN 608), operating as part of Joint Task Force 8 operating near Christmas Island in the Pacific, fires a Polaris A-2 missile with a nuclear warhead that detonates. This is the only full-systems test of a US nuclear missile—land- or sea-based—from launch tube though detonation. The test had the code-name Operation Frigate Bird.

7 MAY
Eight US Navy warships, including the anti-submarine carrier *Wasp* (CVS 18), enter the Baltic Sea. This is the largest American force to enter these waters since World War II. The other US ships are the *John S. McCain* (DL 3), *New* (DD 818), *Holder* (DD 819), *Robert L. Wilson* (DD 847), *Damato* (DD 871), *Basilone* (DD 824), and *Robert A. Owens* (DD 827).

8 MAY
US ballistic missile submarine *Lafayette* (SSBN 616), the first of a new class of Polaris submarines, is launched at General Dynamics/Electric Boat yard in Groton, Conn. She is the largest undersea craft yet launched by a Western shipyard. Mrs. Jacqueline Kennedy, wife of the President, is sponsor.

10 MAY
A Sparrow III air-to-air missile fired from an F4H-1 Phantom fighter scores a direct hit in a head-on attack

on a Regulus II guided missile while both are flying at supersonic speeds. The test, at the Pacific Missile Test Range, marks the first head-on hit scored by an air-launched missile launched against a surface-launched missile.

11 MAY
The ASROC is tested with a nuclear warhead, being fired from the destroyer *Agerholm* (DD 826) in the eastern Pacific in a test known as Swordfish, part of the Dominic test series.

12 MAY
President Kennedy orders a task force from the Seventh Fleet, including amphibious ships with 1,800 Marines embarked, to move toward the Indochina peninsula to back up efforts to support Laos' independence.

24 MAY
Lt. Comdr. M. Scott Carpenter, USN, is launched into orbit from Cape Canaveral, Fla., on the second manned US orbital flight. His spacecraft *Aurora 7* orbits the earth three times and then comes down approximately 200 n.miles (371 km) from its planned impact point. After nearly three hours in his floating capsule, Carpenter is picked up by an HSS-2 Sea King helicopter from the carrier *Intrepid* (CVS 11). Carpenter's capsule was later retrieved by the destroyer *John R. Pierce* (DD 753).

26 JUNE
The ballistic missile submarine *Ethan Allen* (SSBN 608) departs Charleston, S.C., on the first deterrent patrol with the Polaris A-2 missile.

6 JULY
Secretary of Defense Robert S. McNamara directs that a standard designation system for all US military aircraft be established. He assigns primary responsibility for the formulation and application to the Air Force. (*See* 18 Sep 1962.)

7 JULY
Soviet Premier Nikita S. Khrushchev approves the completed plan for the deployment of nuclear-capable ballistic missiles and aircraft, as well as ground combat troops and coastal and air defense forces to Cuba.

26 JULY
The Soviet freighter *Maria Ulyanova* arrives at the port of Cananas, Cuba, carrying the advance party of the Soviet forces being sent to Cuba.

1 AUG

The second US Navy Polaris missile submarine squadron—SubRon 16—is commissioned at the Naval Submarine Base New London, Conn. However, no Polaris submarines will operate from New London although the staff and submarine crews will be based there.

The US Navy releases all reservists who were called to active duty in October 1961; 3,995 officers and enlisted men are involved.

2 AUG

The US nuclear-propelled submarines *Skate* (SSN 578) and *Seadragon* (SSN 584) rendezvous under the polar ice pack and surface together at the North Pole. This is the first two-submarine operation at the North Pole.

4 AUG

The USS *Leahy* (DLG 16), the first of a new class of "double-end" missile frigates, is commissioned at Bath, Maine. These ships will be redesignated as cruisers (CG) in 1974. Named for Fleet Adm. William D. Leahy, USN, the Chief of Staff to Presidents Franklin D. Roosevelt and Harry S. Truman. The ship's first CO is Capt. Robert L. Baughan, Jr., USN.

5 AUG

A CIA U-2 reconnaissance flight over Cuba reveals a sudden increase in Soviet military matériel being unloaded in Cuba, progress in the deployment of surface-to-air missile sites, and the presence of Soviet military personnel.

7 AUG

The launch of an advanced Polaris A-3 missile from Cape Canaveral, Fla., is successful. With a range of more than 2,500 n.miles (4,633 km), the missile will replace the A-1 and A-2 missiles in US submarines and, with a British-developed warhead, will be used by the Royal Navy's strategic missile submarines. The Polaris A-3 has a Multiple Re-entry Vehicle (MRV) warhead that "shotguns" three nuclear projectiles onto a single target.

30 AUG

The twin-engine version of the North American Buckeye trainer, the YT2J-1, makes its first flight. The carrier-capable aircraft will become a mainstay of Navy flight training. (It will be designated T-2 in 1962.) (*See* 31 Jan 1958.)

31 AUG

The last US Navy airship, a ZPG-3W, makes its final flight from NAS Lakehurst, N.J.

8 SEP

The USS *Raleigh* (LPD 1), the first of a new class of amphibious transport docks, is commissioned. She is the first ship of her design, being similar to the dock landing ship (LSD) with increased troop and vehicle capacities. Her first CO is Capt. A. W. Whitney, USN.

10 SEP

The US Navy League's Sea Cadet program is established.

12 SEP

The UF-2G Albatross flying boat sets two amphibian records. Piloted by Lt. Comdr. D. E. Moore, USN, the aircraft climbs to 29,460 feet (8,979 m) over NAS Floyd Bennet Field, N.Y., setting a record for carrying a 2,200-pound (1,000-kg) load; flown by Lt. Comdr. F. A. W. Franke, Jr., USN, the UF-2G lifts 4,400 pounds (2,000 kg) to 27,380 feet (8,345 m). Three days later Lt. Comdr. R. A. Hoffman, USN, will set another record in a UF-2G, carrying a load of 2,200 pounds (1,000 kg) at an average speed of 151.4 mph (244 kmh) on a course from Floyd Bennet Field to Plattsburg, N.Y., to Dupree, S.D., and back to Floyd Bennet.

18 SEP

At the direction of Secretary of Defense McNamara, all US military aircraft designations are merged into a single system based on the Air Force scheme. Under this system the following basic mission designations are established:

A	Attack
B	Bomber
C	Cargo/transport
E	Electronic
F	Fighter
H	Helicopter
O	Observation
P	Patrol
S	Anti-Submarine
T	Trainer
U	Utility
V	VSTOL or STOL
X	Research
Z	Airship

Thus, the Navy's AD Skywarrior becomes the A-1, the AJ Savage the A-2, the A3D Skywarrior the A-3, etc. Where possible, similar numerical sequence is used, as the W2F Hawkeye becomes the E-2, the P3V Orion the P-3, the F4H Phantom the F-4, etc.

3 OCT

The US spacecraft *Sigma 7* carrying Comdr. Walter M. Schirra, Jr., USN, is launched into orbit by a Mercury-Atlas rocket from Cape Canaveral, Fla. His 10-hour, 46-minute flight carries him around the earth six times. Schirra re-enters the atmosphere and comes down in the Pacific Ocean, 275 n.miles (510 km) northeast of Midway Island where he is retrieved by helicopter and delivered to the carrier *Kearsarge* (CVS 33).

4 OCT

Nuclear warheads arrive in the Cuban port of Mariel in the Soviet freighter *Indigiirka*. The ship includes warheads for 36 medium-range ballistic missiles, 80 nuclear warheads for defensive cruise missiles, and six nuclear bombs for Il-28 Beagle light bombers. The unloading of nuclear warheads is not detected by US intelligence activities. (The cargo ship *Alexandrovsk* reaches port with additional nuclear warheads for ballistic missiles, but they are not unloaded.)

6 OCT

The guided missile frigate *Bainbridge* (DLGN 25), the world's first destroyer-type ship with nuclear propulsion is commissioned. Her first CO is Capt. Raymond E. Peet, USN.

9 OCT

The Inter-American Defense College, located at Fort Lesley J. McNair in Washington, D.C., is formally opened in ceremonies led by Secretary of State Dean Rusk.

14 OCT

A USAF U-2 reconnaissance plane photographs a Soviet missile site for nuclear-capable ballistic missiles being constructed at San Cristobal, Cuba, some 100 miles (161 km) west of Havana. This marks the beginning of the Cuban Missile Crisis.

15 OCT

US Navy RF-8A Photo Crusaders (formerly F8U-1P) begin flying missions over Cuba to pinpoint Soviet missile sites; low-level flights by these aircraft begin on 23 Oct.

16 OCT

The photographs taken by the USAF U-2 aircraft on 14 Oct are presented to President John F. Kennedy.

Soon afterward it is also learned that Soviet Il-28 Beagle bombers are being assembled on Cuban airfields.

President Kennedy's key advisors—later designated the Excomm (Executive Committee of the National Security Council)—hold marathon meetings to frame an appropriate response to the Soviet challenge of missiles and bombers in Cuba. Kennedy chooses the option of imposing a naval blockade, which, since the United States and Cuba are not in a state of war, will be called a quarantine.

Chief of Naval Operations Adm. George W. Anderson, Jr., USN, directs that a helicopter minesweeping program be implemented. Originally H-46A Sea Knight (formerly HRB-1) helicopters are to be converted, but the SH-3 Sea King (HSS-2) is later substituted, to be designated RH-3A in the mine countermeasures role.

22 OCT

President Kennedy appears on national television to announce that he is imposing a naval quarantine, effective 24 Oct to block the further entry of Soviet offensive weapons into Cuba. To carry out the quarantine, Task Force 136 is organized under Vice Adm. Alfred G. Ward, USN, the Commander, Second Fleet and Strike Fleet Atlantic. TF-136 consists of the antisubmarine carrier *Essex* (CVS 9), the cruisers *Canberra* (CAG 2) and *Newport News* (CA 148), several squadrons of destroyers, and support ships. At the same time, Task Force 135 is established under Rear Adm. John T. Hayward, USN, Commander, Carrier Division 2, containing the carrier *Enterprise* (CVAN 65); TF 135 stands ready to come to the defense of the US naval base at Guantanamo Bay. Also, Carrier Division 6 under Rear Adm. Robert J. Stroh, USN, with the carrier *Independence* (CVA 62) is positioned to provide additional support to the blockade.

The evacuation begins of 3,190 dependents of US Navy and Marine Corps personnel by air and sea from the naval base at Guantanamo Bay, Cuba.

23 OCT

The UN Security Council holds an emergency session to consider a charge by the United States that the Soviet Union is threatening the peace.

President Kennedy signs a proclamation ordering the interdiction of offensive weapons being shipped to Cuba. Prohibited materials include surface-to-surface missiles, bomber aircraft, bombs, air-to-ground missiles, warheads for any of the above weapons, mechanical or electronic equipment to support or operate the above items, and any other materials that may be designated by the Secretary of Defense.

The Organization of American States (OAS) approves the use of force in carrying out the quarantine of Cuba by a vote of 19 to 0; Uruguay abstains.

24 OCT

The US naval quarantine of Cuba goes into effect. Reconnaissance aircraft reveal 25 merchant ships en route to Cuba, but at mid-morning all but one of those nearing the blockade line are dead in the water. Several hours later most of the ships reverse course.

25 OCT

On the Cuban quarantine line, the US destroyer *Gearing* (DD 710) stops the Soviet tanker *Bucharest,* but allows her to proceed to Cuba upon learning that she is carrying only petroleum and no weapons.

26 OCT

The US destroyers *Joseph P. Kennedy, Jr.* (DD 850) and *John R. Pierce* (DD 753) stop and send crewmen on board a Soviet-chartered, Lebanese-flag freighter, the *Marcula.* After her cargo is inspected, she is allowed to continue to Havana.

At 1800 President Kennedy receives an emotional letter from Soviet Premier Khrushchev, which states that the missiles have been placed in Cuba only to deter an American invasion and promises to remove them if the United States will pledge to lift the blockade and not attack Cuba.

27 OCT

A USAF U-2 reconnaissance aircraft is shot down by a Soviet SA-2 surface-to-air missile while overflying Cuba. The pilot, Maj. Rudolf Anderson, Jr., USAF, is killed, the only US combat casualty of the Cuban Missile Crisis.

President Kennedy receives a second letter from Khrushchev. In this letter, the Soviet Premier adds a

demand for the withdrawl of American missiles from Turkey to his previous terms for the withdrawl of Soviet missiles from Cuba. After several hours of discussion, Attorney General Robert F. Kennedy, the President's brother, suggests that the President agree to the conditions of the first letter received and simply ignore the second. This is done and, at the same time, Robert Kennedy privately informs Soviet Ambassador Anatoly F. Dobrynin that President Kennedy already planned to remove the American missiles from Turkey.

28 OCT

Premier Khrushchev notifies President Kennedy that he is ordering the Soviet offensive missiles in Cuba to be withdrawn.

8 NOV

The Department of Defense announces that the Soviet offensive missile bases in Cuba have all been dismantled.

20 NOV

President Kennedy declares that, having received Premier Khrushchev's promise to withdraw all Soviet Il-28 Beagle bomber aircraft from Cuba within 30 days, he has ended the quarantine of the island.

8 DEC

First flight of the Bell OH-4A helicopter; later variants of this widely flown helicopter are the OH-58 Kiowa and TH-57 SeaRanger.

19 DEC

President Kennedy and British Prime Minister Harold Macmillan begin three days of meetings at Nassau, Bahamas. Because the US government is about to cancel the Skybolt air-launched strategic missile, which was to have been used by Britain, Kennedy offers Macmillan the Polaris missile (less warhead) for the British nuclear deterrence role. The offer is immediately accepted.

1963

24 JAN

Shipboard qualifications are completed by the DASH (Drone Anti-Submarine Helicopter) system on board the destroyer *Buck* (DD 761). The system, employing the QH-50C (formerly DSN-3) unmanned helicopter, is considered operational.

29 JAN

In the first demonstration of its automatic television guidance feature, a Walleye air-to-surface bomb is launched by a YA-4B Skyhawk at the Naval Ordnance Test Station China Lake, Calif. The Walleye makes a direct hit on the target.

27 FEB

First flight of Hughes OH-6 Cayuse (formerly YHO-6) helicopter. Winning the US Army's Light Observation Helicopter (LOH) program, it will be produced in large numbers for that service as well as a score of foreign nations.

28 MAR

The Department of Defense announces the deployment of the first of three Polaris missile submarines to the Mediterranean. This is looked at by defense analysts as a substitute for the dismantling of US Jupiter ballistic missiles in Turkey and Italy.

10 APR

US nuclear-propelled submarine *Thresher* (SSN 593), commanded by Lt. Comdr. John W. Harvey, USN, is lost with all hands—129 officers, enlisted men, and civilian technicians—approximately 240 n.miles (445 km) east of Cape Cod, Mass. Apparently the disaster results from a reactor shut-down ("scram") during a dive to the submarine's test depth of 1,300 feet (396 m). The *Thresher* is the world's first nuclear submarine loss.

14 APR

The Polaris missile submarine *Sam Houston* (SSBN 609), the first US ballistic missile submarine assigned to the Mediterranean, visits Ozmir, Turkey. This is the first foreign port call other than Holy Loch by a US Polaris submarine.

17 APR

The first British nuclear-propelled submarine, the *Dreadnought,* is placed in commission with Comdr. B. F. P. (Peter) Samborne, RN, in command.

23 APR

The USS *Lafayette* (SSBN 616), the first of the third US Polaris submarine class is placed in commission. Her first COs are Comdr. P. J. Hannifin (Blue) and Comdr. James T. Strong (Gold).

24 APR

Secretary of the Navy Fred H. Korth announces the establishment of a Deep Submergence Review Group (DSRG) under Rear Adm. E. C. Stephan, USN, to review and formalize into one program all of the Navy's deep-ocean search, location, rescue, and salvage requirements.

6 MAY

Engineers on board the nuclear-propelled merchant ship *Savannah* unilaterally and without authority commence to shut down the ship's reactor. A scheduled sailing from Galveston to Houston, Texas, the following morning is canceled. On 9 May the engineers shut off the ship's sanitary water, lighting, galley services, and refrigeration.

15 MAY

The first American to fly in space for more than one day, Maj. L. Gordon Cooper, USAF, completes a 22-orbit, 34-hour flight in the *Faith 7* capsule of the Mercury program. The carrier *Kearsarge* (CVS 33) recovers the astronaut in the Pacific Ocean some 80 n.miles (148 km) southeast of Midway Island and less than five n.miles (9.3 km) from the carrier. Cooper is hoisted aboard the carrier in his capsule.

17 MAY

Thirty-four volunteer US Naval Reserve officers are released from a protective fall-out shelter at the National Naval Medical Center, Bethesda, Md., where they have been isolated for a period of five days as part of an exercise to observe their medical and physiological conditions.

The Department of Commerce terminates the general agency agreement with the States Marine Lines to operate the NS *Savannah* and engage Babcock and Wilcox Co., designer and builder of the nuclear reactor in the ship, to care for the reactor until final decision on the ship's future can be taken.

24 MAY

Two single-engine Cessna 180 aircraft of the US Navy's Arctic Research Laboratory make the deepest known penetration of the Arctic Ocean Basin ever made by a light plane. The two planes took off from the laboratory's scientific station on the ice island Arlis-2 and landed at the North Pole after a flight of 170 n.miles (274 km).

4 JUNE

Six Soviet Tu-16 Badger bombers fly near the US carrier *Ranger* (CVA 61), steaming in international waters, 330 n.miles (611 km) east of Japan. The *Ranger* is en route to the United States from Yokosuka, Japan, after completing a deployment with the Seventh Fleet. Aircraft from the carrier intercept the Soviet aircraft at distances of 65 to 100 n.miles (120 to 185 km) from the ship after they are detected by the carrier's radar.

6 JUNE

The US Caribbean Command (CINCARIB) is redesignated the US Southern Command (CINCSO), with responsibilities for US military activities in Central and South America.

7 JUNE

The US Court of Inquiry investigating the loss of the submarine *Thresher* completes its work. Records of the court, together with its findings of facts, opinions, and recommendations, are delivered to Adm. H. P. Smith, USN, Commander in Chief US Atlantic Fleet, the convening authority of the court. After review by Smith, the report will be submitted to the Secretary of the Navy.

10 JUNE

Soviet Premier Nikita S. Khrushchev states that the Soviet Union has ended production of strategic bombers and surface warships because of their vulnerability to missiles. However, according to a subsequent statement by Harold Wilson, Great Britain's Labor Party leader, the Soviet Union is still building bombers.

15 JUNE

The USS *Bronstein* (DE 1037) is commissioned at Charleston, S.C. She is the first of a new concept in escort ships, being the first to carry the large AN/SQS-26 sonar, ASROC rocket launcher, and facilities for the Drone Anti-Submarine Helicopter (DASH). Lt. Comdr. Stanley T. Counts, USN, is the frigate's first CO.

16 JUNE

Valentina Tereshkova of the Soviet Union is launched into orbit in *Vostok 6,* the first woman to enter space.

20 JUNE

The opinion of the US Court of Inquiry into the sinking of the nuclear-propelled submarine *Thresher* is made public. The report states that a flooding casualty in the engine room is believed to be the most probable cause of sinking, brought about by a piping system failure in one of the submarine's salt water systems.

The US and Soviet governments sign the "hot line" agreement in Geneva to establish a teleprinter link between Moscow and Washington. The Washington terminal will be installed in the Pentagon.

1 JULY

The Atlantic Fleet Weapons Range, combining the Guided Missile Operations Control and Gunfire Support Training Unit, is placed in commission at the Naval Station Roosevelt Roads, Puerto Rico.

8 JULY

Rear Adm. Draper L. Kauffman, USN, becomes head of the new Office of Program Appraisal (OPA) under the Secretary of the Navy. OPA provides the Navy Secretary with independent program appraisal and analysis.

19 JULY

A contract is let for a $72-million US Navy Very-Low Frequency (VLF) radio communications facility to be located near Perth, Australia. It will be the largest of its type in the Pacific area.

A pair of Israeli Mirage fighters fire warning shots to force a US RB-57A Canberra to land at Lod (later Ben-Gurion) Airport after the American plane overflew Israeli territory.

22 JULY

The US Navy announces success in permanently stabilizing an orbiting satellite in space, thus improving reception of radio signals from earth.

26 JULY

The Hughes Corporation's *Syncom 2*—prototype of the US Early Bird communications satellite—is "parked" over the Atlantic at an altitude of 22,500 miles (36,202 km) to become the earth's first geosynchronous satellite.

I AUG

US Marine Corps all-weather fighter squadrons (VMF[AW]) flying the F-4B Phantom aircraft are re-designated as all-weather fighter attack squadrons (VMFA). Eventually all 15 Marine fighter squadrons will have the Phantom.

2 AUG

The space probe Sparroair is launched by a US Navy F-3B Demon fighter. It is the first of a series of five such space probes designed to measure the ultraviolet radiation of the stars.

9 AUG

A US Navy P-3A Orion becomes the first maritime patrol aircraft to make a nonstop, trans-Pacific flight. The Orion flies 5,135 n.miles (9,515 km) from NAS Moffett Field, Calif., to Japan in 14 hours, 25 minutes.

13 AUG

The Navy transport *Gen. R. M. Blatchford* (T-AP 153) returns to New York after serving 2½ years overseas with the United Nations and the US-Congo sealift. While serving under UN auspices the *Blatchford* carried 36,809 troops to and from Morocco, India, Pakistan, Malaysia, and Indonesia.

24 AUG

Searching for the sunken submarine *Thresher*, the US Navy's deep-diving bathyscaph *Trieste II* recovers a length of copper tubing and a fitting with markings from the lost submarine.

30 AUG

The French destroyer *Dupetit Thouars*, the first Allied warship to be armed with the US Navy's Tartar surface-to-air missile, arrives in Norfolk, Va., to begin missile training.

I SEP

The US Navy's bathyscaph *Trieste II* and her support ships return to Boston after five dives and 17 days on station in search of the remains of the *Thresher*.

6 SEP

Secretary of the Navy Fred H. Korth directs an end to the operational aspects of the search for the lost submarine *Thresher*. He announces that "the location of structural parts of the *Thresher* on the ocean floor have been positively confirmed by the bathyscaph *Trieste*."

24 SEP

The US Senate votes 80 to 19 in favor of ratification of a treaty between the United States, Great Britain, and the Soviet Union banning all atmospheric nuclear tests and detonations. The ban will go into effect on 10 Oct 1963.

30 SEP

US Marines begin Operation Swampex 1-63, a full-scale counter-guerrilla exercise in North Carolina. Involving 4,500 Marines from 4th Marine Expeditionary Brigade, this is the largest exercise of its type ever held on the East Coast.

25 OCT

US Navy and Marine Corps units depart Port-au-Prince, Haiti, after almost two weeks of relief operations as a result of Hurricane Flora, which inflicted heavy damage on the nation. Cuba is also damaged in the hurricane but refuses an offer of US assistance. The ships involved in the relief operation are *Lake Champlain* (CVS 39), *Liddle* (APD 60), and *Muliphen* (AKA 61).

Secretary of Defense Robert S. McNamara announces that the CVA 67, the aircraft carrier authorized in the FY 1963 shipbuilding program will have conventional propulsion, not nuclear. McNamara states that "this decision was motivated by a desire to avoid further delay, and does not prejudge the larger question of the application of nuclear power to the Navy surface vessels in the future." The CVA 67 will later be named *John F. Kennedy*.

26 OCT

The first Polaris A-3 missile launched from a submarine is fired from the submarine *Andrew Jackson* (SSBN 619).

30 OCT

A US Navy KC-130F Hercules makes 16 touch-and-go landings aboard the carrier *Forrestal* (CVA 59), the first time a four-engine aircraft has "operated" on an aircraft carrier. During the next three weeks the KC-130F will make numerous full-stop landings and deck-run take-offs from the ship, with gross aircraft weight reaching 120,000 pounds (54,432 kg).

10 NOV

US Navy oceanographic survey ship *Rehoboth* (AGS 50) arrives in Nakhodka, Siberia, for a three-day visit. This is the first visit made by a US Navy ship to a Soviet port in the Pacific since the late 1940s.

15 NOV

The US Coast Guard begins testing a new Loran-C station located at the southern tip of Greenland.

When operational, the station will provide complete Loran coverage for the North Atlantic.

16 NOV

President John F. Kennedy watches from the USS *Observation Island* (EAG 154) as the *Andrew Jackson* carries out a submerged launching of a Polaris A-2 missile.

22 NOV

President Kennedy is assassinated in Dallas, Texas. Vice President Lyndon B. Johnson is sworn in as President on board the presidential aircraft before returning to Washington. A former Texas representative and senator, Johnson went on active duty as a naval reserve officer in 1942 and was a passenger in a USAAF bomber attacked by Japanese fighters. (Later that year President Franklin D. Roosevelt ordered all congressmen in the armed forces to return to Washington.)

1 DEC

The US destroyer *Strong* (DD 758) completes a seven-day medical action mission along the southern coast of Iran with the Iranian naval ship *Babr*. The US and Iranian doctors treat 2,335 patients at the three ports visited—Chahbar, Jask, and Bandar Addas.

2 DEC

The Naval Material Support Establishment is activated with Vice Adm. William A. Schoech, USN, as Chief of Navy Material. He reports to the Secretary of the Navy for duty as his assistant for Naval Material Support and assumes supervision and command of the four material bureaus—Naval Weapons, Ships, Supplies and Accounts, and Yards and Docks.

4 DEC

The US Navy discloses details of the new SUBROC (Submarine Rocket) anti-submarine weapon being tested at the Naval Ordnance Test Station China Lake, Calif. SUBROC is an underwater-launched missile with a range of some 25 n.miles (46 km) carrying a nuclear depth bomb. Fired from a standard torpedo tube, the missile has a solid-fuel rocket motor that propels the missile out of the water and through the air toward its target.

20 DEC

The US Navy's designation of Carrier Air Groups (CAG) is changed to Carrier Air Wings (CVW). However, the term CAG—for Commander Air Group—remains in use with the air wings.

21 DEC

The USS *Mars* (AFS 1) is commissioned at the Long Beach Naval Shipyard, Calif., a new-design underway replenishment ship that combines the capabilities of stores ships (AF) and stores-issue ships (AKS). Her first CO is Russell C. Medley, USN.

1964

6 JAN

A new naval supply center responsible for the support of the Polaris missile weapon system throughout the world is commissioned at Charleston, S.C.

7 JAN

The US Navy halts the development of the Typhon shipboard surface-to-air missile. A re-orientation of the Navy's shipboard missile program is announced that will provide for the development of an advanced shipboard missile system and standardization of improved Tartar / Terrier missiles; the resulting systems will be the Aegis fire control system and Standard missile series.

10 JAN

The Military Sea Transportation Service (MSTS) places in service the first Fleet Ballistic Missile (FBM) resupply ship, the USNS *Norwalk* (T-AK 279), in New Orleans, La. A converted Victory freighter, the ship was built in 1945 in Portland, Ore., as the *Norwalk Victory*.

13 JAN

During a revolution in Zanzibar, the US destroyer *Manley* (DD 940) evacuates 55 American citizens and 36 other persons.

15 JAN

US Navy Carrier Divisions 15, 17, and 19 in the Pacific Fleet are redesignated Anti-Submarine Warfare Groups 1, 3, and 5, respectively, reflecting an increased Navy emphasis on anti-submarine operations.

18 JAN

Secretary of the Navy Paul H. Nitze accepts the resignation of President Lyndon B. Johnson as a commander in the US Naval Reserve.

19 JAN

A six-man US Navy medical team under Capt. Robert Philips (Medical Corps), USN, a detachment of Naval Medical Research Unit 2, arrives in Saigon at the request of the South Vietnamese government to help contain a serious epidemic of cholera in that city.

1 FEB

Vice Adm. H. G. Rickover, USN, Assistant Chief of the Bureau of Ships for Nuclear Propulsion, retires from active duty, having reached the mandatory re-

tirement age of 64. He immediately returns to active duty in a retired status.

5 FEB

The US Navy announces plans to base Polaris submarines at Charleston, S.C., and Melville, R.I. In the event, only the Charleston base will be established (the only Polaris base in the continental United States).

Members of the House of Representatives introduce bills calling for Congress to reverse Secretary of Defense Robert S. McNamara's decision against nuclear power for the carrier CVA 67 (later named *John F. Kennedy*). None of these bills become law.

6 FEB

The Cuban government shuts off the fresh water supply to the US Naval Base at Guantanamo Bay, Cuba. The move is described as retaliation for the seizure of four Cuban fishing boats and their crews off Florida on 3 Feb 1964.

In response to the water shut-off at the Guantanamo Bay Naval Base, on 7 Feb President Johnson announces that the base will be made self-sufficient. He issues instructions to Secretary of Defense McNamara to "assure the base control over its own water supply both by conversion of sea water to fresh water and by transportation of water by ship," and to reduce the employment of Cuban nationals at the base.

10 FEB

Australia's worst peacetime maritime disaster occurs when the destroyer *Voyager* is cut in half and sinks in a collision with the aircraft carrier *Melbourne* off the Australian coast; 82 officers and enlisted men in the *Voyager* are lost.

11 FEB

The Department of Defense states that as a further step toward self-sufficiency, and in order to "improve the garrison posture" of Guantanamo, no more dependents will be allowed to go there. Future tours of unaccompanied personnel will be reduced to one year or less, and by a process of attrition, all dependents will be removed from the base by early 1966.

17 FEB

Rear Adm. John D. Bulkeley, USN, Commander Naval Base Guantanamo, orders the pipeline that previously supplied the base with fresh water from the Cuban Yateras Plant to be severed. The action is taken to prove that the base is not stealing water as Cuban Prime Minister Fidel Castro has charged.

24 FEB
The second overseas US Polaris submarine base is established at Rota, Spain, with arrival of the submarine tender *Proteus* (AS 19). She will be replaced at Rota on 1 Apr 1964 by the USS *Holland* (AS 32).

26 FEB
Secretary of Defense McNamara announces that the United States will make available the guided missile destroyer *Biddle* (DDG 5) for a mixed-manning demonstration ship by the personnel of countries interested in the proposal for a multilateral force. The *Biddle*'s current CO, Comdr. Thomas E. Forston II, USN, will remain in command for the initial phase of the experiment, to last from June 1964 through Dec 1965. The US Navy will furnish 49 percent of the ship's company with the remainder to be provided by Great Britain, West Germany, Greece, Italy, the Netherlands, and Turkey. The ship will remain a US warship and under US Navy regulations. The crew members will be paid according to the standards of their own country.

29 FEB
President Johnson announces at a White House news conference that an advanced aircraft capable of flying more than 2,000 mph (3,218 kmh) in sustained flight at an altitude of more than 70,000 feet (21,340 m) has been developed, a performance that "far exceeds that of any other aircraft in the world today." He calls the aircraft the A-11, which is succeeded by the advanced YF-12 in the fighter version and SR-71 Blackbird in the reconnaissance version.

4 MAR
Prime Minister Castro offers to restore water service to the US naval base at Guantanamo Bay. The US government rejects the offer.

10 MAR
A USAF RB-66 Destroyer reconnaissance aircraft is shot down over East Germany by a Soviet fighter. The three-man crew parachutes from the plane with one man being injured; all three are returned to US custody. (The RB-66 is a USAF variant of the A-3 Skywarrior.)

13 MAR
US Navy instructions are issued to redesignate all heavy attack squadrons (VAH) as reconnaissance attack squadrons (RVAH) upon assignment of RA-5C Vigilante aircraft.

23 MAR
West Germany's first destroyer built in-country since World War II, the *Hamburg,* is commissioned at Hamburg. She is Germany's largest warship.

26 MAR
A Canadian White Paper on Defense is presented to the House of Commons by the government that contains a proposal to amalgamate the three military services.

1 APR
Britain's unified Ministry of Defence is established as Defence Minister Peter Thorneycroft becomes Secretary of State for Defence, merging the nation's three services under one organization. Along with the War Office and the Air Ministry, the Admiralty ceases to exist as a separate government department.

2 APR
The Soviet oceanographic research ships *Sergei Vavilov* and *Petr Lebedev* enter Boston, Mass., for fuel and to permit crew and scientists to visit the Woods Hole Oceanographic Institute on Cape Cod. They are the first Soviet ships to enter Boston since World War II.

4 APR
The US Navy's Concord Squadron, consisting of the carrier *Bon Homme Richard* (CVA 31), the destroyers *Shelton* (DD 790), *Frank Knox* (DDR 742), and *Blue* (DD 744), and the oiler *Hassayampa* (AO 145), enters the Indian Ocean from the Pacific to begin a six-week goodwill tour of Africa and Middle East ports. The squadron is commanded by Rear Adm. Robert B. Moore, USN, Commander Carrier Division 5.

20 APR
The submarine *Henry Clay* (SSBN 625) successfully fires a Polaris A-2 missile while surfaced off Cape Kennedy, Fla. This is the first launch of a Polaris missile from a surfaced submarine. (No additional surface Submarine-Launched Ballistic Missile (SLBM) launches by US submarines have been announced.)

24 APR
Secretary of Defense McNamara announces 63 actions to consolidate, reduce, or discontinue Depart-

ment of Defense activities in the United States and overseas. Fifty-five of these actions affect military activities in 29 states and, when completed, are expected to produce annual savings of $68 million and reduce personnel by 10,056 without reducing military effectiveness. Included among the facilities affected are the Naval Auxiliary Air Station New Iberia, La., which will be closed by Jan 1965, and NAS Grosse Isle, Mich., which will be closed by Sep 1967.

28 APR

French President Charles de Gaulle withdraws French naval officers from NATO commands in the Mediterranean and the English Channel. The government communiqué adds, however, that in the event of war, the French fleet will maintain close operational liaison with Allied fleets.

I MAY

Vice Adm. Charles B. Martell, USN, becomes the first Director, Anti-Submarine Warfare Programs (OP-095) in the Office of the Chief of Naval Operations, reflecting the concern for Soviet submarines by the US Navy's leadership.

The USNS *Card* (T-AKV 40), a former escort carrier manned by MSTS civilian seamen and employed as an aircraft transport, is crippled by an explosion while alongside a pier in Saigon, South Vietnam. The ship sinks to the river bottom as a 30-foot (9.1-m) hole is torn in the hull below the water line. There were no casualties among the *Card*'s 73-man crew. The attack is attributed to communist guerrillas. The ship is later raised and towed to Subic Bay in the Philippines for permanent repairs.

5 MAY

The nuclear-propelled merchant ship *Savannah* resumes operations, delayed since an engineers' strike in May 1963, with a cruise from Galveston to Houston, Texas. The ship subsequently sails on her first trans-ocean operations under the management of the American Export Isbrandtsen Lines.

6 MAY

The US destroyer *Decatur* (DD 936) is severely damaged in a collision while pulling away from the carrier *Lake Champlain* (CVS 39) following refueling operations in the Atlantic, 150 n.miles (278 km) east of Cape Henry, Va. No injuries are suffered by the ships' crews, but there is heavy damage to the destroyer's superstructure.

13 MAY

The US Navy disbands its parachute demonstration team, the Chuting Stars, for budgetary reasons.

The first nuclear-powered task force is formed as part of the US Sixth Fleet in the Mediterranean when the attack carrier *Enterprise* (CVAN 65) is joined by the guided missile cruiser *Long Beach* (CGN 9) and the guided missile frigate *Bainbridge* (DLGN 25). The group is commanded by Rear Adm. Bernard M. Strean, USN, Commander Carrier Division 2.

3 JUNE

The US carrier *Lake Champlain* is damaged in a collision with the Norwegian freighter *Skauvaag* in Chesapeake Bay. There are no injuries.

6 JUNE

A US Navy RF-8 Crusader reconnaissance aircraft flying from the carrier *Kitty Hawk* (CVA 63) is shot down over the Plane des Jarres region in Laos. The pilot, Lt. Charles F. Klusmann, USN, parachutes safely to the ground. When it appears that a helicopter sent in to rescue him will also be shot down, Klusmann waves off the rescue. For this action he will be awarded the Distinguished Flying Cross. Communist China radio later reports that he has been captured. (*See* 1 Sep 1964.)

7 JUNE

An F-8 Crusader fighter from the carrier *Kitty Hawk* (CVA 63) is shot down over the Plane des Jarres. The fighter, escorting a photo-reconnaissance mission, is flown by Comdr. Doyle W. Lynn, USN; he is rescued after he parachutes from his plane.

II JUNE

The *George Washington* (SSBN 598), the first submarine to deploy with Polaris missiles, returns to her home port of New London, Conn., after 3½ years of operations from Holy Loch, Scotland. During that period she undertook 15 Polaris deterrent patrols. During a forthcoming overhaul at the General Dynamics/Electric Boat yard in Groton, Conn., she will be modified to carry the Polaris A-3 missile.

13 JUNE

Europe's first nuclear-powered merchant ship, the freighter *Otto Hahn,* is launched at the Kiel Shipyard in Germany. The ship is named for a German Nobel Prize winner and pioneer in the field of nuclear fission.

18 JUNE

The White House announces that the CVA 67 will be named for the late President John F. Kennedy. This will be the second carrier named for a deceased president, the first being the *Franklin D. Roosevelt* (CVB/CVA 42).

19 JUNE

The Italian guided missile destroyer *Impavido* arrives at Norfolk, Va., to begin training with the use of her surface-to-air Tartar missile.

The first foreign nuclear-propelled ship to visit the United States, the British attack submarine *Dreadnought,* arrives at Norfolk, Va., after a submerged transit from Gibraltar. This is also the first time that the *Dreadnought* has entered a port other than in Britain or a British possession.

20 JUNE

The US Coast Guard cutter *Reliance* (WPC 615) is commissioned, the first major ship to be built for the Coast Guard since World War II. (Later redesignated WMEC 615.)

26 JUNE

An unprecedented mid-winter penetration of the South Pole continent is made when a US Navy LC-130 Hercules aircraft lands at McMurdo Station, Antarctica, to evacuate a sailor with a broken back. The ski-equipped aircraft, piloted by Lt. Robert V. Mayer, USN, lands in the mid-winter darkness on an ice runway marked on either side with flaming oil drums. After a stay of two hours, the aircraft returns to Christchurch, New Zealand, with the injured sailor. Two LC-130s from Air Development Squadron (VX) 6, departed Quonset Point, R.I., on 23 June for the emergency flight, the second aircraft serving as backup. The New Zealand frigate *Otago* took station at 60° south latitude to provide weather data and other support on the final leg of the flight.

1 JULY

The Canadian armed forces begin to integrate into a single service, the first step being to combine headquarters organizations, cutting back by an estimated 30 percent the military and civilian staff billets.

9 JULY

The US Navy announces that the multinational manned demonstration ship *Biddle* will be renamed *Claude V. Ricketts* to honor the Vice Chief of Naval Operations who died of a heart attack three days earlier.

10 JULY

The US Senate Committee on Commerce reports that the Soviet Union has advanced, in just five years,

from twelfth to seventh place among the maritime nations of the world in shipping tonnage.

22 JULY

The US carrier *Coral Sea* (CVA 43), while conducting carrier qualifications off the coast of California, records 536 arrested landings between 0800 on 21 July and 0200 the following morning, averaging almost one landing every two minutes for 18 hours. During much of the period, the *Coral Sea* is also launching aircraft.

25 JULY

Commander in Chief of the Soviet Navy Adm. Sergei G. Gorshkov declares that Soviet nuclear-propelled submarines have operated in "distant areas of the ocean, beneath Arctic ice and in equatorial waters."

31 JULY

US Navy Task Force 1, composed of the nuclear-propelled ships *Enterprise, Long Beach,* and *Bainbridge,* departs Gibraltar for an around-the-world, unreplenished cruise dubbed Operation Sea Orbit. Rear Adm. John T. Hayward, USN, is TF1 commander.

The British government announces the withdrawal to home waters of the Royal Navy's Mediterranean-based submarine squadron. The withdrawal is to be offset partially by periodic visits to the Mediterranean by submarines from the Home Fleet.

1 AUG

The US Marine Corps announce that their "senior" and "junior" schools located at Marine Corps Schools, Quantico, Va., are being redesignated as the Marine Corps Command and Staff College, and Marine Corps Amphibious Warfare School, respectively. The change reflects more accurately the level of training and the functions of the two schools.

2 AUG

Three North Vietnamese torpedo craft make a high-speed attack on the US destroyer *Maddox* (DD 731) in international waters of the Gulf of Tonkin, about 30 n.miles (55.6 km) off the coast of North Vietnam. The destroyer and four F-8E Crusader fighter aircraft from the carrier *Ticonderoga* (CVA 14) return fire until 1529, driving the craft away. North Vietnam acknowledges the attacks, but accuses the *Maddox* of being in its territorial waters. The *Maddox* is engaged in Operation DeSoto, the patrolling of destroyers for intelligence collection in the northern Tonkin Gulf.

5 AUG

For the second time in three days, North Vietnamese high-speed torpedo craft attack the *Maddox* at 2130. The *Maddox*, now in company with the *Turner Joy* (DD 951), which is also attacked, commence a counterattack that lasts until after midnight. It is believed that they sink at least two enemy craft and damage two others. Aircraft sent from the US carrier *Ticonderoga* to assist in the action are hampered by darkness and bad weather.

Aircraft launched from the US carriers *Constellation* (CVA 64) and *Ticonderoga*, operating in the South China Sea, bomb North Vietnamese coastal bases, patrol boats, and oil depots, in retaliation for the torpedo attacks on the US destroyers. Secretary of Defense McNamara reports that 64 sorties are flown that destroy or damage 25 North Vietnamese patrol boats and 90 percent of the petroleum stored in the target areas at Phucloi, Loc Chao, Hon Gay, Vihn, and Quang Khe. The *Constellation* loses two of her aircraft, an A-1H skyraider piloted by Lt. (jg) Richard A. Sather, USN, who is lost with the aircraft, and an A-4E Skyhawk, piloted by Lt. (jg) Everett Alvarez, USN, who is reported to have been captured. Another Skyraider from the *Constellation* is damaged as is an F-8E Crusader from the *Ticonderoga*. The air strikes, which begin at approximately 1200 local time, last for four hours.

7 AUG

Congress partially relinquishes its war-making powers to President Johnson by authorizing him to "take all necessary measures to repel any armed attack against forces of the United States . . . [and] to assist any member or protocol state" of the Southeast Asia Treaty Organization. The so-called Tonkin Gulf Resolution passes in the House of Representatives by a vote of 416 to 0 and in the Senate by 88 to 2.

8 AUG

The Soviet press claims that US aircraft have flown at dangerously low altitudes over Soviet ships more than 1,000 times and that US ships have executed dangerous maneuvers in the vicinity of Soviet ships 20 times.

12 AUG

The Sun Oil Company in its 22nd annual Analysis of the World Tankership Fleet reports that for the past decade the nation with the fastest growing carrier capability in relation to the size of its merchant fleet is the Soviet Union. Its average annual rate of increase since 1953 has been 29 percent. The Soviet tanker fleet, with 2,134,700 tons, stands eighth in the world. The United States, with 8,912,600, is in fourth place.

17 AUG

Secretary of Defense McNamara announces that the United States has a four-to-one superiority over the Soviet Union in heavy bombers and ICBMs, and has 256 missiles capable of being launched from submarines, while the Soviet Union has 142.

1 SEP

Navy Lt. Klusmann, a prisoner of the Laotian communists, escapes with several Laotians. He had been held captive since his RF-8 Crusader aircraft, based on the carrier *Kitty Hawk,* was shot down while on a reconnaissance mission over Laos on 6 June 1964.

5 SEP

President Johnson discloses that significant progress has been made in the development of a new propulsion reactor that will be "a significant step in the creation of a nuclear-powered Navy." This is the Westinghouse A4W reactor, being developed for use in the next generation of US aircraft carriers.

6 SEP

The Military Sealift Command's roll-on/roll-off ship *Comet* (T-LSV 7) loads 297 vehicles at Norfolk, Va., in 3 hours, 3 minutes and, after transiting the Atlantic, unloads them at Bremerhaven, Germany, under blackout conditions, in 1 hour, 21 minutes.

8 SEP

The Polaris missile assembly facility for the Pacific Fleet is commissioned at the US Naval Ammunition Depot, Bangor, Wash. The 430-acre (1.7-km) site, known as Polaris Missile Facility, Pacific, serves as the link between industrial producers of the missile and the fleet.

16 SEP

The US Navy announces that the largest anti-submarine warfare exercise since World War II is under way in cooperation with Canada. It involves 100 ships and more than 300 aircraft of the two navies.

The French government reports that a nuclear power plant of the type designed for planned nuclear submarines has been operating for three weeks.

18 SEP

The US destroyers *Morton* (DD 948) and *Parsons* (DD 949) fire on four radar contacts evaluated as fast torpedo craft making a nighttime attack on them in the

Gulf of Tonkin. The destroyers suffer no damage, and damage—if any—to the hostile craft is unknown.

21 SEP
Operation Teamwork begins, the largest exercise in NATO history. Involving eight nations of NATO, Teamwork is a multi-purpose exercise of NATO's Striking Fleet, Atlantic. Twenty-seven US warships and two US merchant ships are to join units of other NATO navies in exercises that include the convoying of merchant ships and a series of coastal mining tasks. Soviet surface ships, aircraft, and submarines are expected to conduct a close and intensive surveillance of Operation Teamwork.

26 SEP
Two French shipbuilding firms are announced as winners of a $6.4-million contract to build two freighters for Communist China. This is the first announcement of a nation signing a shipbuilding contract with China.

28 SEP
US ballistic missile submarine *Daniel Webster* (SSBN 626) departs Charleston, S.C., for a two-month Atlantic patrol on the first deployment of the Polaris A-3 missile.

1 OCT
The US Navy announces that the main wreckage of the nuclear attack submarine *Thresher* (SSN 593), lost with all hands on 10 April 1963, has been located. Photographs are released of the wreckage of the submarine's diving planes and sail structure with hull numbers plainly visible, taken by the bathyscaph *Trieste II.*

3 OCT
The US nuclear-propelled aircraft carrier *Enterprise* accompanied by the nuclear cruiser *Long Beach* arrive at Norfolk, Va., and the nuclear frigate *Bainbridge* arrives in Charleston, S.C., completing the 64-day, around-the-world Operation Sea Orbit. Ports visited include Karachi, Pakistan; Fremantle, Melborne, and Sidney, Australia; Wellington, New Zealand; and Rio de Janerio, Brazil. The ships took on no fuel, food, or supplies during the cruise.

8 OCT
The first large Soviet liner to enter service since World War II, the 19,000-gross-ton *Ivan Franko,* undergoes extensive sea trials in the Baltic Sea. The ship was built in East Germany.

9 OCT
A Soviet floating drydock, capable of lifting ships up to 2,500 tons, arrives in Havana, Cuba, towed by the Soviet motorship *Berdjansk.*

14 OCT
First flight of the Sikorsky CH-53A Sea Stallion heavy-lift helicopter. Developed for the US Marine Corps, the aircraft will also be flown in large numbers by the USAF and foreign services.

15 OCT
Nikita S. Khrushchev is forced to relinquish his posts of Prime Minister of the Soviet Union and General Secretary of the Communist Party. He is replaced by Alexei Kosygin as Prime Minister and Leonid Brezhnev as General Secretary.

China detonates its first atomic bomb. It becomes the fifth nation to do so, after the United States, Soviet Union, Britain, and France.

26 OCT
A US-Spanish amphibious assault exercise named Steel Pike begins in southern Spain. Involving 80 ships and 60,000 men from the US Navy and Marine Corps and Spanish armed forces, Steel Pike is the largest amphibious exercise held to date. Ten US merchant ships are used to transport Marines from the United States to Spain. Landings will take place at Huelva, 50 miles (80 km) northwest of the US naval base at Rota, Spain.

27 OCT
US attack submarine *Seadragon* (SSN 584) arrives in Hong Kong, the first nuclear-propelled ship to visit a Far Eastern port.

28 OCT
In a letter to the Atomic Energy Commission and the Maritime Administration, American Export Isbrandtsen Lines offers to underwrite future nuclear-propelled merchant ships. This is the first time that a private firm has offered to commit its own funds to the development of a nuclear fleet. The firm has been operating the world's only commercial nuclear vessel, the NS *Savannah.*

31 OCT
Japan formally notifies the United States that US nuclear-propelled ships will be permitted to visit Japanese ports. Ships carrying nuclear weapons are still officially prohibited.

1 NOV

Viet Cong forces attack the Bien Hoa air base in South Vietnam with mortars, killing four and wounding 72 American servicemen; 28 US aircraft are destroyed or damaged.

6 NOV

Canada announces plans to arm three squadrons of interceptor aircraft with the Falcon air-to-air missile fitted with a nuclear warhead. Use of the warheads will be controlled by US authorities.

7 NOV

The US guided missile frigate *Belknap* (DLG 26) is commissioned. She is the first of a new class of "single-end" missile ships with a twin Mk 10 Terrier/ASROC missile launcher forward and a 5-inch (127-mm) gun mount aft; a helicopter facility is fitted. Her first CO is Capt. John T. Law, USN.

12 NOV

France announces details of its five-year plan to build a nuclear striking force, including Polaris-type submarines. One such submarine is to be operational by 1970 with two more to be under construction by that date.

The US attack submarine *Seadragon* arrives in Sasebo for the first visit of a nuclear-propelled ship to Japan. Some 2,000 of a threatened 15,000 demonstrators are on hand as the ship arrives in Japanese waters.

18 NOV

First flight of the Grumman YC-2A Carrier On-board Delivery (COD) aircraft, later named Greyhound.

Assistant Secretary of the Navy for Research and Development Robert W. Morse announces that the Navy will increase its development expenditures for anti-submarine warfare, and assign the program a priority second only to that given the fleet ballistic missile submarine program.

6 DEC

The last of three salt water conversion plants become fully operational at Guantanamo Bay, Cuba, making the US naval base completely independent of outside water sources.

18 DEC

President Johnson reveals plans to move ahead, in cooperation with Panama and any other interested Central American governments, in planning for a new sea-level canal. Routes to be considered include the present canal location, one farther east in Panama, one in western Colombia, and another along the border between Nicaragua and Costa Rica. The President also discloses that the US government intends to negotiate a new treaty with Panama for the existing canal.

21 DEC

First flight of the General Dynamics F-111, developed under the designation TFX (for tri-service fighter). The Navy variant was to have been the carrier-based F-111B.

President Johnson orders an end to efforts by the United States to have NATO nations participate in a Multi-Lateral Force (MLF), the mixed-manning of surface ships armed with Polaris missiles.

22 DEC

The Honorable Carl Vinson, 81, returns permanently to Georgia after serving 50 years as a member of the US House of Representatives. He was chairman of the House Naval Affairs Committee from 1933 to 1949, after which he served continuously as chairman of the new Armed Services Committee, except for two years (1954 to 1956) until his 1964 retirement. Known as father of the Two-Ocean Navy bill on the eve of World War II, the aircraft carrier CVN 70 will be named for Vinson.

24 DEC

Two Americans are killed and 63 wounded when a bomb explodes in a car beside the Brink Bachelor Officers Quarters in Saigon, and destroys part of the building.

26 DEC

The first ballistic missile submarine patrol in the Pacific begins when the *Daniel Boone* (SSBN 629) departs Guam armed with Polaris A-3 missiles.

27 DEC

Dependents of US Navy and Marine personnel serving at Guantanamo Bay, Cuba, are permitted to return to the base. Since Feb 1964 military personnel ordered to Guantanamo had not been permitted to be accompanied by dependents, but families already there were permitted to remain until their tour of duty ended.

31 DEC

At year's end there are 23,000 US military personnel in South Vietnam.

1965

9 JAN

The US Joint Congressional Committee on Atomic Energy makes public its investigation of the loss of the US nuclear-propelled submarine *Thresher* (SSN 593). Much of the blame is pinned on the US Navy for allowing the submarine to go to sea in spite of certain indications that her design and workmanship were faulty.

11 JAN

The US Navy states that all 20 of the recommendations that resulted from the congressional study on the loss of the submarine *Thresher* have been carried out, are being carried out, or are scheduled to be carried out.

14 JAN

The Turkish government refuses permission for the US nuclear-propelled merchant ship *Savannah* to visit her ports.

Brazilian President Humberto Branco moves to end a nine-year-old Navy–Air Force dispute by placing all of Brazil's fixed-wing military aircraft, including those capable of being based on Brazil's aircraft carrier, under control of the Air Force. All helicopters, including those previously operated by the Air Force, are to be assigned to the Navy. Brazil's Minister of the Navy promptly resigns in protest.

15 JAN

Vice Adm. H. G. Rickover, USN, receives the Fermi Award for his work on the development of marine reactors. He is the first non-scientist to receive the award, America's highest in atomic science.

18 JAN

In his annual message on defense, President Johnson announces plans to develop the advanced Polaris B-3 missile, which will be deployed as the Poseidon C-3.

23 JAN

The carrier *America* (CVA 66) is commissioned at the Norfolk naval base. She is the Navy's eighth "supercarrier." Her first CO is Capt. Lawrence Heyworth, USN.

6 FEB

The first of three planned large-scale, conventional, explosive charges—part of Project Sailor Hat—is det-

onated off Kahoolawe, Hawaii, to test the resistance of naval ships and weapon systems to high-energy explosions. The main test ships are the specially configured *ex-Atlanta* (IX 304, formerly CL 104), the destroyer *Cochrane* (DDG 21) and the Canadian destroyer escort *Fraser*. The ships are manned during the tests.

7 FEB

Viet Cong guerrillas attack the US barracks area at Pleiku, South Vietnam, killing eight and wounding 126 US Army officers and enlisted men.

In retaliation for the Pleiku attack, 49 aircraft from the aircraft carriers *Hancock* (CVA 19), *Coral Sea* (CVA 43), and *Ranger* (CVA 61) fly strikes against North Vietnamese barracks and staging areas near Dong Hoi. One A-4C Skyhawk is lost in the raid code-named Flaming Dart I.

President Lyndon B. Johnson orders the immediate deployment of the Marine's 1st Light Anti-Aircraft Missile Battalion to Da Nang Airfield in South Vietnam. The unit is armed with Hawk surface-to-air missiles.

9 FEB

The withdrawal of American dependents from Saigon begins on orders of President Johnson.

10 FEB

A US Army enlisted barracks at the helicopter base at Qui Nhon in South Vietnam is bombed by the Viet Cong; 23 Americans are killed and 21 are injured.

11 FEB

In Operation Flaming Dart II, more than 100 aircraft from the carriers *Hancock, Coral Sea,* and *Ranger* strike North Vietnamese barracks and staging areas at Chan Hoa. An F-8D Crusader fails to return to the *Coral Sea* and its pilot, Lt. Comdr. R. H. Schumaker, USN, is subsequently reported by the North Vietnamese government to be a prisoner.

14 FEB

Turkey withdraws her personnel from multinationally manned destroyer *Claude V. Ricketts* (DDG 5).

16 FEB

South Vietnamese A-1H Skyraider attack aircraft sink a 120-foot (36.5-m) steel ship at Vung Ro Bay, about 50 miles (80 km) north of Cam Ranh Bay. The ship is subsequently found to be carrying Viet Cong weapons. Four days later, in a cove adjacent to where the craft was sunk, South Vietnamese troops uncover the largest cache of Viet Cong arms found since the war began. The ordnance is found in crates stacked over an area 100 × 300 yards (91 × 183 m).

17 FEB

The former Chief of the Soviet General Staff, Marshal Vasiliy D. Sokolovskii, claims "virtual parity" with the United States in nuclear-propelled submarines. The retired marshal also claims that, for the first time, the Soviet Union has fewer men in uniform than the United States. Soviet strength is given as 2,423,000 while 2,690,000 Americans are in military uniform.

18 FEB

In his annual statement to Congress, US Secretary of Defense Robert S. McNamara reveals plans to terminate the Atlantic and Pacific radar barrier patrols. At the time 32 radar picket ships, 42 Navy EC-121 early warning aircraft, and three EC-121 pilot training aircraft are scheduled for inactivation by the end of the year.

23 FEB

Operation Silver Lance, a major fleet exercise, begins off the coast of California. Involving more than 50 ships and 65,000 men, Silver Lance is one of the largest peacetime Navy–Marine Corps training exercises, being designed to test the mobility and strike capabilities of the Pacific Fleet. The exercise continues until 12 Mar.

25 FEB

The US discloses for the first time that American pilots have been in action against guerrilla targets in South Vietnam.

Lt. (jg) L. J. Cooper, USN, flying an A-4E Skyhawk, is accidently shot down and killed by a Terrier surface-to-air missile fired from the US frigate *Preble* (DLG 15) during exercise Silver Lance. Flying at about the same altitude and on the same heading as a target drone, Cooper inadvertently enters the missile's envelope and is shot down.

26 FEB

A US government White Paper accuses North Vietnam of aggression in supporting Viet Cong guerrillas and threatens air strikes against North Vietnam.

2 MAR

US Navy and Air Force aircraft begin the sustained bombing of military targets in North Vietnam. These raids—Operation Rolling Thunder—are an application of the theory of "graduated response" in which pressure will be incrementally increased until North Vietnam feels that it can accept no more damage and will then cease supporting the Viet Cong guerrillas. The operation will continue until 31 Oct 1968.

6 MAR

A US Navy SH-3A Sea King helicopter piloted by Comdr. J. R. Williford, USN, takes off from the carrier *Hornet* (CVS 12) berthed at NAS North Island, San Diego, Calif., and 15 hours, 51 minutes later lands on the carrier *Franklin D. Roosevelt* (CVA 42) at sea off Mayport, Fla. The flight surpasses the existing distance record for helicopters by more than 700 miles (1,126 km).

8 MAR

A force of 3,500 US Marines begin landing on the beaches near Da Nang in South Vietnam as President Johnson orders the 9th Marine Expeditionary Brigade to defend the air base at Da Nang, near the northern border of South Vietnam.

11 MAR

The operation later given the name Market Time begins when the Seventh Fleet destroyers *Black* (DD 666) and *Higbee* (DD 806) are ordered to inspect native junk traffic off the coast of South Vietnam to prevent the infiltration of men and arms to the south. More ships as well as patrol aircraft are soon assigned to this mission with Task Force 71 (Vietnam Patrol Force) being established to control their activities. By the end of Nov 1965, Market Time ships will have made 73,000 junk sightings, of which approximately 15,000 have been visually inspected at close quarters and another 6,000 boarded and searched.

12 MAR

The American International Longshoremen's Association of the AFL-CIO institutes a boycott against foreign ships that have traded with North Vietnam.

15 MAR

Two US Marines are killed and a third is wounded at Da Nang when a Marine sentry mistakes them for Viet Cong guerrillas and fires on them.

Aircraft launched from the carriers *Hancock* and

Ranger strike an ammunition depot at Phu Qui, 100 miles (161 km) south of the North Vietnamese capital of Hanoi. An A-1H Skyraider comes down at sea, its pilot killed.

18 MAR

Operation Jungle Drum III begins in Thailand as US Navy and Marine personnel join Thailand's Marine Corps in an exercise involving 3,000 troops in counter-guerrilla warfare training.

Man's first "walk" in space is accomplished by Soviet cosmonaut Alexei Leonov from the spacecraft *Voskhod 2.*

22 MAR

The US Navy announces plans to transfer nuclear surface ships from Atlantic bases to the Pacific. The carrier *Enterprise* (CVAN 65) and the frigate *Bainbridge* (DLGN 25) will arrive on the US West Coast in Oct 1965; the cruiser *Long Beach* (CGN 9) and the frigate *Truxtun* (DLGN 35) will be transferred in 1966.

23 MAR

Astronauts Lt. Col. Virgil I. Grissom, USAF, and Lt. Comdr. John W. Young, USN, ride the first manned two-place Gemini space capsule, named *Molly Brown,* into orbit. After three orbits, including the first orbital deviation made by a manned space vehicle controlled entirely from the capsule, the *Molly Brown* splashes down into the Atlantic Ocean six miles (9.6 km) from the waiting Coast Guard cutter *Diligence* (WPG 616). The astronauts are taken by helicopter to the primary recovery ship, the carrier *Intrepid* (CVS 11).

26 MAR

Forty aircraft from the carriers *Hancock* and *Coral Sea* strike four radar sites in North Vietnam as part of Operation Rolling Thunder. Their targets are Back Long Vi Island, about 80 miles (129 km) south of Communist China, and Vinh Son, Ha Tinh, and Cap Mui Ron, all on the North Vietnamese mainland. One A-4E Skyhawk and one F-8E Crusader are lost with their pilots being recovered by US forces.

29 MAR

Forty-two aircraft from the carrier *Coral Sea* strike the radar site on Long Vi Island off North Vietnam. Three planes are lost but two of the pilots are recovered. One, Comdr. W. M. Donnelly, USN, pilot of an F-8D Crusader, spends 45 hours in the water before rescuers find him.

A bomb thrown by a Viet Cong explodes outside the US Embassy in Saigon, killing 20 people, including two Americans, and wounding 65 Americans and nearly 100 Vietnamese.

31 MAR

One hundred ten aircraft from the carriers *Hancock* and *Coral Sea* strike radar sites and anti-aircraft positions in North Vietnam. One aircraft is lost in the action.

3 APR

A strike from the carriers *Hancock* and *Coral Sea* destroy the Dong Phuong highway bridge, 65 miles (105 km) south of Hanoi. This is the first strike against a North Vietnamese target whose importance is primarily economic. It is also the first time that North Vietnamese MiG-type fighters are seen aloft in the target area. The MiGs, however, offer no opposition to the strike aircraft. Two aircraft from the *Hancock* are lost in the strike, an A-1H Skyraider and an A-4C Skyhawk, both downed by ground fire.

8 APR

President Johnson, in a nationwide speech delivered in Baltimore, Md., reveals his willingness to begin diplomatic discussions, with no prior conditions and with any nation, to end the conflict in Vietnam. At the same time he asks Congress to approve a $1-billion investment in a Southeast Asian development program that can eventually be applied to North Vietnam. Within the week China, North Vietnam, and the Soviet Union reject both offers.

9 APR

Four F-4 Phantom fighters from US carriers in the South China Sea are attacked by several MiG-17 aircraft of undetermined nationality about 35 n.miles (65 km) southwest of Hainan Island (China). The F-4s are flying cover for Navy attack aircraft on a mission over North Vietnam. One MiG is believed to be shot down and one F-4 fails to return to the carriers. The last report from the missing F-4 pilot states that he is running low on fuel; both crewmen are lost.

10 APR

At the request of the South Vietnamese government, the US 2nd Battalion, 3rd Marines, begins landing north of Da Nang to assist in protecting the Da Nang air base from Viet Cong attack.

Marine F-4 Phantom aircraft from Marine Fighter Attack Squadron (VMFA) 531 arrive at Da Nang to provide air support for the Marines. Other US squadrons soon follow.

14 APR

The 3rd Battalion, 4th Marines begin landing at Da Nang, bringing the total Marines there to more than 8,000 troops.

15 APR

For the first time, the Navy and Marine Corps planes join Army, Air Force, and South Vietnamese Air Force aircraft to strike Viet Cong positions in South Vietnam. Attack aircraft from the carriers *Midway* (CVA 41) and *Coral Sea* fly in this, the largest strike against the Viet Cong to date. All carrier aircraft return safely to their ships.

16 APR

The US Navy reveals the first combat use of the Bullpup air-to-ground guided missile in a successful strike against two North Vietnamese bridges by planes from the carrier *Midway.*

19 APR

Six US Navy and two Marine aviators emerge from two sealed chambers at a Philadelphia laboratory after a 34-day test to determine the physical effect of prolonged stays in confined quarters and a low-pressure, pure oxygen atmosphere.

22 APR

US Marines are involved in their first extended clash with Viet Cong guerrillas near Da Nang, South Vietnam. The skirmish lasts several hours, but there are no serious Marine casualties. Viet Cong casualties are unknown.

27 APR

The Department of Defense announces that harbor and port facilities in South Vietnam are to be developed in cooperation with the local government to accommodate expanding military operations. The effort will include improvement of Da Nang Harbor, Cam Ranh Bay, and six smaller harbors. The channel to Saigon will also be deepened.

The South Vietnamese government establishes a three-mile (4.8-km) limit for its territorial waters. It had no limit previous to this announcement. In addition, the Saigon government claims jurisdiction over the passage of vessels within 12 miles (19.3 km) of its coast.

Two North Korean MiG-17 aircraft attack an Air Force RB-47 Stratojet reconnaissance aircraft flying parallel to the coast more than 50 miles (80 km) offshore over the Sea of Japan. Although damaged, the plane returns safely to Yokota Air Base in Japan; none of its six crewmen are injured.

In response to a threatened revolt in the Dominican Republic, the US helicopter carrier *Boxer* (LPH 4) sends Marines ashore while embarked Marine helicopters begin the evacuation of 1,000 Americans to US ships standing offshore. The 400-man *Boxer* force is from the 3rd Battalion, 6th Marines (forming the 4th Marine Expeditionary Brigade).

29 APR

Reinforcements raise the strength of US Marines in the Dominican Republic to 1,600.

Seventeen 82-foot (25-m) US Coast Guard cutters of the *Point* class and their crews are assigned duty in Vietnam as Coast Guard Squadron 1. Coming under the operational control of the Seventh Fleet, these Coast Guard units are the first to be assigned combat duty since the Korean War.

3 MAY

The first of 3,500 paratroopers from the US Army's 173rd Airborne Brigade arrive in Saigon. They are the first US Army combat troops to be committed to the Vietnam War, and their arrival brings the total number of US military personnel in Vietnam to 36,000. The brigade's two infantry battalions, one artillery battalion, and support troops are transported from Okinawa to Saigon in Navy landing ships.

The 9th Marine Expeditionary Brigade in Vietnam is reinforced and reorganized as the III Marine Amphibious Force under Lt. Gen. Lewis W. Walt, USMC. The Marines will be responsible for the northernmost of the four military districts into which the country is divided, with the district's five provinces compromising the I Corps Tactical Zone.

5 MAY

Mediators of the Organization of American States persuade the warring Dominican factions to sign a ceasefire agreement, despite which fighting continues in Santo Domingo.

7 MAY

The 1st and 2nd Battalions, 4th Marine Regiment, and several hundred Seabees of Mobile Construction Battalion 10, begin landing at Chu Lai, Vietnam, to secure an area for establishing an expeditionary airfield.

9 MAY

Exercise Sea Horse sponsored by the Southeast Asian Treaty Organization (SEATO) begins. The exercise seeks to move a large convoy across 2,000 n.miles (3,218 km) of open sea with protection against submarine, air, and surface attack. Thirty ships and 130 aircraft from Australia, New Zealand, the Philippines, Thailand, Great Britain, and the United States participate in the transit from Manila Bay to the Gulf of Thailand.

10 MAY
The first shipboard test of the Sea Sparrow surface-to-air missile is carried out from the landing ship *Tioga County* (LST 1158) on the Pacific missile test range. The Sea Sparrow—adopted from the air-to-air Sparrow III missile—is in response to the threat to US ships from Soviet missiles.

11 MAY
With the arrival of units of the US Army's 82nd Airborne Division, the number of US troops in the Dominican Republic rises to more than 11,000, including 6,000 Marines.

12 MAY
President Johnson suspends air attacks on North Vietnam and calls upon the Hanoi government to negotiate. There is no response.

Some 1,400 troops of the 3rd Battalion, 3rd Marine Regiment land at Chu Lai, South Vietnam, from amphibious ships.

16 MAY
A chain of accidental explosions at Bien Hoa Airfield in South Vietnam kills 27 Americans and injures another 103. More than 40 aircraft are destroyed or damaged in the mishap, which takes more American lives than have been lost previously in any single incident to date in Vietnam.

A carrier operating station—code-name Dixie—is established approximately 100 n.miles (185 km) southeast of Cam Ranh Bay, from which strikes can be launched in support of allied forces inside South Vietnam. It will be discontinued 15 months later because of the buildup of US air strength ashore.

20 MAY
Destroyers of the Seventh Fleet begin shore bombardment of suspected Viet Cong along the South Vietnamese coast. This is the first US Navy shore bombardment since the Korean War.

26 MAY
US Marines begin to withdraw from the Dominican Republic following arrangements of the Organization of American States to have an inter-American peacekeeping force replace US troops in the country. In the course of the crisis, the Marines have lost ten men killed and 26 wounded in scattered street fighting in Santa Domingo. Troops of the Army's 82nd Airborne Division remain part of the inter-American force.

27 MAY
In one of the largest air strikes in South Vietnam to date, 129 sorties flown from the carriers *Bon Homme Richard* (CVA 31) and *Oriskany* (CVA 34) attack Viet Cong targets.

1 JUNE
US aircraft begin operating from the Chu Lai Airfield, 52 miles (84 km) south of the major base at Da Nang, South Vietnam.

2 JUNE
Two Navy A-4 Skyhawk aircraft and their pilots are lost to anti-aircraft fire over North Vietnam. A third aircraft, a Navy A-1 Skyraider, is shot down while searching for the pilots of the Skyhawks. These losses combined with the loss of two Navy F-8 Crusaders on the previous day make a total of five aircraft downed in two days, the heaviest Navy losses suffered in the air war since the strikes over North Vietnam began.

The US guided missile cruiser *Canberra* (CAG 2) becomes the first US warship to fire 8-inch (203-mm) guns in combat since the end of the Korean War. The *Canberra* fires five rounds at a range of seven n.miles (13 km) to assist a US Marine patrol attacking heavily defended Viet Cong positions.

4 JUNE
Gemini 4 astronauts Maj. Edward H. White, USAF, and Maj. James A. McDivitt, USAF, perform the first American space walk. Launched on 3 June, they also fly a record-breaking 62-orbit flight that lasts 97 hours, 56 minutes. The Gemini capsule comes down in the Atlantic, 48 n.miles (89 km) short of its planned target area on 7 June. The astronauts are picked up by helicopter and taken to the carrier *Wasp* (CVS 18).

7 JUNE
Secretary of the Navy Paul H. Nitze reports that US ships are involved in "stopping, boarding, and searching" missions along the coast of South Vietnam in efforts to halt the infiltration of arms for the Viet Cong.

8 JUNE
Pole Star, a NATO convoy and anti-submarine warfare exercise, begins in the western Atlantic. Pole Star

involves ships of the US, Canadian, British, and Dutch navies and includes six submarines, 15 surface ships, and three aircraft squadrons. Four of the ships—a destroyer type from each of the participating nations—have been operating together in Matchmaker, another NATO exercise, since February. The four ships are sailing together to test the sharing of their combined facilities and resources over a period of several months.

9 JUNE

The US Army's 35th Engineer Group lands at Cam Ranh Bay, South Vietnam, to begin construction of a major deep-water port.

16 JUNE

Secretary of Defense McNamara announces the immediate addition of 20,000 combat troops in Vietnam. This will bring the total US combat strength there to almost 75,000.

The Department of Defense authorizes the creation of the 101st Airmobile Division within the Army's force structure of 16 active divisions. The new, highly mobile division will consist of 15,787 men with 428 helicopters and six fixed-wing aircraft. Initially most of the troops will be paratroopers, but those "jump qualified" will later be reduced to the division's reconnaissance unit.

17 JUNE

Two US Navy F-4B Phantom aircraft from Fighter Squadron (VF) 21 on the carrier *Midway* shoot down two North Vietnamese MiG-17 aircraft with Sidewinder air-to-air missiles some 50 n.miles (92.7 km) south of Hanoi. These are the first confirmed kills of enemy aircraft since strikes into North Vietnam began. No US aircraft are lost in the action.

18 JUNE

The first USAF B-52 Stratofortress bombing mission over South Vietnam is carried out by 27 B-52F Stratofortress bombers based on Guam. They attack a Viet Cong jungle redoubt with 750-pound (340-kg) and 1,000-pound (454-kg) bombs. Few if any Viet Cong are killed. Two B-52s are lost in a mid-air collision en route to the target. Additional B-52 strikes follow in this Operation Arc Light.

US aircraft strike north of Hanoi for the first time in the war when Air Force F-105 Thunderchief fighter-bombers attack barracks at Son La, 150 miles (241 km) northwest of Hanoi and only 80 miles (129 km) from the Chinese border.

21 JUNE

The US Secretary of Commerce announces the creation of an interdepartmental task force to develop a new US maritime policy. Representatives from the Departments of State, Defense, Agriculture, and Labor, the Budget Bureau, and the Council of Economic Advisors will participate.

23 JUNE

In possibly a naval first, the US seaplane tender *Currituck* (AV 7), armed with 5-inch (127-mm) guns, carries out a shore bombardment of Viet Cong positions in the Mekong Delta area of South Vietnam.

28 JUNE

US combat troops are committed to battle in South Vietnam for the first time as a unit when troops of the 173rd Airborne Brigade are helicopter-lifted into battle against the Viet Cong.

30 JUNE

Seven years after its establishment, the Pacific extension of the US air defense barrier system is abolished. Included are the Navy commands Barrier Force Pacific, and Airborne Early Warning Barrier Squadron Pacific.

1 JULY

US Navy Helicopter Utility Squadrons (HU) are redesignated Helicopter Combat Support Squadrons (HC) and Utility Squadrons (VU) are redesignated Fleet Composite Squadrons (VC).

Anti-Submarine Warfare Fighter Squadron (VFS) 1 is established at Alameda, Calif., to provide air defense detachments to ASW aircraft carriers operating in forward areas. VFS-1 flies the A-4 Skyhawk light attack aircraft.

4 JULY

The carrier *Independence* (CVA 62) launches the first A-6A Intruder aircraft to fly a combat mission. The strike, made into North Vietnam, is flown by aircraft of Attack Squadron (VA) 75.

7 JULY

An additional 8,000 US Marines begin landing in South Vietnam, bringing the total Marine force ashore to 25,000, about 13 percent of total Marine Corps strength.

13 JULY

US Maritime Administrator Nickolas Johnson notifies the nation's leading subsidized steamship companies that 54 merchant ships are needed immediately to transport supplies to Vietnam. He announces that 28 will come from private industry and the remainder from the National Defense Reserve Fleet.

16 JULY

A team of Royal Navy divers make a successful experimental escape from a submerged submarine at a depth of 500 feet (152 m). This is a new escape record.

First flight of the Rockwell International OV-10 Bronco, a twin-turboprop aircraft developed specifically for Counter-Insurgency (COIN) operations.

20 JULY

The *Alvin*, a US Navy research submersible, is successfully tested at a depth of 6,000 feet (1,829 m) for 20 minutes off Andros Island in the Bahamas. The craft is operated for the Navy by the Woods Hole Oceanographic Institution.

21 JULY

The US Department of Defense and Department of Treasury announce the transfer of all Navy icebreakers to the Coast Guard. The *Burton Island* (AGB 1), *Edisto* (AGB 2), *Atka* (AGB 3), *Glacier* (AGB 4), and *Staten Island* (AGB 5), are to join the four icebreakers already operated by the US Coast Guard.

28 JULY

The US Navy announces that beginning in Oct 1965 it will accept draftees for the first time in more than nine years.

President Johnson announces that the draft will be increased from 17,000 to 35,000 men per month and that the strength of ground forces in Vietnam will be increased from about 70,000 to 125,000. He also announces the decision not to call reserve personnel to active duty for the Vietnam conflict.

In a television address to the nation, President Johnson reveals that he has ordered the 1st Cavalry Division (Airmobile) and other smaller combat and support units to South Vietnam. The arrival of these forces will increase the American commitment to approximately 125,000 men.

30 JULY

Six Atlantic-based MSTS troop transports are transferred to the Pacific, bringing the Navy's entire 16-ship transport fleet under the Pacific command.

1 AUG

The remaining nine of 17 82-foot Coast Guard *Point*-class cutters arrive in Vietnam. The 17 cutters form

Coast Guard Squadron 1, and are divided between Coast Guard Division 11 operating out of An Thoi, Phu Quoc Island, off the southern tip of Vietnam, and Coast Guard Division 12, operating out of Da Nang in northern South Vietnam.

3 AUG

The Military Advisory Command Vietnam (MACV) announces that units from the US Seventh Fleet expended 12,088 rounds of ammunition in 340 gunfire support missions between 3 July and 2 August 1965.

5 AUG

The Esso facility at Da Nang, Republic of Vietnam, is damaged by a Viet Cong attack with two oil storage tanks destroyed and two damaged. The destroyer *Stoddard* (DD 566) fires on the Viet Cong positions.

9 AUG

The Commander Seventh Fleet is assigned responsibility for the operation of port facilities at Da Nang, Vietnam. Previously operated by the Headquarters Support Activity, Saigon, the port is placed under the operational control of Task Force 76.

China accuses the US Navy of attacking Chinese fishing craft twice within 22 days and claims six fishermen missing.

11 AUG

The first US Navy plane definitely known to be downed by a surface-to-air missile, an A-4 Skyhawk flying from the aircraft carrier *Midway*, is lost over North Vietnam.

13 AUG

Five US carrier aircraft are lost on armed reconnaissance missions over North Vietnam. Three of the aircraft are from the *Coral Sea* and two are from the *Midway*. All five aircraft are downed by ground fire.

14 AUG

Secretary of the Navy Nitze orders a four-month involuntary extension of active duty Navy and Marine Corps enlisted personnel, beginning 20 Aug for the Marine Corps and 15 Sep for the Navy.

18 AUG

Operation Starlight, the first large-scale amphibious assault in Vietnam, begins as US Marines land 14 miles (23 km) south of Chu Lai in an area that has been held by the Viet Cong for two years. The largest ground combat operation since the Korean War follows as elements of the 3rd, 4th, and 7th Marine Regiments land over the beach and father inland by helicopters. They are supported by naval gunfire from the cruiser *Galveston* (CLG 3) and two destroyers. Marine Corps aircraft fly more than 1,000 close air support missions and deliver over 1,000 tons (907,200 kg) of bombs. In the three-day battle about 50 Marines are killed and estimates of enemy casualties run as high as 1,000.

19 AUG

The Department of Defense announces plans to reactivate 20 Navy ships from the reserve fleet: four replenishment ships (AO/AOG), two attack cargo ships (AKA), and 14 tank landing ships (LST) as well as 13 utility landing craft (LCU).

The US Navy and Marine Corps request inactive reserve officers to volunteer for active duty due to the Vietnam War.

20 AUG

The nuclear-propelled merchant ship *Savannah* ends her "demonstration operations" and begins "experimental commercial operation" under charter to Fast Atomic Transport, Inc. During her first year of commercial operation the ship will make seven transits across the Atlantic to European and Mediterranean ports.

21 AUG

Astronauts Col. L. Gordon Cooper, USAF, and Comdr. Charles C. Conrad, USN, begin an eight-day space flight in *Gemini V*. The capsule will come down in the Atlantic, 90 n.miles (145 km) from the prime recovery ship, the carrier *Lake Champlain* (CVS 39). The astronauts arrive on board the *Lake Champlain* by Navy helicopter 45 minutes after splashing down.

24 AUG

US Marine Corps C-130 Hercules aircraft with 71 personnel on board crashes into the water off Hong Kong shortly after take-off, killing 58 on board. The flight is returning troops to Vietnam after a rest period when the crash occurs.

26 AUG

Navy Airborne Early Warning Squadron (VAQ) 11 flies the last North Atlantic barrier patrol with an EC-121J Warning Star aircraft. (The squadron is formally decommissioned on 7 Oct 1965.)

27 AUG

President Johnson signs an executive order ending draft exemptions for married men.

British and US officials reveal a slight increase in the level of radiation at the US Polaris submarine base at Holy Loch, Scotland. Although the level is below that considered a health hazard, it is announced that action is being taken to reduce the radioactivity, which is caused by discharge from the cooling agent coming from submarine reactors.

The destroyer *Newman K. Perry* (DD 883) and the aircraft carrier *Shangri-La* (CVA 38) collide in the Mediterranean Sea, killing one sailor on the destroyer and injuring another. The destroyer suffers bow damage and the *Shangri-La* has minor hull damage. Both ships are repaired at Naples and return to duty with the Sixth Fleet.

The crew of the Mexican freighter *El Mexicano* refuses to sail from San Diego, Calif., with a cargo for Vietnam when the Mexican government protests to the use of the ship on the Vietnam run. The following day the crew of the Greek freighter *Stamatios S. Embiricos* refuses to sail from San Diego with a cargo bound for Vietnam.

28 AUG

Ten US Navy aquanauts, including astronaut Comdr. M. Scott Carpenter, USN, enter the Sealab II capsule at a depth of 205 feet (62 m) on the seafloor off La Jolla, Calif. Three ten-man teams of aquanauts are to inhabit the capsule for 15-day periods. Carpenter is to be the only aquanaut to remain continuously in the capsule for 30 days. Lt. R. Sonnenburg (Medical Corps), USN, a doctor, is to spend two 15-day periods in the underwater laboratory, but the two bottom sessions will spend 15 days on the surface. The experiment in underwater living and working is intended to develop procedures for manned construction and salvage operations on the ocean floor.

31 AUG

Vice Adm. Charles Martell, USN, Director of Anti-Submarine Warfare Programs in the Office of the Chief of Naval Operations, announces that Soviet submarines are moving from their traditionally defensive role, and are now operating freely in the Mediterranean, Norwegian, and Philippine Seas. He also states that recent Soviet operations in the Norwegian Sea made use of more submarines than are available in the entire US Atlantic Fleet. To date, according to Martell, no Soviet submarines have been detected in the South China Sea.

President Johnson signs into law a bill authorizing hazardous-duty pay for carrier flight deck crews. Navy statements indicate that flight deck duty is one of the most dangerous in the Navy; it ranks first in injuries and second only to flying in the number of deaths.

The President also approves a policy on the promotion and decoration of military astronauts; upon the competition of his first space flight, a one-grade promotion up to and including colonel in the Air Force and Marine Corps and captain in the Navy, and Gemini astronauts completing a successful space flight would receive the NASA Medal for Exceptional Service (or cluster for subsequent awards).

I SEP

The US Marine Corps announces the compression of recruit training from 12 to eight weeks because of the requirement for combat troops. The reduction is to be accomplished by intensifying training and increasing the number of training hours in each week.

The Department of Defense states that US aircraft have flown 1,224 sorties over North Vietnam during the month of August, the highest monthly total to date.

2 SEP

For the first time, three US aircraft carriers launch strikes on the same day against Viet Cong troops in South Vietnam. Aircraft from the *Oriskany, Coral Sea,* and *Independence* fly 256 missions against the Viet Cong.

5 SEP

After a lengthy study, President Johnson's Committee on the Economic Impact of Defense Disarmament reports that neither reduction in defense expenditures nor a complete disarmament will present major problems for the US economy.

6 SEP

The Indian government announces that Soviet government has agreed to provide India with an undisclosed number of submarines. India has not previously operated submarines. (*See* 6 July 1968.)

7 SEP

A study released by the Committee of American Steamship Lines indicates that aircraft carry less than four percent of the cargo moved in overseas trade; the remainder goes by ship.

I I SEP

The lead elements of the Army's 1st Cavalry Division (Airmobile) go ashore at Qui Nhon, South Vietnam, from the helicopter carrier *Boxer,* which had trans-

ported the division's helicopters and light aircraft from Mayport, Fla.

I 5 SEP

The communications relay ship *Annapolis* (AGMR 1), the first such ship to enter US service, arrives in the South China Sea. The *Annapolis* serves as a mobile communications and relay station. She was converted from the escort carrier *Gilbert Islands* (CVE 107/ AKV 39).

Chief of Naval Operations Adm. David L. McDonald, USN, announces that there is no evidence that North Vietnamese supplies are still being shipped to the Viet Cong by sea. But the flow of arms into the south by sea continues.

I 7 SEP

The Department of Defense requests the Selective Service System to provide 36,450 men in November, including 4,000 for the Navy and 4,050 for the Marine Corps. The Navy's requirement is subsequently canceled. The Marines do not accept draftees in December but begin doing so in Jan 1966.

26 SEP

The destroyer *Rowan* (DD 782) is commended by the government of the Republic of Vietnam, by the Commander US Military Advisory Command, Vietnam, and by the Commander Seventh Fleet, for having fired 26 support missions in five days in support of Vietnamese operations.

27 SEP

First flight of the Vought A-7 Corsair carrier-based light attack aircraft. It will be flown mainly by the US Navy and US Air Force Reserve; several foreign air forces will also fly the plane, but not the US Marine Corps.

I OCT

The US First Fleet begins Operation Ragweed, a seven-day training exercise in the Pacific. It involves US Navy ships in a variety of operations.

6 OCT

The US Department of Defense authorizes a Vietnamese Service Medal and makes the award retroactive to 3 July 1965.

9 OCT

The first elements of a 15,000-man combat division from South Korea arrive at Cam Ranh Bay, South

Vietnam, on board the transport *Gen. LeRoy Eltinge* (T-AP 154). The Korean National Assembly earlier voted 101 to 1 to send the troops to support South Vietnam.

13 OCT

The nuclear-propelled submarines *Sargo* (SSN 583) and *Barb* (SSN 596) collide while submerged on a training exercise 15 n.miles (24 km) west of Oahu, Hawaii. No injuries are reported and both submarines return to port under their own power.

14 OCT

The Polaris A-1 missile is retired as the ballistic missile submarine *Abraham Lincoln* (SSBN 602) arrives in the United States to begin overhaul and modification to launch the Polaris A-3 missile.

Two US Navy LCM landing craft collide in the river at Da Nang, South Vietnam, killing one enlisted man and injuring 11.

15 OCT

US Naval Support Activity Da Nang is established in South Vietnam, under the Commander Service Force, Pacific Fleet. With about 3,500 naval personnel, the organization is designed to provide logistic support for US and allied units in Vietnam.

16 OCT

The US Navy hospital ship *Repose* (AH 16) is recommissioned at San Francisco Bay Naval Shipyard. The 700-bed hospital ship is the first of two to be returned to active duty, and will be the first to deploy to Southeast Asia.

17 OCT

A-6 Intruder and A-4 Skyhawk attack aircraft, flying from the carrier *Independence,* destroy a surface-to-air missile site 50 miles (80 km) northeast of Hanoi. Military officials report that the strike, carried out "with almost flawless precision," is the first one known to be successful against an operational mobile missile site. No enemy missiles are launched and no aircraft are lost in the strike.

18 OCT

The Department of Defense releases data showing that voluntary enlistments in the Marine Corps have almost doubled over 1964.

23 OCT

The US Coast Guard icebreaker *Northwind* (WAGB 282) returns to New York at the end of a late summer and early fall cruise into the Arctic, during which she makes the first major US oceanographic survey of the Barents and Kara Seas.

26 OCT

A powder case explodes in a 5-inch (127-mm) gun mount on the destroyer *Turner Joy* (DD 951) during a gunfire support mission off Vietnam. Three of the gun crew are killed, and three other sailors are injured.

Thirty-six Soviet fishing and whaling ships are reported in the area of the Aleutians where the United States plans to detonate an underground nuclear test device on 29 Oct.

27 OCT

Chief of Naval Operations Adm. McDonald states that 98 percent of the military cargo moving to Vietnam is going by sea, and that in the preceding six months, two out of every three fighting men of major combat units were moved to Vietnam by MSTS.

More than 40 US aircraft are destroyed or damaged in two Viet Cong raids on Marine airfields at Da Nang and Chu Lai, Vietnam. The Marines suffer light casualties, but report killing 39 Viet Cong.

28 OCT

The US Navy takes delivery of its first Mark 46 lightweight anti-submarine torpedo. Built by Honeywell Corp., the Mk 46 is used from Mk 32 tubes and ASROC launchers on surface ships, is dropped by ASW aircraft, and is launched by the Encapsulated Torpedo (CAPTOR) mine.

31 OCT

The first Swift boats (designated PCF) for coastal and riverine operations arrive in South Vietnam. Within hours these craft exchange fire with Viet Cong forces.

7 NOV

The Soviet Union displays what is claimed to be an orbital nuclear weapon that can "deliver its first blow on the first or any other loop around the earth." This is the SS-9 Mod 3 Scarp ICBM developed for the Fractional Orbital Bombardment System (FOBS) mode. The FOBS mode could reduce the time of flight to US targets or, by overflying the south polar area, outflank US ground-based early warning radars.

9 NOV

Secretary of Defense McNamara issues an order exempting 17-year-old servicemen from duty in Vietnam. The directive does not apply to 17-year-olds on board ships in the Seventh Fleet.

12 NOV

The US Army's 1st Cavalry Division (Airmobile) begins a six-day clash with three regiments of North Vietnamese regular troops in the Iadrang Valley, 200 miles (322 km) north of Saigon. A total of 1,285 North Vietnamese bodies are counted after one of the hardest contested battles of the conflict. Approximately 200 US troops are killed.

14 NOV

The Taiwan government claims that two of its warships sank four Chinese gunboats, damaged a fifth, and drove off three others in a two-hour battle in the Formosa Strait. The Nationalists lost a minesweeper in the exchange.

17 NOV

A broken cable between the Ballistic Missile Early Warning System (BMEWS) at Thule, Greenland, and North American Air Defense Command (NORAD) headquarters in Colorado Springs, Colo., is restored to use. The ends are recovered from Baffen Bay, 600 n.miles (1,112 km) north of the Arctic Circle by the Canadian cable-layer *John Cabot,* assisted by the Canadian icebreaker *d'Ilberville* and the US Coast Guard icebreaker *Westwind* (WAGB 281).

25 NOV

Deputy Assistant Secretary of Defense (Logistics) Robert Moot reports that the volume of military cargo delivered by sea to Southeast Asia has more than doubled since 1965 and is averaging 725,000 measurement tons monthly. According to Moot, 174 cargo ships are operating in support of the Vietnam War.

26 NOV

The nuclear-propelled carrier *Enterprise* and the nuclear-propelled frigate *Bainbridge* join other Seventh Fleets units operating in the South China Sea. This is the first deployment of nuclear-propelled warships to a combat zone.

30 NOV

The Department of Defense states that US ships on coastal surveillance patrol in Vietnam under Operation Market Time have sighted 73,000 Vietnamese junks in the past seven months. Of these, about 15,000 were inspected from close aboard and about 6,000 more have been boarded and searched. Market Time surveillance forces are composed of destroyers, escorts, minesweepers, Coast Guard cutters, and the new Swift boats.

1 DEC

The US destroyer *Claude V. Ricketts* arrives in Norfolk, Va., bringing to a close the one-year demonstration of a multinationally manned warship. The *Ricketts* project was intended to test the feasibility of NATO ships armed with ballistic missiles and manned by multinational crews; that effort will not be pursued.

2 DEC

The nuclear-propelled carrier *Enterprise* with Carrier Air Wing 9 embarked begins its first combat operation with strikes on Viet Cong positions near Bien Hoa, South Vietnam. The carrier launches 118 during the day; two aircraft are lost in these strikes.

4 DEC

The *Gemini 7* spacecraft is launched on a record-breaking, 14-day orbital mission with astronauts Comdr. James A. Lovell, Jr., USN, and Lt. Col. Frank Borman, USAF, on board. On 15 Dec the *Gemini 7* will rendezvous with *Gemini 6* (launched on that date with Capt. Walter M. Schirra, Jr., USN, and Maj. Thomas P. Stafford, USAF, on board) in the first meeting of two manned space vehicles in orbit. The two Gemini capsules keep station with each other for 3½ orbits. Both capsules are recovered by the carrier *Wasp* (CVS 18) in the western Atlantic near Puerto Rico—the *Gemini 6* on 16 Dec and *Gemini 7* on 18 Dec.

7 DEC

Fire breaks out in a machinery room on board the carrier *Kitty Hawk* (CVA 63) while operating in the South China Sea. Two sailors die and 28 are injured in the fire. As a result of the blaze, a nearby ammunition magazine is flooded as a precautionary measure.

8 DEC

An amphibious and anti-submarine warfare exercise involving 50 ships and 12,000 men of the US Atlantic Fleet begins with landings on Vieques Island off Puerto Rico.

12 DEC

While operating in the South China Sea, the carrier *Enterprise* launches a record 165 combat sorties in one day.

18 DEC

The US Coast Guard cutter *Hamilton* (WPG 715) is launched by Avondale Shipyards, New Orleans, La. The lead ship of a new class, the *Hamilton*, 378 foot (115 m) long with a standard displacement of 2,700 tons, is the largest Coast Guard cutter launched in 20 years. The 12 ships of this class are later classified as high-endurance cutters (WHEC).

The US Navy River Patrol Force is activated in South Vietnam. Its operations are given the name Game Warden.

22 DEC

The North Vietnamese power plant at Uong Bi is struck by 100 aircraft from the carriers *Enterprise, Kitty Hawk,* and *Ticonderoga* (CVA 14). Two planes are lost in this first raid on an industrial target in North Vietnam.

23 DEC

The Department of Defense announces the cancellation of Operation Polar Sweep, Alaska's annual military exercise, because of increased commitments in Southeast Asia.

24 DEC

US forces begin a 30-hour Christmas ceasefire in Vietnam.

1966

I JAN

The USAF Military Air Transport Service (MATS) is renamed the Military Airlift Command (MAC).

4 JAN

The Department of Defense announces that during the last ten months of 1965, Navy aircraft flew more than 61,000 sorties over North and South Vietnam. Air Force aircraft flew almost 50,000 sorties over Vietnam during the same time period.

5 JAN

A Department of Defense statement places the total number of American servicemen killed in combat in Vietnam during 1965 at 1,365 compared to 146 Americans the previous year.

II JAN

Six destroyers and escorts/frigates from the navies of Great Britain, Canada, the Netherlands, and the United States begin Exercise Matchmaker II, an extended exercise concerned primarily with anti-submarine warfare to evaluate the feasibility of long-duration multinational operations. The same four nations also participated in the Matchmaker exercise of 1965.

12 JAN

The West German cabinet agrees to charter and equip a ship to provide hospital services and place it at the disposal of the Red Cross for use off Vietnam. Only civilian patients are to be treated on board.

13 JAN

The US carrier *Bon Homme Richard* (CVA 31) and her embarked Carrier Air Wing 19 return to the United States from a deployment with the Seventh Fleet off Vietnam. They are awarded Navy Unit Commendations, the ship having launched 12,328 combat missions, more than any other carrier in the history of carrier aviation in a single deployment.

17 JAN

A USAF B-52G Stratofortress strategic bomber and a USAF KC-135 tanker collide near Palomares, Spain, at an altitude of 30,500 feet (9,296 m). Four B28 thermonuclear bombs tumble from the stricken bomber, three fall to earth and one into the Mediterranean Sea. Both planes crash with three of the seven crewmen of the B-52G and all four in the KC-135 being

killed. The Navy initiates a major search/recovery effort for the H-bomb that fell into the sea.

20 JAN

The United States begins a three-day ceasefire to honor the Vietnamese lunar new year, Tet.

21 JAN

Turkey's Anatolia news agency announces that two US missile-armed warships have sailed through the Turkish Straits for "training in the international waters" of the Black Sea. The Pentagon says only that destroyers of the Sixth Fleet have been in the international waters of the Black Sea, "from time to time." The Soviet Union charges that the US warships *Harry E. Yarnell* (DLG 17) and *Forrest Royal* (DD 872) have been engaged in "suspicious muscle-flexing and intelligence operations in the Black Sea."

The Soviet news agency Tass announces that for the first time a Soviet fishing flotilla has entered the Gulf of California on an experimental fishing expedition.

29 JAN

The US Selective Service System announces that for the first time since the Korean War the agency would again use national tests and class standings in determining student draft deferments.

30 JAN

US Marine Corps units in South Vietnam begin the largest amphibious operation since the landing at Inchon, Korea, in 1950. Approximately 10,000 Marines and 18 ships are directly involved in the operation. Only light contact is made with the Viet Cong forces.

31 JAN

After a 37-day lull in bombing, US aircraft resume strikes against targets in North Vietnam. During the lull, the United States makes unsuccessful efforts through many channels to establish negotiation contacts concerning the war in Vietnam.

I FEB

The US Navy's Deep Submergence Systems Project (DSSP) becomes a separate activity under the Chief of Naval Material. The project had previously been managed by the Navy's Special Projects Office (SPO), which is responsible for strategic missile systems.

Capt. William Nicholson, USN, is named director of DSSP, succeeding Dr. John Craven, who was additionally the chief scientist for SPO.

2 FEB

The nuclear-propelled submarine *George Washington* (SSBN 598) completes an 18-month overhaul. The pioneer Polaris submarine has also been modified to launch the Polaris A-3 missile. All of the first ten Polaris submarines are being upgraded to the A-3 capability.

3 FEB

Six US Navymen are killed in the Antarctic when their C-47 Skytrain aircraft crashes while landing on the Ross ice shelf. It is the worst accident in the 11-year history of the Navy's Operation Deepfreeze.

The Soviet unmanned space vehicle *Luna 9* makes the first "soft" landing on the moon and transmits photographs back to earth.

5 FEB

The US destroyers *Waddell* (DDG 24) and *Brinkley Bass* (DD 887) collide in the South China Sea; both sustain heavy damage. Three crewmen from the fleet oiler *Navasota* (AO 106) are killed while returning to their ship after assisting the destroyers when the helicopter in which they are flying crashes into the sea. Both destroyers return to port under their own power.

14 FEB

The first US Navy patrol boat to be lost in action in Vietnam is the Swift boat *PCF 4*, sunk by an underwater explosion in the Gulf of Thailand off South Vietnam. Four of the six crewmen are killed; the two others are wounded.

16 FEB

The US Navy hospital ship *Repose* (AH 16) arrives off Chu Lai, South Vietnam, to provide medical support for US forces.

The Military Sea Transportation Service (MSTS) announces that the recent charter of six ships has brought to 87 the number provided to MSTS since an appeal for more vessels to support Vietnam operations was made on 2 Nov 1965.

22 FEB

Nine additional 82-foot (24.9-m) US Coast Guard *Point*-class cutters arrive in South Vietnam, bringing the number on coastal surveillance operations to 26. The nine new cutters comprise Coast Guard Division

13 and are based at Vung Tau, near the seaward approach to Saigon.

The British government announces plans to discard all five Royal Navy aircraft carriers during the 1970s. Overseas commitments will be fulfilled with 50 American-built F-111A strike aircraft. Defence Minister Dennis Healy says that the move reflects the fact that Britain can no longer mount a major military operation on her own outside of Europe. Navy Minister Christopher Mayhew and First Sea Lord Adm. Sir David Luce resign in protest at the decision to discard the carriers. (In the event, the F-111s will not be procured by Britain.)

The first unmanned spacecraft of the Apollo series is launched into sub-orbital flight by a Saturn 1B rocket from Cape Kennedy, Fla. It is recovered in the southeast Atlantic, 200 n.miles (370.4 km) east of Ascension Island by a helicopter from the USS *Boxer* (LPH 4).

28 FEB

The US Department of Agriculture announces imposition of a ban on the shipment of most food and farm products on foreign-flag ships that have called at any North Vietnamese port since 24 Jan 1966. The action also applies to Food for Peace and World Food Program shipments.

1 MAR

The US Marine Corps reactivates the 5th Marine Division with the reestablishment of the 26th Marine Regiment and supporting elements at Camp Pendleton, Calif. The Division will be at full strength in about one year. Its activation is part of the increase of Marine manpower from 190,000 to 278,000. The 5th Marine Division, which participated in the capture of Iwo Jima and raised the flag on Mount Suribachi, was deactivated after World War II.

3 MAR

The Greek government bans all merchant ships under her flag from sailing to or from North Vietnamese ports.

5 MAR

Gen. Maxwell D. Taylor, USA (Ret.), former Chairman of the Joint Chiefs of Staff and former ambassador to South Vietnam, publicly calls for the mining of Haiphong Harbor, North Vietnam's major seaport.

8 MAR

Australian Prime Minister Harold E. Holt announces plans to increase his nation's military force in Vietnam from 1,500 to 4,500. This is a larger commitment than Australia made during the Korean War.

10 MAR

President Charles de Gaulle announces France's intention to withdraw from the integrated NATO military structure.

12 MAR

The guided missile escort ship *Brooke* (DEG 1) is commissioned, the US Navy's first escort/frigate-type ship armed with guided missiles, being fitted with a Mk 22 launcher for the Tartar surface-to-air missile. The ship retains a full anti-submarine capability, differing from the similar *Garcia* (DE 1040) class in having the Tartar launcher in place of a second 5-inch (127-mm) gun. The *Brooke*'s first CO is Comdr. Robert L. Walters, USN.

16 MAR

Marine CH-46 Sea Knight helicopters enter combat for the first time carrying cargo and troops in support of Marine operations near Da Nang, South Vietnam.

Following their launch from Cape Kennedy, astronauts Neil A. Armstrong and Maj. David R. Scott, USAF, perform the first manual docking maneuver in space during a rendezvous with an Agena booster rocket. However, shortly after the evolution their *Gemini 8* capsule tumbles out of control due to a malfunction. The flight is terminated prematurely after 6½ orbits and a flight of 10 hours, 42 minutes, and they come down without incident 500 n.miles (926.5 km) east of Okinawa. The astronauts and their spacecraft are recovered by the destroyer *Leonard F. Mason* (DD 852), which delivers them to Okinawa.

17 MAR

First flight of the Bell X-22A Vertical Take-Off and Landing (VTOL) aircraft. This unusual vehicle has four ducted turboshaft engines that tilt to transition from vertical to horizontal flight.

20 MAR

The National Assembly of South Korea approves plans to double that nation's troop commitment to the war in Vietnam by dispatching 20,000 additional combat troops.

26 MAR

Operation Jackstay begins in the Rung Sat Special Zone, 35 miles (56.3 km) south of Saigon, South Vietnam. This is the first full-scale US amphibious operation to be conducted in the Mekong River Delta. The amphibious forces offshore include the helicopter carrier *Princeton* (LPH 5) with air support being provided by the carrier *Hancock* (CVA 19), subsequently replaced by the *Kitty Hawk* (CVA 63). The assault force, landed by helicopters and landing craft, is supported by Navy and Coast Guard small craft, and Army UH-1 Huey helicopters and OV-1 Mohawk reconnaissance aircraft as well as Navy and Marine aircraft; Air Force B-52 bombers flying from Guam provide saturation bombing of suspected Viet Cong areas. The assault force consists of a landing team based of the 1st Battalion, 5th Marine Regiment, followed up by two battalions of South Vietnamese Marines. The operation, completed early the following month, has a body count of 53 dead Viet Cong. The cost to US forces is five killed and 31 wounded plus two presumed to have drowned. The operation is considered a success in securing the area and providing lessons for combat in an unusual environment.

29 MAR

The Department of Defense announces that the four Army combat divisions remaining in the United States have been reduced to training status and are no longer combat ready.

Ens. Gale Ann Gordon (Medical Corps), USN, becomes the first woman in the history of the US Naval Air Basic Training Command to make a solo flight. Gordon has been given flight training as part of her instruction in aviation experimental psychology.

31 MAR

The lead elements of the 1st Marine Division begin the move from Okinawa to Chu Lai, South Vietnam. This marks the first deployment of two US Marine divisions in a single combat area since World War II. The 3rd Marine Division is already in Vietnam.

Lt. Comdr. Marcus A. Arnheiter, USN, is relieved of command of the US Navy escort ship *Vance* (DER 387) off the coast of Vietnam. Subsequently Arnheiter protests that he has been victimized by a cabal of disloyal officers, and the incident attracts nationwide publicity. Hearings and suits continue for several years.

1 APR

The command US Naval Forces Vietnam is established under Rear Adm. Norvell G. Ward, USN, who exercises operational control over virtually all US

Navy forces in South Vietnam as well as certain units afloat off the coast of Vietnam for the Commander, Military Advisory Command Vietnam (MACV). Previously Ward was Naval Component Commander, MACV, a position that is disestablished.

The US Seventh Air Force is reactivated in Vietnam. The Seventh Air Force had been inactive since Jan 1957. It will be responsible for all Air Force combat operations in Southeast Asia. This responsibility was formally assigned to 2nd Air Division, which has more than 29,000 officers and enlisted personnel and operates about 500 combat aircraft.

2 APR

The US Army helicopter repair ship *Corpus Christi Bay* (T-ARVH 1), the former Navy seaplane tender *Albemarle* (AV 5), arrives in South Vietnamese waters to provide depot maintenance for the more than 1,500 Army aircraft in the country. The ship is operated by an MSTS civilian crew and carries 300 Army aircraft technicians.

5 APR

Secretary of the Navy Paul H. Nitze announces that involuntary active-duty extensions of enlisted personnel will be phased out gradually and that the process will be completed by 30 Sep 1966 for the Navy and 31 Oct 1966 for the Marine Corps.

The US Army announces that the new light-observation helicopter OH-6A Cayuse has broken 21 unofficial world records for rotary-wing aircraft. The Hughes-built OH-6A claims more world records than any other helicopter with 12 new speed records and three new records each in distance, climbing, and sustained altitude.

Secretary of Defense Robert S. McNamara approves a request from the Secretaries of the Air Force and Navy that naval air transport units be withdrawn from the Military Airlift Command (MAC). The withdrawal will be completed by mid-1967.

7 APR

A US B28 thermonuclear weapon is recovered from the waters off Palomares, Spain, following an intensive 80-day search and recovery operation after the weapon was lost in a B-52 collision with a KC-135 tanker. The weapon is located in 2,500 feet (762 m) of water by the *Alvin,* a Navy deep-diving research submersible. The Navy's Cable-controlled Underwater Research Vehicle (CURV), designed for the recovery of experimental torpedoes, is used to attach lines to

the bomb. Once the lines are secured, the bomb is brought to the surface by the submarine rescue ship *Petrel* (ASR 14).

9 APR

For the first time in the Vietnam War, more American than South Vietnamese servicemen are killed during a one-week period (ending this date). American casualties are 95 killed while 67 South Vietnamese soldiers reportedly die during the same period.

10 APR

The first two 31-foot (9.4-m) river patrol craft (PBR) begin operating in South Vietnam. During their first day of operation, the boats halt and inspect 18 Vietnamese junks in river waters about 30 miles (48.3 km) south of Saigon.

12 APR

USAF B-52 Stratofortress bombers strike targets near the Mu Gia Pass, 65 miles (104.6 km) south of Vinh. This marks the first time that B-52s attack North Vietnam. The pass will be struck by B-52s again on 26 Apr.

Exercise Grey Ghost, the first major exercise of the year for the US First Fleet, begins off the coast of California. Forty-eight ships participate in the 11-day exercise, which encompasses most aspects of naval warfare.

17 APR

The cruiser *Canberra* (CAG 2), operating off Vietnam, becomes the first US ship to relay an operational message via satellite. The *Canberra* uses the *Syncom III* communications satellite to relay a message to the Naval Communications Station in Honolulu, Hawaii, some 4,000 n.miles (7,412 km) away.

22 APR

Marine Regimental Landing Team (RLT) 7, based in the 7th Marine Regiment, becomes the first Marine ground unit to receive the Navy Unit Commendation for action in Vietnam. The award is made for its part in the previous year's Operation Starlight, which was the first direct field confrontation between a major US unit and a main force Viet Cong unit. RLT-7 was credited with killing 600 and capturing 125 communist troops, virtually annihilating a Viet Cong regiment.

25 APR

The British Far East Command announces that Indonesian shore batteries have fired on the coastal minesweeper *Puncheston* while in Singapore's territorial waters. The shells miss the ship and the minesweeper does not return fire.

A USAF F-4C Phantom fighter downs a North Vietnamese MiG-21 aircraft over North Vietnam with a Sidewinder air-to-air missile. This is the first confirmed kill of a MiG-21 over Vietnam.

26 APR
As part of the withdrawal from the Military Airlift Command (MAC), the US Navy announces that Naval Air Transport Squadron (VR) 3 at McGuire AFB, N.J., will be decommissioned in July 1967, while VR-7 and VR-22, both at NAS Moffett Field, Calif., will be decommissioned in Jan and Apr 1967, respectively. Air Transport (Maintenance) Squadron (VR) 8, also at Moffett Field, will be decommissioned in June 1967. The squadrons' 48 C-130E Hercules transport aircraft will transfer to the Air Force.

I MAY
The Navy Department is reorganized into an unilinear framework, with the Office of Naval Material, Bureau of Naval Personnel, and Bureau of Medicine and Surgery placed under the direct command of the Chief of Naval Operations. The Bureau of Naval Weapons, Bureau of Yards and Docks, Bureau of Supplies and Accounts, and Bureau of Ships are reconstituted into six functional commands under the Chief of Navy Material, respectively the Air, Ship, Electronics, Ordnance, and Supply Systems Commands, and Facilities Engineering Command. This ends the Navy's bureau structure that dates to 1842.

The US anti-submarine carrier *Intrepid* (CVS 11) arrives off South Vietnam to serve in a "limited attack" role. Her ASW aircraft have been "beached" and she is assigned two squadrons of A-1 Skyraider and two of A-4 Skyhawk attack aircraft. She will conduct strikes in South Vietnam.

The US Coast Guard redesignates its larger cutters (WPG) as high-endurance cutters (WHEC) and the small patrol craft (WPC) as medium-endurance cutters (WMEC).

9 MAY
Three US Navy patrol air-cushion vehicles (PACV) begin operating in South Vietnam as units of the coastal surveillance (Market Time) force. Grouped as PACV Division 107, part of Boat Squadron 1, the vehicles are the first such craft to become operational with the US armed forces.

Ten river patrol boats (PBR) begin to patrol the Bassac River in South Vietnam. This is the first of many US military operations to counter Viet Cong activity in the Mekong Delta.

II MAY
The nuclear-propelled missile cruiser *Long Beach* (CGN 9), operating in the northern Tonkin Gulf, fires Talos missiles against North Vietnamese MiG fighter aircraft in the first US attempt to use surface-to-air missiles against hostile aircraft. (*See* 23 May 1966.)

US Navy and South Vietnamese Air Force aircraft join US surface units in sinking the first large, steel-hull freighter caught attempting to supply Viet Cong units, the first such action since Feb 1965. The US escort ship *Brister* (DER 327), the minesweeper *Vireo* (MSC 205), and the Coast Guard patrol boat *Point Grey* (WPB 82324), all of the Market Time Force, join the aircraft in destroying the ship, which is carrying over 50 tons of supplies.

North Vietnamese MiG-17 aircraft make the first Communist air-to-air missile attack of the Vietnam War. The attack, against a USAF rescue helicopter and its A-1H Skyraider escort, is unsuccessful.

In an air strike made closer to the port city of Haiphong than any since the start of the Vietnam War, A-4 Skyhawks from the carrier *Enterprise* (CVAN 65) strike two surface-to-air missile sites ten miles (16 km) from that city. Three SAMs are launched against the aircraft, but all return safely.

A Marine A-4 Skyhawk is catapult launched from the Marine expeditionary airfield at Chu Lai, South Vietnam. It is the first combat use of the field catapult system, capable of launching a fully loaded tactical aircraft from runways less than 3,000 feet (914 m) long.

Flight tests of the British P.1127 Kestrel VSTOL aircraft begin aboard the US landing ship *Raleigh* (LPD 1) and carrier *Independence* (CVA 62). The aircraft, designated XV-6A for US test purposes, conducts seven days of operations from the two ships. It is the progenitor of the Harrier VSTOL aircraft.

12 MAY
The first guided firing of the US Navy's Phoenix air-to-air missile is conducted on the Pacific Missile Range off Point Mugu, Calif. The long-range missile, intended for the F-14 Tomcat fighter, is launched from an A-3B Skywarrior aircraft against a target drone; all test objectives are met.

The US Department of Defense in Saigon announces that air sorties in support of ground operations in South Vietnam have increased from about 3,000 a month in 1965 to the current 16,000 a month.

18 MAY

The XC-142A VSTOL cargo aircraft is flight tested aboard the carrier *Bennington* (CVS 20), operating off San Diego, Calif. The Ling-Temco-Vought experimental aircraft, powered by four turboprop engines, flies in both vertical and the short take-off and landing configurations. Army, Marine, and Navy pilots fly the aircraft during the tests.

22 MAY

The US Navy patrol boat *PCF 41* is sunk by 57-mm recoilless rifle fire while patrolling the Dinh Ba River in the Rung Sat Special Zone of South Vietnam. There are no fatalities in the Viet Cong attack.

The recently reactivated inshore fire support ship *Carronade* (IFS 1) provides rocket fire support in South Vietnam for the first time.

23 MAY

The cruiser *Long Beach,* in the northern Tonkin Gulf, fires two Talos missiles two minutes apart at a pair of MiG fighters some 65 n.miles (120 km) away. The first missile destroys an aircraft and the second missile detonates on the falling wreckage. The *Long Beach* will repeat the feat against a MiG at a range of 61 n.miles (113 km). Additional US warships will engage North Vietnamese aircraft with Talos and Terrier missiles during the Vietnam conflict, scoring several additional kills.

24 MAY

About 1,000 tons of obsolete ordnance are detonated 4,000 feet (1,219 m) underwater at a location 75 n.miles (139 km) off Cape Mendocino, Calif. The Navy explosives are in the sunken hull of the Liberty ship *Isaac Van Zandt* and are part of the Vela Uniform seismic research program of the Defense Advanced Research Projects Agency (DARPA).

30 MAY

An estimated 12,000 Japanese stage a protest demonstration when the nuclear-propelled attack submarine *Snook* (SSN 592) arrives at Yokosuka, Japan. The *Snook* is the first nuclear ship to call at Yokosuka, although such ships have called at the US base at Sasebo, Japan, on several occasions.

31 MAY

A US Navy official gives support to legislation to extend the fisheries jurisdiction of the United States to 12 miles (19.3 km) offshore. In announcing the support to the House Fisheries Subcommittee, Navy Judge Advocate Rear Adm. Wilfred A. Hearn, USN, stresses that the Navy feels it imperative to continue the three-mile (4.8 km) sovereignty limit, but supports the State Department's contention that sovereignty and fishing rights can be separated.

6 JUNE

The carrier *Wasp* (CVS 18) recovers astronauts Lt. Comdr. Eugene A. Cernan, USN, and Lt. Col. Thomas P. Stafford, USAF, following their *Gemini 9* orbital flight. Cernan is the second American to walk in space, spending more than an hour on his space "walk." The spacecraft, launched on 3 June, flies 21 orbits during the 72-hour, 21-minute flight before splashdown 345 n.miles (639 km) east of Cape Kennedy. The astronauts elect to remain in their spacecraft during the recovery and are hoisted aboard the *Wasp* in their capsule.

12 JUNE

The US Navy scores its first aerial victory of the year and the first ever by an F-8 Crusader when Comdr. Harold L. Marr, USN, flying off the carrier *Hancock,* destroys a MiG-19 fighter over North Vietnam with a Sidewinder missile.

16 JUNE

Aircraft from the carrier *Hancock* strike North Vietnamese petroleum facilities in an area 24 miles (38.6 km) west of Thanh Hoa. This is the first carrier attack on petroleum facilities since 1964 and the beginning of what will be a systematic effort to destroy the country's oil storage system.

20 JUNE

Near the Co Chien River at the mouth of the Mekong Delta, the Coast Guard cutters *Point League* (WPB 82304) and *Point Slocum* (WPB 82313) encounter and receive fire from a 120-foot (36.6-m) steel-hull trawler, which they drive aground ablaze. The Chinese vessel is found to be carrying 250 tons of munitions destined for the Viet Cong. The *Point Slocum* takes a hit from a mortar shell in the course of the action.

22 JUNE

The US Army announces plans to reactivate 11 T-2 oil tankers from the National Defense Reserve Fleet and convert them into floating power plants for use in Vietnam. The ships, using their own 150,000-barrel

(22,624-ton) oil capacity, will be able to provide shore power for about two years without refueling. Civilian crews will sail the ships to Vietnam, and then return to the United States when the ships have been permanently moored in five protected areas.

25 JUNE

The US Navy minesweeper *Stalwart* (MSO 493) catches fire, and after firemen fight the blaze for eight hours, capsizes alongside a pier at San Juan, Puerto Rico. The ship is salvaged the following month.

28 JUNE

The British Ambassador to the United States, Sir Patrick Dean, accepts the first F-4K Phantom fighter aircraft for the Royal Navy. More than 46 percent of the parts being used in the F-4K are produced by Great Britain.

29 JUNE

Forty-six Navy and Air Force strike aircraft inflict heavy damage on North Vietnam's major petroleum storage area on the outskirts of Hanoi and Haiphong. This is the first strike so near those cities, whose combined oil capacity represents 60 percent of the nation's total. Navy aircraft, flying from the aircraft carriers *Ranger* (CVA 61) and *Constellation* (CVA 64), attack targets near Haiphong, and Air Force planes strike near Hanoi. In announcing the air strikes, Secretary of Defense McNamara discloses that enemy truck movements to South Vietnam during the first five months of 1966 are double the number for the same period in 1965.

1 JULY

France conducts its first nuclear explosion at Mururoa Atoll near Tahiti in the Pacific. (Previous French nuclear tests were conducted in Algeria.) French officials state that the US technical research ship *Belmont* (AGTR 4), the missile range ship *Richfield* (T-AGM 4), and possibly a US submarine spied on the experiment.

Three North Vietnamese torpedo boats come out to attack the US frigate *Coontz* (DLG 9) and destroyer *Rogers* (DD 876) operating some 40 n.miles (74 km) offshore on search-and-rescue operations. Aircraft from the carriers *Hancock* and *Constellation* attack the small craft, sinking all three with bombs and cannon fire. The *Coontz* picks up 19 survivors.

Detachment Alfa of Mine Squadron 11 is established at Nha Be, South Vietnam. Composed of 12 57-foot (17.4-m) minesweeping boats (MSB), the detachment is to keep the Long Tau River channel to Saigon free of mines.

2 JULY

Operation Jay by the 2nd Battalion, 1st Marine Regiment, and 2nd Battalion, 4th Marine Regiment in the Thua Thien Province of South Vietnam ends after 82 enemy are killed. The operation began on 25 June.

4 JULY

Operation Macon begins in Thua Thien and Quang Nam Provinces of South Vietnam. This three-month long operation will involve five Marine battalions at various times.

6 JULY

A-4 Skyhawk attack aircraft from the carrier *Constellation* exchange fire with two North Vietnamese torpedo boats at night, 38 n.miles (70.4 km) southeast of Haiphong. The aircraft fire rockets but there is no verification that they hit the craft. One A-4 is lost in the attack with the pilot being rescued.

7 JULY

Some 8,000 US Marines from the III Marine Amphibious Force and 3,000 South Vietnamese troops begin a brigade-sized search-and-destroy operation—code-named Hastings III—in Quang Tri Province, to counter units of the North Vietnamese Army's 324B Division, which had moved across the Demilitarized Zone (DMZ). The operation will end on 3 Aug 1966, with a reported 824 Viet Cong killed.

The III Marine Amphibious Force in South Vietnam will grow to the largest combined combat force ever commanded by a Marine general, reaching a peak of some 163,000 Army, Navy, and Marine personnel.

Aircraft from the carriers *Hancock* and *Constellation* sink two North Vietnamese torpedo boats and heavily damage two others moored near Hon Gay Island, 30 n.miles (55.6 km) east of Haiphong. No US aircraft are lost. Aircraft from the *Hancock* also attack the only two pumping stations in North Vietnam capable of transferring petroleum from ships to tanks ashore.

The US Department of Defense announces that it will release servicemen who are the sole surviving sons in their families. This is in line with Selective Service System policy, which has ceased drafting sole surviving sons.

8 JULY

Exercise Belaying Pin, an eight-day fleet exercise involving 43 ships and 25,000 personnel of the US First Fleet, begins off the coast of California.

9 JULY

The US Navy patrol boats *PCF 57* and *PCF 66* are fired on by a junk 40 n.miles (74 km) north of Qui Nhon. The Swift boats return fire and capture the junk and eight Viet Cong.

10 JULY

Two US Marine A-4 Skyhawks flying from Chu Lai sink an armed motor sampan heading toward two downed USAF crewmen awaiting rescue eight n.miles (14.8 km) off the DMZ.

12 JULY

British Defence Minister Healy states that Britain will maintain "a substantial military capability" in the Far East after Indonesia's confrontation with Malaysia comes to an end, provided that Malaysia and Singapore want the forces in the area.

15 JULY

US Navy and Air Force pilots set a daily record by flying 121 missions over North Vietnam.

16 JULY

Operation Deckhouse II begins when the Special Landing Force of the III Marine Amphibious Force makes an amphibious assault in Quang Tri Province, 40 miles (64.4 km) north of Hue in South Vietnam.

US Navy and Air Force pilots equal the 121-mission record over North Vietnam set on 15 July 1966.

18 JULY

In a protest to the International Control Commission, the North Vietnamese government charges that in raids conducted on 17 July, US planes made provocations against foreign ships in Haiphong Harbor.

Operation Deckhouse II ends after two days. The US Marine operation in South Vietnam kills a reported three enemy soldiers.

HMS *Valiant,* the Royal Navy's first "all-British" nuclear-propelled fleet submarine, is commissioned. (The previous *Dreadnought* had an American-designed propulsion system.)

19 JULY

Two US Navy river patrol boats (PBR) sink a 30-foot (9.1-m) junk on the Co Chien River, one of the mouths of the Mekong, when the junk fires upon the patrol boats.

21 JULY

The helicopter carrier *Guadalcanal* (LPH 7) recovers *Gemini 10* astronauts Comdr. John W. Young, USN, and Maj. Michael Collins, USAF, after they land 460 n.miles (852.4 km) east of Cape Kennedy. The astronauts have spent 70 hours, 47 minutes in space, docked with an Agena satellite, and Collins made a space walk during the 43-orbit flight.

23 JULY

Four US Navy river patrol boats (PBR) engage a 30-foot (9.1-m) sampan at night in the Mekong River east of My Tho. Eight Viet Cong are killed. The sampan is captured and found to contain mines, munitions, and numerous military documents.

25 JULY

The US destroyer *O'Brien* (DD 725) steams 180 n.miles (333 km) up the Columbia River. She is the largest ship ever to navigate the river above the Bonneville Dam. The transit takes 14 hours, during which the destroyer crosses two mountain ranges and passes through the locks of the Bonneville Dam.

28 JULY

The US Military Assistance Command Vietnam (MACV) announces that Lt. (jg) Dieter Dengler, USN, a Navy pilot who had been shot down six days earlier, has escaped from Viet Cong captivity.

The US Navy and Defense Advanced Research Projects Agency (DARPA) conduct an underwater seismic test 4,000 feet (1,219 m) down, 75 n.miles (138.9 km) off the North Carolina coast. The test, named Vela Uniform, is the fourth in a series, and 300 tons of conventional explosives are set off in a World War II Liberty ship, which is scuttled for the test.

The third and final phase of the US Navy's test known as Project Neptune to determine the feasibility of employing merchant ships as research ships of opportunity begins with the departure of the American Export Isbrandtsen Lines ship *Exilona* from Detroit, Mich., to European ports. Project Neptune began in the summer of 1964.

2 AUG

Aircraft from the carrier *Constellation* bomb oil installations at Haiphong for the third time and meet one of the heaviest anti-aircraft barrages of the Vietnam War. The Soviets later charge that "large caliber bullets" from the attacking American planes hit the Soviet merchant ship *Madyn* during the attack; the United States denies the charge.

Operation Prairie, a brigade-sized operation involving the III Marine Amphibious Force in Quang Tri Province, begins. The operation seeks to stop North Vietnamese forces of the 324B division from crossing into the province through the DMZ.

4 AUG

The US Navy halts carrier strikes in South Vietnam and moves the Dixie Station carrier to Yankee Station to join the two carriers that have been carrying out operations against North Vietnam.

5 AUG

Aircraft from the carrier *Constellation* attack a petroleum storage point at Do Son, 13 miles (21 km) southeast of Haiphong, destroying three large oil tanks and damaging others.

6 AUG

The US Navy patrol gunboat *Asheville* (PGM 84), the lead ship in a new class of motor gunboats, is commissioned. Her commanding officer is Lt. Henry Dale, USN. Redesignated PG from PGM in 1967, these ships will see extensive service off Vietnam and in the Caribbean.

A-4 Skyhawks and A-6 Intruders from the carrier *Constellation* sink four North Vietnamese torpedo boats and damage a fifth some 40 to 50 n.miles (74 to 93 km) northeast of Haiphong.

A reinforced battalion of the 5th Marine Regiment begins Operation Colorado in the Quang Nam and Quang Tri Provinces of South Vietnam.

7 AUG

US officials announce that seven US aircraft, one of them a Navy A-1 Skyraider, have been lost over North Vietnam, making this the worst single day for US pilots since the air war began over North Vietnam. Six of the aircraft are lost to anti-aircraft fire; the cause of the loss of the seventh plane is unknown.

8 AUG

US Navy and Air Force pilots set a record of 139 bombing missions against North Vietnam. The previous record was 121 missions set on 15 July.

The US Department of Defense announces that while one member of a family is serving in South Vietnam, another member of the same family (either parent, brothers, or sisters) upon request, will be deferred from assignment in South Vietnam until completion of the first member's tour. The order is not applicable to personnel assigned to ships of the Seventh Fleet.

9 AUG

President Johnson states that, despite the recent rise in air losses over North Vietnam, the United States is losing fewer planes than had been expected.

11 AUG

USAF aircraft accidently attack and damage the 82-foot (25-m) US Coast Guard patrol boat *Point Welcome* (WPB 82329) at night off the northern coast of South Vietnam, killing the commanding officer and one crewman and wounding five others.

13 AUG

A-4 Skyhawk aircraft from the carrier *Oriskany* (CVA 34) sink two North Vietnamese torpedo boats 25 n.miles (46 km) northeast of Haiphong.

The US naval transports *Gen. A. M. Patch* (T-AP 122) and *Gen. William O. Darby* (T-AP 127) end the longest single point-to-point trooplift in the 17-year history of MSTS by transporting the Army's 3,124-man 196th Light Infantry Brigade the 12,358 n.miles (22,899 km) from Boston to Vung Tau, Vietnam. Both ships departed Boston on 15 July and traveled via the Panama Canal and Long Beach, Calif.

15 AUG

A-4 Skyhawk aircraft from the carrier *Oriskany* strike the Tuc Tranh petroleum facility, three miles (5 km) south of Thanh Hoa.

Thirty-one ships and 15,000 personnel from Great Britain, France, Norway, the Netherlands, and the United States begin NATO exercise Straightlaced in the Norwegian Sea.

16 AUG

The 1st Battalion, 26th Marine Regiment begins Operation Deckhouse III in Binh Tuy Province in the II Corps Tactical Zone. It will end on 20 Aug with no enemy reported killed.

North Vietnamese MiG fighters, engaging in combat farther south than ever before, attack a flight of bomb-laden A-4 Skyhawks flying from the carrier *Constellation* as they are about to bomb a supply relay point near Haiphong. The US aircraft suffer no damage.

The US Navy's PM-3A nuclear power plant at McMurdo Station, Antarctica, sets a new record of 2,100 hours (over 12 weeks) of continuous operation, surpassing the previous shore reactor record of 2,000.5 hours which was set earlier in 1966 by an Air Force reactor at Sundance, Wyo.

The MSTS asks that 20 more Victory ships and one Liberty ship be reactivated from the reserve fleet to bring to 142 the number of vessels removed from mothballs because of the Vietnam conflict.

The US Department of Defense announces that the Air Force paid $5.43 million to the US Navy for recovering the hydrogen bomb lost off Palomares, Spain, in early 1966.

17 AUG

On take-off from Da Nang Air Base, a US Marine F-8E Crusader crashes into a village about a mile south of the runway. The pilot ejects, but casualties in the village are 30 killed and 15 wounded.

18 AUG

The US communications relay ship *Annapolis* (AGMR 1, ex–CVE 107) opens the first permanent shipboard operational satellite link between operating forces afloat and a communication station ashore. Using *Syncom III* satellite, she communicates from the South China Sea to Pacific Fleet headquarters in Honolulu. The same day, the *Annapolis* receives the first broadcast radio signals relayed from the Naval Communications Station Philippines via *Syncom II* over the Indian Ocean.

Aircraft from the carriers *Oriskany* and *Constellation* destroy a 20-car train, 20 miles (32 km) northeast of Thanh Hoa, North Vietnam.

20 AUG

A battalion-sized unit of the 3rd Marine Regiment begins Operation Allegheny in Quang Nam Province.

21 AUG

Gen. William Westmoreland, USA, the US commander in Vietnam, restricts the conditions under which US warplanes are permitted to open fire on small vessels in order to "prevent the recurrence" of incidents such as the one on 11 Aug in which three US aircraft accidently strafed the Coast Guard patrol boat *Point Welcome*.

22 AUG

Phase Two of Operation Deckhouse III begins with a US Marine assault on the beaches 100 miles (161 km) east of Saigon. Coming ashore from the helicopter carrier *Iwo Jima* (LPH 2), the Marines provide a blocking force for a sweep already under way by US and Vietnamese paratroopers engaged in Operation Toledo, which began on 10 Aug. This phase of Deckhouse III will end on 24 Aug; four Viet Cong are reported killed.

23 AUG

The MSTS-chartered merchant ship *Baton Rouge Victory* hits a mine in the Long Tau River, 20 miles (32 km) east of Saigon, and is beached outside the channel. Seven crewmen are killed. She is the third ship mined in or near Saigon. The first, an aircraft transport, sank at her berth in Saigon in May 1964; the second, another freighter, was beached in May 1965 near Nha Be, ten miles (16 km) from Saigon.

A-4 Skyhawks aircraft from the carrier *Oriskany* sink a North Vietnamese torpedo boat and damage two camouflaged torpedo boats near an island south of Hon Gai.

24 AUG

A force of six US river patrol boats (PBR) kill two Viet Cong and capture 91 documents in a sampan attempting to cross the My Tho River in the Mekong Delta.

25 AUG

American planes stage their heaviest raids over North Vietnam, flying 146 missions. The Air Force flies 71, the Navy 68, and the Marines seven missions. No planes are lost.

The anti-submarine carrier *Hornet* (CVS 12) recovers the second unmanned spacecraft of the Apollo series after its suborbital flight; the recovery takes place some 500 n.miles (926.5 km) southeast of Wake Island.

26 AUG

US pilots fly a record 156 missions against North Vietnam.

28 AUG

An electrically detonated mine sinks a South Vietnamese minesweeper in the Long Tau River. Two US Navy advisors are wounded in the incident.

29 AUG

The Viet Cong attack two river patrol boats (PBR) with mines and automatic weapons in the Co Chien River, 55 miles (88.5 km) southwest of Saigon. The US craft are undamaged.

A Viet Cong mine in the Long Tau River explodes just off the bow of the minesweeping boat *MSB 54*, causing minor damage. This is the first Viet Cong attempt to sink a US minesweeper.

A battalion of the 3rd Marine Regiment ends Operation Allegheny, which began on 20 Aug in Quang Nam Province, after killing 113 of the enemy.

Aircraft from the carrier *Constellation* sink one and damage two North Vietnamese torpedo boats northeast of Haiphong. The Chinese government later asserts that US planes sank one Chinese merchant vessel and damaged another. The US State Department states that the vessels were presumed to be North Vietnamese, and that the US planes attacked only after being fired on.

30 AUG

The US Navy assumes responsibility from the Army for flying armed UH-1B Huey helicopters in support of Operation Game Warden in South Vietnam. This is the first time that Navy helicopter crews participate in offensive missions in Vietnam; the Navy helicopters are referred to as Seawolves.

The merchant ship *Baton Rouge Victory* breaks loose from her salvage mooring in a flood tide, causing temporary closing of the Long Tau River. She is later towed to Vung Tau and the river is cleared.

2 SEP

US Army, Air Force, and Marine Corps units participate in Exercise Bar Frost, a joint combined exercise with British and Norwegian forces in Norway.

The US destroyers *Stribling* (DD 867) and *Jonas Ingram* (DD 938) begin a four-day visit to Port Said. This is the first visit by US warships to an Egyptian port in more than 12 years.

5 SEP

Having traveled from Pusan on board the US naval transports *Gen. A. M. Patch, Gen. William O. Darby,* and *Gen. H. J. Gaffey* (T-AP 121), 5,542 Korean troops arrive at Nha Trang, South Vietnam, bringing to 46,000 the number of Korean troops in Vietnam.

7 SEP

About 800 students engage in a rock-throwing melee with 2,000 riot police in Yokosuka, Japan, during a demonstration against the US nuclear-propelled submarine *Seadragon* (SSN 584) visiting the Japanese port.

The Viet Cong explode a mine in the Long Tau River 40 feet (12 m) from the US minesweeper *MSB 49*. This is the fourth unsuccessful Viet Cong mining attempt in four days. The other three attempts have been made against South Vietnamese minesweeping and river assault craft.

9 SEP

A-4 Skyhawk and A-6 Intruder aircraft from the carrier *Constellation* sink a North Vietnamese torpedo boat and damage two others with bombs and Zuni rockets.

11 SEP

US pilots log a record 171 missions over North Vietnam without the loss of a plane. This is 15 more missions than the previous record set on 26 Aug 1966.

Two US river patrol boats (PBR) are ambushed by the Viet Cong in the Co Chien River in the Delta area of South Vietnam. One PBR crewman is killed, the first fatality in the Game Warden river patrol operation.

13 SEP

An eight-day US First Fleet exercise—Eager Angler—involving 29 ships, begins off southern California.

The 150-bed German hospital ship *Helgoland* arrives in Saigon to treat South Vietnamese civilians. The West German Red Cross operates the ship on a grant from the West German government.

In ceremonies at the White House, President Lyndon B. Johnson posthumously presents the Medal of Honor to Construction Mechanic 3rd Class Marvin Shields, USN, for conspicuous gallantry at Dong Xoai, South Vietnam, on 10 June 1965. This is the first Medal of Honor awarded to a Navy man in the Vietnam War. A frigate will be named for him (FF 1066).

15 SEP

Desert Frost, a nine-day, combined US-British amphibious landing exercise begins in the Bomba area of Libya.

The amphibious assault ship *Guam* (LPH 9) recovers *Gemini 11* astronauts Lt. Comdr. Richard Gordan, USN, and Comdr. Charles C. Conrad, USN, at sea 700 n.miles (1,297 km) southeast of Cape Kennedy. Their flight, launched on 12 Sep, lasted 71 hours, 17 minutes and made 44 orbits. During the flight they achieved a first-orbit rendezvous with an Agena target rocket and established an altitude record of more than 850 miles (1,368 km); Gordon made a space walk during the flight.

Operation Deckhouse IV begins with a battalion landing made by US Marines in the Quang Tri Province of South Vietnam. It will be completed on 18 Sep with an estimated 83 Viet Cong killed.

16 SEP

US Secretary of State Dean Rusk and Philippine Foreign Secretary Narciso Ramos sign an agreement in

Washington reducing to 25 years the remaining period of US rights to four bases in the Philippines. The original term of 99 years began in 1951. The bases are Clark Field, Camp John Hay at Baguio, and naval bases at Subic Bay and Sangley Point.

The US carrier *Oriskany* rescues all 44 crew members of the British-registry merchant ship *August Moon*, which runs aground 175 n.miles (324 km) southeast of Hong Kong. One helicopter from the *Oriskany* crashes during the rescue when it is engulfed by a gigantic wave. The helicopter's crewmen survive the crash. Philippine Navy landing ships carrying 730 troops arrive at Cam Ranh Bay, South Vietnam; this is the first contingent of Philippine troops to serve in Vietnam.

17 SEP

A battalion of the 7th Marine Regiment begins Operation Golden Fleece 7-1, a rice harvest protection/search-and-destroy operation in Quang Ngai Province of South Vietnam. When completed on 27 Sep, an estimated 244 enemy are killed and 7,620 tons of rice are harvested under the protection of the US Marines and South Vietnamese forces.

19 SEP

In response to Chinese charges, the US State Department states that "there is a possibility that some inadvertent intrusions of China may have taken place during breakoff from air engagements over North Vietnam."

20 SEP

A-6 Intruder aircraft from the carrier *Constellation* sink a North Vietnamese torpedo boat 52 n.miles (96 km) northeast of Haiphong.

In a speech to the Fleet Reserve Association, Secretary of the Navy Nitze says that about 12 percent of the US Navy's active-duty force of nearly three-quarters of a million personnel are "involved in, or directly supporting, combat operations in Vietnam."

22 SEP

Secretary of Defense McNamara announces the reprogramming of about $700 million of FY 1967 funds to increase tactical aircraft production by about one-third to meet the needs of the conflict in Vietnam. He notes that most of the aircraft will be for the Navy, which has lost more aircraft than anticipated.

Two US Navy minesweeping boats (MSB) are ambushed on the Long Tau River by recoilless weapons

and rocket fire. The *MSB 15* takes a hit in her pilothouse, killing one and wounding 11 others. They are the first casualties to be inflicted on US mine force personnel in Vietnam. The second minesweeper is not hit.

25 SEP

A-4 Skyhawk aircraft from the carrier *Oriskany* destroy a North Vietnamese torpedo boat 50 n.miles (93 km) northeast of Haiphong.

27 SEP

US Navy river patrol boats (PBR) and helicopters begin operations in the Plain of Reeds, west of Saigon, in support of US Special Forces and Vietnamese Civilian Irregular Defense Groups. The operation, which lasts until 17 Oct, results in the capture or destruction of tons of ammunition and supplies, and the killing of a number of enemy troops.

A-6 Intruder aircraft from the carrier *Oriskany* sink two North Vietnamese torpedo boats 25 n.miles (46 km) southeast of Haiphong.

28 SEP

A-4 Skyhawk aircraft from the carrier *Constellation* attack a North Vietnamese torpedo boat 25 miles (40 km) southeast of Haiphong.

29 SEP

US Atlantic Fleet amphibious ships *Boxer* (LPH 4), *Rankin* (AKA 103), *Plymouth Rock* (LSD 29), *Ruchamkin* (APD 89), and *Suffolk County* (LST 1173) begin six days of relief operations in the Dominican Republic and Haiti after Hurricane Inez struck the island of Hispaniola with winds up to 150 miles per hour (241 kmh).

A US military spokesman in Saigon confirms that a foreign freighter was damaged during the attack on torpedo boats conducted by US Navy aircraft on 27 Sep, but denies that any bombs or rockets from the US planes caused the damage to the freighter. The spokesman says that an anti-aircraft round fired at the aircraft, which were flying 50 feet (15 m) above the water, burst about 100 feet (30.5 m) from the freighter.

3 OCT

Japan begins its largest naval maneuvers since World War II. The exercise will involve 300 aircraft and numerous ships, and last until 9 Oct.

Swedish Navy ships and aircraft begin a hunt for foreign submarines believed to be observing Swedish naval maneuvers. Warning shots are fired from a

Swedish helicopter near the submarines, which subsequently head out to sea submerged. The incident takes place north of the Island of Vinga, off Göteborg.

5 OCT

A Swedish Navy helicopter drops small charges near a submarine to "scare the vessel away from maneuvers taking place within Swedish territorial waters." Swedish defense officials state that they do not know whether any damage has been done to the submarine but that it is unlikely. The event takes place west of Stora Poelsan lighthouse, inside Swedish territorial waters.

13 OCT

A daily record of 173 bombing missions over North Vietnam are flown by US planes. The previous record of 171 was set on 11 Sep 1966.

14 OCT

President Johnson signs Public Law 89-658, which extends the exclusive US fishing zone from 3 miles (4.8 km) off the coast to 12 miles (19.3 km).

15 OCT

Three deep-draft piers are dedicated at Da Nang, Vietnam, transforming Da Nang into a deep-water port. The piers double the cargo capacity of the port.

16 OCT

President Johnson signs the bill creating the Department of Transportation. Among the agencies incorporated into the new department is the Coast Guard. In a sea battle off the Min River estuary in Fukien Province, near the island of Matsu, China, Nationalist forces reportedly sink two Chinese gunboats and damage two others.

17 OCT

The experimental French submarine *Gymnote* is completed. Although she has diesel-electric propulsion, the *Gymnote* is fitted with four launch tubes for ballistic missiles, serving as a test platform for the French Navy's *Le Redoutable* class of strategic missile submarines.

19 OCT

The US Navy announces that the PM-3A nuclear power plant at McMurdo Station, Antarctica, has broken the record for the longest continuous run for any military or naval nuclear plant by operating without interruption for 3,356 hours or nearly 20 weeks.

22 OCT

The US State Department states that a series of underwater explosion detection tests will begin later in October in the North Pacific, 75 n.miles (139 km) from the nearest land mass, and 212 n.miles (393 km) from Soviet territory. A temporary network of 13 ocean-bottom seismographs are being placed in an arc running northward from Hokkaido, Japan, along the Kurile Islands for a distance of some 500 n.miles (926.5 km).

25 OCT

The US destroyer *Mansfield* (DD 728) returns North Vietnamese gunfire north of Dong Hoi after she and the destroyer *Hanson* (DD 832) are fired on while they are in international waters. North Vietnam protests to the International Control Commission that the incident is an "escalation of the war."

Swedish helicopters again drop warning charges near a reported submarine inside Swedish territorial waters, according to Swedish officials.

The US Seventh Fleet begins Operation Sea Dragon. The operation seeks to destroy supply vessels along the coast of North Vietnam.

Acting Maritime Administrator James Gulick announces that the 1967 classes of cadets at federal and state academies will graduate early in order to meet the anticipated need for manpower in US merchant ships to support the Vietnam War.

26 OCT

A fire caused by a parachute flare breaks out on the hangar deck of the carrier *Oriskany* operating off Vietnam, resulting in serious damage and the death of 44 officers and enlisted men.

The US minesweepers *MSB 15* and *MSB 31* are ambushed by Viet Cong on the Mong Tau River, 15 miles (24 km) southeast of Saigon. No casualties are reported.

The US river patrol boats *PBR 34* and *PBR 40*, assisted by *PBR 37* and *PBR 38*, Army and Navy helicopters, and Vietnamese naval craft disrupt what is estimated to be a battalion-sized attempt by the Viet Cong to cross the Bassac River, 42 miles (68 km) below Can Tho.

29 OCT

A battalion of the 3rd Marine Division begins Operation Pawnee III in Thua Thien Province. It ends on 24 Dec 1966 with 32 enemy reported killed.

31 OCT

A Game Warden force captures or sinks 57 enemy junks and sampans on the Mekong River, 10 miles (16 km) west of My Tho. The encounter begins as patrol boats *PBR 105* and *PBR 107* each sight a single sampan. After following them, the PBRs come upon several enemy junks and sampans in a canal. At the end of a three-hour engagement, in which six more patrol boats and US Navy UH-1B Seawolf helicopters participate, 43 sampans and eight junks are sunk, and three sampans and three junks captured. No US casualties are reported.

The US minesweeper *MSB 54* is mined and sunk on the Long Tau River. Two of the seven crewmen are reported missing and four are wounded. A second boat, the *MSB 49*, operating in company with the *MSB 54*, receives heavy automatic weapons fire but suffers no casualties. This is the first sinking of a US minesweeping boat in the war.

1 NOV

Secretary of Defense McNamara initiates a comprehensive study effort called STRAT-X to examine future strategic missile basing concepts and the missile performance needed to counter potential Soviet Anti-Ballistic Missile (ABM) proliferation. This study will be the origins of the US Trident strategic missile system. The study will be completed in Aug 1967.

4 NOV

A flash fire in a storage compartment containing oil and hydraulic fluid four decks below the hangar deck of the carrier *Franklin D. Roosevelt* (CVA 42) kills seven crewmen and injures four. The fire is extinguished in 15 minutes and the routine of the carrier, operating on Yankee Station in the South China Sea, is not interrupted.

The US destroyers *Braine* (DD 630) and *Perkins* (DD 877), patrolling about 15 n.miles (28 km) north of the Demilitarized Zone (DMZ), are fired on by North Vietnamese shore batteries. Both ships return fire for nearly 20 minutes. Air strikes are called in and attack the shore battery for 40 minutes. No casualties are reported on the ships, although the *Braine* receives minor splinter damage.

The US Department of Defense announces the start of a series of simulated deep-ocean dives, including physiological experiments under high pressure, to be conducted by the US Navy Experimental Diving Unit at the Washington Navy Yard. The dives are part

of the research and training for the Navy's SEALAB III seafloor living experiment scheduled for 1967.

6 NOV

A North Vietnamese torpedo boat is sunk 50 n.miles (93 km) northeast of Haiphong by A-6 Intruder aircraft flying from the carrier *Constellation*.

Sniper fire is encountered by one of the Navy's air-cushion vehicles (PACV) undergoing operational evaluation in South Vietnam. The three Navy PACVs arrived in South Vietnam in May and will depart in Dec 1966.

10 NOV

The US nuclear-propelled attack submarine *Nautilus* (SSN 571) has an underwater collision with the ASW carrier *Essex* (CVS 9) during an exercise 360 n.miles (667 km) east of Morehead City, N.C. The *Essex* sustains a gash in her port bow, and the *Nautilus* sustains damage to her conning tower. Both ships return to their home ports under their own power. The only casualty resulting from the accident is a minor injury to one man in the *Nautilus*.

Thailand's Deputy Defense Minister announces that Thailand will send two ships, a patrol boat, and a tank landing ship to South Vietnam to help in the war.

11 NOV

The last flight of the Gemini series—*Gemini 12*—is launched from Cape Kennedy carrying astronauts Capt. James A. Lovell, Jr., USN, and Lt. Col. Edwin E. Aldrin, Jr., USAF, on a 59-orbit flight that will last 94 hours, 35 minutes. Aldrin carries out a lengthy space walk and the astronauts practice docking with an Agena rocket. Splashdown is in the Atlantic on 15 Nov, three miles (4.8 km) from the recovery ship, the carrier *Wasp*.

13 NOV

The first US jet aircraft flight to Antarctica touches down at the McMurdo Station. The USAF C-141 Starlifter transport completes the 2,300-mile (3,700-km) trip from Christchurch, New Zealand, to McMurdo without incident, off-loads 25,000 pounds (11,340 kg) of cargo in two hours, and returns to Christchurch.

14 NOV

The US destroyers *Hamner* (DD 718) and *John R. Craig* (DD 885) are fired on by North Vietnamese shore batteries. There are no casualties or damage reported, and the shore batteries are neutralized by air strikes and naval gunfire.

15 NOV

The US Navy Swift boat *PCF 77* broaches and sinks in heavy turf at the entrance to Hue River in South Vietnam.

16 NOV

Adm. R. L. Johnson, USN, Commander in Chief US Pacific Command, discloses in Saigon that "about two" US submarines have been patrolling off North Vietnam carrying out surveillance and other classified missions.

18 NOV

The US destroyers *John R. Craig* and *Hamner* fire on a North Vietnamese radar site two miles (3.2 km) north of the DMZ. It is the first time in the war that US warships have fired upon a shore target without being fired upon first. Both destroyers also attack 12 cargo barges that have been beached in the same area, destroying six of them.

22 NOV

Aircraft from the US carrier *Coral Sea* (CVA 43) attack a surface-to-air missile storage and repair site five miles (8.1 km) southwest of Haiphong.

The North Korean government charges that US naval ships bombarded its eastern coast on 22 November. US Defense Department officials state that US warships were not involved. In another incident, South Korea reports that North Korean shore batteries have fired 43 shells at a South Korean fishing fleet just south of the Demarcation Line. Three South Korean naval ships return fire for about 20 minutes.

23 NOV

The US destroyers *Mullany* (DD 528) and *Warrington* (DD 843) attack a convoy of 60 enemy supply barges off the North Vietnamese coast, sinking or damaging 47 of them. This attack raises to 230 the number of enemy vessels sunk since warships of the Seventh Fleet began intercepting supply craft on 25 Oct 1966.

25 NOV

The US Department of Defense confirms the existence of a new policy for the use of naval gunfire against North Vietnamese targets. According to the policy, a commanding officer is authorized to bombard North Vietnamese radars if he has reason to believe the enemy is tracking him to fire on the ship. The announcement is made in reference to the 18 Nov attack on a North Vietnamese radar site.

28 NOV

Lantflex 66, the largest US Atlantic Fleet exercise to be conducted in 1966, begins in the mid-Atlantic and Caribbean. Involved in the exercise are 91 ships of the US Second Fleet, three destroyers of the Canadian Navy, 19 US naval air squadrons, and some 42,000 US sailors and Marines. The exercise will continue until mid-Dec 1966.

29 NOV

A reinforced battalion of the 9th Marine Regiment begins Operation Mississippi in Quang Nam and Quang Tri Provinces of South Vietnam.

Four North Korean patrol boats raid a group of 30 South Korean fishing boats just south of the armistice line in the Sea of Japan.

30 NOV

Premier Nguyen Cao Ky of South Vietnam announces that US naval and air bombardment of North Vietnam will be suspended and that no offensive action will be initiated by South Vietnamese or other allied troops for 48 hours over Christmas and for 48 hours over the Solar New Year.

Following the second North Korean raid on South Korean fishing fleets within a week, the South Korean Chief of Naval Operations, Kim Yung Kwan, orders the sinking of any North Korean craft that attacks South Korean boats.

2 DEC

Planes from the US carriers *Ticonderoga* (CVA 14) and *Franklin D. Roosevelt* strike the Van Diem vehicle depot five miles (8.1 km) south of Hanoi. This is the first raid close to the capital of North Vietnam since 10 Aug 1966. USAF aircraft attack oil storage depots four miles (6.4 km) outside of Hanoi. Eight planes and 13 pilots and crewmen, none from the Navy, are lost, making this the heaviest single-day toll of US fliers of the war to date.

5 DEC

While patrolling 11 miles (17.7 km) northeast of Dong Hoi, the US destroyer *Ingersoll* (DD 652) is slightly damaged by a North Vietnamese shore battery; no one is injured in the ship. The destroyer returns fire and continues on patrol.

The China News Agency charges that US planes attacked and sank six Chinese fishing boats in the Gulf of Tonkin on 30 Nov and 1 Dec 1966, killing 17 Chinese fishermen and wounding 29 others.

6 DEC

Sgt. Robert Emmet O'Malley, USMC, is presented the Medal of Honor by President Johnson at Austin, Texas. O'Malley receives the award for heroism on 18 Aug 1965, during Operation Starlight, near Chu Lai, South Vietnam. He is the first US Marine to receive the Medal of Honor for heroism in the Vietnam War.

The USS *Queenfish* (SSN 651) is commissioned, the first of 37 submarines of the *Sturgeon* (SSN 637) class to join the fleet. This class is an enlarged version of the *Permit* (SSN 594) design, featuring a taller sail structure (to provide more space for masts), improved electronics, and an under-ice capability. Her first CO is Comdr. Jackson B. Richard, USN.

7 DEC

While the US destroyer *Manley* (DD 940) is engaged in gunfire support of Marines off the coast of South Vietnam, a 5-inch (127-mm) shell explodes in her forward gun mount. Three crewmen are injured.

Operation Mississippi, which began on 29 Nov in Quang Nam and Quang Tri Provinces of South Vietnam, is terminated. Eight enemy are reported killed.

8 DEC

Elements of the 1st Marine Regiment begins Operation Trinidad II in the Quang Nam Province of South Vietnam. When it ends on 11 Dec the enemy body count is 33.

Adm. Thomas H. Moorer, USN, Supreme Allied Commander Atlantic, announces the establishment of a new NATO command to protect Allied shipping in the western approaches to the Mediterranean. Located in Lisbon, Portugal, and known as the Iberian Atlantic Command (IBERLANT), the new staff will be composed of Portuguese, British, and American naval officers and headed by Rear Adm. Edwin Miller, USN.

9 DEC

The Grumman C-2 Greyhound Carrier On-board Delivery (COD) aircraft makes its first operational delivery in a combat zone when it lands aboard the carrier *Kitty Hawk* (CVA 63) in the Gulf of Tonkin.

11 DEC

Two US PBRs on the Mekong River west of My Tho sight a sampan with two uniformed Viet Cong on board and pursues her into a canal where they find 40 more sampans and a large number of uniformed Viet Cong apparently waiting to cross the canal. The patrol boats open fire, killing nine enemy and destroy-

ing 28 sampans. This is the second major river fight in the Delta. (*See* 31 Oct 1966.)

12 DEC

Gunfire from the US destroyers *Ingersoll* and *Keppler* (DD 765) destroy a North Vietnamese radar site northwest of Dong Hoi.

13 DEC

After an eight-day investigation, a US State Department spokesman denies that US warplanes have bombed and sunk Chinese fishing boats off North Vietnam on 30 Nov and 1 Dec 1966. He declines to identify the nationality of the vessels encountered by the Americans on the days in question but says it has been determined that they were not Chinese.

15 DEC

A-4 Skyhawk pilots from the US carrier *Kitty Hawk* report that a North Vietnamese surface-to-air missile fired at their flight had come down on a North Vietnamese junk and demolished her.

16 DEC

US carrier-based aircraft attack 12 beached cargo barges 13 miles (20.9 km) south of Thanh Hoa, North Vietnam, and reports damaging six of them with Zuni rockets. Other pilots from the carrier *Kitty Hawk* report that they have destroyed a large, three-masted cargo junk, 17 miles (27.4 km) northeast of Vinh.

18 DEC

The US nuclear-propelled carrier *Enterprise* rejoins the Seventh Fleet's Yankee Station and launches the first strikes of her second cruise to Vietnam waters.

19 DEC

US naval ships assist a sinking Chinese fishing boat from Hainan, sailing off the Vietnamese coast with 48 fishermen on board. The men and their boat, which had been damaged in a storm, are taken to the South Vietnamese port of Nha Trang.

20 DEC

A battalion of the 4th Marine Regiment begins Operation Chinook in Quang Tri Province of South Vietnam; a battalion of the 1st Marine Regiment begins Operation Shasta II in Quang Nam Province. Shasta II ends the following day with 11 enemy troops reported to have been killed.

23 DEC

The US destroyer *O'Brien* (DD 725) is hit twice by North Vietnamese shore batteries as she patrols in the Tonkin Gulf, about three miles (4.8 km) north of Dong Hoi. Two crewmen are killed and four wounded. This is the first time a US destroyer has sustained direct hits from North Vietnamese guns.

24 DEC
At 0700 Saigon time, the two-day Christmas truce begins.

31 DEC
A three-day New Year stand-down begins at 0700 Saigon time.

The US minesweeper *MSB 52* recovers a Soviet-made contact mine in the Long Tao River south of Saigon.

The US tank landing ship *Mahnomen County* (LST 912) runs aground near Chu Lai, South Vietnam, and is subsequently split in two by heavy seas.

Twelve damage-control men from the US destroyer *Perkins* volunteer to extinguish a fire aboard the Panamanian freighter *Oriana* in Kaohsiung Harbor, Taiwan. The merchant ship is saved by their efforts.

At year's end there are 385,000 US troops in South Vietnam.

1967

2 JAN

The three-day New Year stand-down ends at 0700 Saigon time. Less than two hours later, the US destroyer *Ingersoll* (DD 652) is fired upon by North Vietnamese gun batteries located on Hon Mat Island. The *Ingersoll* returns fire and heads out of range, but a large secondary explosion from her fire is observed in the target area.

In what is described by a US spokesman in Saigon as "the largest air battle of the war," USAF F-4 Phantom fighters serving as escorts for F-105 Thunderchief strike aircraft attacking surface-to-air missile sites in the Red River Delta shoot down seven North Vietnamese MiG fighters.

4 JAN

F-4 Phantom aircraft from the US carrier *Kitty Hawk* (CVA 63) make a rocket attack and possibly destroy a 70-foot (21.3-m) North Vietnamese patrol boat, 23 n.miles (43 km) east of Haiphong.

5 JAN

Exercise Snatch Block, the first US First Fleet exercise of 1967, begins off the coast of southern California. The nine-day exercise includes 25 ships and 27 air units.

6 JAN

Marines of the US Seventh Fleet's Special Landing Force and South Vietnamese Marines begin operation Deckhouse V in the Mekong Delta area of South Vietnam. This is the first direct American ground commitment to the Delta area in the Vietnam War. The operation terminates on 16 Jan and is considered to have been unproductive.

9 JAN

Using two command-detonated charges, Viet Cong frogmen sink the 170-foot (51.8-m) dredge *Jamaica Bay,* fourth largest in the world, in about 20 feet (6 m) of water, southwest of My Tho on the Mekong River. Two US civilians are killed. The dredge is later salvaged, but will sink in deeper water.

The British tanker *Haustrum* receives nine hits from recoilless-rifle fire from Viet Cong positions along the Long Tau River, 14 miles (22.5 km) southeast of Saigon. One crewman is killed in the incident. The *Haustrum* proceeds to Saigon after the action.

13 JAN

While patrolling northeast of the island of Quemoy, Nationalist Chinese F-104 Starfighter fighters shoot down two Chinese MiG-19s fighters. This is the first aerial clash over the Taiwan Strait to be reported in more than a year, and the first reported clash between Nationalist and Communist Chinese jets since 1958.

Master Chief Gunner's Mate D. D. Black, USN, is named the Navy's first Senior Enlisted Advisor. His primary mission is to advise the Chief of Naval Personnel on enlisted men's problems and policies.

14 JAN

The US minesweeper *MSB 14* sinks in the Long Tau River, 30 miles (48.3 km) south of Saigon following a collision with the Norwegian motor ship *Mui Finn.*

19 JAN

The 967-ton South Korean patrol ship *Tang Po* (ex-USS *Maria* [PCE 842]) is sunk by North Korean shore batteries after reportedly attempting to lead about 70 South Korean fishing boats, which had strayed into North Korean territorial waters, back to home waters. Twenty-eight of her crew of 79 are reported missing. She is the first South Korean warship sunk under fire since the Korean Armistice in 1953.

Matchmaker III, a six-month exercise designed to test combined naval operations and the capabilities of various NATO nations to provide base and logistic support to a small international force for prolonged periods, begins in Bermuda.

20 JAN

The US minesweeper *MSB 43* strikes a submerged dolphin while running the Charleston, S.C., degaussing range, and sinks with no personnel injuries. The boat is later raised and returned to service.

The flagship of the US Sixth Fleet, the USS *Springfield* (CLG 7) departs her home port of Villefranche, France, for the last time. Villefranche has been home port of the Sixth Fleet since 1956. The home port of the new Sixth Fleet flagship, the *Little Rock* (CLG 4), which relieves *Springfield,* is Gaeta, Italy. The change is made necessary by the request of the French government. The *Little Rock* will arrive at Gaeta on 3 Feb 1967.

The US destroyers *Stoddard* (DD 566) and *Benner* (DD 807) are taken under fire by coastal gun batteries, 21 n.miles (39 km) from Vinh, North Vietnam. Both ships return fire and neutralize the shore battery and then damage five enemy waterborne craft. There are no American casualties.

23 JAN
As a result of a "target plotting error," the US destroyer *Norris* (DD 859) mistakenly shells the friendly South Vietnamese hamlet of Dong Ruy, killing four Vietnamese civilians and wounding four.

25 JAN
The US Navy displays a contact mine found at Nha Be, South Vietnam, in the main shipping channel of Saigon. The 4,000-pound (1,814-kg) weapon, reportedly of Soviet manufacture, had been swept from Long Tau River on 31 Dec 1966. This was the first contact mine to be found in South Vietnamese waters.

27 JAN
Astronauts Lt. Col. Virgil I. Grissom, USAF, Lt. Col. Edward White, USAF, and Lt. Comdr. Roger B. Chaffee, USN, are killed as fire sweeps through the *Apollo 1* command module during a ground rehearsal at Cape Kennedy. The flash fire occurs as the spacecraft sits atop a Saturn rocket. Major redesigns of the Apollo spacecraft are initiated after the accident.

Off Bridgeport, Conn., Sikorsky Aircraft and American Export Isbrandtsen Lines hold the first demonstration of the use of helicopters for discharging containers from a cargo ship. During the demonstration Sikorsky S-64 Flying Crane helicopters lift more than 500 measurement tons of freight in 20-foot (6-m) containers from an offshore cargo ship.

31 JAN
The US escort ship *McMorris* (DE 1036) and the small oiler *Tombigbee* (AOG 11) collide during night exercises, 75 miles (121 km) southeast of Honolulu. Two in the *McMorris* are killed and seven injured.

1 FEB
Three US Marine battalions begin Operation Prairie II, designed to counter North Vietnamese infiltration and Viet Cong activities in northern Quang Tri Province. Operation Independence which involves two Marine battalions also begins southwest of Da Nang on this date. Prairie II ends on 18 Mar 1967, and the same five battalions begin Operation Prairie III.

2 FEB
Secretary of the Navy Paul H. Nitze announces that all strategic warfare activities in the Navy have been

placed under a central authority within the Office of the Chief of Naval Operations. The new authority, called the Office of the Director for Strategic Offensive and Defensive Systems (OP-97), will be headed by Rear Adm. George H. Miller, USN.

4 FEB
The US river patrol boat *PBR 113* is set on fire by a Viet Cong grenade while on patrol three miles (4.8 km) north of Phu Vinh on the Co Chien River. The boat is abandoned, but later towed to base, where she is stripped of her salvageable parts. This is the first PBR lost to enemy fire.

8 FEB
A four-day ceasefire to mark the celebration of Tet commences at 0700 Saigon time.

The US destroyer *Stoddard* exchanges fire with shore batteries while on patrol six miles (9.7 km) southeast of Hon Mat Island, near Vinh, North Vietnam. The incident takes place several hours after the Tet truce begins.

10 FEB
HMS *Resolution,* Great Britain's first nuclear-propelled, ballistic missile submarine (SSBN), is placed in service. She will be armed with 16 Polaris A-3 missiles, fitted with British warheads.

The US Navy announces the first assignment of a WAVE to duty in South Vietnam. Lt. Elizabeth Wylie, USN, is ordered to duty on the staff, Commander Naval Forces Vietnam, in Saigon.

14 FEB
The US destroyer *Joseph Strauss* (DDG 16) is fired on by two shore batteries located on Ho Nieu and Hon Mat Islands in the Gulf of Tonkin, opposite Vinh. The destroyer returns fire and silences the gun batteries.

15 FEB
US minesweepers in the main shipping channel leading to Saigon come under heavy Viet Cong attack. In four separate incidents the *MSB 45* is destroyed by an enemy mine, the *MSB 49* is severely damaged, and two other craft are hit by Viet Cong fire. US casualties are one killed and 16 wounded.

16 FEB
The US Navy's River Assault Flotilla 1 begins offensive operations in the Rung Sat Special Zone of South Vietnam in conjunction with elements of the US Army's 9th Infantry Division. Marines of the Seventh

Fleet Special Landing Force begin Operation Deckhouse VI, 60 miles (96.5 km) south of Chu Lai, South Vietnam. These Marines, from the 1st Battalion, 4th Marine Regiment, terminate the operation on 3 Mar 1967.

17 FEB

Operation Rio Grande, an operation involving Korean and South Vietnamese troops and a battalion of US Marines, begins 17 miles (27.4 km) southwest of Da Nang against the 21st Viet Cong Regiment and elements of the support battalion of the 2nd North Vietnamese Army Division.

20 FEB

The US Coast Guard cutter *Hamilton* (WPG 715, later WHEC 715) is commissioned. She is the first in a new class of large, long-endurance cutters, the first major US ships to have gas-turbine propulsion. A class of 36 of the 378-foot (115.4-m) cutters is planned, but in the event only 12 are completed through 1972.

23 FEB

The US destroyer *McKean* (DD 784) sets a record for in-flight helicopter refueling operations. During a 30-day period while operating in the Gulf of Tonkin the ship participates in 100 refueling operations of Seventh Fleet and transfers more than 175,000 pounds (79,380 kg) of JP-5 fuel.

26 FEB

In the first aerial mining operation of the Vietnam War, seven A-6 Intruder attack aircraft from the carrier *Enterprise* (CVAN 65) plant mines in the mouths of the Song Ca and Song Giang Rivers. The mines are intended to stop the movement of coastal barge traffic.

The US cruiser *Canberra* (CAG 2) along with the destroyers *Benner* (DD 807) and *Joseph Strauss* begin bombarding North Vietnam coastal targets, striking 16 targets in an area from 10 to 20 miles (16 to 32 km) southeast and east of Thanh Hoa. This is the first time US warships have bombarded North Vietnamese targets without the enemy having fired first or having indicated by radar tracking that they were going to fire on the ships. The destroyers *Picking* (DD 685) and *Duncan* (DDR 874) also fire on ammunition dumps, a barracks area, and a shore battery north of Vinh.

28 FEB

The US Army-Navy Mobile Riverine Force (Task Force 117) is established in the Mekong Delta to control the area and clear it of enemy forces.

1 MAR

North Vietnamese shore batteries score hits on the US cruiser *Canberra*, 15 miles (24 km) north of Dong Hoi. Damage to the ship is slight and the batteries are later silenced by gunfire from the *Canberra* and the destroyers *Joseph Strauss* and *Benner*.

The Viet Cong attack the minesweeping boats *MSB 17* and *MSB 18* with automatic weapons, 13 miles (21 km) southeast of Saigon, on the Lonh Tau River. No US casualties or damage are reported.

2 MAR

The US Coast Guard cutter *Storis* (WAGB 38) seizes the 178-foot (54.3-m) Soviet fishing trawler *STRM-8-413* for violating US territorial waters by fishing one mile off the coast of the Shumagin Islands, off the southeast coast of Alaska. The captain of the Soviet vessel enters a plea of "no contest," and is fined $5,000. This is the first time the United States has seized a Soviet ship and prosecuted her captain for violating US territorial waters.

7 MAR

The US Navy approves a 20 percent increase in the number of WAVES, bringing their total strength to 600 officers and 6,000 enlisted women. The increase is made to ease the rotation of male personnel, especially those in the aviation community.

8 MAR

The US cruiser *Canberra* and the destroyers *Ingersoll* (DD 652) and *Keppler* (DD 765) are taken under enemy fire as they fire against 17 targets along the coast of North Vietnam, 41 miles (66 km) southwest of Vinh. They are credited with destroying one coastal battery and a river port facility, and with setting off large secondary explosions.

9 MAR

The US destroyers *Ingersoll* and *Keppler*, operating off Cape Falaise, south of Hon Me Island, fire on enemy shore batteries. Two of the batteries return fire, but are silenced by the destroyers, which suffer no damage.

10 MAR

The US destroyer *Ingersoll* is fired upon by a North Vietnamese gun battery 31 miles (50 km) north of Vinh. The American ship returns fire and silences the battery. No damage to the *Ingersoll* is reported.

11 MAR

The US destroyer *Keppler* is hit by an enemy shore battery, suffering damaged to her forward 5-inch

(1267-mm) gun mount while conducting Sea Dragon operations 30 miles (48 km) north of Vinh. Six of her crewmen are injured in the incident.

The Walleye television-guided, air-to-surface glide bomb is first used in combat, being launched from aircraft flying from the carrier *Oriskany* (CVA 34). The target is the barracks at Sam Son, North Vietnam.

14 MAR

A steel-hull North Vietnamese trawler is spotted by a US Navy P-2 Neptune aircraft while attempting to infiltrate weapons into South Vietnam. The vessel is forced to beach by the US ships *Brister* (DER 327) and *Point Ellis* (WPB 82330), and the patrol craft *PCF 78*. The trawler explodes after running aground; several tons of arms and other supplies are captured.

15 MAR

The US Coast Guard begins enforcing Public Law 89-658, under which the limit of US territorial waters for fishing operations is nine miles (14.5 km) beyond the regular three-mile (4.8-km) limit.

The US destroyer *Stoddard,* while firing on gun batteries at Han Hung and Ngoai, North Vietnam, some 24 miles (38.6 km) southeast of Thanh Hoa, comes under fire from the Han Hung gun battery. No damage is sustained by the destroyer.

16 MAR

Flying in darkness and clouds, a single A-6 Intruder strike aircraft flying from the US carrier *Kitty Hawk* dodges a hail of gunfire and four surface-to-air missiles during an attack on the Bac Giang power plant, 20 miles (32.2 km) from Hanoi. The plane drops 13 1,000-pound (454-kg) bombs on the target, which is North Vietnam's newest power plant, reportedly generating nine percent of the country's power.

The Viet Cong ambush the 22-year-old US Liberty ship *Conqueror* in the Long Tau River, three miles (4.8 km) below Nha Be. The cargo ship sustains hits from seven recoilless-rifle rounds and small arms fire. The ship, laden with rice and cement, is able to proceed to Saigon.

17 MAR

Rear Adm. D.C. Richardson, USN, Commander Task Force 77, states that "the quantities of flak our pilots are getting are heavier than ever—about one-third heavier than last summer." US intelligence officers estimate that the North Vietnamese have some 6,000 anti-aircraft guns and missile launchers.

A Phoenix long-range, air-to-air guided missile is fired for the first time from a US Navy F-111B aircraft at Point Mugu, Calif. It scores a hit on a jet target drone. The missile will be deployed on the F-14 Tomcat.

The US destroyers *Ingersoll* and *Stoddard* attempt to rescue a downed US Navy pilot off the coast of Vietnam. While engaged in the rescue the *Stoddard* is hit by enemy shore fire approximately 10 miles (16.1 km) north of the Demilitarized Zone (DMZ); the ship is holed above the waterline on her starboard side. There are no injuries. The destroyers' guns silence the enemy batteries and the rescue proceeds.

18 MAR

Master Sgt. Barbara Dulinsky, USMC, becomes the first woman Marine to report for duty in Vietnam. She is assigned to the US Military Assistance Command Vietnam.

20 MAR

Operation Beacon Hill I, the third amphibious assault of the year, begins four miles (6.4 km) south of the DMZ. The amphibious ships *Monticello* (LSD 35), *Ogden* (LPD 5), and *Princeton* (LPH 5) launch the landing of the Seventh Fleet's Special Landing Force.

22 MAR

The US Coast Guard seizes a Soviet trawler 5½ miles (8.9 km) off the coast of Alaska. It is the first arrest of a foreign ship for violation of the US established law establishing a 12-mile (19.3-km) offshore fisheries limit that went into effect on 15 Mar.

24 MAR

The US minesweeping boat *MSB 31* is damaged by an explosion from a mine or recoilless rifle in the Rung Sat Special Zone, 27 miles (43.5 km) southeast of Saigon. There are no casualties.

25 MAR

The US destroyer *Ozbourn* (DD 846), patrolling off the coast of South Vietnam, just south of the DMZ, is taken under fire by North Vietnamese shore batteries. She is hit twice and returns fire. The *Ozborne* suffers minor damage but no injuries.

26 MAR

The US destroyers *Stoddard* and *Turner Joy* (DD 951) are taken under fire while conducting a strike on coastal defenses in the area of Hon Me Island, Cape Bouton, and Cape La Tus, North Vietnam. They begin counter-battery fire. No damage is suffered by the ships and there are no injuries.

31 MAR
Headquarters of NATO's Supreme Headquarters Allied Powers Europe (SHAPE) is opened at Casteau, near Mons, Belgium.

1 APR
After almost 177 years as a part of the Treasury Department, the US Coast Guard becomes part of the newly created Department of Transportation.

The Australian guided missile destroyer *Hobart* begins operations with the US Seventh Fleet off Vietnam. She is the first Australian warship to participate in the Vietnam conflict.

The US cruiser *Providence* (CLG 6) and the destroyers *Waddell* (DDG 24), *Alfred A. Cunningham* (DD 752), *Duncan* (DDR 874), and *Turner Joy* bombard North Vietnamese coastal targets, among them points along the supply line to the south and barges on the southern coast of North Vietnam in the war's largest single-day shore bombardment operation.

The USS *Will Rogers* (SSBN 659) is placed in commission, the 41st and last Polaris submarine. Her first COs are Capt. R. Y. (Yogi) Kaufman, USN (Blue Crew), and Comdr. W. J. Cowhill, USN (Gold Crew).

10 APR
The US Navy hospital ship *Sanctuary* (AH 17) becomes the second hospital ship to operate off South Vietnam.

20 APR
Aircraft from the US carriers *Ticonderoga* (CVA 14) and *Kitty Hawk* attack power plants within two miles (3.2 km) of the center of Haiphong. This is the closest planes have struck to the center of the North Vietnamese capital.

21 APR
Operation Beacon Star begins, a sweep through Thua Thien Province by the Special Landing Force of the US Seventh Fleet. The operation will end on 12 May with Viet Cong fatalities listed at 764.

24 APR
The US carriers *Bon Homme Richard* (CVA 31) and *Kitty Hawk* participate in the first strikes against MiG bases in North Vietnam flown by US aircraft. The carrier planes attack the airfield at Kep, 37 miles (59.5 km) northeast of Hanoi, while USAF planes attack Hoa Lac, 19 miles (30.6 km) to the west of Kep. Navy F-4B Phantoms flying cover for the strike aircraft are credited with two "probable" MiG-17 kills in aerial combat.

North Vietnamese forces attack a small unit of US Marine riflemen and artillery observers near the Laotian border and the DMZ, commencing what will become a bloody, 12-day battle for several hills in the area. US Marine casualties total 138 dead and 397 wounded. Enemy casualties are counted at 554 dead with another 600 estimated killed but carried away from the battlefield.

28 APR
Operation Beaver Cage begins as the 1st Battalion, 3rd Marine Regiment comes ashore to sweep a long-established enemy stronghold 25 miles (40.2 km) south of Da Nang. More than 200 Viet Cong are killed in the operation which ends on 13 May 1967.

1 MAY
A-4 Skyhawks attack aircraft from the carriers *Bon Homme Richard* and *Kitty Hawk* shoot down two MiG-17 fighters in aerial combat and destroy four more on the ground in a second carrier attack on the airfield at Kep.

13 MAY
The 26th Marine Regiment begins Operation Crockett in Quang Tri Province. The two-month long operation will end on 16 July 1967 and accounts for 206 Viet Cong dead.

15 MAY
The number of US Coast Guardsmen in Vietnam waters is doubled by the arrival of the large cutters *Barataria* (WHEC 381), *Bering Strait* (WHEC 382), and *Gresham* (WHEC 387).

19 MAY
Two A-7A Corsair attack aircraft, piloted by Capt. Alex Gillespie, USN, and Comdr. Charles Fritz, USN, make a trans-Atlantic crossing from NAS Patuxent River, Md., to Evreux, France, establishing an unofficial distance record for light jet aircraft. The 3,327-mile (5,354-km) flight is made in 7 hours, 1 minute.

24 MAY
The seaplane tender *Currituck* (AV 7) returns to San Diego, Calif., completing a ten-month deployment in the Western Pacific. This is the last combat deployment of a US seaplane tender.

30 MAY
The Soviet Navy commissions the first of 34 Yankee-class strategic missile nuclear-propelled submarines. Fitted with 16 SS-N-6 Serb ballistic missiles, this is

the Soviet Union's first "modern" strategic missile submarine.

31 MAY

Operation Prairie IV, another sweep through Quang Tri Province by the 3rd Marine Division, is completed, yielding 489 enemy dead. Marine casualties are 164 killed and almost 1,000 wounded.

1 JUNE

The 13th Marine Regiment launches a major drive in Quang Tri Province. Known as Operation Cimarron, the name is later changed to Operation Buffalo from 2 July 1967 until its termination on 14 July.

2 JUNE

The Soviet government complains that the Soviet merchant ship *Turkestan* has been attacked by American aircraft in port at Cam Pha, North Vietnam. One crewmen is said to have been killed and several wounded.

3 JUNE

The US strategic missile submarine *Abraham Lincoln* (SSBN 602), the last of five submarines that carried the Polaris A-1 missile, completes her conversion to carry the A-3. The submarine will deploy on her first A-3 deterrent patrol on 26 Oct 1967.

5 JUNE

Israel launches a massive preemptive strike against Arab air bases with Israeli fighter and attack planes destroying about 300 Egyptian, 50 Syrian, and 20 Jordanian aircraft, mostly on the ground. The action, which virtually eliminates the Arab air forces, is immediately followed by Israeli ground forces advancing into Sinai, the Gaza strip, and Syria.

8 JUNE

While in international waters some 15 n.miles (27.8 km) north of the Sinai Peninsula, the US Navy intelligence collection ship *Liberty* (AGTR 5) is strafed by flights of Israeli jet fighters and attacked by three Israeli torpedo boats. The latter fire five torpedoes, one of which strikes the ship, inflicting severe damage. Of the *Liberty*'s crew of 297, 34 are killed and 171 wounded. Israel apologizes for the attack, caused by misidentification by Israeli Air Force pilots (with the American Embassy in Tel Aviv confirming that no US ships were in the area). The Israeli government will pay more than $3 million to families of the men killed. In reply to the Israeli apology, the US State De-

partment condemns the attack as a "literally incomprehensible . . . act of military recklessness reflecting wanton disregard of human life." Capt. William McGonagle, USN, the ship's commanding officer, is awarded the Medal of Honor for his conduct during the attack.

10 JUNE

At 1830 Israeli accepts a UN-imposed ceasefire in the Middle East. Israeli forces have seized the entire Sinai Peninsula to the east bank of the Suez Canal, the west bank of Jordan, including east Jerusalem, and the Golan Heights of Syria.

17 JUNE

China successfully detonates its first thermonuclear (hydrogen) weapon. Although China is the fifth nation to test a thermonuclear weapon, it occurs only 32 months after its first atomic test; the US span between these two key milestones was 86 months, for the Soviet Union 75 months, Great Britain 61 months, and France 105 months.

25 JUNE

The US Navy patrol boat *PCF 97* is sunk by recoilless rifle and automatic weapons fire on the east coast of the Ca Mau Peninsula, South Vietnam. Only one is wounded in this attack on the third Swift boat to be lost in action.

1 JULY

The US Naval Intelligence Command is established with the Director of Naval Intelligence also assuming the position of Commander Naval Intelligence Command. The command is established as part of a general Navy reorganization to reduce Navy headquarters personnel and to establish unified direction and oversight for the increasing number of intelligence subcommands.

15 JULY

A 120-foot (36.6-m) steel-hull trawler ignores the challenge of US Navy and Coast Guard ships on Market Time patrol and is driven ashore at Cape Batangan, 11 miles (17.7 km) north of Quang Ngai City, South Vietnam. She is found to be carrying arms and ammunition for the Viet Cong.

21 JULY

Three MiG-17 fighters are shot down by F-8 Crusaders from the carrier *Bon Homme Richard* during a raid on the oil storage plant at Ta Xa, 30 miles (48.3

km) north of Haiphong. F-8 pilots from this carrier have now downed nine MiG-type fighters.

29 JULY

Fire erupts on the flight deck of the carrier *Forrestal* (CVA 59) steaming off the coast of Vietnam after a rocket ignites while aircraft are being armed. The ensuing fires engulfs the ship's fantail and below-deck spaces, touching off bomb and ammunition explosions. The fires are extinguished after eight hours. Casualties are 134 dead or missing and 62 injured; 21 aircraft are destroyed. Severely damaged, the *Forrestal*, which arrived off Vietnam on her first combat deployment on 26 July, leaves the war zone for repairs.

1 AUG

The decision is made to bring the US battleship *New Jersey* (BB 62) back into service to add weight to the gun line conducting shore bombardment off Vietnam. The decision is made on the day Adm. Thomas H. Moorer, USN, becomes Chief of Naval Operations. His predecessor, Adm. David L. McDonald, USN, had opposed the return of the battleship to active service.

30 AUG

The carriers of Task Force 77 begin a campaign to isolate the port of Haiphong with an attack by aircraft from the *Oriskany* on one of four major bridges linking the city to Hanoi.

The former US light carrier *Cabot* (AVT 3, ex–CVL 28) is transferred to Spain for use as a helicopter carrier. Renamed *Dedalo,* she is the third and last US CVL of World War II construction to be transferred to another navy, the French Navy having earlier received two CVLs.

28 SEP

A US Navy river patrol boat (PBR) sinks after being hit by a rocket in a canal off the Mekong River. Two crewmen are killed and four wounded in the incident.

16 OCT

Formal opening of the new NATO political headquarters in Brussels.

21 OCT

The Israeli destroyer *Eilat*, steaming 4½ miles (7.2 km) off the Egyptian coast from Port Said, is struck by two Soviet-made Styx missiles, fired from Komar-type missile boats inside the harbor. The ship is fatally damaged and sinks after about two hours, with a third missile striking the ship as she goes down.

Forty-seven Israelis are killed and more than 100 injured in this first sinking of a ship in action by surface-to-surface missiles. (German air-launched guided weapons sank several ships in World War II, including the Italian battleship *Roma*.)

25 OCT

US carrier pilots destroy or damage at least ten MiG fighter aircraft on the ground in a strike on Phuc Yen Airfield in North Vietnam.

28 OCT

Adm. Sergei G. Gorshkov, Deputy Minister of Defense and Commander in Chief of the Soviet Navy, is promoted to Admiral of the Fleet of the Soviet Union (*Admiral Flota Sovetskogo Soyuza*), corresponding to the rank of Marshal of the Soviet Union. The rank, introduced on 3 Mar 1955, previously had been awarded to two flag officers.

31 OCT

The seaplane tender *Currituck,* the US Navy's last seaplane tender, is decommissioned and transferred to the mothball fleet.

1 NOV

Operation Kentucky begins, a 16-month operation by the 3rd Marine Division. Ending on 28 Feb 1969, the operation will produce a reported 3,821 enemy kills. American casualties are 520 killed and 3,079 wounded.

5 NOV

Battalions of the 3rd Marine Division, the Army's 196th Light Infantry Brigade, and the 1st Brigade, 5th Infantry Division (Mechanized) begin Operation Napoleon Saline in South Vietnam. Lasting until 9 Dec 1967, the operation kills a reported 3,495 enemy troops in operations east of Gio Linh. American losses at the end of the operation are 395 killed and 1,680 wounded.

6 NOV

An SP-5B Marlin of Patrol Squadron (VP) 40 at NAS North Island, San Diego, makes the last operational flight of a US Navy seaplane. (*See* 12 July 1968.)

9 NOV

The US carrier *Bennington* (CVS 20) recovers the unmanned *Apollo 4* spacecraft about 600 n.miles (1,111 km) northwest of Hawaii after an 8½-hour orbital flight.

14 NOV

Maj. Gen. Bruno Hochmuth, USMC, Commanding General of the 3rd Marine Division, is killed when his

UH-1 Huey helicopter crashes five miles (8.1 km) northwest of Hue in South Vietnam.

3 DEC

The US carrier *Ranger* (CVA 61) arrives on Yankee Station in the Tonkin Gulf, marking the combat debut of the A-7A Corsair light attack aircraft. The plane, derived from the F-8 Crusader, will replace the A-4 Skyhawk as the Navy's carrier-based light attack aircraft.

4 DEC

In Dinh Tuong Province, 66 miles (106.2 km) south of Saigon, the US Army-Navy Mobile Riverine Force kills 235 Viet Cong in one day's fighting.

13 DEC

A two-day meeting begins of the NATO Defense Planning Committee that adopts a new strategic concept of flexible respoonse and the establishment of the Standing Naval Forces Atlantic (STANAVFOR-LANT).

31 DEC

As of this date the strength of US forces in South Vietnam is 486,000.

1968

15 JAN

President Lyndon B. Johnson initiates a four-day suspension of US bombing of targets in the vicinity of Haiphong, North Vietnam.

21 JAN

The US base at Khe Sanh in Quang Tri Province, garrisoned by 3,500 men of the 26th Marine Regiment, is isolated from overland access when North Vietnamese forces cut highway Route 9. In the following days the 1st Battalion, 9th Marine Regiment, a South Vietnamese Ranger battalion, and two 105-mm howitzer batteries are airlifted into Khe Sanh as reinforcements. By 29 Jan 1968, Khe Sanh's garrison numbers 6,000 men. Surrounding it are 15,000 to 20,000 troops of the North Vietnamese 324B and 325C Divisions. US air power plays a large role in the defense of the garrison and the North Vietnamese never succeed in closing Khe Sanh's airfield. Only four transports are shot down during the course of the siege, which lasts until early April. American aircraft, ranging from US Air Force B-52s to Navy carrier aircraft, drop 100,000 tons of bombs on enemy positions surrounding the base during the course of the siege.

22 JAN

The US intelligence collection ship *Pueblo* (AGER 2), commanded by Comdr. Lloyd Bucher, USN, is surrounded and fired on by North Korean patrol boats in international waters off the east coast of North Korea. One crewman is mortally wounded and three others, including Bucher, are wounded. With no means of defense, Bucher accedes to North Korean demands and follows them into Wonsan harbor. Bucher and his crew of Navy, Marine Corps, and National Security Agency (NSA) personnel will be imprisoned until 23 Dec 1968. They are released into South Korea after the US government apologizes for the ship entering North Korean territorial waters.

27 JAN

In response to the emergency situation caused by the North Korean seizure of the US intelligence ship *Pueblo,* six Naval Reserve carrier squadrons are called into active service.

30 JAN

North Vietnam chooses the most important Vietnamese holiday, the lunar new year (Tet), to launch its largest offensive of the war. In the past a truce has been observed during this period; thus approximately half of South Vietnam's 730,000-man Army is on leave. Within a period of 48 hours, attacks are made on Saigon, Hue, Quang Tri, Da Nang, Kontum, and virtually every other major city in South Vietnam. Television coverage centers American domestic attention on Saigon, where a suicide squad of 15 sappers penetrates the American Embassy, killing five servicemen before being wiped out. In purely military terms the effort ends in a major defeat for North Vietnam. Some 32,000 North Vietnamese and (mostly) Viet Cong troops—at least 50 percent of the attacking force—are killed and 5,800 captured, compared to 1,000 American and 2,800 South Vietnamese combat deaths. A popular uprising against the Americans, for which Tet was expected to provide the impetus, fails to occur, and Hue is the only important position the attackers succeed in holding for any length of time. But the offensive's psychological impact on the American public transforms North Vietnam's military defeat into its political victory and American public opinion now turns strongly against the war.

31 JAN

A battalion of the 5th Marine Regiment aids South Vietnamese troops in bitter street fighting during the month-long battle to recover the former imperial capital of Hue. Marine casualties are 142 dead and 857 wounded. While the North Vietnamese have control of the city they execute 5,000 civilians as "political enemies."

10 FEB

The British strategic missile submarine *Resolution,* the Royal Navy's first SSBN, successfully launches a Polaris A-3 missile down the Atlantic Missile Test Range while operating submerged off Cape Kennedy.

31 MAR

In a television address to the nation, President Johnson declares that he will not seek reelection and calls for the beginning of peace talks. As a token of good faith, he orders the bombing of North Vietnam to be restricted to the "panhandle" area south of the 20th parallel.

3 APR

Radio Hanoi announces the willingness of the government of North Vietnam to hold peace talks.

4 APR

Following an orbital flight the *Apollo 6* unmanned spacecraft is recovered by the helicopter carrier *Okinawa* (LPH 3) some 380 n.miles (703.8 km) north of Hawaii.

6 APR

The US battleship *New Jersey* (BB 62) is recommissioned; her CO is Capt. J. Edward Snyder, Jr., USN.

10 APR

The propeller-driven A-1 Skyraider attack aircraft, which first entered US Navy service in 1945, is removed from the Navy's aircraft inventory. The plane was flown extensively in the Korean and Vietnam Wars, in the latter conflict by the USAF and South Vietnamese Air Force as well as by the Navy. (Skyraiders were also flown by British and French forces and several Third World countries.)

14 APR

The US Army's 1st Cavalry Division (Air Mobile) and a South Vietnamese airborne battalion reestablish overland contact with the Marine garrison of Khe Sanh in Operation Pegasus/Lam Son 207. Route 9 was reopened on 12 Apr and action around Khe Sanh ends two days later. It is estimated that approximately 10,000 North Vietnamese have been killed in the course of the siege; American–South Vietnamese casualties are 205 dead and some 800 wounded.

15 APR

In Quang Tri Province of South Vietnam, Operation Scotland II undertaken by units of the 3rd Marine Division is carried out through 28 Feb 1969. The operation claims a total of 3,304 enemy dead; American losses are 463 killed and 2,553 wounded.

3 MAY

The North Vietnamese government agrees to begin preliminary peace talks in Paris.

The US Naval Safety Center is established at Norfolk, Va., consolidating the existing aviation and submarine safety centers, located in Norfolk and New London, Conn., respectively.

18 MAY

Operation Mameluke Thrust, a major search-and-clear operation, is launched by the 1st Marine Division and the 26th Marine Regiment in an area 25 miles (40.2 km) to the west and south of Da Nang. During the operation, which lasts until 23 October, 2,728 enemy troops are reported killed. Marine losses are 267 killed and 1,730 wounded.

22 MAY

The nuclear-propelled attack submarine *Scorpion* (SSN 589), en route to Norfolk, Va., from a deployment with the Sixth Fleet in the Mediterranean, is lost. She is reported overdue on 27 May and declared to be presumed lost with all hands—99 officers and enlisted men—on 5 June. (*See* 30 Oct 1968.)

The keel is laid for the nuclear-propelled aircraft carrier *Nimitz* (CVN 68) at Newport News Shipbuilding in Virginia, the first US nuclear-propelled carrier under construction since completion of the carrier *Enterprise* (CVAN 65) in 1961.

25 MAY

A Soviet Tu-16 Badger naval reconnaissance aircraft, after making four passes over the US carrier *Essex* (CVS 9) steaming in the North Sea, crashes as the aircraft banks and a wingtip strikes the water. There are no survivors from the plane's crew of about six. The Soviet government does not protest the incident.

First flight of the Grumman EA-6B Prowler, an electronic countermeasures aircraft developed from the A-6 Intruder attack aircraft. The Prowler is a highly capable jammer with four crewmen compared to the two-place EA-6A Intruder.

10 JUNE

The South Vietnamese Navy assumes responsibility for sweeping command-detonated mines from the Long Tau River channel to Saigon. Fourteen US small craft are turned over to South Vietnam for this purpose. This event marks the beginning of the turnover program through which the South Vietnamese Navy is to be trained and equipped to fight the "brown-water" war on its own.

16 JUNE

The US missile cruiser *Boston* (CAG 1) and the Australian missile destroyer *Hobart* are slightly damaged and the patrol craft PCF *19* is sunk by USAF planes that mistake them for low-flying enemy helicopters while operating off the coast of Vietnam.

22 JUNE

The first British SLBM patrol begins with the *Resolution* carrying 16 Polaris A-3 missiles. The missiles were produced in the United States and fitted with British warheads.

30 JUNE

First flight of the Lockheed C-5A Galaxy, a long-range, heavy-lift cargo aircraft to be flown by the USAF Military Airlift Command.

1 JULY

President Johnson announces that the United States and the Soviet Union have agreed to open talks in the near future aimed at reducing offensive nuclear weapons and defensive anti-missile systems.

A-4 Skyhawks from the US carrier *Ticonderoga* (CVA 14) attack a truck park five miles (8.1 km) east of Vinh, inflicting major damage on the facility.

2 JULY

Aircraft from the US carrier *Bon Homme Richard* (CVA 31) attack an oil storage area 43 miles (69.2 km) south of Vinh, North Vietnam. Aircraft from the carrier *Constellation* (CVA 64) strike railroad facilities 30 miles (48.3 km) south of Vinh. Other aircraft from these carriers knock down or damage six bridges and other North Vietnamese facilities in a "typical" day on the Yankee carrier station.

The US destroyer *Ozbourn* (DD 846) sinks three supply ships off the coast of North Vietnam.

The US guided missile destroyer *Henry B. Wilson* (DDG 7) destroys Viet Cong support facilities with gunfire near Hue, Vietnam, in support of the 1st South Vietnamese Division.

3 JULY

US Navy UH-1B Seawolf helicopters kill 16 Viet Cong and damage or destroy 18 sampans and junks during the course of Operation Game Warden in Kien Hoa Province, South Vietnam, 55 miles (88.5 km) south of Saigon.

6 JULY

India's first submarine, the Soviet-built *Kalvari,* arrives at New Delhi. The Foxtrot-class submarine is the first of a large number of Soviet-built submarines that will be operated by the Indian Navy.

The US Coast Guard cutters *Androscoggin* (WHEC 68) and *Point Slocum* (WPB 82313) destroy or damage 60 structures, 33 sampans, and two bunkers in An Xuyen and Vinh Binh Provinces southwest of Saigon, South Vietnam.

A Soviet naval squadron arrives in Colombo, Ceylon, for a four-day visit. The ships are a cruiser, frigate, and tanker from the Pacific Fleet. This is the first visit by Soviet warships to Ceylon.

9 JULY

Operation Sneaky Pete, a US anti-submarine and mine warfare exercise begins off the coast of Georgia. Involved are 14 surface ships, 5 submarines, and 28 aircraft from the US Atlantic Fleet.

The US Army-Navy Mobile Riverine Force begins operations in the Co Chien River of South Vietnam. This is the only branch of the Mekong River where the Mobile Riverine Force had not previously operated.

10 JULY

A stop-work order is issued to General Dynamics, Fort Worth, Texas, the prime contractor of the F-111B aircraft. The Navy had opposed procurement of the naval variant of the F-111, claiming that it was too large for effective carrier operation.

11 JULY

The British government announces its plans to turn over one of its last military footholds in the Far East. The Singapore naval base will be turned over to the government of Singapore by Dec 1968.

12 JULY

The last US Navy seaplane, a P-5B Marlin, is retired from active service at NAS Patuxent River, Md.

16 JULY

The US destroyer *Blue* (DD 744) is damaged by shore fire off the coast of North Vietnam, near Dong Hoi. No casualties are reported and damage to the ship is minor.

19 JULY

A US patrol craft carrying 11 Army personnel and one South Vietnamese serviceman is seized by the Cambodian Navy after it inadvertently strays into Cambodian territory on the Mekong River. The US State Department apologizes, explaining that the boat entered Cambodian territory as a result of a navigational error.

The Vietnamese Navy takes possession of four US Navy Swift boats (PCF) in ceremonies held at An Thoi, Phu Quoc Island in the Gulf of Thailand. These are among the first of several hundred US naval craft that will be transferred to South Vietnam.

20 JULY

The British anti-submarine frigate *Exmouth* is recommissioned after conversion to all-gas-turbine propulsion, the first Western warship to have such a power plant. Originally completed in 1957 as a unit of the Blackwood class, she has a single turbine system for full speed and a two-turbine system for cruising. The Soviet navy has had the all-gas-turbine destroyers of the Kashin class at sea since 1962.

22 JULY
Comdr. Samuel R. Chessman, USN, age 42, commanding officer of Attack Squadron (VA) 195 aboard the US carrier *Ticonderoga* (CVA 14), flies his 306th Vietnam combat mission, breaking the record of 305 set by his predecessor, Comdr. Charles Hathaway, USN, in Apr 1967. Chessman also flew 77 combat missions during the Korean War.

At least 15 Viet Cong are killed, and eight sampans damaged or destroyed in the first operation of the newly trained Vietnamese Navy SEALs.

28 JULY
The US Navy's Special Projects Office (SPO) is redesignated the Strategic Systems Project Office (SSPO) to reflect additional responsibilities assigned by the Chief of Naval Operations for strategic offensive and defensive systems.

29 JULY
Operation Game Warden patrols are expanded to the upper reaches of the Mekong and Bassac Rivers; Game Warden now covers the Mekong Delta waterways from the Cambodian border to the sea.

14 AUG
The US designation CVT is established for training aircraft carrier; it will be assigned to the carrier *Lexington* (CVS 16) on 1 Jan 1969. (The designation will be replaced by AVT in 1978.)

16 AUG
The first flight test model of the Poseidon C-3 missile (designated C3X-1) is successfully launched from Cape Kennedy.

17 AUG
The US research submarine *Dolphin* (AGSS 555) is commissioned. She can operate at a greater depth than any US operational submarine. The submarine is not armed. Her first CO is Lt. Comdr. John R. McDonnell, USN.

20 AUG
Soviet, Bulgarian, East German, Hungarian, and Polish troops invade Czechoslovakia.

24 AUG
France detonates its first two-stage, thermonuclear device, code-named Canopus, at its Mururoa test facility in the Pacific. (France had tested low-yield fission devices in 1967 and early 1968, but this is the first true thermonuclear detonation.)

7 SEP
The carrier *John F. Kennedy* (CVA 67) is placed in commission. The "JFK" is the fourth ship of the *Kitty Hawk* class but is officially listed as a separate class. The *Kennedy* will be the last conventional (fossil-fuel) carrier to be built by the US Navy in the 20th Century. Her first CO is Capt. Earl P. Yates, USN.

18 SEP
In Quang Tin Province, 35 miles (56.3 km) south of Da Nang, the US Navy patrol boat *PCF 21* destroys or damages 44 junks and 4 sampans and kills four Viet Cong.

19 SEP
An F-8 Crusader fighter from the carrier *Intrepid* (CVS 11) shoots down a MiG-21 fighter northwest of Vinh. This victory is the Navy's 29th aerial kill and the last officially credited to an F-8; 110 enemy aircraft have been claimed by US forces so far in the war.

29 SEP
The US battleship *New Jersey* begins operations off the coast of Vietnam, firing 20 16-inch (406-mm) shells at enemy positions north of Con Thien near the northern boundary of the DMZ.

6 OCT
A search-and-clear operation called Maui Peak begins around An Hoa, South Vietnam, by units of the US 1st Marine Division and the South Vietnamese 51st Regiment. More than 350 enemy are reported to killed in the operation.

11 OCT
The first American three-man space flight, *Apollo 7*, is launched from Cape Kennedy. Featuring new safety systems following the *Apollo 1* fire, the spacecraft is manned by Capt. Walter M. Schirra, Jr., USN, Maj. Donn F. Eisele, USAF, and civilian scientist R. Walter Cunningham. The flight lasts 10 days, 20 hours, 9 minutes, and travels 163 orbits around the earth in preparation for a flight to the moon. The spacecraft is recovered by the carrier *Essex* (CVS 9) on 22 Oct, about 285 n.miles (528 km) south of Bermuda.

15 OCT

The previously independent efforts of Operation Game Warden forces and the Army-Navy Mobile Riverine Force are combined in a joint operational plan against the enemy in the Mekong Delta. The new combined operation is known as Operation Sealords indicating South-East Asia Lake, Ocean, River, Delta Strategy.

23 OCT

Units of the US 1st Marine Division kill 700 enemy troops and detain 94 suspects in a sweep west of Hoi An—Operation Henderson Hill—which continues through 7 Dec 1968. Marine losses are 35 killed and 231 wounded.

29 OCT

Seven US Navy PCF patrol boats, the Coast Guard cutter *Wachusett* (WHEC 44), the Market Time support ship *Washoe County* (LST 1165), and South Vietnamese Air Force A-1 Skyraiders team up in a surprise attack against enemy positions in the Cua Lon-Bo De River areas at the extreme southern tip of South Vietnam. In five hours, 242 enemy structures are damaged or destroyed. US casualties are five wounded.

30 OCT

Wreckage of the US nuclear-propelled submarine *Scorpion* is located at a depth of more than 10,000 feet (3,048 m) some 400 n.miles (740.8 km) southwest of the Azores by the US research ship *Mizar* (T-AGOR 11). The cause of her loss is determined to be a torpedo that began running in a torpedo tube; an attempt was made to launch the weapon, which then circled back to strike the submarine.

31 OCT

President Johnson orders a complete cessation of all air, sea, and land bombardment of North Vietnam, effective on 1 Nov at 0900 Saigon time.

20 NOV

In Operation Meade River, a sweep through Quang Nam Province by units of the US 1st Marine Division,

841 enemy soldiers are reportedly killed and 2,710 suspects are detained. US losses are 107 killed and 385 wounded in the operation that lasts until 9 Dec 1968.

6 DEC

Operation Giant Slingshot begins when US Navy inshore and coastal operations in South Vietnam are expanded by the initiation of regular patrols on the Vam Co Dong and Vam Co Tay Rivers, which extend westward from their divergence 23 miles (37 km) south of Saigon to enclose the "parrot's beak" of the Cambodian border. In the first year, forces committed to the operation will kill a reported 1,894 enemy troops and capture 517 tons of supplies.

7 DEC

Units of the US 1st Marine Division conduct a search-and-clear operation, code-name Taylor Common, ten miles (16.1 km) west of An Hoa in South Vietnam. An estimated 1,398 enemy are killed; American losses are 151 killed and 1,324 wounded by the time the operation ends on 8 Mar 1969.

21 DEC

The *Apollo 8* spacecraft carrying astronauts Col. Frank Borman, USAF, Comdr. James A. Lovell, Jr., USN, and Maj. William A. Anders, USAF, is launched on the first manned flight to escape earth gravity and enter lunar orbit. The spacecraft circles the moon and comes down in the Pacific in a pre-dawn splashdown on 27 Dec after a flight of 6 days, 3 hours. Helicopters from the carrier *Yorktown* (CVS 10) recover the astronauts and their capsule. This flight technically set an altitude record of 234,772 miles (377,828 km).

23 DEC

Attacking enemy base camps in An Xuyen Province, not previously attacked by naval forces, a task force of four PCF patrol boats supported by Army gunship helicopters destroy or damage 167 sampans, 125 structures, and eight bunkers.

1969

I JAN

The US Navy's large amphibious ships are redesignated from the A-series to L-series designations; thus amphibious command ships (AGC) become LCC; attack cargo ships (AKA) become amphibious cargo ships (LKA); attack transports (APA) become amphibious transports (LPA); and high-speed transports (APD) become amphibious transports (small) (LPR). US Navy Air Development Squadron (VX) 6, originally commissioned on 17 January 1955, is redesignated Antarctic Development Squadron (VXE) 6 specifically for Antarctic operations (Operation Deepfreeze). Air Development Squadron (VX) 8, originally part of Airborne Early Warning Training Unit, becoming VX-8 on 1 July 1967, is changed to Oceanographic Development Squadron (VXN) 8.

3 JAN

US Navy Light Attack Squadron (VAL) 4, the first squadron of its type, is commissioned at NAS North Island, San Diego, Calif., to operate the OV-10A Bronco COIN aircraft. Deploying to South Vietnam in Mar 1969, VAL-4 will support Navy "brown-water" operations.

13 JAN

Operation Bold Mariner, the largest amphibious assault of the Vietnam War, begins when more than 2,500 Marines from the Seventh Fleet land on the Batangan Peninsula, a Viet Cong stronghold ten miles (16.1 km) north of Quang Ngai City in the I Corps area. The operation is supported by gunfire from the battleship *New Jersey* (BB 62) and two destroyers. US Army and South Vietnamese troops are positioned inland in an attempt to trap the enemy on the peninsula. Some 12,000 Vietnamese are screened and 239 Viet Cong are killed during the operation.

14 JAN

The flight deck of the carrier *Enterprise* (CVAN 65) is racked by fire and explosions as the carrier steams some 70 n.miles (130 km) south of the Hawaiian island of Oahu. A rocket ignited on the flight deck during routine operations, firing into an armed aircraft. The fires are brought under control in 45 minutes. The disaster takes the lives of 27 men, injures 344, and destroys 15 aircraft.

In preparation for the first joining of two manned spacecraft in flight and the transfer of crew, the Soviet Union launches the *Soyuz 4* spacecraft carrying Lt. Col. Vladimir Shatalov, civilian engineer Alexei Yeliseyev, and Lt. Col. Yevgeny Khrunov. Their spacecraft, which will fly 2 days, 23 hours, 14 minutes in a 48-hour flight, will dock in space with *Soyuz 5*. The latter craft is carrying Lt. Col. Boris Volynov on a 3-day, 46-minute flight of 49 orbits. After the craft mate in space, Yeliseyev and Khrunov will transfer to the *Soyuz 5* and land in that vehicle on 18 Jan (the *Soyuz 4* lands on 17 Jan).

20 JAN

Richard M. Nixon, the third successive US president with prior naval service, is inaugurated. During World War II he was assigned to the Naval Air Transport Service, having received a direct commission as a lieutenant (j.g.). After training, he was sent to New Caledonia, a Pacific island that served as a landing site for US aircraft being ferried to Australia. In Oct 1945 he entered the Naval Reserve; he was a commander in the reserve in 1953 when he took office as Vice President under President Dwight D. Eisenhower. Prior to becoming vice president he served in the House of Representatives and Senate.

A sweep by the 9th Marine Regiment begins through the Da Krong valley in southwestern Quang Tri Province of South Vietnam. Known as Operation Dewey Canyon, it claims more than 1,600 communists killed during the sweep, which lasts until 19 Mar 1969.

25 JAN

Representatives of the United States and North Vietnam begin formal negotiations in Paris to end the Vietnam War.

31 JAN

The strength of US forces in Vietnam reaches a peak of 542,000 personnel "in country."

I FEB

Twenty-five US Navy river gunboats are transferred to the South Vietnamese Navy in the Mekong Delta.

3 FEB

The US strategic missile submarine *James Madison* (SSBN 627), the first of 31 Polaris missile submarines scheduled for conversion to carry the Poseidon C-3 missile, enters the General Dynamics/Electric Boat yard at Groton, Conn., for overhaul and conversion.

15 FEB
The habitat for the long-delayed SEALAB III seafloor living/research operation is lowered to the ocean floor off San Clemente, Calif. As the first US Navy aquanauts attempt to enter the habitat two days later, Navy civilian diver Berry Canon is killed. The project is aborted.

3 MAR
The *Apollo 9* spacecraft is launched from Cape Kennedy carrying Col. James A. McDivitt, USAF, Col. David R. Scott, USAF, and civilian Russell L. Schweikart (a USAF reserve officer). During their flight of 10 days, 1 hour, 1 minute, the astronauts are able to transfer to the attached lunar landing vehicle. After 151 orbits the *Apollo 9* and its crew come down to be recovered by helicopters from the carrier *Guadalcanal* (LPH 7).

5 MAR
The US carrier *Ticonderoga* (CVA 14) begins her fifth operational tour off Vietnam, the first carrier to do so.

15 MAR
The US 3rd Marine Regiment begins Operation Maine Crag, a search-and-clear operation six miles (9.7 km) south of Khe Sanh.

31 MAR
The battleship *New Jersey* leaves the gun line at the conclusion of a six-month tour off the coast of Vietnam.

The US 7th Marine Regiment launches Operation Oklahoma Hills, a search-and-clear operation southwest of Da Nang, South Vietnam. The operation lasts until 29 May 1969.

12 APR
The escort ship *Knox* (DE 1052) is commissioned, the first of a class of 48 ocean escort ships. This was the largest class of surface warships built in the West prior to the US *Oliver Hazard Perry* (FFG 7) class during the post–World War II era. The *Knox* design provides for the large AN/SQS-26 sonar as well as ASROC and helicopter facilities. The ship's first CO is Comdr. William A. Lamm, USN.

14 APR
An unarmed, four-engine US Navy EC-121 Warning Star electronic surveillance aircraft carrying a crew of 31 is shot down by North Korean aircraft over the Sea of Japan. The plane, which took off from Japan, disappears from US radar screens approximately 90 n.miles (167 km) southeast of Chongjin. An intensive air-sea search is mounted. There are no survivors.

18 APR
The US carrier *Bon Homme Richard* (CVA 31) begins her fifth tour off Vietnam.

20 APR
Task Force 71 is activated as a partial US response to the shoot-down of the EC-121. Initially TF 71 consists of the carriers *Hornet* (CVS 12), *Ticonderoga* (CVA 14), *Ranger* (CVA 61), and *Enterprise* with a cruiser-destroyer screen, all under the command of Rear Adm. Malcolm W. Cagle, USN.

26 APR
At the end of its demonstration, Task Force 71 passes through the Straits of Tsushima into the Yellow Sea and is soon deactivated.

5 MAY
US Marines join South Vietnamese and South Korean forces in an amphibious operation 20 miles (32.2 km) south of Da Nang, South Vietnam. The operation—known as Daring Rebel—terminates on Barrier Island on 20 May.

15 MAY
The US nuclear-propelled attack submarine *Guitarro* (SSN 665), being built at the San Francisco Bay Naval Shipyard in Vallejo, Calif., sinks at dockside in 35 feet (10.7 m) of water. The submarine flooded through a hatch left open by the negligence of workmen; no one was on board at the time of sinking. The submarine was subsequently raised and completed for service.

16 MAY
The US Coast Guard patrol boats *Point Garnet* (WPB 82310) and *Point League* (WPB 82304) are the first US Coast Guard cutters to be transferred to the South Vietnamese Navy.

18 MAY
Man's first flight to the moon is launched: The *Apollo 10* spacecraft carrying astronauts Col. Thomas P. Stafford, USAF, Capt. John W. Young, USN, and Comdr. Eugene A. Cernan, USN, are launched into lunar orbit. While Young remains with the command

module orbiting the moon, Stafford and Cernan are detached in the lunar landing vehicle *Snoopy* and come to within 9½ miles (15.1 km) of the moon. After the lander is recovered, the astronauts return to earth with recovery on 26 May by helicopters from the carrier *Princeton* (LPH 5). The flight lasts 8 days, 3 minutes and includes 1½ earth orbits and 31 moon orbits.

28 MAY

NATO establishes the Naval On-Call Force Mediterranean (NAVOCFORMED). (It will be replaced by the Standing Naval Force Mediterranean [STANAVFORMED] on 30 Apr 1992.)

1 JUNE

The South Vietnamese Navy assumes full responsibility for patrolling the Fourth Coastal Zone, which extends more than 400 n.miles (741 km) along the South China Sea and the Gulf of Thailand.

Lt. Col. R. Lewis, USMC, and Maj. C. L. Phillips, USMC, pilot an OV-10 Bronco to a world record of 2,539.8 miles (4,087.3 km) for a light turboprop aircraft. Their record flight is from Stephenville, Newfoundland, to Midenhall, England.

2 JUNE

Lt. Gen. Lewis W. Walt, USMC, Assistant Commandant of the Marine Corps, is promoted to full general. This is the first time in its history that the Marine Corps has been authorized two four-star officers. (Alexander A. Vandegrift became the first four-star Marine officer in Mar 1945.)

The US destroyer *Frank E. Evans* (DD 754) is struck and cut in two by the Australian aircraft carrier *Melbourne* in the South China Sea, approximately 650 n.miles (1,204 km) southwest of Manila. The two ships are engaged in a SEATO naval exercise. The bow section of the *Evans* sinks in two minutes with the loss of 74 of her 273 crewmen; the after section is quickly secured alongside the *Melbourne*. There are no Australian casualties.

8 JUNE

While meeting with South Vietnamese President Nguyen Van Thieu at Midway Island, President Nixon announces that 25,000 US combat troops will be withdrawn from Vietnam by 31 Aug 1969.

9 JUNE

A joint board of investigation composed of three American and three Australian naval officers begins hearings at Subic Bay Naval Base into the 2 June collision of the *Frank E. Evans* and *Melbourne*. The board will find that primary responsibility for the collision rests with the destroyer, but that the carrier was partly to blame. The *Evan's* captain and officer of the deck are court-martialed, found guilty of dereliction in the performance of duty, and reprimanded. The captain of the *Melbourne* is honorably acquitted by a Royal Australian Navy courtmartial.

24 JUNE

An advanced "hands off" arrested landing system is tested on the carrier *Saratoga* (CVA 60). The first plane to come aboard with the AN/SPN-42 system controlling the landing is an F-4 Phantom piloted by Lt. Dean Smith, USN. The system is an outgrowth of the AN/SPN-10 first tested in 1957 but not found to meet all fleet requirements.

30 JUNE

The Royal Air Force V-bomber force is taken off the strategic deterrent alert at 2400; the principal deterrent role is taken over by the Royal Navy's three strategic missile submarines at 0001 on 1 July. (The fourth SSBN, the *Revenge*, will be completed in Dec 1969; a planned fifth Polaris SSBN will not be built.) The submarines carry Polaris A-3 missiles.

12 JULY

The nuclear-propelled attack submarine *Narwhal* (SSN 671) is commissioned. The one-of-a-kind craft is similar to the *Los Angeles* (SSN 688) class, but has a natural-circulation (S5G) reactor plant to reduce pump noises at slow speeds. Her first CO is Comdr. Willis A. Matson III, USN.

16 JULY

The first flight to the surface of the moon begins with the launch of *Apollo 11* from Cape Kennedy carrying astronauts Neil A. Armstrong; Col. Edwin E. Aldrin, Jr., USAF; and Lt. Col. Michael Collins, USAF. Their lunar lander *Eagle* successfully detaches carrying Armstrong and Aldrin and lands on the surface of the moon; Armstrong descends to the moon's surface at 0256 GMT on 21 July, followed by Aldrin. The lander ascends to the command module *Columbia*, operated by Collins, and the astronauts return to earth with 48 pounds (21.8 kg) of moon rocks. After a flight of 8 days, 3 hours, 18 minutes (with the *Eagle* on the moon for 21 hours, 36 minutes) the craft comes down in the South Pacific on 24 July, to be recovered by the carrier

Hornet. The spacecraft flew 1½ earth orbits and 30 moon orbits. Armstrong and Aldrin walk on the moon eight years after President John F. Kennedy's promise that America would land a man on the moon before the end of the decade.

5 AUG
North Vietnam releases the first three American prisoners of war: Lt. Robert F. Frishman, USNR; Seaman Douglas B. Hegdahl, USN; and Capt. Wesley L. Rumble, USAF. Frishman, a pilot in Navy Attack Squadron (VA) 121, was shot down and captured on 24 Oct 1967; Seaman Hegdahl was captured on 6 Apr 1967 after falling overboard from the cruiser *Canberra* (CAG 2) in the Gulf of Tonkin. In a press conference at the Bethesda (Md.) Naval Hospital on 3 Oct 1969, they report that American prisoners are being beaten and tortured by the North Vietnamese.

21 AUG
Secretary of Defense Melvin Laird announces that up to $3 billion will be cut from defense expenditures for FY 1970. Part of the savings comes from the deactivation of more than 100 naval ships, including the battleship *New Jersey.*

16 SEP
President Nixon announces that 35,000 more troops will be withdrawn from Vietnam by 15 Dec 1969. This will include 5,200 Navy personnel and 18,500 Marines. The number of American forces remaining in Vietnam will be 484,000.

4 OCT
The US Chief of Naval Operations establishes the Underwater Long-range Missile System (ULMS) program. This will later be renamed as the Trident missile program.

10 OCT
Eighty US Navy PBRs are turned over to the South Vietnamese Navy. This is the largest single transfer to date and raises to 229 the total number of ships and craft turned over to the South Vietnamese since June 1968.

22 OCT
The US Naval Air Systems Command and the British government execute a memorandum of understanding whereby the Hawker-Siddely Harrier VSTOL aircraft will be procured for the US Marine Corps. The

aircraft will be given the US designation AV-8 with the British name Harrier being retained.

26 OCT
The US carrier *Coral Sea* (CVA 43) begins her fifth combat tour off Vietnam.

27 OCT
The nuclear-propelled submersible *NR-1* is placed in service. With a submerged displacement of 372 tons and an overall length of 136⁵⁄₁₆ feet (41.6 m), and manned by a crew of seven, the *NR-1* has an operating depth of approximately 3,000 feet (915 m). The *NR-1* was originally built as a test platform for a small submarine nuclear power plant, but subsequently has been employed as a deep-ocean research and recovery vehicle. Her first officer in charge is Lt. Comdr. Dwaine C. Griffith.

14 NOV
For the second lunar landing mission, the *Apollo 12* spacecraft is launched from Cape Kennedy with an all-Navy astronaut crew composed of Comdr. Charles C. Conrad, Comdr. Richard Gordon, and Lt. Comdr. Alan Bean. Conrad and Bean descend from the lunar-orbiting spacecraft to the moon's surface on 19 Nov and remain there for 31½ hours. The return flight leads to the spacecraft being recovered in the Pacific Ocean by the carrier *Hornet* on 24 Nov after a mission lasting 10 days, 4 hours, 36 minutes, having flown 1½ earth orbits and 45 moon orbits.

29 NOV
In the Mekong Delta, the US naval base at My Tho is turned over to the South Vietnamese Navy. This is the first naval base to be transferred.

15 DEC
President Nixon directs the withdrawal of another 50,000 from Vietnam, bringing the total ordered home in 1969 to 110,000.

17 DEC
The battleship *New Jersey* is decommissioned.

24 DEC
On Christmas Eve, Israeli Navy men "steal" five Saar-type missile boats (unarmed) from the French port of Cherbourg. The French-built craft, already paid for by Israel, were embargoed following the 1967 Middle East War. All five craft safely reach Israel on 31 Dec, having been replenished at sea by Israeli merchant ships.

1970

I JAN

US and South Vietnamese naval forces fight throughout New Year's night on the Saigon River, 25 miles (40.2 km) northwest of the city to defend a sunken South Vietnamese river patrol craft from Viet Cong swimmers. Later, 12 enemy dead are counted; the patrol craft is salvaged.

9 JAN

A US Navy Sealords patrol encounters enemy forces estimated at battalion strength in Tay Ninh Province of South Vietnam. Navy UH-1B Seawolf helicopters and OV-10 Bronco aircraft are called in to provide fire support. A total of 32 Viet Cong are killed in the action.

28 JAN

Near Vung Tau, in South Vietnam's III Corps area, the destroyer *Mansfield* (DD 728) heavily damages enemy positions while firing in close support of the 1st Australian Task Force.

3 FEB

Merchant shipping on the Long Tau River in the Rung Sat Special Zone of South Vietnam comes under enemy small arms and rocket fire for the first time in six months. No serious damage is done.

28 FEB

Eleven PCF fast patrol boats are transferred to the South Vietnamese Navy at Da Nang; South Vietnam takes over all coastal patrols operating off the country's five northern provinces.

5 MAR

The Non-Proliferation Treaty (NPT) on Nuclear Weapons, signed on 1 July 1968, comes into force.

7 MAR

The South Vietnamese Navy assumes control of Operation Tran Hung Dao I in the IV Corps area, which had been established in Feb 1969 to interdict the infiltration of enemy personnel and supplies from Cambodia.

14 MAR

The US Navy hospital ship *Repose* (AH 16) departs South Vietnam after four years of almost uninterrupted service in the combat area.

18 MAR

The left-leaning, neutralist Cambodian government of Prince Norodom Sihanouk is overthrown in a bloodless coup by Gen. Lon Nol, whose anti-communist stance attracts the sympathy of the Nixon Administration.

19 MAR

First flight of the Martin Marietta X-24A lifting-body research aircraft, designed to develop technology for Shuttle-type spacecraft that can re-enter the earth's orbit like an aircraft and land on conventional runways. The X-24A is rocket powered and is carried aloft and launched by a modified B-52.

20 MAR

The first NATO military communications satellite—designated *NATO 1*—is launched from Cape Kennedy, Fla.

28 MAR

The US destroyer *Orleck* (DD 886) damages or destroys 44 enemy structures while firing in support of the South Vietnamese 21st Infantry Division operations near Rach Gia in the IV Corps area. In the course of the week ending 3 Apr 1970, the *Orleck,* other Seventh Fleet destroyers, and the Coast Guard cutters *Dallas* (WHEC 716) and *Chase* (WHEC 718) hit 105 enemy structures, 48 bunkers, and 22 sampans.

II APR

Major Soviet task forces began deploying for Exercise Okean (Ocean), the largest peacetime naval operation in history. The month-long exercise will involve more than 200 surface ships and submarines plus hundreds of land-based aircraft. There are combinations of anti-carrier, amphibious assault, anti-submarine, and other exercises in the Northern Fleet and Pacific Fleet areas and the Mediterranean, with some ship movements in the Indian Ocean although the Soviets do not list that area in their pronouncements. As in previous exercises, submarines and intelligence ships deploy before the major task forces go to sea.

The lunar landing flight *Apollo 13* is launched from Cape Kennedy and experiences a near-catastrophic failure en route to the moon, 205,000 miles (329,915 km) from earth. Astronauts Capt. James A. Lovell, USN, and civilians Fred W. Haise, Jr., and John L.

Swigert, are able to return to earth after a flight of 5 days, 22 hours, 54 minutes. The are recovered by helicopters from the carrier *Iwo Jima* (LPH 2), having flown 1½ earth orbits and "looped" around the moon.

12 APR

The nuclear-propelled Soviet submarine *K-8* of the November class sinks in the Atlantic off Cape Finisterre, Spain. This is the first Soviet nuclear-propelled submarine to be lost at sea. The submarine suffered an engineering casualty while operating submerged on 11 Apr; she was able to surface and most of her crew was removed before the craft sank.

16 APR

The US and Soviet governments begin negotiations in Vienna known as the Strategic Arms Limitation Talks (SALT).

20 APR

President Richard M. Nixon announces plans to withdraw 150,000 US troops from Vietnam during the next 12 months. This will leave approximately 285,000 in the country.

29 APR

US and South Vietnamese forces launch spoiling attacks into six Communist staging areas, one only 33 miles (53.1 km) from Saigon, inside the Cambodian border. Large quantities of munitions and supplies are captured and destroyed in the operation that lasts until 30 June 1970.

4 MAY

The US invasion of Cambodia sparks anti-war demonstrations throughout the United States. At Kent State University, where the Ohio National Guard has been sent to maintain order after the burning of the Reserve Officers Training Corps (ROTC) building, a detachment of Guardsmen fire on a group of protesters. Four students and visitors are killed. The tragedy provokes a new wave of campus disorders. By the week's end, 450 colleges and universities are closed by student or faculty strikes.

5 MAY

A joint US–South Vietnamese Navy patrol of the Vam Co Dong and Vam Co Tay Rivers north of Saigon is turned over to the South Vietnamese in ceremonies at Ben Luc. Known as Operation Giant Slingshot, since its inception in Dec 1968, forces in the operation have engaged in 1,200 fire fights and killed an estimated 2,400 enemy troops.

6 MAY

A flotilla of 40 US Navy river patrol craft enters Cambodia on the Kham Span River, some 65 miles (104.6 km) northwest of Saigon. The craft come under fire less than two miles (3.2 km) inside the border.

8 MAY

A force of 100 US and South Vietnamese patrol craft move up the Mekong River into Cambodia. The US boats are to stay inside the 21¾-mile (35-km) limit President Nixon has established for the American penetration of Cambodia.

12 MAY

Operating in the Gulf of Thailand, US and South Vietnamese ships and craft establish a blockade of the Cambodian coastline west to Sihanoukville to prevent North Vietnamese and Viet Cong vessels from reaching Cambodia.

9 JUNE

Sikorsky pilot James R. Wright and copilot Col. Henry Hart, USMC, flying a Marine CH-53D Sea Stallion helicopter establish a New York to Washington, D.C., record of 156.43 mph (251.74 kmh) with an elapsed time of 1 hour, 18 minutes, 41 seconds from downtown to downtown. The next day they establish a New York to Boston record of 162.72 mph (115.86 kmh) with a time of 1 hour, 9 minutes, 24 seconds.

23 JUNE

The US Navy transfers 273 river patrol craft to the South Vietnamese Navy, bringing the total of ships and small craft turned over to 525. The 125 craft still being operated by the US Navy are scheduled for transfer in Dec 1970.

28 JUNE

The *James Madison* (SSBN 627) completes the first strategic missile submarine conversion to a Poseidon C-3 capability.

1 JULY

The nuclear-propelled merchant ship *Savannah* is removed from commercial service and is laid up at Savannah, Ga. She had steamed more than 454,000 n.miles (841,262 km) and visited ports in 25 countries outside of the United States. She carried 261,000 revenue tons of cargo from 1965 to 1970 earning about $11.7 million in revenues.

22 JULY

Sixty South Vietnamese are graduated from the US Navy's Officer Candidate School at Newport, R.I.

They are the first South Vietnamese to attend the school.

30 JULY
Immediately prior to becoming Chief of Naval Operations, Adm. Elmo R. Zumwalt, Jr., USN, declares that the United States has between a 45 and 55 percent chance of winning a conventional naval war with the Soviet Union. (In the spring of 1973, Adm. Zumwalt will estimate the probability of winning against the Soviet Navy as only 25 percent.)

1 AUG
The Military Sea Transportation Service (MSTS) is renamed the Military Sealift Command (MSC) to bring the name in line with the Air Force's Military Airlift Command (MAC). The Military Airlift Command, however, is a specified command within the Defense establishment while MSC remains a Navy command, reporting to the Chief of Naval Operations, with responsibilities for defense-wide transportation and special mission services.

3 AUG
The first submerged launching of the multi-warhead Poseidon C-3 missile is made by the ballistic missile submarine *James Madison* off Cape Kennedy. The launch is observed by the Soviet intelligence collection ship *Khariton Laptev.*

12 SEP
The Soviet Union launches the first unmanned spacecraft to land on the moon's surface and take off again to return samples to earth. The *Luna 16* was controlled from earth during its lunar activities and returned to earth on 24 Sep.

14 SEP
A Pentagon report places the strength of the South Vietnamese Navy at 35,000 plus 1,500 ships and craft, including 600 former US river patrol craft.

17 SEP
The US Navy announces plans to deactivate 58 ships, including the carrier *Shangri-La* (CVA 38). Together

with previous deactivations, these will raise the number of ships retired from active service since Jan 1969 to 286 units.

23 SEP
Chief of Naval Operations Adm. Zumwalt establishes the CNO Executive Panel to help provide "a clear understanding of the Navy's mission."

20 NOV
A US Army–Air Force commando force lands from helicopters 23 miles (37 km) west of Hanoi in an attempt to free American prisoners of war at Son Tay, North Vietnam. The prisoners had been moved from the area a few days earlier. There are no US casualties in the operation.

21 NOV
In response to attacks on US reconnaissace aircraft overflying North Vietnam, more than 200 US aircraft carry out strikes against North Vietnamese missile and anti-aircraft gun sites south of the 19th parallel. Navy aircraft from the carriers *Hancock* (CVA 16), *Oriskany* (CVA 34), and *Ranger* (CVA 61) participate with land-based USAF and Marine aircraft.

15 DEC
The US State Department announces that a $19 million naval communications facility will be constructed on the British island of Diego Garcia in the Indian Ocean.

21 DEC
First flight of the Grumman F-14A Tomcat carrier-based fighter. The aircraft has a variable-sweep wing and the advanced Phoenix air-to-air weapon system. It will replace the F-4 Phantom and F-8 Crusader to become the principal US carrier-based fighter.

31 DEC
The Tonkin Gulf Resolution, through which President Lyndon B. Johnson introduced US troops into Vietnam, is repealed by the House of Representatives; the Senate had approved repeal of the resolution on 24 June 1970. President Nixon signs the bill into law on 14 Jan 1971.

1971

4 JAN

President Richard M. Nixon states that if the Soviet Union services nuclear-propelled submarines in or from Cuban ports it risks creating an international crisis.

The Polish passenger liner *Stefan Batory* docks in New York City, the first Eastern bloc passenger ship to do so in 20 years.

6 JAN

The US Marine Corps accepts the first VSTOL aircraft for operational use by the US armed forces at Dunsfold, England. The AV-8A Harrier is intended for shipboard use in the light attack role.

8 JAN

Scheduled passenger ship service out of New York City ends with the final voyage of the SS *Santa Rosa,* a Prudential-Grace liner.

10 JAN

Cuba completes the erection of barbed wire fences around the US naval base at Guantanamo Bay.

22 JAN

A US Navy P-3C Orion maritime patrol aircraft sets a world turboprop flight distance record, flying 5,963 n.miles (11,049 km) in 15 hours, 21 minutes, flying the great circle route from Atsugi, Japan, to NAS Patuxent River, Md. (In order to avoid overflying the Soviet Union's Kamchatka Peninsula, the aircraft actually flies 6,095.6 n.miles (11,295 km). Comdr. Donald H. Lilienthal, USN, commanded the aircraft. On 23 Jan the P-3C will set a turboprop speed record of 501.44 mph (806.97 kmh) over the 15- to 25-km course, and on 4 Feb, Lilienthal's P-3C will set a world record for turboprop horizontal flight at an altitude of 45,018 feet (13,725 m). On 8 Feb he will set a series of turboprop aircraft climb records: 2 minutes, 51.7 seconds to 9,843 feet (3,000 m); 5 minutes, 46.3 seconds to 19,685 feet (6,000 m); 10 minutes, 26.1 seconds to 29,528 feet (9,000 m); and 19 minutes, 42.2 seconds to 39,370 feet (12,000 m). The aircraft will also maintain level flight at a record 46,214.5 feet (14,086.2 m).

27 JAN

The US Navy turns over eight river patrol boats to Cambodia, the first US combat craft to be given to Cambodia.

31 JAN

The third moon landing will be accomplished by the *Apollo 14* spacecraft, launched from Cape Kennedy with astronauts Capt. Alan B. Shepard, Jr., USN; Col. Stuart A. Roosa, USAF; and Maj. Edgar J. Mitchell, USAF. The craft's lunar module *Antares* lands Shepard and Mitchell on the moon. The spacecraft comes down in the South Pacific and is recovered by the helicopter carrier USS *New Orleans* (LPH 11) after a flight of 8 days, 22 hours, 2 minutes.

5 FEB

The US Navy announces the first successful firing of a Condor air-to-surface missile armed with a live warhead. However, the missile will not become operational.

8 FEB

South Vietnamese troops enter southern Laos to attack North Vietnamese forces on the Ho Chi Minh Trail in Operations Lam Son 719 and Dewey Canyon II.

11 FEB

Representatives of the United States and Soviet Union sign a treaty barring nuclear weapons from being intentionally placed on the ocean floor.

2 MAR

A US Navy spokesman announces that its first Reserve Officers Training Corps (ROTC) program in Florida will begin in the fall at Jacksonville State University as part of a Navy policy to increase the number of black officers.

5 MAR

Adm. Elmo R. Zumwalt, Jr., reorganizes the Office of the Chief of Naval Operations, including the establishment of Deputy Chiefs of Naval Operations (DCNO) for Air (OP-05), Surface (OP-3), and Submarine (OP-02) activities, all vice admirals. Previously the only "platform" DCNO was for Air (established in 1944).

6 MAR

An 80-knot-plus, 100-ton Surface Effect Ship (SES) is christened at Operation Bell Aerospace Division of Textron in New Orleans. The test craft program is a major phase in a US Navy effort to determine the feasibility of building and operating 100-knot, combat-configured surface effect ships of 4,000 to 5,000 tons.

9 MAR

Construction begins on the joint US-British naval air and communications complex on the Diego Garcia Atoll in the Indian Ocean. US Navy Mobile Construction Battalion 40 arrives later in the month to undertake the major portion of the work.

10 MAR

The US carriers *Ranger* (CVA 61) and *Kitty Hawk* (CVA 63) launch a one-day record of 233 strike sorties over North Vietnam.

16 MAR

First flight of the SH-2D LAMPS (Light Airborne Multi-Purpose System) helicopter. A program to convert 115 SH-2 Seasprite utility helicopters to the LAMPS I configuration is approved as the Navy seeks to improve the long-range detection and attack capability of anti-submarine ships.

18 MAR

Deputy Secretary of Defense David Packard testifies to a House Appropriations Defense subcommittee that the Soviet Union has reached "a rough overall parity" with the United States in strategic nuclear capacity.

29 MAR

Singapore Prime Minister Lee Kuan Yew says that a Soviet fleet in the Southeast Asian area could be a useful counterweight against both China and Japan.

First firing of an active AIM-9G variant of the Sidewinder missile from an NUH-2H Seasprite helicopter.

31 MAR

The strategic missile submarine *James Madison* (SSBN 627) departs Charleston, S.C., the first US submarine to deploy with the Poseidon C-3 missile fitted with multiple warheads. The patrol will last until 10 May 1971.

The Undersea Long-range Missile System (ULMS —later named Trident) Project Manager (PM-2) is established under the Chief of Naval Material. Polaris-Poseidon development was under the direction of the Special Project Office (SPO), later designated PM-1.

I APR

Helicopter Mine Countermeasures Squadron (HM) 12 is established at NAS Norfolk, Va., as the Navy's first squadron devoted exclusively to the mine countermeasures role. The squadron initially flies Marine CH-53A Sea Stallion helicopters.

19 APR

The Soviet Union launches the unmanned *Salyut 1*, the world's first orbiting space research station. On 7 June a spacecraft will dock with *Salyut 1* and transfer three crewmen who will operate the laboratory until 29 June. The *Salyut 1* will remain in orbit less than six months, being followed by similar manned space stations, the last *Salyut 7*, being placed in orbit on 19 Apr 1982; that 21-ton spacecraft will remain in orbit until early 1991.

21 APR

The Secretary of the Navy John H. Chafee announces the establishment of the Navy Recruiting Command as a field activity under the Chief of Naval Personnel.

28 APR

The Navy announces the selection of its first black admiral, Capt. Samuel L. Gravely, Jr., USN, and the first astronaut to be selected for flag rank, Capt. Alan B. Shepherd, Jr., USN. Shepherd, one of the original seven astronauts, was a member of the Mercury and Apollo programs, and was the first American in space.

22 MAY

The Soviet Union announces that a submarine and an auxiliary ship would visit Cuban ports later in May. The report states that the ships will take on supplies and give the crews liberty.

4 JUNE

The Washington Post reports that US satellite intelligence has detected what appears to be construction of China's first nuclear-propelled submarine.

II JUNE

Soviet leader Leonid Brezhnev offers to negotiate a mutual limitation of naval forces with the United States.

7 JULY

The US Navy retires its last active US Navy A-1 Skyraider piston-engine attack aircraft, an NA-1E research aircraft assigned to the Naval Air Test Center, Patuxent River, Md.

15 JULY

The first shipment of almost 13,000 tons of American poison gas weapons is removed from Okinawa.

26 JULY

The fourth US moon landing team is launched in Apollo *15* from Cape Kennedy. Astronauts Col. Alfred M. Worden, USAF; Col. David R. Scott, USAF; and Col. James B. Irwin, USAF, make the flight, with Scott and Irwin descending to the moon's surface in the lunar module *Falcon*. The astronauts are in flight for 11 days, 7 hours, 12 minutes, making 1½ orbits of the earth and 75 moon orbits. They land at sea in the Pacific and are recovered by helicopters from the carrier *Okinawa* (LPH 3) on 7 Aug 1971.

2 AUG

Secretary of State William P. Rodgers announces that the United States is changing its 21-year policy and will vote to admit the People's Republic of China to the United Nations.

8 AUG

The US Navy accepts its first Deep Submergence Rescue Vehicle (DSRV) from the Lockheed Missiles & Space Company. The craft is the first of two such submersibles that can rescue submarine survivors down to depths of 3,500 feet (1,066.8 m) that were developed in the aftermath of the sinking of the submarine *Thresher* (SSN 593) in 1963. The original DSRV program called for 12 submersibles, each with a capacity of 12 rescuees; the program was later changed to six craft with a 24-man capacity, but in the event only the DSRV-1 *Mystic* and DSRV-1 *Avalon* will be built.

31 AUG

The US Naval Station at Sangley Point in the Philippines is turned over to the Philippine government, marking the end of the 73-year US Navy presence in the Philippine Islands.

25 SEP

Full endurance trials of the Soviet Papa-type cruise missile submarine *K-162* begin. The trials for the submarine, which will last through 4 Dec 1971, include the craft achieving an underwater speed of 44.7 knots —still the world record for submarine speed. The one-of-a-kind nuclear submarine, completed in late 1969, was also the first to have a titanium hull.

6 OCT

The United States relinquishes the final portion of its former naval base in Trinidad, ending the 30-year American naval presence on the island.

8 OCT

About 100 officers and enlisted men and four CH-53 Sea Stallion helicopters are airlifted from NAS Norfolk, Va., and Charleston, S.C., to Suda Bay, Crete, by C-5 Galaxy transport aircraft in a demonstration of the long-range, quick-reaction capability of mine countermeasure helicopters. From 2 to 7 Nov 1971

the helicopters will operate in the Mediterranean from the landing ship *Coronado* (LPD 11).

29 OCT

Helicopter Sea Control Squadron (HS) 15 is commissioned at NAS Lakehurst, N.J. The only unit of its kind, HS-15 will operate from the helicopter carrier *Guam* (LPH 9) during a test of Sea Control Ship (SCS) concepts. Working with HS-15 will be AV-8A Harriers from Marine Attack Squadron (VMA) 513.

2 NOV

The first US Defense Satellite Communications System Phase II (DSCS II) satellites are launched in synchronous orbits by a Titan IIIC booster.

6 NOV

The Soviet publication *Soviet Diplomatichesky Slovar* (Diplomatic Lexicon), whose chief editor is Foreign Minister Andrei Gromyko, demands that the Baltic Sea be closed to the naval units of all non-Baltic powers.

7 NOV

US Navy Mobile Construction Battalion 5, the last Seabee unit to serve in South Vietnam, arrives at its home port of Port Hueneme, Calif.

DEC

The Soviet Navy completes the first Alfa-class submarine, a highly automated, high-speed (43 knots), deep-diving nuclear submarine. The prototype will have extensive technical problems and modifications, and will be scrapped about 1974. The Alfa prototype will be followed by six production SSNs, completed from 1979 to 1983.

1 DEC

The French Navy places in service the first of that country's strategic missile submarines, *Le Redoutable*. She will carry 16 M4 ballistic missiles. *Le Redoutable* is also the first French nuclear-propelled submarine to go to sea.

8 DEC

Australia becomes the first participating country to withdraw all of its combat troops from South Vietnam with the departure by ship of the 4th Battalion of the Royal Australian Rifles.

31 DEC

The 147-year-old rope walk at the Boston Naval Shipyard, at Charlestown, Mass., closes its doors. Authorized by President Andrew Jackson in 1834, it was the Navy's only rope-making facility. The Navy will now buy its rope from commercial firms.

1972

1 JAN

Warrant rank or *michman* is introduced in the Soviet Navy (equal to *praporshchik* in the other military services) to help counter the limitations of enlisted conscripts in a fleet that demands increasing technical competence. The program is open to qualified enlisted men under age 35 as well as to qualified civilians; most enlisted candidates have completed a term of service as a conscript, but some with sufficient prior training are recruited directly from "boot" camp to warrant military technical schools. (*Michman* was first introduced in the Russian Navy in 1716 and was used almost continuously until 1917 as the initial officer grade, corresponding to 2nd lieutenant in the army; the Soviet government reintroduced the rank of *michman* in the Navy on 30 Nov 1940 as the highest rank for petty officers).

5 JAN

The US Navy states that 500 gallons (1,893 liters) of slightly radioactive water were accidentally spilled into the Thames River near New London, Conn., during a routine transfer between two ships.

The New York Times reports that the United States has entered into an unpublicized agreement with the government of Bahrain to establish a permanent naval station there. Bahrain is a strategically located island nation in the Persian Gulf.

17 JAN

The New York Times reports that military analysts say the large ship under construction in a Soviet Black Sea shipyard may be the Soviet Union's first aircraft carrier.

18 JAN

The helicopter carrier *Guam* (LPH 9) begins the first in a series of Sea Control Ship (SCS) tests operating AV-8A Harrier VSTOL aircraft and SH-3 Sea King helicopters. Capt. Staser Holcomb, USN, is the ship's CO for the tests.

21 JAN

First flight of the Lockheed S-3A Viking carrier-based, anti-submarine aircraft. The turbojet aircraft will replace the S-2 Tracker piston-engine aircraft.

14 MAR

Turkish Premier Nihat Erim says his government will reopen Turkish ports to US Sixth Fleet ships. These

visits were halted in 1969, following the injury of several sailors in anti-American riots.

18 MAR

The escort ship *Jesse L. Brown* (DE 1089) is launched at Avondale Shipyards in New Orleans, La. This is the first US naval ship to be named after a black naval officer.

23 MAR

Secretary of Defense Melvin Laird suggests that Japan may have to establish a naval presence in the Indian Ocean to protect its Middle East oil supplies.

26 MAR

Following nine months of discussion over terms, Malta and Great Britain sign a seven-year defense agreement banning island facilities to Warsaw Pact nations. The agreement gives Malta an income of $35 million yearly, $13 million to be paid by Great Britain and the rest by other NATO nations.

31 MAR

North Vietnamese forces make a massive attack across the DMZ in what becomes known as the "Easter Offensive." President Richard M. Nixon orders a buildup of US naval forces off Vietnam and of B-52 bombers on Guam in preparation for large-scale US combat operations.

1 APR

The last US Navy combat unit is withdrawn from South Vietnam—Light Attack Squadron (VAL) 4 flying the OV-10A Bronco aircraft.

6 APR

For the first time since 1968, hundreds of US Navy and Air Force planes strike military targets in North Vietnam in a resumption of heavy air strikes. This is in retaliation for the invasion of South Vietnam by six North Vietnamese divisions.

F-4 Phantom fighters from Marine Fighter-Attack Squadrons (VMFA) 115 and 232 fly from Iwakuni, Japan, to Da Nang, South Vietnam, as part of the US support of South Vietnamese troops. In addition, F-4s of VMFA-212 from Kaneohoe, Hawaii, will arrive on 14 Apr.

14 APR

The Navy ends a week of intensive carrier strikes in support of South Vietnamese forces. An average of

191 sorties per day have been launched from the carriers *Hancock* (CVA 16), *Coral Sea* (CVA 43), *Kitty Hawk* (CVA 63), and *Constellation* (CVA 64).

16 APR
The *Apollo 16* spacecraft carrying astronauts Capt. John W. Young, USN, Lt. Comdr. Thomas K. Mattingly II, USN, and Lt. Col. Charles F. Duke, Jr., USAF, are launched from Cape Kennedy on the fifth US moon mission. Young and Duke descend to the moon's surface in the lunar module *Orion* to undertake astronomical observations. The spacecraft returns to earth after a flight of 11 days, 1 hour, 50 minutes, coming down in the Pacific on 27 Apr, with the primary recovery ship being the carrier *Ticonderoga* (CVA 14).

27 APR
Capt. Alene Buertha Duerk (Nurse Corps), USN, is among 50 captains selected for promotion to rear admiral. She will be the US Navy's first female flag officer.

28 APR
First launch of a Phoenix air-to-air missile from an F-14 Tomcat occurs off the California coast.

4 MAY
The US Defense Department states that a Soviet diesel-electric submarine of the Golf class armed with three ballistic missiles recently entered a port of Cuba's north coast. The submarine is accompanied by a destroyer and a submarine tender.

5 MAY
The US Navy's 100th nuclear-propelled submarine, the *Silversides* (SSN 679), is commissioned at Groton, Conn. Her first CO is Comdr. John E. Allen, USN.

8 MAY
Operation Pocket Money, the mining campaign against North Vietnam ports, begins as aircraft from the carriers *Coral Sea* and *Kitty Hawk* strike targets in North Vietnam. Three Marine A-6A Intruders and six Navy A-7E Corsairs from the *Coral Sea* mine the outer approaches of Haiphong Harbor. Each aircraft carrier lays four Mk 52-2 mines. It required only two minutes for the planes to lay their "strings" of 36 mines. The mines were programmed to arm 72 hours after being laid to permit foreign merchant ships to safely leave North Vietnam ports. Over the next eight months more than 11,000 Mk 36 Destructor and 108 Mk 52-2 mines will be planted along the North Vietnamese coast.

Rear Adm. Rembrandt C. Robinson, USN, Commander Cruiser-Destroyer Flotilla 11, is killed in a helicopter crash in the Tonkin Gulf. He is the only US Navy flag officer killed in the Vietnam War.

In the second most active aerial combat day of the Vietnam War, Navy carrier-based F-4 Phantoms shoot down two MiG-17 and two MiG-21 fighters. Navy pilots from the carriers *Coral Sea* and *Kitty Hawk* score the kills, two per ship.

10 MAY
In the most intensive day of aerial combat in the Vietnam War, Navy F-4 Phantoms shoot down eight MiG fighter aircraft. The kills are scored by planes from the carriers *Coral Sea* (one) and *Constellation* (seven).

Lt. Randy Cunningham, USN, and Lt. (jg) William Driscoll, USN, flying an F-4 Phantom shoot down three MiGs to become the first MiG aces of the war. However, after scoring their third kill of the day their plane is hit by a surface-to-air missile; both fliers eject over the Gulf of Tonkin and are rescued. (A total of 41 MiG fighters were believed to have been airborne during the day.)

13 MAY
US Marine CH-46 Sea Knight and CH-53 Sea Stallion helicopters based aboard the helicopter carrier *Okinawa* (LPH 3) lift 1,000 South Vietnamese marines from a landing area near Hue to an area 24 miles (38.6 km) behind North Vietnamese lines.

14 MAY
The island of Okinawa is returned to Japanese administrative control after approval by the US Senate and the Japanese Diet. The agreement for return of Okinawa was reached in November 1969 at a meeting between Prime Minister Eisaku Sato and President Nixon.

16 MAY
Secretary of Defense Laird approves a Navy proposal to rename the ULMS program the Trident program.

17 MAY
US Marine Attack Squadrons (VMA) 211 and 311, both flying A-4 Skyhawks, arrive from Japan at the reactivated air base at Bien Hoa, South Vietnam.

22 MAY
President Nixon arrives in Moscow, the first US President to visit the Soviet Union. Mr. Nixon had previously visited the Soviet Union in 1959 while the vice president.

25 MAY

Secretary of the Navy John W. Warner and Commander in Chief of the Soviet Navy Adm. of the Fleet of the SU Sergei G. Gorshkov sign the Incidents at Sea Agreement in Moscow. The agreement seeks to prevent accidents involving the two navies.

26 MAY

Representatives of the United States and the Soviet Union sign the interim SALT, an agreement on Anti-Ballistic Missile (ABM) systems in Moscow. The SALT agreement sets limits on numbers of land-based and submarine-launched missiles each country may have. (No curbs are placed on strategic bombers.)

1 JUNE

The US Navy announces that the Greek government has approved the assignment of Navy personnel and their families to home ports in Greece. The Navy plans to base an aircraft carrier and a modified hospital ship in Greek ports. In the event, only the carrier will not be based in a Mediterranean port, and the hospital ship—serving as a dependent's support ship—will be at Pireaus only briefly.

28 JUNE

President Nixon orders that, from this date, no draftees will be sent to Vietnam unless they volunteer for duty there.

12 JULY

A Navy UH-2C Seasprite helicopter begins a three-day demonstration of the feasibility of launching Sparrow III air-to-air missiles against surface targets. Four missiles are fired during the demonstration.

18 JULY

Egyptian President Anwar Sadat orders the immediate withdrawal of Soviet military advisors from Egypt. He also places Soviet bases and equipment under the exclusive control of Egyptian forces.

23 JULY

The first US Earth Resources Technology Satellite (ERTS A) is launched; it will later be renamed *Landsat 1.*

31 JULY

Commandant of the Marine Corps Gen. Robert E. Cushman, Jr., USMC, orders an end to the "voluntary segregation" by race of Marines' living quarters at shore bases and aboard ships.

3 AUG

The US Senate approves, by a vote of 88 to 2, the treaty with the Soviet Union that limits each nation to two Anti-Ballistic Missile (ABM) sites. (The Soviet Union will establish one ABM system, around Moscow; the United States does not deploy an ABM system.)

8 AUG

A US Navy spokesman announces that the service will send women to sea as regular ship's crew for the first time in history. The sea-going assignments will be in auxiliary ships. Previously women served only in hospital ships and transports carrying military dependents.

11 AUG

The first US Navy women other than nurses to be assigned to ships are named: Ens. Rosemary E. Nelson, USN, is named to become the assistant supply officer, and Lt. (jg) Ann Kerr, USN, will become personnel officer on board the hospital ship *Sanctuary* (AH 17).

18 AUG

The ballistic missile submarine *Ulysses S. Grant* (SSBN 631) launches four Poseidon C-3 missiles in the first quadruple missile launch by a US submarine. Previously the largest number of SLBM launches in a single day from a US submarine was two.

28 AUG

President Nixon and Secretary of Defense Laird announce that there will be no further draft calls after 30 June 1973.

The first USAF fighter aces of the Vietnam War, Capt. Steve Ritchie, USAF, and his radar operator Capt. Charles DeBellevue, USAF, flying an F-4 Phantom, gain their fifth and sixth MiG kills. This is more than three months after the first Navy aces score their fifth kill. (*See* 10 May 1972.)

11 SEP

The only Marine aviators to score a MiG kill in the Vietnam War are Maj. Less Lasseter, USMC, and his radar intercept officer, Capt. John Cummings, USMC, flying an F-4 Phantom. They shoot down a MiG north of Hanoi while flying from the carrier *America* (CVA 66). After the kill the fliers abandon their damaged aircraft and are rescued.

14 SEP

NATO's largest land, sea, and air exercise yet conducted—Operation Strong Express—begins. Lasting until 28 Sep, it involves more than 50,000 personnel and 300 ships from 11 NATO nations, including France.

25 SEP

The House of Representatives approves and sends to the White House an interim US-Soviet agreement to freeze a major part of their nuclear arsenals for a period of five years. This agreement clears the way for a second round of talks (SALT II), which are expected to begin later in 1972.

3 OCT

President Nixon and Soviet Foreign Minister Andrei Gromyko sign documents putting into effect the nuclear arms limitation agreements reached at the Moscow summit.

6 OCT

Secretary of Transportation John A. Volpe says that women will enter the US Coast Guard officer candidate program in 1973 for the first time since World War II.

12 OCT

Racial rioting breaks out on the carrier *Kitty Hawk,* en route from the Philippines to the Gulf of Tonkin. The troubles began about 2000 when a young black sailor, summoned to the ship's investigative office, brought nine friends with him and refused to answer questions. Returning to their spaces, the men beat up a white mess attendant, leading to rampaging and looting that lasted until 0500 on 13 Oct. Sixty men were injured, three of whom required evacuation to hospitals ashore. At 0758 the ship commenced air strikes against North Vietnam. This was the most serious of several instances of racial disturbances in the Navy in this period.

14 OCT

The United States and the Soviet Union sign a three-year maritime agreement to open 40 ports in each nation to civilian-manned ships from each country. Ships must give four days notice prior to arrival.

16 OCT

Secretary of the Navy Warner says that women will soon be able to fly naval aircraft as part of the Navy's equal opportunity program. However, they will not be permitted to fly combat aircraft.

A dozen black sailors on the US fleet oiler *Has-*

sayampa (AO 145), dock at Subic Bay in the Philippines, tell the ship's executive officer they will not sail at 1600 as scheduled, and accused unnamed white sailors of stealing money from them. That afternoon white sailors were assaulted by several blacks, with five sailors requiring medical treatment. A Marine detachment restored order. At 2115 the *Hassayampa* puts to sea.

17 OCT

First test flight of the US Navy's Harpoon anti-ship missile. The weapon will enter service in 1977 and become the most widely used anti-ship missile in the West. It was originally developed to attack Soviet cruise missile submarines while on the surface.

23 OCT

The United States ends all tactical air sorties over North Vietnam above the 20th parallel, bringing a close to the Linebacker I operations.

15 NOV

The first agreements to permit US-flag ships to carry grain to the Soviet Union are signed.

21 NOV

Negotiations between the US and Soviet governments for a SALT II accord begin in Geneva.

7 DEC

Apollo 17—the last US lunar flight and sixth moon mission—is launched from Cape Kennedy. Manned by astronauts Capt. Eugene A. Cernan, USN, Comdr. Ronald E. Evans, USN, and civilian geologist Harrison H. Schmidt, their lunar module *Challanger* lands Cernan and Schmidt on the moon. After a flight of 12 days, 13 hours, 52 minutes, the astronauts come down in the Pacific on 19 Dec. The carrier *Ticonderoga* is the recovery ship.

11 DEC

The governments of Australia and New Zealand announce details of their plans for final withdrawal of their forces in South Vietnam.

18 DEC

Linebacker II bombing operations are initiated over North Vietnam when negotiations in Paris between the US and North Vietnamese governments stall. Massive strikes will be conducted by USAF B-52s and F-111s as well as carrier aircraft. The Navy flies 505 sorties from the carriers *Oriskany* (CVA 34), *Saratoga* (CVA 60), *Ranger* (CVA 61), and *Enterprise* (CVAN 65) before the strikes are halted on 29 December when the peace talks resume. (Bad weather was a limiting factor in the Linebacker II operation.)

30 DEC
President Nixon announces the halt of aerial bombing and naval bombardment of North Vietnam above the 20th parallel as well as the resumption of private peace negotiations in Paris.

1973

3 JAN

The North Vietnamese delegation to the Paris peace talks says Hanoi has agreed to resume negotiations with the United States because of the cessation of bombing and mining above the 20th parallel.

8 JAN

A USAF F-4D Phantom downs a MiG-21 over North Vietnam, the last Air Force MiG "kill" of the war. (*See* 12 Jan 1973.)

11 JAN

Soviet maritime officials say that one of the first US ships bringing American grain to the Soviet Union will sail back with the first Russian oil to be imported by the United States since the end of World War II.

12 JAN

A Navy F-4 Phantom from the carrier *Midway* (CVA 41) downs a MiG-21 over North Vietnam, the last kill by a US aviator in the Vietnam War. (A *Midway* fighter had shot down the first MiG downed in the war; *see* 17 June 1965.) During the war 58 MiG fighters were shot down by Navy carrier pilots and one by a Marine flying from the carrier *America* (CVA 66); land-based Air Force fighters shot down 135 MiG-type aircraft and B-52 tail guns were credited with two MiGs. Several additional MiGs are downed by US ship-launched Terrier and Talos missiles.

23 JAN

The US and Japanese governments announce a major consolidation of American military bases in Japan. US officials say that the agreement will keep large US bases and forces in Japan for at least five more years.

US Secretary of State Dr. Henry A. Kissinger and North Vietnam's chief negotiator Le Duc Tho initial the Paris agreement on Ending the War and Restoring Peace in Vietnam ". . . to end the war and bring peace with honor in Vietnam and Southeast Asia." Under terms of the accord, all American prisoners of war will be released, and the remaining 23,700-man American force in South Vietnam will be withdrawn within 60 days.

27 JAN

A US–North Vietnamese ceasefire goes into effect.

Operation Homecoming begins with 591 US pris-

oners of war being released through 1 Apr 1973 (of those, 566 were military personnel, the remainder civilians).

US Navy Task Force 78 is formed under the command of Rear Adm. Brian McCauley, USN, to conduct minesweeping operations in North Vietnamese waters under the code-name Endsweep. The US force consists of surface ships and Navy Helicopter Mine Countermeasures Squadron (HM) 12 and Marine squadrons, all employing CH-53 Sea Stallion helicopters.

Secretary of Defense Melvin Laird sends the following message to the service secretaries: "With the signing of the peace agreement in Paris . . . I wish to inform you that the Armed Forces henceforth will depend exclusively on volunteer soldiers, sailors, airmen, and Marines. Use of the draft has ended."

28 JAN

Aircraft from the US carriers *Ranger* (CVA 61) and *Enterprise* (CVAN 65) fly 81 combat sorties on the first day of the Vietnam ceasefire against communists targets in Laos. The corridor for these overflights of South Vietnam are between Hue and Da Nang. The strikes are flown in support of the Laotian government, which had requested US assistance. Later the carriers *Oriskany* (CVA 34) and *Constellation* (CVA 64) will fly strikes against Laotian targets and, in late Feb 1973, these ships will also fly missions over Cambodia.

1 FEB

The US Third Fleet is reactivated at Pearl Harbor with the merger of the First Fleet and Anti-Submarine Warfare Forces, Pacific Fleet. The Third Fleet has responsibility for Pacific operations from the US West Coast to beyond Midway Island.

2 FEB

The National Aeronautics and Space Administration (NASA) announces that it will cooperate during February with the Soviet Academy of Sciences in a joint study of the Bering Sea. Aircraft and ships are to be used to measure surface and atmospheric conditions and sea ice.

3 FEB

The Task Force 78 flagship *New Orleans* (LPH 11) and other ships and helicopters begin a six-day mine countermeasures exercise in Subic Bay, Philippines, in preparation for Operation Endsweep.

5 FEB
The first meeting is held between military representatives of the US Navy and North Vietnam to discuss US minesweeping efforts—Operation Endsweep—in the North. The session is held in Haiphong.

7 FEB
Following the Commonwealth Senate, the Puerto Rican House of Representatives unanimously adopts a resolution demanding immediate withdrawal of the US Navy from Culebra and Vieques, two small offshore islands used by the US Navy for gunnery and amphibious training.

13 FEB
A Soviet official in Moscow says that the Soviet Union has delivered its first shipload of postwar aid to North Vietnam despite US mines still blocking the port of Haiphong.

16 FEB
The Navy announces that a $550-million Trident submarine base will be built at Keyport, Wash., on Puget Sound near Bangor, Wash.

21 FEB
The New York Times reports that Iran has contracted to buy more that $2 billion in military equipment from the United States. Defense Department officials call it the biggest single arms deal ever arranged by the Pentagon.

27 FEB
The US Navy begins airborne mine countermeasures efforts off the port of Haiphong. However, all operations are abruptly halted and the minesweeping task force moves to sea as President Richard M. Nixon calls for "clarification . . . on a most urgent basis" of Hanoi's delay in releasing American prisoners of war.

1 MAR
The Navy's SES-100B Surface Effect Ship (SES) reaches a speed of more than 70 knots during a test run on Lake Pontchartrain at New Orleans, La. This is a world record for this type of craft.

4 MAR
US minesweeping operations resume off Haiphong.

13 MAR
The Department of Defense announces that the first ship to enter Haiphong Harbor since it was mined in

May 1972 is a Soviet freighter carrying flour that enters the port without incident.

20 MAR
An eight-ship convoy, carrying gasoline, ammunition, and food, arrives in Phenom Phen, Cambodia, after sailing up the Mekong River under the protection of US aircraft.

28 MAR
The London-based International Institute for Strategic Studies (IISS) estimates that the Vietnam War has cost the United States more the $108 billion in military aid and expenditures. The IISS estimates that aid to the North Vietnam from the Soviet Union and China to have been $1.66 billion and $670 million, respectively.

29 MAR
The remaining US combat forces depart South Vietnam and the US Military Assistance Command Vietnam is disbanded, ending US military involvement in South Vietnam.

5 APR
A bomb severely damages the living quarters of 13 US Marines assigned to the American Embassy in Rome. There are no injuries.

19 APR
The US Navy announces suspension of all minesweeping operations along the coast of North Vietnam, and charges that Hanoi was violating terms of the ceasefire agreement.

28 APR
The US submarine rescue ship *Pigeon* (ASR 21) is placed in commission. The *Pigeon* and her sister ship *Ortolan* (ASR 22) are built to a catamaran (twin-hull) design to support Deep Submergence Rescue Vehicles (DSRVs) and deep-diving operations, part of the Navy's rescue and salvage program developed after the 1963 loss of the *Thresher* (SSN 593). The original deep-submergence plan called for six such ships.

30 APR
The last US Marine enlisted Naval Aviation Pilot (NAP) on active duty is retired. Master Gunnery Sgt. Patrick J. O'Neil had served on active duty for 30 years.

11 MAY
Prime Minister Lee Kuan Yew of Singapore suggests, in a Tokyo news conference, that the United States,

Australia, and Japan, form a naval task force to counter Soviet influence in the Indian Ocean and western Pacific.

The NATO Standing Naval Force Channel (STANAVFORCHAN) is activated.

14 MAY

The Supreme Court rules that female members of the armed forces are entitled to the same dependency benefits for their husbands as male servicemen receive for their wives.

The 118-foot (35.9-m) unmanned US *Skylab 1* orbiting laboratory is launched into earth orbit from Cape Kennedy. NASA officials announce that a set of solar panels failed to deploy on the space laboratory, causing the delay in the launching of the Apollo spacecraft that would have carried an all-Navy crew on a 28-day mission in the space laboratory. (*See* 25 May 1973.)

18 MAY

President Nixon marks Armed Forces Day with a speech attacking North Vietnam for not accounting for Americans missing in action and congressional doves for cutting the defense budget. The speech is delivered at the Norfolk (Va.) Naval Station.

20 MAY

In a move to counter the British decision to send warships to protect British trawlers in disputed Icelandic waters, Iceland's premier bans all British military planes from landing at the NATO airfield at Keflavik.

23 MAY

Iceland extends the 20 May ban on British military aircraft to all Icelandic airports and airspace.

25 MAY

After a ten-day delay, the all-Navy US *Skylab 2* crew is launched into space for a 28-day mission aboard the first US orbiting space laboratory. The astronauts Capt. Charles C. Conrad, USN, Comdr. Joseph P. Kerwin, USN, and Comdr. Paul J. Weitz, USN, repaired damage to the *Skylab* caused during its launch, and conducted experiments in the weightless environment. They come down on 22 June 1973, in the Pacific Ocean and are recovered by helicopters from the carrier *Ticonderoga* (CVA 14).

13 JUNE

The Hughes Aircraft Co. claims a distance record for an air-to-air missile kill: 126 n.miles (233.4 km) by a Phoenix missile fired from an F-14 Tomcat fighter.

25 JUNE

Rear Adm. James B. Stockdale, USN, a former North Vietnamese prisoner of war, files misconduct charges against two other former prisoners, Capt. Walter E. Wilbur, USN, and Lt. Col. Edison W. Miller, USMC.

26 JUNE

US Marines raise the American flag over the US liaison office in Peking, China, as it formally opens for business.

Two Greek ships, one of which later sinks, are reported to have hit mines in Tripoli Harbor during the past week. The mines were reportedly planted by the Libyan government to protect the port from possible Israeli attacks.

30 JUNE

The largest merchant ship ever built in the United States, the 230,000-deadweight-ton, 1,094-foot (333.5-m) tanker *Brooklyn,* is launched at the former naval shipyard in Brooklyn, N.Y., which is now is operated by Seatrain Shipbuilding Corp.

2 JULY

The first female chaplain in the US military services, Florence Dianna Pohlman, is sworn into the Navy.

6 JULY

The fastest Pacific crossing on record is achieved by the container ship *SeaLand Commerce* in 6 days, 1 hour, 27 minutes from Yokohama, Japan, to Long Beach, Calif., a distance of 4,840 n.miles (8,968.5 km); her average speed was 33.27 knots.

22 JULY

A US Navy spokesman reports that racial fighting among black and white sailors occurred on board the carrier *Franklin D. Roosevelt* (CVA 42) while the ship was in the Caribbean.

24 JULY

Maj. Edward W. Leonard, Jr., USAF, files mutiny charges against seven Army and Marine enlisted men who were prisoners of war in North Vietnam.

27 JULY

The US Navy's Operation Endsweep ends and Task Force 78 is disbanded. During six months of operation, the helicopter mine countermeasures effort made 3,554 sweep runs totaling 1,134.7 sweeping hours in 623 sorties. The surface craft made 208 sweep runs of 308.8 hours' duration.

28 JULY

The *Skylab 3* team consisting of astronauts Capt. Alan Bean, USN, Maj. Jack Lousma, USMC, and civilian Dr. Owen Garriott is launched into space from Cape Kennedy to rendezvous with the orbiting space laboratory. The three *Skylab 3* astronauts make a successful splashdown in the Pacific on 25 Sep 1973, ending a record 59-day flight in the orbiting *Skylab* laboratory. Bean, the commander of the team, sets a new aggregate record for US space flight, eclipsing the previous record of 49 days, 3 hours, 37 minutes set by Capt. Charles C. Conrad, USN.

31 JULY

Light Helicopter Anti-Submarine Squadron (HSL) 33, the Navy's first squadron dedicated to providing Light Airborne Multi-Purpose System (LAMPS) helicopters to surface warships, is commissioned at NAS Imperial Beach, Calif. The squadron flies the SH-2D helicopter.

8 AUG

The first Soviet tanker to moor in the United States in 25 years arrives in Delaware City, Del., with 320,000 barrels (48,265 tons) of Egyptian crude oil.

10 AUG

The Polaris missile is phased out of US Navy service in the Atlantic-Mediterranean area with the transfer of the submarine *Robert E. Lee* (SSBN 601) to the Pacific. Four British SSBNs continue to operate in the Atlantic with the Polaris A-3 missile (fitted with British warheads).

15 AUG

All American offensive operations in Southeast Asia end with the halt in US bombing of targets in Cambodia, as voted by Congress on 30 June 1973.

17 AUG

Secretary of Defense James R. Schlesinger says that the Soviet Union has successfully flight tested a Multiple Independently targeted Re-entry (MIRV) warhead system comparable to those of the United States.

25 AUG

Ship traffic through the Panama Canal comes to a near halt as 96 American canal pilots strike because of a labor dispute with the Panama Canal Co., an American firm.

29 AUG

US Navy Helicopter Mine Countermeasures Squadron (HM) 12 receives the first specialized RH-53D Sea Stallion helicopters. They are configured to tow various mine countermeasures devices.

1 SEP

The last squadron of US Marine F-4 Phantoms on the Asian mainland departs Thailand. This squadron is also the last Marine combat unit to leave, ending an 11-year US military commitment to Indochina.

7 SEP

The US government seizes the Soviet research ship *Belogorsk* at Woods Hole, Mass. The seizure is a result of a suit brought by a lobster firm in 1971 for damages to lobster lines.

26 SEP

The Center for Women's Policy Studies, a national women's rights group, files a class action suit to force the Naval and Air Force Academies to admit women.

27 SEP

Secretary of the Navy John W. Warner dismisses mutiny and other misconduct charges against one Navy and one Marine officer. He does, however, issue letters of censure for ". . . failing to meet the standards expected of officers." Both men will be retired ". . . in the best interests of the naval service."

2 OCT

British Minister of Defence Lord Carrington warns that the Soviet naval buildup could give it the dominance of the seas that the British fleet had possessed in the 19th Century.

5 OCT

Secretary of the Navy Warner dismisses charges of misconduct against two enlisted Marines while they were prisoners of war in North Vietnam.

The US carrier *Midway* with embarked Carrier Air Wing 5 arrives at Yokosuka, Japan, the first homeporting of a US carrier in a foreign port. (Plans to similarly base a carrier in Greece are dropped.)

6 OCT

Fighting breaks out between Israel and Egypt and Syria, beginning with a surprise crossing of the Suez Canal by Egyptian forces to assault Israeli positions in the Sinai. Liberty for the US Sixth Fleet is canceled, but the Navy says that no American ships have been ordered to the conflict area. The conflict is termed the Yom Kippur War because the Arab states attack Israeli on the holiest Jewish holiday, Yom Kippur (the day of atonement).

13 OCT

The USAF Military Airlift Command (MAC) begins the airlift of high-priority munitions to Israel.

15 OCT

The US government announces that it has begun re-supplying Israel with military equipment to prevent a "massive airlift" by the Soviet Union to Egypt and Syria from upsetting the military balance in the Middle East.

Two Soviet warships arrive at Taranto, Italy, in the first visit of Soviet naval units to an Italian port since World War II.

19 OCT

President Nixon asks Congress for $2.2 billion in emergency military aid for Israel, to maintain the military balance and achieve stability in the Middle East.

US Navy pilots begin ferrying A-4 Skyhawk attack aircraft from the United States to Israel. The aircraft stage through the Azores and the US carrier *Franklin D. Roosevelt,* located south of Sicily. NATO nations will not allow the jets to refuel at their bases, except for Portugal's permission to use the Azores.

20 OCT

The Middle East state of Bahrain cancels an agreement providing mooring and other facilities to the US Navy because of US support of Israel in the Middle East War.

23 OCT

Israel and Egypt accept a ceasefire sponsored by the United States and the Soviet Union. By this time Israeli forces have pushed back the Syrian and Egyptian forces and destroyed or encircled most of the surviving Egyptian army.

24 OCT

President Nixon orders all US armed forces to increase their readiness posture to Defense Condition Three in response to Soviet moves in the Middle East crisis.

26 OCT

Secretary of Defense Schlesinger announces that the United States has begun removing some forces from Defense Condition Three.

30 OCT

Nineteen countries from the Atlantic Alliance and the Warsaw Pact begin negotiations in Vienna in an effort to reduce forces in Central Europe. The conference is known as the Mutual and Balanced Force Reductions (MBFR).

The US Department of Defense ends the world-wide military alert for all units except the Sixth Fleet in the Mediterranean.

13 NOV

The press reports that five major international oil refineries in Singapore have been directed to stop all sales to US Navy ships or ships chartered by the Navy. A. J. Hurlton, chairman and managing director of the Mobil refinery in Singapore, is quoted as saying: "The Singapore government has directed that oil will not be sold to countries embargoed by the Arabs. The US is included in this."

15 NOV

The US destroyer *Johnston* (DD 821) steams out of Philadelphia following modification to be the first ship in history to use coal-derived oil to power her engines. The project is called Seacoal.

16 NOV

The *Skylab 4* team commanded by Lt. Col. Gerald P. Carr, USMC, and carrying Lt. Col. William R. Pogue, USAF, and civilian Edward G. Gibson is launched from Cape Kennedy. The astronauts will board the *Skylab* orbiting laboratory to study the Comet Kohoutek, the sun, and earth resources. The mission is scheduled for 56 days but is considered to be "open ended." The astronauts come down in the Pacific after a record-setting 84-day orbital flight in the *Skylab* laboratory. They were recovered by the helicopter carrier *New Orleans* (LPH 11).

19 NOV

The Department of Defense says that the US Sixth Fleet has been taken off an alert and returned to "normal training condition" status.

21 NOV

It the first test of a full load-out of six Phoenix air-to-air missiles, an F-14 Tomcat operating over the Pacific missile test range launches all six weapons and guides them to six separate targets 50 n.miles (93 km) away; four are direct hits.

3 DEC

Vice Adm. H. G. Rickover, USN (Ret.), head of the Navy's nuclear-propulsion program, is promoted to full admiral.

5 DEC

The Marine Corps changes its regulations to allow women to command units made up mostly of men; it is the last US military service to do so.

6 DEC

President Nixon signs a bill calling for the full integration of women into the Coast Guard. The bill eliminates all discriminatory laws and creates a single Coast Guard Reserve of both male and female members.

10 DEC

Col. Mary E. Bane, USMC, is named commanding officer of Headquarters and Service Battalion at Camp Pendelton, Calif. She is the first woman in the Marine Corps to be given direct command over men. (*See* 5 Dec 1973.)

19 DEC

The cargo ship *Mason Lykes* sails from Baltimore, Md., en route to the Black Sea port of Odessa, to become the first American-flag cargo ship to call at a Soviet port in more than a decade.

20 DEC

Two women physicians, Lt. Jane O. McWilliams, USN, and Lt. Victoria M. Voge, USN, graduate from the Naval Flight Surgeon Training Program, to become the first women naval flight surgeons.

1974

9 JAN

The US and Australian governments announce an agreement whereby the United States will turn control of the naval communications installation at North West Cape in western Australia over to the Australian Navy.

10 JAN

Secretary of Defense James R. Schlesinger says that he plans to improve the accuracy of US long-range missiles and re-target some of these missiles against Soviet military targets as well as the currently targeted population and industrial centers.

22 JAN

The US Maritime Administration announces a change in policy to permit women to attend the Merchant Marine Academy at King's Point, N.Y., beginning in July 1974.

23 JAN

The Department of the Interior issues a permit for the building of the 789-mile (1,270-km) oil pipeline running from Alaska's north coast to the ice-free port of Valdez. From there tankers will carry the oil to US West Coast ports. Among the concepts rejected for exploiting the Arctic oil are submarine tankers.

24 JAN

Secretary of Defense Schlesinger confirms reports that US oil companies, under Arab pressure, reduced oil supplies to US military forces during the 1973 Middle East War.

6 FEB

The strategic missile submarine *George Washington* (SSBN 598) launches five Polaris A-3T missiles in the first quintuple missile launch by a US submarine; previously the largest number of SLBM in a single day was four.

13 FEB

Ten black sailors charged with a Nov 1973 disturbance on board the cruiser *Little Rock* (CLG 4) hold a news conference in Naples to state that they are victims of discrimination and cannot receive a fair trial in their scheduled court martial.

14 FEB

The South Korean Defense Ministry reports that North Korean ships shelled two South Korean trawlers off the west coast of Korea. One of the trawlers was sunk, the other wrecked.

21 FEB

The last of the Israeli soldiers occupying the western bank of the Suez Canal pull back from the canal in accord with Israeli-Egyptian agreement.

22 FEB

Lt. (jg) Barbara Ann Allen, USN, becomes the first woman to be designated as a naval aviator, receiving her wings of gold in ceremonies at NAS Corpus Christi, Texas.

1 MAR

The YCH-53E Super Stallion helicopter, the most powerful helicopter in the West, makes its first flight. The "E" model of the CH-53 has three turboshaft engines in place of the two found in the earlier models.

5 MAR

The Martin Marietta–built X-24B research aircraft, designed to test the approach and landing techniques for the US space shuttle, makes its first flight. The rocket-powered aircraft originally flew as the X-24A and was stripped down to its basic structure and rebuilt in 1972–1973. (*See* 19 Mar 1970.)

22 MAR

A US military planning staff led by Rear Adm. Brian McCauley, USN, arrives in Cairo, Egypt, to help plan the clearing of the Suez Canal of mines and other ordnance. The project—a joint effort of Egypt, France, Great Britain, and the United States—has the codename Nimbus Star.

2 APR

The last C-54 Skymaster four-engine transport flown by the US Navy is retired. This is the military version of the Douglas DC 6. Originally flown as the R5D, the last naval aircraft of this type was a 29-year-old C-54Q that served with the Naval Test Pilot School at NAS Patuxent River, Md.

9 APR

The Soviet Union launches its first supertanker, the 150,500-deadweight-ton *Krym* at the Zaliv/B. Ye. Butoma Shipyard at Kerch' on the Crimean Peninsula.

11 APR

A P-3A Orion fires a Harpoon air-to-surface missile in the first test of this weapon from a maritime patrol aircraft. The missile scored a direct hit on a remote-controlled target boat.

14 APR

Four Soviet cosmonauts depart Moscow for Houston, Texas, in preparation for the joint US–Soviet space mission, to take place in 1975.

21 APR

Egyptian President Anwar Sadat states that his country has stopped relying on Soviet weapons because the Soviet Union has used them as a lever to influence Egyptian policy.

22 APR

Twelve RH-53D Sea Stallion helicopters from US Navy Helicopter Mine Countermeasures Squadron (HM) 12 begin mine clearing operations in the Suez Canal as part of Nimbus Star.

6 MAY

The government of Prime Minister Olafur Johannesson of Iceland falls, causing an end to plans for the ousting of American forces from Iceland.

13 MAY

In an interview published in *The New York Times,* Chief of Naval Operations Adm. Elmo R. Zumwalt, Jr., USN, says he is convinced that the United States has lost control of the sea lanes to the Soviet Union.

18 MAY

India conducts a successful test of a nuclear device. It is the sixth nation to explode a nuclear device, following the United States, Soviet Union, Britain, France, and China.

3 JUNE

The US Navy completes its portion of the mine-sweeping operations in the Suez Canal as part of Operation Nimbus Star.

6 JUNE

The US strategic missile submarine *John Marshall* (SSBN 611) completes the final Polaris A-2 deterrent patrol. All eight submarines that carried the Polaris A-2 are undergoing conversion to the Polaris A-3 or Poseidon C-3 missile and the A-2 is phased out of service.

27 JUNE

The United States and the Soviet Union agree to further limits on anti-ballistic missile systems, and begin bargaining over the problems of permanent limits on offensive strategic weapons.

1 JULY

The 174-year-old Boston Naval Shipyard, the oldest active yard in the United States, closes. (The older Washington Navy Yard, the nation's first naval shipyard, remains in service albeit not as a shipyard.)

4 JULY

The *Hughes Glomar Explorer* (later US Navy AG 193) arrives at the mid-Pacific location where a Soviet Golf-class ballistic missile submarine sank in 1968. In a clandestine, month-long operation, the *Glomar Explorer* will lift the forward portion of the submarine from a depth of three miles (4.8 km) in a clandestine operation given the code-name Jennifer. (The ship's cover story was a seafloor mining operation under the aegis of millionaire Howard Hughes through the Summa Corporation for his Global Marine Development firm.)

5 JULY

Maj. John H. Pierson, USMC, and Maj. David Shore, USMC, fly an OV-10A Bronco aircraft 2,784 miles (4,480 km) from NAS Whidbey Island, Wash., to Homestead AFB, Fla., to set a world record for straight-line distance in this class of turboprop aircraft.

21 JULY

Soviet General Secretary Leonid Brezhnev says that the Soviet Union has proposed withdrawal from the Mediterranean Sea of all Soviet and US ships carrying nuclear weapons.

22 JULY

US Marine and British Navy helicopters evacuate more than 400 citizens of the United States, Great Britain, and other countries from Cyprus to the amphibious ship *Coronado* (LPD 11), which transports the evacuees to Beirut, Lebanon.

28 JULY

Turkish naval and merchant ships and helicopters continue landing more forces on Cyprus, but do not advance beyond the Turkish-held area between Nicosia and Kyrenia.

6 AUG

The world's largest unmanned balloon is launched from Fort Churchill in Manitoba, Canada, the flight sponsored by the US Office of Naval Research (ONR) and NASA. The balloon, carrying an 800-pound (363-kg) instrument package, will reach an altitude of 155,000 feet (47,244 m).

9 AUG

As a result of the Watergate scandal, President Richard M. Nixon resigns, turning over the presidency to Vice President Gerald Ford. (This was the first resignation of a US president and Ford was the first appointed vice president in US history.) Ford is the fourth successive US president to have served in the Navy; having been in the light carrier *Monterey* (CVL 26) in the Pacific during World War II. He left the Navy in Jan 1946 and subsequently served in the House of Representatives.

The Navy accepts its first EC-130 Hercules TACAMO (Take Charge And Move Out) aircraft into squadron service. The TACAMO aircraft provide airborne relay for communications to US strategic missile submarines at sea.

10 AUG

A YCH-53E Super Stallion helicopter flies in hover at a gross weight of 71,700 pounds (32,523 kg) carrying an external load of 35,600 pounds (16,148 kg). This is the heaviest gross weight ever flown by a helicopter and the heaviest payload ever lifted by a Western helicopter.

14 AUG

The Greek government withdraws its armed forces from the military structure of NATO.

25 AUG

Japanese fishermen tie 60 of their boats to Japan's first nuclear-powered ship, the *Mutsu,* to protest against feared radioactive pollution of the sea.

29 AUG

The new government of Iceland announces a reversal of the plans to close down the NATO base at Keflavik. The previous government had championed the closedown.

30 AUG

Israel announces that Soviet minesweeping efforts in the Gulf of Suez would be coordinated with Israel,

thus ending confrontations between the craft of the two nations in the area.

The Soviet guided missile destroyer *Otvazhnyi* of the Kashin class suffers a fire and, after almost six hours of her crew trying to control the conflagration, blows up, and sinks in the Black Sea near the base of Sevastopol. The cause of the catastrophe is reported to be a surface-to-air missile booster that ignites in the after missile magazine. Six crewmen are reported to have been killed in the fire and another shot himself.

6 OCT

Japanese demonstrators march through the streets of Yokosuka for three hours to demand that the US carrier *Midway* (CVA 41) leave Japan.

17 NOV

Four Egyptian passenger ships begin the 100-mile (161-km) Port Said to Suez trip, the first attempt at this voyage since the 1967 Arab-Israeli War.

19 NOV

The Central Treaty Organization (CENTO) begins exercise Midlink 74, the largest naval exercise ever held in the Arabian Sea. Forces from Great Britain, Iran, Pakistan, Turkey, and the United States participate. The US Navy participation includes the carrier *Constellation* (CVA 64) and seven other ships.

23 NOV

President Ford and Soviet General Secretary Leonid Brezhnev meet at the Siberian port of Vladivostok. During the two-day session the leaders sign an agreement to put limits on the number of ICBMs, submarine-launched missiles, and heavy bombers that each country can have; each country is permitted to arm 1,320 missiles with Multiple Independently targeted Re-entry Vehicles (MIRV). During the conference Brezhnev states that the Soviet Union is building a new strategic missile submarine called the *Tayfun* (Typhoon) as a response to the US Trident submarine program.

25 NOV

The USS *Constellation* enters the Persian Gulf, the first time in 26 years that a US aircraft carrier has operated in that area. She is accompanied by two guided missile destroyers for the "familiarization deployment."

14 DEC

The US frigate *Elmer Montgomery* (DE 1082) arrives in Aquaba, Jordan, for a five-day visit. This is the first

US Navy ship visit to Jordan since the 1967 Arab-Israeli War.

18 DEC
French officials announce that France will begin construction of a nuclear-propelled helicopter carrier in Apr 1975, to be operational in 1980. This would make France the third nation to have nuclear-propelled surface naval ships. (This ship will not be constructed.)

23 DEC
First flight of the Rockwell International B-1A supersonic strategic bomber; only four prototypes will be built before the aircraft is canceled by President James E. Carter, Jr., in 1977. The strategic bomber will be resurrected during the Reagan Administration.

25 DEC
The Soviet news agency Tass reports that the Soviet Union has put the first atomic-powered lighthouse into service. The lighthouse is on the Baltic Sea.

1975

8 JAN

Egyptian President Anwar Sadat criticizes the Soviet Union for the Soviet refusal to replace weapons lost by the Egyptians in the 1973 Arab-Israeli War.

22 JAN

President Gerald Ford signs the Geneva Protocol of 1925 [sic] that prohibits the use of asphyxiating, poisonous, or other gases in war. The protocol does not prohibit the production of chemical warfare agents, the development of weapons that deliver chemical agents, the stockpiling of chemical munitions, or the development of chemical warfare protective material and decontamination equipment. The signatories further reserve the right to retaliate with chemical weapons should chemical warfare be initiated against them.

27 JAN

The US destroyer *Richard E. Byrd* (DDG 23) departs Corfu after two of her officers are attacked by a mob demonstrating against the alleged anti-Greek policies of the US government.

29 JAN

Egyptian President Sadat announces that France has agreed to sell Mirage F-1 fighters to Egypt, marking a shift in Egypt's major weapons supply from the Soviet Union to NATO countries.

31 JAN

The Soviet news agency Tass reports that the Soviet Union has agreed to sweep mines from the Mediterranean approaches to Port Said.

1 FEB

The Associated Press reports that the Soviet Union has asked Portugal to make a seaport available for use by its fishing fleet.

4 FEB

The Soviet news agency Tass reports that the Soviet Union has not sought a naval foothold in Portugal, but does not rebut a report that the Soviet Union has asked for fishing port facilities.

24 FEB

Soviet Defense Minister Marshal of the SU Andrei A. Grechko, Chief Marshal of Aviation Pavel Kutankov, and Adm. of the Fleet of the SU Sergei G. Gorshkov arrive in India on a four-day visit to study and assess Indian military requirements.

3 MAR

The Thai government announces that it wants all US troops and aircraft withdrawn from Thailand within 18 months.

25 MAR

President Ford directs Army Chief of Staff Gen. Fredrick C. Weyand, USA, to fly to South Vietnam to make an assessment of the military situation there and make recommendations regarding further American assistance as North Vietnamese forces take large portions of the country.

30 MAR

The New York Times reports that several freighters and landing ships have arrived in southern South Vietnamese ports with an estimated 30,000 people fleeing from Da Nang. One US Navy cargo ship, the *Sgt. Andrew Miller* (T-AK 242), carried more than 9,000 refugees.

1 APR

The Associated Press reports that South Vietnamese marines aboard the US Military Sealift Command–chartered cargo ship *Pioneer Contender* executed about 25 persons they said were Viet Cong suspects. The ship was the last able to carry refugees out of Da Nang before communist shelling forced cessation of the sealift.

5 APR

The SS *Greenville Victory,* a cargo ship on charter to the US Military Sealift Command to carry Vietnamese refugees to Phu Quoc Island in the Gulf of Thailand, is hijacked by South Vietnamese soldiers and forced into the port of Vung Tau.

7 APR

The US Department of Defense announces that US Marines have been put on four civilian merchant ships on charter to the Military Sealift Command to prevent their takeover by South Vietnamese refugees.

12 APR

Operation Eagle Pull is activated in Cambodia for the removal of US officials. Twelve Marine CH-53 Sea Stallion helicopters evacuate 287 persons from Phnom Penh to the helicopter carrier *Okinawa* (LPH 3), among them Cambodian President Saukhm Khoy as well as journalists and foreign nationals. Subsequently, the helicopters evacuate troops of the 31st Marine Amphibious Unit, which had established a defensive perimeter from which the evacuees were rescued.

14 APR

Israel unveils its first homebuilt turbojet fighter-bomber, the Kfir (Young Lion), at Tel Aviv. The aircraft reportedly flies at Mach 2 speeds and has a combat ceiling of 50,000 feet (15,240 m). The Kfir is a refinement of the Dassault Mirage 5 design, with a more powerful engine of American origins. (During the 1980s, 25 of the Kfir C1 variant will serve as F-21A aggressor training aircraft for the US Navy and Marine Corps.)

21 APR

With the military and political situation deteriorating rapidly in South Vietnam, President Nguyen Van Thieu resigns after ten years in office, denouncing the United States as untrustworthy. He appoints his vice president, Tran Van Huong, to replace him.

22 APR

The Ford Administration reports that the number of Americans in South Vietnam has been reduced to about 1,500. Meanwhile, the US Navy has deployed more than 40 ships in the South China Sea to aid in evacuation if required; these include the aircraft carriers *Hancock* (CVA 19), *Midway* (CVA 41), *Coral Sea* (CVA 43), and *Enterprise* (CVAN 65), and the helicopter carrier *Okinawa*. The North Vietnamese government, which now controls some two-thirds of South Vietnam, pronounces the carrier presence a brazen challenge and a violation of the 1973 Paris peace accords.

29 APR

US Navy, Marine, and Air Force flying helicopters from Seventh Fleet ships evacuate Americans from Saigon in Operation Frequent Winds—which lasts for three hours. Helicopters are the only means of rescue because of North Vietnamese troop actions. Fighter aircraft from the offshore carriers provide protective cover while the helicopters take out all but a handful of the 900 Americans believed still in the Saigon area. The main helicopter landing zone at Tan Son Nhut Airport is protected by Marines from the 9th Marine Amphibious Brigade, flown in for that purpose. The last helicopter lifts off the roof of the US Embassy in Saigon at 1952 carrying Marine security guards, ending US military presence in South Vietnam.

The carrier *Enterprise,* participating in these operations, carries Fighter Squadrons (VF) 1 and 2 flying the F-14A Tomcat fighter. This is the combat debut of the aircraft.

Greece and the United States announce they have agreed to end the agreement providing home port facilities to Sixth Fleet ships and to close the US Air Force base near Athens.

MAY

The Soviet VSTOL carrier *Kiev* enters service. With a full-load displacement of 43,000 tons, she is the largest warship yet built in the Soviet Union. The four ships of the *Kiev* class are completed from 1975 to 1988. They have heavy gun and missile batteries and can operate some 30 Yak-38 Forger VSTOL aircraft and Ka-25 Hormone/Ka-25 Helix helicopters.

2 MAY

The US carrier *Midway* offloads more than 40 USAF helicopters at Utapao, Thailand, which were used to in the Saigon-area evacuation. At the same time, the carrier loads almost 100 South Vietnamese Air Force aircraft that had flown into Utapao when South Vietnam fell to the Communists. These aircraft will be transported to Guam.

The Navy selects a derivative of the Northrop Corporation's YF-17 lightweight fighter for production as the F-18 for carrier use. Congress had directed that the Navy select the winner of the Air Force lightweight fighter competition; the Air Force selected the YF-16. The Navy's selection will become the F/A-18 Hornet series.

3 MAY

The carrier *Nimitz* (CVAN 68) is placed in commission at the Norfolk Naval Station in Virginia. *Nimitz* is the first nuclear-powered attack aircraft carrier designated for series production. Improvements over the *Enterprise* include greater protection, reduction of reactors from eight to two, and advanced aircraft support systems. The carrier is expected to steam for 13 years on her original set of reactor cores. Her first commanding officer is Capt. Bryan W. Compton, Jr., USN.

4 MAY

More than 26,000 refugees from South Vietnam reach Subic Bay in the Philippines on board 11 ships of the American evacuation fleet.

7 MAY

The United States and the Soviet Union exchange warship visits for the first time. The US frigate *Leahy* (DLG 16) and destroyer *Tattnall* (DDG 19) arrive at Leningrad while the Kanin-class destroyers *Boykiy* and *Zhguchiy* arrive in Boston for goodwill visits.

12 MAY

The US merchant ship *Mayaguez*, owned by the SeaLand Corp., is fired on and seized by a Cambodian gunboat under control of the Communist Khmer Rouge. The ship is taken in international waters in the Gulf of Thailand. President Ford warns of "serious consequences" unless the ship and her 40-man crew are released promptly.

13 MAY

Secretary of State Henry A. Kissinger states that all diplomatic efforts to obtain release of the *Mayaguez* from Cambodia will be exhausted before any other action is taken.

14 MAY

Protective air strikes are flown against Cambodian naval and air installations by aircraft from the US carrier *Coral Sea* as 288 US Marines are launched in USAF helicopters from Utapao, Thailand, to rescue the *Mayaguez* crew from an offshore island. Other Marines board the *Mayaguez* from the US frigate *Harold E. Holt* (DE 1074). Eighteen Marines, airmen, and Navy hospital corpsmen are killed in the operation and another 50 American servicemen are injured.

19 MAY

The Polish fishing trawler *Kalamar* is charged with violating American territorial waters after being seized by the US Coast Guard cutter *Modoc* (WMEC 194) 1.2 miles (1.9 km) inside US waters. The 2,600-ton trawler and her crew of 79 are brought to San Francisco.

22 MAY

The State Department grants asylum to the 20 Cambodian naval officers who came to the United States before the communist takeover in their country. They had recently graduated from Navy Officer Candidate School at Newport, R.I.

24 MAY

The New York Times reports that US submarines have been conducting electronic surveillance operations near the Soviet Union, frequently within the three-mile (4.8-km) limit for nearly 15 years in an operation called Holystone.

28 MAY

The Associated Press reports a claim by China that the Soviet Union has asked the new Communist government in Saigon for the use of former US military bases in Vietnam, particularly Cam Ranh Bay, in compensation for the aid provided by the Soviet Union during the Vietnam War.

5 JUNE

The Suez Canal is formally reopened with the US Sixth Fleet cruiser-flagship *Little Rock* (CLG 4) the only foreign warship in the official Egyptian flotilla that sails down the canal toward Ismalia.

23 JUNE

The US Department of Defense announces that the armed services have been authorized to give enlistment preference to qualified Cambodian and Vietnamese evacuees who have been previously trained by US armed forces as well as those in training by the United States when their governments fell.

27 JUNE

The heavy cruiser *Newport News* (CA 148) is decommissioned. The 21,500-ton ship, which served as a gunfire support ship in the Vietnam War, is the world's last heavy cruiser in operational service.

30 JUNE

The US Navy reclassifies 24 frigates (DLG/DLGN) as guided missile cruisers (CG/CGN) with their same hull numbers; the ten ships of the *Farragut* class (DLG 6–15) are changed to guided missile destroyers (DDG 37–46). There was some internal Navy debate over whether to classify the latter ships as cruisers or destroyers with the DDG decision being based on their commanding officers having the rank of commander while all other DLG/DLGNs were commanded by captains.

All US Navy escort ships (DE/DEG/DER) are reclassified as frigates (FF/FFG/FFR).

1 JULY

President Ford asks Congress to give commonwealth status to the Mariana Islands. This would be the first addition to US territory in 50 years.

The President nominates Lt. Gen. Daniel (Chappie) James, Jr., USAF, for promotion to the rank of full general. James is the first black officer to reach four-star rank in the US armed forces.

Rabbi Bertram W. Korn becomes the first clergyman of the Jewish faith to reach flag rank when he is promoted to rear admiral in the Chaplain Corps of the US Naval Reserve.

The US Navy ship designation CVA for attack aircraft carrier is replaced by CV indicating multipurpose aircraft carrier. The change is made to reflect the assignment of anti-submarine helicopters and fixed-wing aircraft to large-deck carriers in addition to fighter, attack, and special-mission aircraft.

2 JULY

Secretary of Defense Schlesinger is reported to have said that under some war conditions the United States might make first use of strategic weapons against selected targets in the Soviet Union.

6 JULY

Senator Dewey F. Bartlett (R-Okla.) says that his on-site inspection in Somalia with a group of American experts confirms Department of Defense allegations that the Soviet Union is installing a missile facility there.

7 JULY

President Ferdinand E. Marcos declares that the Philippines plans to assume control of US air and naval bases in his country but will still allow the United States to use them subject to negotiated arrangements.

15 JULY

US astronauts Col. Thomas P. Stafford, USAF, civilian Vance Brand, and Col. Donald K. Slayton, USAF, are launched from Cape Kennedy in the *Apollo 18* spacecraft to rendezvous with a Soviet spacecraft in history's first multinational space operation. Simultaneously, from Tyuratam the Soviets launch cosmonauts Alexei Leonov and Valeri Kubasov in the *Soyuz 19* spacecraft. The *Soyuz 19* remains in space for 5 days, 22 hours, and 3 minutes, coming down on 21 July. The *Apollo 18* remains aloft for 9 days, 1 hour, 28 minutes, splashing down on 24 July and being recovered by the helicopter carrier *New Orleans* (LPH 11). This is the final at-sea space recovery planned by the United States. The space shuttle—key to future US manned space activities—will land on conventional runways.

19 JULY

Two American civilian technicians from a US naval communications station in Asmara, Ethiopia, are among four persons kidnapped by members of the Eritrean Liberaton Front.

23 JULY

The Department of Defense announces the end of US military participation in Suez Canal clearing operations. The departure of the salvage ship *Opportune* (ARS 41), the last ship of the US task force working in the canal, marks the completion of over 15 months of US naval activity in that area.

1 AUG

A Navy KA–3B Skywarrior tanker aircraft completes the longest nonstop flight ever made by a carrier-type aircraft. The flight originated at Rota, Spain, and ends at NAS Alameda, Calif. The plane took 13 hours to fly the 6,100 miles (9,815 km). The Conference on Security and Cooperation in Europe (CSCE) "Final Act" is signed in Helsinki, Finland, by Soviet and NATO officials. The agreement provides for prior notification of large-scale maneuvers and exercises, and other actions in an attempt to reduce East-West tensions.

5 AUG

The wingless US NASA X–24B experimental aircraft makes a 200-mph (321.9-kmh) landing at Edwards AFB, Calif., in a test of forthcoming space shuttle landing techniques. The X–24B makes both rocket-powered and unpowered flights in the tests.

14 AUG

The Greek government withdraws its forces from NATO command in frustration at not being able to halt Turkey's advances on Cyprus.

British troops are flown to two bases on Cyprus, but are not ordered to restore the ceasefire.

Japanese newspapers report that an American sailor charged with unauthorized absence from the carrier *Midway* said at his court martial that he had refused to return to the ship because the carrier had brought nuclear weapons to Japan.

12 SEP

The American communicaations station in Asmara, Ethiopia, is reported heavily damaged in an attack by Eritrean guerrillas.

20 SEP

The destroyer *Spruance* (DD 963), the US Navy's first major gas-turbine-powered warship, is placed in commission. Her first CO is Comdr. Raymond J. Harbrecht,

USN. The *Spruance* is the basis for the subsequent *Kidd* (DDG 993) class of missile destroyers and *Ticonderoga* (CG 47) class of Aegis missile cruisers.

13 OCT
President Ford signs a congressional resolution authorizing the stationing of up to 200 American civilian technicians to operate an early warning station in the Sinai to provide mutual defense for Egypt and Israel.

7 NOV
Crewmen on the Soviet frigate *Storozhevoy* in the Baltic Fleet mutiny on the night of 7–8 November, led by the ship's political officer, Capt. 3rd Rank V. M. Sablin. They attempt to take the ship to Sweden but are intercepted by Soviet air and surface forces and surrender. Sablin will be tried and executed by firing squad as will be several enlisted men; another officer is sentenced to 15 years in a labor camp.

22 NOV
During the night operations in the Mediterranean, the guided missile frigate *Belknap* (CG 26) is severely damaged in a collision with the carrier *John F. Kennedy* (CV 67). Six sailors in the *Belknap* and one in the *Kennedy* are killed, and 47 *Belknap* men are injured.

The *Belknap*'s aluminum superstructure is crushed and burned in the accident and the ship will undergo repairs until late 1980, when she returns to service, modified to serve as flagship for the Sixth Fleet in the Mediterranean.

2 DEC
Appearing before the House Select Committee on Intelligence, Adm. Elmo R. Zumwalt, Jr., USN (Ret.), the former Chief of Naval Operations, accuses the Soviet Union of gross violations of the 1972 strategic arms limitation agreement and claims that Secretary of State Kissinger had concealed the breaches from Congress and the President.

19 DEC
The US Senate votes to cut off funds for covert military aid to Angola even though the Soviet Union and Cuba are providing large amounts of assistance to rebel forces. President Ford deplores the Senate action.

29 DEC
The Soviet Union and Turkey announce that they will soon sign a "political document on friendly relations and cooperation."

1976

2 JAN

The US State Department warns all countries that the United States objects to any nation allowing Cuban aircraft to use airfields or airspace for activities related to the war in Angola.

3 JAN

The Moroccan Navy stops and searches a Soviet cargo ship. On board are discovered three Algerian officers and a shipment of arms, intended for anti-government forces in Morocco.

8 JAN

The Soviet Union denies it has warships in the area of Angola, saying that such reports were "without foundation . . . and clearly provocative in character."

11 JAN

Icelandic fishermen block the road to the Keflavik military base to demand NATO intervention in the Icelandic-British fishing dispute.

12 JAN

The Icelandic government tells NATO that if the Royal Navy does not leave Icelandic waters, Iceland will reconsider its membership in NATO.

14 JAN

Reversing the policy of the former government, the new Australian government announces that it will allow allied nuclear-propelled ships to visit the Cockburn Sound naval facility when it is completed in 1978.

An Associated Press report quotes Vice Adm. Robert B. Baldwin, USN, Commander Naval Air Force Pacific, as stating that about 20 percent of his aircraft are grounded because of a shortage of spare parts, caused partly by the lack of funds.

19 JAN

The Coast Guard icebreaker *Polar Star* (WAGB 10) is commissioned in Seattle, Wash. She is the first US government icebreaker commissioned since 1955 and the largest yet built in the United States. A sister ship, the *Polar Sea* (WAGB 11), will follow in 1978.

Great Britain announces that all British warships will withdraw from Icelandic waters.

Officials of Old Dominion University in Virginia

confirm that Iran has proposed establishment of an Iranian naval academy at the school.

24 JAN

The United States and Spain sign a five-year treaty of friendship in which the United States agrees to remove its Poseidon submarines from the base at Rota in 1979.

4 FEB

The Argentine destroyer *Almirante Storni* fires a warning shot across the bow of the British research ship *Shackleton* when the latter reportedly ignores radio warnings to heave to off the coast of the Falkland Islands in the South Atlantic.

12 FEB

Capt. Fran McKee, USN, becomes the first US Navy woman line officer to be nominated for promotion to rear admiral.

16 FEB

The House Intelligence Committee is reported to have learned that US nuclear-propelled submarines have collided with nine Soviet "vessels" in Soviet waters during the past ten years.

22 FEB

The Vietnamese government releases the bodies of two US Marines killed during the American evacuation of Saigon in May 1975.

23 FEB

Icelandic coast guard patrol boats cut the trawls of two British fishing vessels; the Icelandic government declares the vessels were fishing within the country's self-proclaimed 200-n.mile (370-km) fishing rights limits.

2 MAR

An 11-day exercise under the aegis of the US Third Fleet begins off the coast of southern California; ships from Australia, Canada, Great Britain, and New Zealand as well as the United States participate in the exercise.

21 MAR

The United States ends operations at all bases in Thailand in preparation for final US military withdrawal from that country.

26 MAR

The United States and Turkey sign a four-year agreement to give Turkey $1 billion in military aid in return for permission for the United States to reopen its bases in Turkey.

31 MAR

Great Britain completes withdrawal of its military forces from Singapore.

4 APR

Egyptian President Anwar Sadat states that he has canceled Soviet Navy rights to use Egyptian ports and that he fears that the Soviet Union might be establishing military bases in Libya.

8 APR

US Secretary of State Henry A. Kissinger presents a plan for world revenue sharing in profits from exploitation of sea resources. This plan is part of a package of compromises intended to avoid a world scramble over resources on the ocean floor.

10 APR

The keel for the first Trident submarine, the *Ohio* (SSBN 726), is laid down at the General Dynamics/Electric Boat yard in Groton, Conn. This event occurs nine years after completion of the previous US strategic missile submarine, the *Will Rogers* (SSBN 659).

15 APR

The United States and Greece sign a four-year agreement that will give Greece $700 million in arms aid in return for use of four military bases in Greece. This agreement follows a similar agreement, signed in March, between the United States and Turkey.

18 APR

The US Navy's *SES-100B* Surface Effect Ship (SES) fires a Standard SM-1 missile while traveling at a speed of 70 mph (112.65 km/h) off the coast of Florida in the Gulf of Mexico. This is the first firing of an operational weapon from a high-speed marine craft and the first vertical launch of an SM-1 from any Navy ship.

26 APR

The US Marine Corps announces that the service has abolished the "motivation platoon," a special unit for troublesome recruits, following the death of a recruit assigned to the platoon by beating with Pugil sticks at San Diego on 5 Dec 1975. Other changes are also made in Marine training procedures.

28 APR

The US guided missile destroyer *Mahan* (DDG 42) arrives in Haifa, Israel. This is the first call by a US warship at an Israeli port in 13 years.

28 MAY

The US and Soviet governments sign a pact that limits nuclear underground explosions and provides for American observation of some Soviet nuclear tests.

29 MAY

The amphibious assault ship *Tarawa* (LHA 1) is placed in commission. She is the largest specialized amphibious ship yet built by any nation, with a full-load displacement of 39,300 tons. The *Tarawa* can carry 1,900 Marines and operate some 30 large helicopters and AV-8 Harrier VSTOL aircraft. Unlike the earlier LPH-type helicopter carriers, the LHA design provides for a large docking well for landing craft. Her first CO is Capt. James H. Morris, USN.

1 JUNE

Britain and Iceland sign a temporary agreement ending the seven-month dispute over fishing rights off Iceland.

4 JUNE

Australian Prime Minister Malcolm Fraser tells Parliament that he is opening Australian ports to US nuclear-propelled ships.

10 JUNE

The US Navy *SES-100B*, in trials off Panama City, Fla., reaches 101 mph (162.5 km/h), setting a speed record for this type of ship. On 30 June, the *SES-100B* will establish another speed record, reaching 103 mph (165.8 km/h).

20 JUNE

US Navy amphibious ships evacuate 263 Americans and several foreigners from Beirut.

25 JUNE

The Washington Post reports that 37 sailors from the crew of the ballistic missile submarine *Thomas Jefferson* (SSBN 618) were removed from the submarine when she arrived at Bangor, Wash., as part of a marijuana investigation.

28 JUNE

Thirty-eight women and 289 men enter the US Coast Guard Academy, marking the first time women are sworn in as cadets.

3 JULY

An Israeli commando unit conducts a raid on Entebbe Airport in Uganda, rescuing 103 hostages who are being held there following the hijacking of an Air France airliner. Four of the hostages, seven of the ten hijackers, and about 20 Ugandan soldiers are killed in the raid as is one Israeli officer. The raid, conducted by commandos carried in C-130 Hercules aircraft flying from bases in Israel, becomes a model for counter-hostage operations.

4 JULY

President Gerald Ford commemorates the 200th birthday of the United States in a gala ceremony on board the carrier *Forrestal* (CV 59) anchored in New York Harbor amidst an international flotilla of 53 naval ships representing 22 countries.

6 JULY

Eighty-one women join the US Naval Academy class of 1980, becoming the first women admitted to that institution.

7 JULY

The Soviet government cancels plans for further American port visits for the sail training ships *Krusenshtern* and *Tovarich* following the poor treatment of their crews in Newport, R.I., and threats against the ships in New York.

12 JULY

The US frigate *Donald B. Beary* (FF 1085) arrives at the Kenyan port of Mombassa in what a Department of Defense official describes as a "courtesy port call." But the news media views the visit—combined with the presence of a P-3 Orion patrol aircraft at Nairobi —as a show of US support for Kenya in the dispute between that country and Uganda.

13 JULY

The Department of Defense announces that B-52 bombers of the Strategic Air Command have begun flying ocean patrols over the Atlantic to supplement the Navy in its sea control operations.

18 JULY

The Soviet VSTOL carrier *Kiev* sails into the Mediterranean from the Black Sea for the first time. She will subsequently be assigned to the Soviet Northern Fleet.

28 JULY

In another evacuation of Americans and other foreign nationals from Beirut, US Navy amphibious ships take off 308 persons from the strife-torn country.

I AUG

The Soviet Navy publication *Morskoi Sbornik* rebuts Western objections to the passage of the aircraft carrier *Kiev* through the Turkish straits, claiming the right of the Soviet Union to send any ships it chooses through the straits despite the Montreaux Convention explicitly banning aircraft carriers according to some interpretations.

15 AUG

The US submarine *Snook* (SSN 592) arrives at Perth, Australia, the first nuclear-propelled submarine to visit that country. Australian maritime union demonstrators protest the visit. (Three US nuclear-propelled surface warships had already visited Australia.)

18 AUG

Two US Army officers are killed by axe-wielding North Korean guards while supervising the trimming of a tree in the demilitarized zone at Panmunjom. (A heavily armed US force will cut down the tree on 21 Aug.)

27 AUG

The US guided missile cruiser *Truxtun* (CGN 35) arrives in Auckland, the first nuclear-propelled ship to visit New Zealand in ten years. The arrival sparks demonstrations by port labor unions against nuclear ship visits.

28 AUG

A Soviet guided missile submarine of the Echo II class collides with the US frigate *Voge* (FF 1047) in the Ionian Sea. The *Voge* suffers damage to her propeller and is towed to Suda Bay, Crete. The Soviet craft suffers minor damage. A US Navy report of the accident released on 11 Mar 1977 will say that the Soviet submarine was at fault for the incident.

I SEP

Capt. Pauline M. Hartington, USN, becomes the first woman to hold the position of Secretary to the Joint Chiefs of Staff.

2 SEP

Australian Prime Minister Fraser supports construction of a US naval base on the British island of Diego Garcia in the Indian Ocean. He states that the Indian Ocean should not become the private preserve of the Soviet Union.

6 SEP

A Soviet Air Forces officer lands a MiG-25 fighter aircraft at an airfield in northern Japan and asks for asylum in the United States. He is granted asylum the following day. The aircraft will be disassembled and shipped back to the Soviet Union after examination by US and Japanese technicians.

7 SEP

The US State Department announces that Israeli gunboats fired the previous week on an American oil prospecting vessel in a disputed area of the Gulf of Suez.

14 SEP

An F-14 Tomcat fighter carrying a Phoenix missile rolls off the deck of the carrier *John F. Kennedy* (CV 67) and sinks in 1,890 feet (576 m) of water off the coast of Scotland. The aircraft is located on 21 Oct 1976, with the help of the nuclear-propelled research submersible *NR-1*. The aircraft and missile are recovered on 11 Nov 1976.

The carrier *Kennedy* and the destroyer *Bordelon* (DD 881) collide during night underway refueling operations in the Atlantic, 100 n.miles (185 km) north of Scotland. Damage to the carrier is minor but the *Bordelon* suffers major damage. (The *Bordelon* will be decommissioned in early 1977 because of the high cost to repair the damage.)

20 SEP

The US Navy states that the deep-ocean salvage ship *Glomar Explorer* (AG 193) is being "mothballed" in the reserve fleet at Suisun Bay, Calif. The CIA-sponsored ship had earlier salvaged portions of a Soviet missile submarine from record depths.

27 SEP

At a news conference Secretary of Defense Donald H. Rumsfeld warns that Soviet weapon programs appear to be intended to win, not just deter nuclear war, as are US nuclear weapons.

30 SEP

The US carrier *Oriskany* (CV 34) is decommissioned at Alameda, Calif. She is the last carrier of the *Essex* (CV 9) class in active service except for the training ship *Lexington* (CVT 16, later AVT 16).

2 OCT

The arrival of the US nuclear-propelled cruiser *Long Beach* (CGN 9) in Auckland, New Zealand, sets off further strikes and protests against nuclear ship visits.

3 OCT

The Swedish Navy reports that Swedish ships fired warning shots in a futile attempt to force an unidentified submarine to surface in Swedish waters 60 n.miles (111 km) south of Stockholm.

5 OCT

A US General Accounting Office study of the *Mayaguez* affair concludes that the US government did not exhaust all diplomatic options before ordering military action in recovering the ship and crew. Inadequate intelligence is blamed on the loss of 41 American lives in the operation.

7 OCT

The Navy announces a reduction in the number of naval district headquarters from 12 to four, to be located in Philadelphia, Penn.; Washington, D.C.; Seattle, Wash.; and Great Lakes, Ill.

10 NOV

The American Civil Liberties Union and the League of Women Voters Education Fund announce that a class action suit has been filed against the US Navy charging discrimination in training, assignments, and promotion because women are barred from shipboard duty.

13 NOV

The lead ship of *Los Angeles* (SSN 688) class is commissioned at Newport News Shipbuilding and Dry Dock Co. in Newport News, Va. With a speed of about 33 knots, the *Los Angeles* is the fastest US nuclear submarine to enter service since the *Skipjack* (SSN 585) class, completed 1959–1961. The first CO of the *Los Angeles* is Comdr. John Christensen, Jr., USN.

5 DEC

Fire in a hangar at the naval air station in Nowra, Australia, destroys 12 of the Australian Navy's 13 S-2E Tracker ASW aircraft that flew from the carrier *Melbourne*.

9 DEC

Rohr Marine Inc. is awarded a $159,887,011 contract for the design of a prototype, 3,000-ton Surface Effect Ship (SES). The ship, to have been a prototype for future frigate-type warships, will not be built.

1977

I JAN

Reuters News Service reports that Great Britain has joined the ranks of those enforcing a 200-n.mile (370-km) fishing zone. Other countries instituting similar fishing zones on this date include Canada, Denmark, West Germany, France, Ireland, Norway, and the Soviet Union.

The US Navy ends the issuance of undesirable discharges to enlisted personnel.

2 JAN

The Washington Post reports that a new National Intelligence Estimate (NIE) of Soviet military intentions developed by the US intelligence community states that the goal of the Soviet Union is to strive for military superiority over the United States rather than military "parity." A panel of civilian and retired military experts, including former Secretary of the Navy Paul H. Nitze, assisted in preparation of the NIE.

10 JAN

President Gerald Ford presents the nation's highest civilian award, the Medal of Freedom, to Adm. Arleigh A. Burke, USN (Ret.), former Chief of Naval Operations.

14 JAN

For the first time, all-nuclear-propelled task groups are operating in both US deployed fleets—the Sixth Fleet in the Mediterranean and the Seventh Fleet in the western Pacific. The Sixth Fleet group consisted of the *Nimitz* (CVN 68), *California* (CGN 36), and *South Carolina* (CGN 37); the Seventh Fleet group contained the *Enterprise* (CVN 65), *Long Beach* (CGN 9), and *Truxtun* (CGN 35).

16 JAN

A 56-foot (17-m) mechanized landing craft from the *Trenton* (LPD 14) collides with the Spanish merchant ship *Urlea* and overturns in Barcelona Harbor. Forty-nine sailors and Marines are killed.

18 JAN

The US Navy successfully launches the first Trident C-4 SLBM test missile from Cape Canaveral, Fla.

20 JAN

James E. Carter, Jr., is sworn in as the 39th President of the United States. A Naval Academy graduate, Carter is the fifth US president to have served in the

Navy. He qualified in diesel submarines and was undergoing nuclear training when he resigned from the Navy.

Australian Defense Minister James Killen announces that a 19-year-old Australian sailor has been charged in connection with the fire on 5 Dec 1976 that destroyed 12 naval aircraft.

21 JAN

President Carter issues a Proclamation of Pardon for violators of the Military Selective Service act during the Vietnam era (4 Aug 1964 to 28 Mar 1973). This pardon does not cover deserters, whose cases are to be reviewed on an individual basis.

22 JAN

A Navy spokesman acknowledges that nine sailors from the strategic missile submarine *Casimir Pulaski* (SSBN 633) have been charged with drug offenses and removed from submarine duty, at Holy Loch, Scotland.

I FEB

US Secretary of Defense Harold Brown announces the establishment of the Military Airlift Command (MAC) as a specified command that will report to the National Command Authorities through the Joint Chiefs of Staff; MAC will remain under Air Force control for administration and logistics support.

Tenneco, Inc., owner of Newport News Shipbuilding and Dry Dock Co., signs a letter of intent with Globtik Tankers Ltd. to construct the world's first nuclear-propelled oil tankers. However, the ships will not be built.

7 FEB

President Carter announces the nomination of Adm. Stansfield Turner, USN, the Commander in Chief Allied Forces Southern Europe, to be Director of Central Intelligence (DCI). Turner, who will serve in that post from Mar 1977 to Jan 1981, will be the fourth naval officer to serve as DCI.

8 FEB

According to the *Wall Street Journal*, Robert Blackwell, Assistant Secretary of Commerce for Maritime Affairs, has stated that the Soviet government has agreed that US cargo ships will carry one-third of the US grain shipped to the Soviet Union.

26 FEB

A Navy spokesman announces a legislative proposal from Secretary of the Navy W. Graham Claytor, Jr., to amend Title 10 US Code to allow women temporary duty on any Navy ship not engaged in combat missions and to allow permanent assignment to ships such as hospital ships and transports that cannot be assigned combat missions.

1 MAR

The US government extends the nation's fishing zone to 200 n.miles (370 km). The Soviet government announces that it has put into effect a similar fishing zone along its lengthy Pacific and Arctic coasts.

24 MAR

The US State Department announces that the United States and Cuba held talks in New York City on fishing rights and maritime boundaries. These are the first such officially announced meetings since the suspension of diplomatic relations between the two countries in the late 1960s.

28 MAR

US Secretary of Defense Brown announces President Carter's approval of a new program by service discharge review boards to consider, on a case by case application basis, the possible upgrading of former Vietnam era service personnel who received undesirable discharges. Also, boards are asked to consider applications from recipients of administrative general discharges in light of the President's request that these discharges be reexamined in a spirit of compassion.

31 MAR

The White House acknowledges that President Carter has requested Secretary of Defense Brown to sell the presidential yacht *Sequoia* (AG 23) as part of an austerity campaign. Built in 1925–1926, the *Sequoia* was taken into naval service in 1933.

6 APR

US Secretary of Defense Brown directs the Secretary of the Navy to end the patrol hydrofoil ship (PHM) program, canceling five ships that have been authorized but not yet constructed. The prototype *Pegasus* (PHM 1) is to become a test craft.

10 APR

The Soviet trawler *Taras Shevchenko* is seized 130 n.miles (241 km) off Nantucket by a boarding party from the US Coast Guard cutter *Decisive* (WMEC 629) for violations of the US 200-n.mile (370-km) fishing zone regulations.

This is the first such seizure. The trawler is taken to Boston, Mass. The trawler's captain will plead guilty to the charges on 2 May 1977 and be fined $10,000 and given a suspended nine-month jail sentence.

14 APR

A Soviet Tu-20 Bear-D naval surveillance aircraft flies closer to the East Coast of the United States than such aircraft have previously flown. It passes near US warships exercising off Charleston, S.C.

23 APR

The Ethiopian government orders the closing of several American facilities in Ethiopia, including the Kagnew naval communications unit near Asmara and the US Naval Medical Research Center in Addis Ababa.

3 MAY

First flight of Bell XV-15, one of two technology demonstration aircraft for the tilt-rotor concept. The technology permits a turboprop aircraft to combine helicopter and conventional aircraft flight profiles in a single aircraft. The V-22 Osprey will be developed as the production aircraft employing this technology concept.

A US Navy spokesman acknowledges that 33 enlisted men or about one-quarter of the crew of the nuclear-propelled attack submarine *Los Angeles* (SSN 688) have been transferred from the ship following an investigation into alleged drug use.

4 MAY

The UN Command in South Korea reports that North Korean troops have fired upon a South Korean border patrol near the demilitarized zone, killing one soldier and wounding another. This is the first major incident since 18 Aug 1976, when two US Army officers were killed by North Korean guards near Panmunjon.

25 MAY

US Secretary of Transportation Brock Adams announces in a speech at the Coast Guard Academy commencement that for the first time in the Coast Guard's history, women will be assigned to cutters beginning in the fall of 1977.

27 MAY

Reuters News Service reports that the USS *Bluefish* (SSN 675) had arrived in Haifa, Israel, marking the first nuclear-propelled submarine visit to Israel.

President and Mrs. Carter embark in the attack submarine *Los Angeles* for a cruise off Cape Canaveral,

Fla. This is the first time President Carter has been in a nuclear-propelled undersea craft, having earlier served in diesel-electric submarines.

22 JUNE

Soviet-American talks on the demilitarization of the Indian Ocean begin in Moscow.

28 JUNE

Queen Elizabeth II reviews 150 British and foreign naval ships during the Silver Jubilee Naval review off Portsmouth, England. Present are the US cruiser *California* (CGN 36) and the submarine *Billfish* (SSN 676). Other US ships in British ports at the time are the *Conyngham* (DDG 17), *Milwaukee* (AOR 2), *Julius A. Furer* (FFG 6), *Jesse L. Brown* (FF 1089), and *Francis Marion* (LPA 249).

30 JUNE

SEATO closes its headquarters in Bangkok, Thailand, formally marking the dissolution of the 23-year-old alliance organization.

9 JULY

The US Navy's first missile-armed hydrofoil patrol craft, the *Pegasus* (PHM 1), is placed in commission at Seattle, Wash. Her first CO is Lt. Comdr. Wilson J. Erickson, USN.

14 JULY

An unarmed US Army CH-47 Chinook helicopter strays into North Korea and is shot down. Three crewmen are killed and one is captured by the North Koreans. The captured copilot and the three bodies are released to US authorities two days later.

1 AUG

US Chief of Naval Operations Adm. James L. Holloway III, USN, announces the return to the Navy of the traditional bell-bottom trousers and jumper uniform for enlisted men after a one-year test by 20,000 sailors.

North Korea puts into effect a 200-n.mile (370-km) "economic sea zone," and forbids any fishery or exploitation of this zone by foreigners in these waters. North Korea also sets up a "military sea boundary" of up to 50 n.miles (92.7 km) beyond the starting line of its territorial waters within which foreign military vessels and aircraft are prohibited and permission is required for civilian ships and aircraft to operate.

10 AUG

Secretary of Defense Brown reverses a 6 Aug decision to cancel five *Pegasus* (PHM 1) hydrofoil missile craft since Congress refused to approve the action. He releases $272.7 million in previously appropriated funds to complete four as missile craft and one as an unarmed test craft; however, the fifth unit will also be armed.

12 AUG

The US space shuttle *Enterprise* makes its first free flight after release from a modified Boeing 747 aircraft at an altitude of 22,800 feet (6,950 m).

Secretary of the Navy Claytor announces a six-month delay in the completion of the first Trident missile submarine, the *Ohio* (SSBN 726), until Oct 1979, due to construction, manpower, and production problems at the Electric Boat yard in Groton, Conn.

17 AUG

The Soviet nuclear-propelled icebreaker *Arktika* becomes the first surface ship in history to break through the polar ice pack to reach the North Pole. The ship spends 15 hours at the North Pole; her round trip from Murmansk will take 13 days. (Her sister ship *Sibir'* will become the second surface ship to reach the North Pole, in May 1987.)

26 AUG

The US Navy unveils its new single-engine, single-seat XFV-12A Thrust Augmented Wing (TAW) prototype aircraft designed for vertical take-off and landing operations. The aircraft, built by Rockwell International Aircraft Division at Columbus, Ohio, will never fly.

7 SEP

President Carter and Panamanian President Brig. Gen. Omar Torrijos sign two Panama Canal treaties that will turn over control of the canal to Panama in the year 2000 and which will guarantee the neutrality of the canal in the event of war.

The *Los Angeles Times* reports that for the first time since Greece pulled out of the military structure of NATO in 1974, Greek naval and air force units will participate in a NATO naval exercise. The exercise, named Display Determination, is scheduled for late Sep 1977.

9 SEP

A US Navy spokesman announces approval of maternity uniforms for women officers and enlisted personnel. These uniforms will be available beginning in early 1978.

20 SEP

The US nuclear-propelled submarine *Ray* (SSN 653) strikes bottom in the Mediterranean Sea, south of Sardinia. Three crewmen suffer minor injuries. Following the accident the *Ray* surfaces and proceeds under her own power to Sardinia.

21 SEP

Reuters News Service reports that the United States and Australia have signed an agreement for construction of the final Omega navigation station in the state of Victoria. This will complete the world-wide Omega network.

26 SEP

The final round of United States–Soviet talks on limitation of naval forces in the Indian Ocean begins in Washington, D.C.

30 SEP

The US Coast Guard ends 37 years of ocean weather station patrols when the cutter *Taney* (WHEC 37) departs Ocean Station Hotel, some 200 n.miles (370 km) east of the Maryland-Virginia line. An automatic weather buoy replaced the cutter.

3 OCT

The US-Soviet Strategic Arms Limitation Talks (SALT I) agreement, signed in 1972, expires, but both countries issue "unilateral" declarations to respect SALT I arms ceilings while negotiations for a SALT II treaty are under way.

4 OCT

Secretary of Defense Brown announces that the Soviet Union has an operational anti-satellite capability.

6 OCT

Secretary of Defense Brown issues department Directive 1354.1, prohibiting members of the Armed Forces from engaging in labor strikes.

18 OCT

The US aircraft carrier *Dwight D. Eisenhower* (CVN 69) is placed in commission at Norfolk, Va. This is the second nuclear-propelled carrier of the *Nimitz* (CVN 68) class. The ship's first CO is Capt. William E. Ramsey, USN.

21 OCT

A US Marine Corps CH-53 Sea Stallion helicopter, with 37 on board, crashes and burns 100 miles (161

km) south of Manila on Mindoro Island during a combined US Seventh Fleet–Philippine training exercise. Twenty-three US Marines and one sailor are killed; another 13 are injured.

27 OCT

According to *The Washington Post,* the US Navy has acknowledged the highest enlisted desertion rate in its history during FY 1977, with 31.7 desertions per 1,000 enlisted personnel (14,539 desertions out of a total enlisted force of 459,8576), which was almost six times the World War II high of 5.5 desertions per 1,000, more than triple the Korean War high of 8.7, and more than double the Vietnam War peak (FY 1973) of 13.6. Most of the deserters, 72 percent, were between ages 18 and 20, and 92 percent were on their first tour of duty; 79 percent were assigned to ships and 66 percent were in the lower mental categories.

31 OCT

The Associated Press reports that the British nuclear-propelled submarine *Dreadnought* was refused transit through the Suez Canal because Egypt objected to nuclear ships using the canal.

13 NOV

The Somalian government orders all Soviet advisors to leave that country within seven days, ends Soviet use of all naval facilities, including the base at Berbera, and breaks off diplomatic relations with Cuba.

29 NOV

The Navy states that the first Trident strategic missile submarine, the *Ohio,* is one year behind schedule and that her cost would be some 50 percent higher than the originally estimated cost of $800 million for a total cost of $1.2 billion. Completion is now expected in the spring of 1980.

17 DEC

The first ship of the *Oliver Hazard Perry* (FFG 7) class is commissioned at Bath, Maine. A total of 51 ships of this class will be built for the US Navy and four for the Australian Navy, more than any other post–World War II surface combatant design except for the 72-ship Soviet *Skoryy* class (completed 1950–1953). Similar ships to the *Perry* design will be built in Spain and Taiwan. The *Perry* is designed primarily for open-ocean convoy escort, but will be a very flexible warship. The *Perry's* first CO is Comdr. Stephen J. Avich, USN.

1978

24 JAN
The Soviet radar ocean surveillance satellite *Cosmos 954* re-enters earth's atmosphere and scatters radioactive debris over Canada.

26 JAN
Secretary of the Navy W. Graham Claytor, Jr., announces the choice of Kings Bay, Ga., as the site of a new submarine support base for fleet ballistic missile submarines. The base is scheduled to open in May 1979.

1 FEB
A Tomahawk cruise missile is successfully launched from the USS *Barb* (SSN 696) operating off the coast of California. This is the first Tomahawk launch from a submerged submarine.

6 FEB
The United Press International reports that the frigate *Truett* (FF 1095) has been dispatched from the Sixth Fleet to reinforce two ships of the Middle East Force operating in the Red Sea as the war between Ethiopia and Somalia heats up in the "horn" of Africa.

16 FEB
Under Secretary of Defense for Research and Engineering William J. Perry states in his annual report to Congress that the first five Trident submarines of the *Ohio* (SSBN 726) class would be delayed because of "inefficiencies and lower than expected productivity" at the Electric Boat yard in Groton, Conn. He anticipated that the Trident program would be back on schedule in FY 1983 with delivery of the sixth Trident submarine.

19 FEB
The Boston Globe reports an unofficial study that the newspaper calls an "alarming rate of cancer deaths" among Portsmouth (New Hampshire) naval shipyard workers, whose jobs brought them into the area of nuclear submarine reactors. The alleged death rate is more than twice the national average and nearly 80 percent higher than the rate for other shipyard workers who did no nuclear-related work.

21 FEB
The fourth round of US–Soviet talks on limiting Indian Ocean military activities ends in Bern, Switzerland, with no announced agreements and no date set for future talks.

3 MAR
The Washington Post reports that the governor of Puerto Rico and the mayor of Vieques Island have filed suit against the Defense Department and the Navy, claiming that the Navy violated environmental laws by bombing and strafing the target areas of Vieques.

11 MAR
The *Abraham Lincoln* (SSBN 602) becomes the first US strategic missile submarine to complete 50 deterrent patrols. During the submarine's 17 years of service, one-half of her operating time was submerged (74,571 hours) and she steamed 420,666 n.miles (790,073 km), the equivalent of circumnavigating the globe almost 17 times.

15 MAR
The Wall Street Journal reports that West Germany will build six submarines valued at $500 million for Iran. The 1,000-ton submarines are to be delivered between 1982 and 1984. Subsequent political pressure from other countries will lead to cancellation of the sale.

16 MAR
The US Senate ratifies the Panama Canal Neutrality Treaty by a vote of 68 to 32. The Senate will subsequently vote to turn the canal over to Panama on 31 Dec 1999.

17 MAR
President James E. Carter, Jr., visits the US Atlantic Fleet during operations off the East Coast, embarking in the carrier *Dwight D. Eisenhower* (CVN 69). Other ships in the task group are the cruiser *Virginia* (CGN 38), destroyer *Peterson* (DD 969), and frigate *Ainsworth* (FF 1090).

23 MAR
Ingalls Shipbuilding at Pascagoula, Miss., receives a $796 million contract from Iran for the construction of four modified *Spruance* (DD 963)–class destroyers. These ships are to be the guided missile (DDG) variant of the *Spruance,* which is not being procured by the US Navy. They are assigned US hull numbers DDG 993–996 for accounting purposes.

27 MAR
Three naval aircraft accidents occur in the San Diego area: An F-14 Tomcat fighter crashes on the freeway

near the Miramar Naval Air Station, killing one and seriously injuring the other; an A-4 Skyhawk crashes into the Pacific Ocean about 50 miles (80 km) from San Diego and the pilot is recovered; and an S-3A Viking explodes and crashes into the Pacific Ocean near San Diego, killing two.

4 APR

A four-nation naval exercise—RimPac 78—begins in the mid-Pacific consisting of 42 ships, 225 aircraft, and 22,000 personnel from Australia, Canada, New Zealand, and the U.S. Third Fleet.

6 APR

President Carter nominates Col. Margaret A. Brewer, USMC, to become the Marine Corps' first female general officer.

The USS *Nimitz* (CVN 68) is the first US aircraft carrier to visit Haifa, Israel.

7 APR

America's last all-passenger ocean-going ship, the Pacific Far East Line's SS *Mariposa* docks at San Francisco, ending American regular all-passenger ship service.

22 APR

The Associated Press reports a Navy study on radiation hazards in shipyards and on nuclear-powered ships indicates that radiation exposure to shipyard workers resulted in less than one death per 100,000 people, compared to the industrial accident rate at naval shipyards of seven per 100,000. The annual death rate attributed to smoking is 150 per 100,000. The Navy report criticizes a *Boston Globe*–sponsored study which alleged that Portsmouth, N.H., shipyard workers who were involved in the nuclear areas of submarines had twice the normal cancer rates. (*See* 19 Feb 1978.)

20 MAY

McDonnell Douglas delivers the 5,000th F-4 Phantom to be built; this is the largest post–World War II production run of any US fixed-wing military aircraft except for the F-86 Sabre. McDonnell Douglas will produce 5,057 Phantoms for US and foreign service while Japan builds 125 F-4EJ variants, including 11 from parts produced by McDonnell Douglas; all production will end in 1979. The last of 1,264 aircraft delivered to the US Navy and Marine Corps was completed in Dec 1971.

5 JUNE

The United States and Canada begin excluding each other's commercial fishing vessels from their respective waters after talks aimed at solving US–Canadian fishing management problems break down.

9 JUNE

The US Navy and General Dynamics Corp. announce a settlement of claims over the construction of *Los Angeles* (SSN 688)–class submarines, averting a threatened halt in submarine work at the Groton, Conn., yard and the layoff of 8,000 workers.

23 JUNE

The US Navy announces that three destroyers, the *William C. Lawe* (DD 763), *Robert A. Owens* (DD 827), and *Davis* (DD 937) will conduct a six-week Great Lakes cruise in August 1978 to train Naval Reserve crews and to bring a fleet presence to the lakes.

26 JUNE

The first eight women to graduate from a US service academy receive their diplomas and commissions in the Naval or Coast Guard Reserve at the Merchant Marine Academy, King's Point, Long Island, N.Y.

The 5,000-lb (2,268-kg) ocean research satellite *Seasat-A* is launched from Vandenburg Air Force Base, Calif., to determine if radar and other sensors in space could provide useful information for oceanographers, weather forecasters, and commercial users of the sea. The project is managed for NASA by the Jet Propulsion Laboratory, Pasadena, Calif.

15 JULY

The US Navy's training carrier *Lexington* (formerly CVT 16) becomes AVT 16, indicating auxiliary aircraft landing training ship. The change to AVT is to avoid confusion with operational carrier listings. (The "Lex" had been changed from CVS 16 to CVT 16 on 29 Dec 1968.)

27 JULY

US District Court Senior Judge John J. Sirica rules in a suit filed by several Navy women that it was unconstitutional for Congress to bar women arbitrarily from serving on Navy combatant ships. Instead, the judge said, it should be up to the Navy to assign its personnel—both men and women—as it deems appropriate.

7 AUG

The salvage ship *Preserver* (ARS 8) becomes the first US Navy ship to undergo a routine shipyard repair in Yugoslavia, at the Tivat shipyard.

17 AUG

President Carter vetoes the $36.9 billion defense bill for FY 1979, citing the $2-billion nuclear-propelled aircraft carrier in the bill as his reason for the veto.

30 AUG

Coast Guard Commandant Adm. John B. Hayes announces an equal opportunity program that removes all restrictions based solely on sex in training, assignment, and career opportunities of Coast Guard personnel. The new policy includes provisions that all women graduates of the Coast Guard Academy, like their male counterparts, will initially be assigned to sea duty and that mixed-sex crews can be assigned to any Coast Guard unit, afloat or ashore, which could provide reasonable privacy for each sex in berthing and personal hygiene.

31 AUG

The International Institute for Strategic Studies (IISS) in London states in its 1978–1979 *Military Balance* reports that although NATO remains strong enough to repel an attack by the Warsaw Pact, it is weaker in sea power than before and no longer in a position to control all sea areas of importance to the alliance at the start of a conflict.

7 SEP

The US House of Representatives votes 206 to 191 to override President Carter's veto of the FY 1979 defense bill, thus providing funds for the fifth nuclear-propelled aircraft carrier (CVN 71).

17 SEP

President Carter, Egyptian President Anwar Sadat, and Israeli Prime Minister Menachem Begin sign the Camp David Peace Accords, producing peace between Egypt and Israel. This is the first treaty signed by Israel with an Arab state since Israel was established in 1948. The accords call for the return of Sinai to Egypt, with the withdrawal of all Israeli forces and settlements. US troops will be indefinitely deployed to the Sinai to monitor the accords and the United States will build several bases in the Negev desert to replace the Israeli bases given up in Sinai.

29 SEP

The Baltimore Sun reports that a Japanese shipyard is prepared to deliver to the Soviet Union a 1,082 × 275.5-foot (330 × 84-m) floating drydock to be towed to Vladivostok. Japanese defense analysts state the drydock could be used to service a *Kiev*-class aircraft carrier.

30 SEP

The US Navy closes the last US military installation in Africa when the naval communications station at Kenitra, 25 miles (40 km) north of Rabat, is formally returned to the Moroccan government.

5 OCT

The FBI discloses the breakup of a plot to steal the nuclear-propelled attack submarine *Trepang* (SSN 674) and sell the submarine to an undisclosed purchaser. Three men are arrested in the investigation. One becomes a prosecution witness; the others are tried for fraud in US District Court in St. Louis, Mo.

The US Navy announces settlement of almost all $2.7 billion in ship construction contract claims in a settlement with Newport News Shipbuilding and Dry Dock Co. in Virginia related to the construction of nuclear-propelled surface ships and attack submarines.

10 OCT

The first US scientific satellite built to observe the world's oceans—the *Seasat-A*—suffers a massive short circuit and is rendered useless. (*See* 26 June 1978.)

20 OCT

President Carter signs the 1979 Defense Authorization Act which makes the Commandant of the Marine Corps a full member of the Joint Chiefs of Staff.

The 125-foot (38-m) US Coast Guard training cutter *Cuyahoga* (WIX 157) sinks in a collision with the Argentine freighter *Santa Cruz II* in Chesapeake Bay, three miles (4.8 km) from Smith Point, Va. The 51-year-old cutter sinks with 11 of her crew; 18 others are rescued by the freighter, which suffers no injuries and only minor damage. The *Cuyahoga*'s commanding officer, CWO Donald K. Robinson, USCG, will be found guilty of dereliction of duty in the sinking and a US District Court judge will rule that the collision is entirely the fault of the *Cuyahoga*.

21 OCT

The US Navy announces plans for assigning women to sea duty with 55 officers and 375 enlisted women to be assigned to 20 auxiliary ships during FY 1979.

1 NOV

For the first time in US Navy history, nine women report for regular sea duty in ships other than hospital or troop transports. The women, all ensigns, report aboard the Atlantic Fleet ships *L. Y. Spear* (AS 36), *Vulcan* (AR 5), and *Puget Sound* (AD 36); and the Pacific Fleet ships *Dixon* (AS 37) and *Norton Sound* (AVM 1).

9 NOV

The YAV-8B prototype of the US Marine Corps AV-8B Harrier VSTOL aircraft flies for the first time at the McDonnell Douglas Corp. in St. Louis, Mo. This aircraft is one of two AV-8B protoypes converted from AV-8A aircraft. The "B" variant is a significantly more capable aircraft.

14 NOV

A major US Atlantic Fleet exercise—GulfEx 79—begins in the Gulf of Mexico and western Caribbean. The exercise involves 20,000 personnel of the US Air Force, Navy, and Coast Guard, both active and reserve, as well as British forces. Nearly 300 aircraft participate in the exercise.

15 NOV

The US cruiser *Sterett* (CG 31), the destroyer *Waddell* (DDG 24), and the frigate *Bradley* (FF 1041) accompanied by the fleet oiler *Passumpsic* (T-AO 107) enter the Indian Ocean. This marks the beginning of an almost continuous US naval presence in that area through the remainder of the century.

17 NOV

United Press International reports that the Soviet guided missile cruiser *Dzerzhinsky*, with the Commander of the Black Sea Fleet embarked, has arrived in Istanbul, becoming the first Soviet warship to visit the Turkish port in 40 years.

18 NOV

First flight of McDonnell Douglas–Northrop F-18 Hornet carrier-based fighter aircraft. It will subsequently be redesignated F/A-18 (indicating strike-fighter) and will be widely used by the US Navy and Marine Corps as well as several foreign air forces.

4 DEC

HMS *Ark Royal*, the last conventional carrier in the Royal Navy, is paid off and decommissioned. The ship was laid down in 1943 but was not launched until after the war and was completed in 1955. Hereafter the Royal Navy will operate only VSTOL aircraft and helicopters from ships.

1979

1 JAN

The US Navy announces that Submarine Squadron 16 and the strategic missile submarine support facility at Rota, Spain, has begun moving to Kings Bay, Ga., in accord with provisions of the 1976 Treaty of Friendship and Cooperation with Spain.

16 JAN

As fighting increases in the streets of Iranian cities, the Shah of Iran, Mohammad Reza Pahlevi, flees Iran. This ends the close US military and intelligence ties with the nation.

22 JAN

President James E. Carter, Jr., announces his FY 1980 budget, which includes $6.1 billion for 15 new Navy ships, including funds for a $1.5-billion conventionally propelled 60,000-ton aircraft carrier (designated CVV). The carrier will not be built.

23 JAN

Secretary of the Navy W. Graham Claytor, Jr., announces plans to retire 37 ships during FY 1980. The ships consist of eight active Navy ships, five Military Sealift Command (MSC) ships, one oceanographic ship, and 23 Naval Reserve Force (NRF) ships. The Sixth Fleet flagship *Albany* (CG 10), and the Seventh Fleet flagship *Oklahoma City* (CG 5) are among the active ships to be retired.

24 JAN

A US federal district judge enjoins fisherman from interfering with naval operations on the gunnery range and landing areas of Vieques Island, Puerto Rico. The fisherman had been conducting "fish ins" and "camp ins" to stop the Navy from using the island. However, on 4 Feb 1979 the fisherman occupy Navy landing areas on the island.

14 FEB

Armed Iranian rebels shoot their way into the US Embassy compound in Tehran. Two US Marines are wounded in the incident.

17 FEB

Chinese forces invade northern provinces in Vietnam.

21 FEB

US Navy ships help in the evacuation of 440 people, including 200 US citizens, from the Iranian ports of Bandar Abbas and Char Bahar. Involved are the flagship *La Salle* (AGF 3), the destroyers *Blandy* (DD 943), *Decatur* (DDG 31), *Hoel* (DDG 13), and *Kinkaid* (DD 965), and the frigate *Talbot* (FFG 4).

6 MAR

A Soviet landing ship is reported by United Press International to have arrived at the Vietnamese port of Da Nang. It is the first visit by a Soviet naval ship to that port, which was formerly a US naval base.

8 MAR

The US Department of Defense announces that the aircraft carrier *Constellation* (CV 64) along with the *Sterett* (CG 31), *Waddell* (DDG 24), and *Kansas City* (AOR 3) have deployed to the western Indian Ocean in a show of support for North Yemen in its fight with the People's Democratic Republic of (South) Yemen.

The Baltimore Sun reports that the Carter Administration is considering the formation of an expanded Indian Ocean force, to be called the Fifth Fleet, with the mission of protecting vital Western oil supply routes from the Persian Gulf. However, the Fifth Fleet will not be established at this time. (The Fifth Fleet was originally established in Mar 1944 under the command of Adm. Raymond A. Spruance, USN, for operations against the Japanese; it was disestablished in Nov 1945.)

22 MAR

Private 1st Class Robert R. Garwood, USMC, arrives in Thailand for return to US authorities. He had spent the last 14 years as a prisoner of war in Vietnam, after disappearing in Sep 1965. It was alleged by other former US prisoners of war that Garwood had collaborated with the enemy.

25 MAR

Three Soviet Navy warships—a *Kresta*-class guided missile cruiser, a *Petya*-class frigate, and a minesweeper—arrive at Cam Ranh Bay, Vietnam. This is the first time that Soviet warships had called at that port, formerly a major US base.

30 MAR

The Baltimore Sun reports that a submarine base is being built at Cienfuegos on the southern coast of Cuba.

31 MAR

The British flag is lowered for the last time on the island of Malta in the central Mediterranean. This ends the association of Malta with Great Britain, which began in 1800.

1 APR

Lt. (jg) Beverly Kelly, USCG, becomes the first woman to command a US government ship as she takes command of the Coast Guard cutter *Cape Newagen* (WPB 95318). She is 26 years old.

9 APR

Five fires set by an arsonist on the US aircraft carrier *John F. Kennedy* (CV 67) kill one civilian shipyard employee and injure 34 other people while the ship is undergoing an overhaul at the Norfolk (Va.) Naval Shipyard. There is no serious damage to the ship.

10 APR

The USS *Francis Scott Key* (SSBN 657) carries out the first submerged launch of a Trident C-4 missile off the coast of Florida near Cape Canaveral.

11 APR

The USS *Patrick Henry* (SSBN 599) launches three Polaris A-3TA missiles off the Florida coast. These are the last US submarine launches of Polaris missiles. The first Polaris A-1 launch from a submarine occurred from the USS *George Washington* (SSBN 598) on 20 July 1960.

14 APR

The US Department of State reveals that two Soviet Tu-20 Bear-D reconnaissance aircraft had landed at Da Nang Air Base in Vietnam, apparently the first time Soviet combat aircraft had landed at that base. A spokesman states that the US government would be deeply concerned if Soviet ships and aircraft regularly use Vietnamese bases.

18 APR

The first Chinese merchant ship to enter a US port in 30 years, the 632-foot (192.7-m) *Liu lin Hai,* calls at Seattle, Wash.

5 MAY

The US frigate *Robert E. Peary* (FF 1073) rescues 440 Vietnamese refugees from their disabled craft some 400 n.miles (740 km) south of Thailand.

12 MAY

The US Atlantic Command begins exercise Solid Shield 79 with more than 19,000 Army, Navy, Air Force, and Marine personnel participating.

The NATO command Allied Forces Southern Europe begins a 12-day, eight-nation exercise named Dawn Patrol 79. Participants include 100 ships and 400 aircraft from France, Great Britain, Greece, Italy, the Netherlands, Portugal, Turkey, and the United States. Greece and France participate although neither is a part of NATO's military structure.

15 MAY

Two Soviet Il-38 May maritime patrol aircraft fly so close to the US carrier *Midway* (CV 41), operating in the Arabian Sea, that aircraft in the ship's landing pattern have to take evasive action. The US government protests the incident under the US-Soviet Incidents at Sea Agreement.

16 MAY

A US Coast Guard HC-130 Hercules aircraft sights the Soviet stern trawler *Zereche* anchored about five miles (8 km) inside the 200-n.mile (370-km) fishing zone off the coast of Alaska. When the Coast Guard cutter *Midgett* (WHEC 726) arrives on the scene and attempts to board the Soviet ship, the *Zereche* steams away from the zone, refusing to comply with Coast Guard signals.

Twelve protesting fishermen are arrested by US authorities for camping out on a Navy target range on Vieques, Puerto Rico.

17 MAY

Sixteen Puerto Rican fishing boats enter restricted waters off Vieques, disrupting a scheduled US Navy practice bombardment exercise as part of their protest against use of the island for military training.

19 MAY

Twenty-one persons are arrested on a restricted beach on Vieques Island used for Navy bombardment practice.

5 JUNE

Five small fires break out on the carrier *John F. Kennedy* located at the Norfolk (Va.) Naval Shipyard. There is only minor damage from the fires, with arson suspected. (*See* 9 Apr 1979.)

10 JUNE

The US submarine tender *Canopus* (AS 34) departs Rota, Spain, with Commander Submarine Squadron 16 embarked. Her sailing marks the complete withdrawal of US Polaris-Poseidon support facilities from Rota.

16 JUNE

The US Navy announces the reestablishment of the Merchant Marine Reserve program to provide direct commissions to qualified merchant marine officers, providing them with specialized training, including periodic active duty for training.

18 JUNE

President Carter and Soviet President Leonid Brezhnev sign the Strategic Arms Limitation Treaty (SALT II) in Vienna. (The agreement will not be ratified by the US Congress.)

26 JUNE

The US aircraft carrier *Forrestal* (CV 59) suffers three minor fires in which arson is suspected. The carrier is in port at Mayport, Fla., at the time.

30 JUNE

The Associated Press reports that the Navy is investigating Ku Klux Klan activities on board two unidentified Atlantic Fleet ships.

1 JULY

Lloyd's of London announces that because of the danger of terrorist attacks, oil tankers traveling through the Persian Gulf must have special "war-zone" insurance in order to be properly covered.

3 JULY

A fire sweeps through two berthing spaces of the helicopter carrier *Iwo Jima* (LPH 2), causing $1.5 million in damages and injuries to five sailors. The ship was berthed at the Norfolk (Va.) Naval Shipyard. A sailor will be arrested on 6 July and charged with setting the fire.

6 JULY

The US strategic missile submarine *James Monroe* (SSBN 622) arrives at Kings Bay, Ga., for the first SSBN refit at that base. The submarine had departed on patrol from the former tender site at Rota, Spain. The refit base at Kings Bay was activated on 2 July, one day after the required closure of the base at Rota, and will be formally designated as a submarine base on 1 Apr 1982.

8 JULY

A fire breaks out in the diesel generator space on the amphibious ship *Charleston* (LKA 113), moored at the Norfolk, Va., naval base. There is minor damage and no injuries. On 11 July three crewmen are detained in connection with the fire.

19 JULY

President Carter announces that he will use the Seventh Fleet to aid the Vietnamese "boat people" and bring refugees to safety.

21 JULY

United Press International reports that the replenishment ship *Concord* (AFS 5) sailed for the Mediterranean amid reports of racial troubles on board, sparked by alleged Ku Klux Klan activities in the ship.

23 JULY

The US replenishment oiler *Wabash* (AOR 5) rescues 19 Vietnamese refugees from a small boat in the South China Sea. This is the first of several hundred rescues of Vietnamese "boat people" by US Navy ships and those of foreign navies during the coming months.

24 JULY

The US Navy formally acquires four guided missile destroyers, a modification of the *Spruance* (DD 963) class, under construction for Iran at Ingalls Shipbuilding, Pascagoula, Miss. Congress provided $1.35 billion in the FY 1979 supplemental budget for the purchase of these ships, to be completed in 1981–1982 as the US *Kidd* (DDG 993) class.

27 AUG

Adm. of the Fleet Lord Louis Mountbatten, who had begun World War II as a destroyer squadron commander and ended it as Supreme Allied Commander in Southeast Asia, is killed by a terrorist bomb explosion on his boat, in Irish waters at the time.

31 AUG

The Associated Press reports that three white sailors on the US carrier *Independence* (CV 62), operating in the Mediterranean, have been arrested after they appeared in Ku Klux Klan–type robes and hoods in a living compartment, prompting a disturbance with black sailors.

1 SEP

The Washington Post reports that the US Department of State has confirmed revised intelligence assessments that conclude there are still 2,000 to 3,000 Soviet troops in Cuba.

8 SEP

The Associated Press reports that the Soviet intelligence collection ships *Gidrograf* and *Gavril Sarychev* have been operating some 35 n.miles (65 km) off the coast of southern California, closer than Soviet spy ships had been reported in several years.

10 SEP

The Greek state-controlled Neorion Shipyard signs an agreement with the Soviet government to repair Soviet merchant and naval auxiliary ships.

Thirteen midshipmen at the US Naval Academy are expelled on drug charges after a five-month investigation that involved 38 midshipmen.

11 SEP

The US Navy repair ship *Vulcan* (AR 5) departs Norfolk, Va., for a six-month deployment in the Mediterranean. She carries 55 women in her crew, the first US Navy ship other than a hospital ship or transport to deploy overseas with women on board. The deployment will last until the *Vulcan* returns to Norfolk on 1 Mar 1980.

14 SEP

The Spanish fishing trawler *Cudillero* is boarded and seized some 90 n.miles (167 km) east of Cape May, N.J., by the US Coast Guard cutter *Bibb* (WHEC 31). The trawler was charged with violating fishing limits within the 200-n.mile (370-km) fishing zone.

22 SEP

An atmospheric nuclear detonation occurs over the southern Indian Ocean, detected by a US Vela nuclear detection satellite. The detonation was from an Israeli nuclear weapon, reportedly the third weapon exploded in the test. This was said to be the test of a low-yield nuclear artillery round. Israel thus became the seventh country to test a nuclear device, following the United States, Soviet Union, Britain, France, China, and India.

23 SEP

The NATO Mediterranean exercise Display Determination 79 begins with 50 Allied ships and 400 aircraft from the US, British, Italian, Portuguese, and Turkish navies taking part. A combined amphibious landing in Turkey puts ashore 7,000 American, Italian, and Turkish troops as part of the exercise.

24 SEP

The NATO Atlantic exercise Ocean Safari 79 begins with ships from the US, Belgium, Canadian, Dutch, West German, Norwegian, and Portuguese navies participating.

A combined US–Canadian air, land, and sea exercise called Kernel Potlatch begins in the northeastern Pacific. The exercises includes 45 ships from the two navies with a combined US Marine–Canadian Army amphibious landing on Vancouver Island in British Columbia.

27 SEP

Fireman Muriel Macbride, a 22-year-old enlisted woman crewmember on board the US missile test ship *Norton Sound* (AVM 1), is lost at sea in the Pacific, 230 n.miles (426 km) southwest of Vancouver Island. She is the first Navy woman to be lost at sea since the service assigned women to ships in Dec 1978.

30 SEP

The US government turns over control of the Panama Canal Zone at midnight to the Panamanian government, ending three-quarters of a century of American control of the canal.

US Navy Reconnaissance Heavy Attack Squadron (RVAH) 7, flying the RA-5C Vigilante, is disestablished, ending the use of "heavy attack" aircraft in the fleet except for electronic surveillance and test variants of the A-3B Skywarrior.

1 OCT

President Carter announces that the United States would respond to the continued presence of a Soviet combat brigade in Cuba with several actions, including establishment of a permanent Caribbean Joint Task Force headquarters at Key West, Fla.; increased surveillance of Cuba; and more military exercises in the Caribbean area. Carter also announced that the United States had reinforced its naval presence in the Indian Ocean.

6 OCT

The New York Times reports that the Soviet 7,500-ton cargo ship *Kiodo* has arrived at the Greek Siros Island shipyard, the first ship to undergo repairs under the agreement with the Soviet Union. (*See* 10 Sep 1979.)

17 OCT

A force of 1,800 US Marines come ashore at the US naval base at Guantanamo, Cuba, in a demonstration of naval power in the wake of the Soviet refusal to withdraw its combat brigade from Cuba.

19 OCT

The Wall Street Journal reports that the US Navy will require some officers to enter nuclear-power training involuntarily to help overcome the acute shortage of officers for nuclear submarines. Only 42 percent of the nuclear-trained officers remain after their initial tour of duty in 1978 despite bonus pay.

About 70 US Marines, sleeping in their barracks at Mount Fuji, Japan, are burned—37 of them seriously —when flaming oil spills through their barracks. A 5,000-gallon (19,000-liter) rubber fuel container ruptured and the fuel ignited during typhoon Tip.

20 OCT

The strategic missile submarine *Francis Scott Key* begins the first US deterrent patrol with C-4 Trident missiles, departing Charleston, S.C.

24 OCT

Coast Guard Academy Cadet 1st Class Linda Johansen becomes the first woman to command a cadet corps at a US service academy. She is named regimental commander of the 817 Coast Guard cadets, of whom 83 are women.

28 OCT

South Korean President Chung Hee Park is assassinated. The US government responds by ordering a carrier task force, led by the *Kitty Hawk* (CV 63), into the area and deploying two Air Force E-3A Airborne Warning And Control System (AWACS) aircraft to South Korea.

4 NOV

Iranian militant students seize the US Embassy in Tehran, taking 66 Americans as prisoners, including 14 Marines and three Navy personnel. The students demand the return of the deposed Shah, who is in a New York hospital, to Iran for trial in exchange for the hostages.

In the joint US–Spanish exercise CrisEx 79, more than 3,000 Marines from the two countries land on the southeast Spanish coast.

5 NOV

Radio Hanoi announces the arrival in Haiphong, Vietnam, of a Soviet cruiser and two destroyers to celebrate the first anniversary of the Vietnam-Soviet Friendship Treaty.

8 NOV

The Canadian–US naval exercise Canus Marcor 79 begins in the North Atlantic with ships and planes of both nations.

19 NOV

Iranian militants free three American hostages at the US Embassy in Tehran—one female and two black Marines. Another ten Americans will be released the following day. All but one of the 53 remaining hostages will be held in captivity for more than a year.

21 NOV

A mob attacks and burns the American Embassy in Islamabad, Pakistan. One Marine and one US soldier are killed in the attack.

23 NOV

Secretary of Defense Harold Brown announces that he has ordered the Air Force and Navy to halt the training of 251 Iranian pilots and navigators in the United States.

1 DEC

A US Department of Energy (DOE) official reveals that about three-quarters of warheads of the Polaris A-1 SLBMs probably would not have functioned during the mid-1960s because of a mechanical defect. The disclosure was made as part of the debate over the comprehensive nuclear test ban. The problem, attributed to the aging of materials used in a missile safety device, was first detected in 1965 during a routine examination of Polaris missiles. In Nov 1966 broader Polaris testing of A-1 missiles revealed, according to a DOE official, that "three were bad to one good."

3 DEC

A US Navy bus en route to a communications station on Puerto Rico is attacked by terrorists. Two sailors are killed and ten are injured by gunfire.

12 DEC

The NATO ministers announce their decision to modernize European theater nuclear weapons by deploying 108 Pershing II launchers and 464 Tomahawk-type Ground-Launched Cruise Missiles (GLCMs). The Pershings are to be based in West Germany and the GLCMs in Belgium, Great Britain, Italy, and the Netherlands. The deployments are to counter Soviet deployment of improved theater nuclear weapons.

First flight of the US Navy's SH-60B Seahawk, the LAMPS (Light Airborne Multi-Purpose System) III that will be carried on board cruisers, destroyers, and frigates. The IBM/Sikorsky helicopter will fly from surface combatants in the SH-60B variant and from aircraft carriers in the modified SH-60F version. Several other navies will also procure the helciopter for shipboard operation.

22 DEC
The New York Times reports that the Somali government has offered the United States access to the former Soviet naval and air bases at Berbera.

27 DEC
Soviet forces invade Afghanistan in carrying out in effect a coup d'etat against the government of President Hafizullah Amin. Soviet *Spetnaz* (commandos) begin the invasion with a strike against the palace; Amin is killed and Babrak Karmal becomes president of Afghanistan. Soviet troop strength in Afghanistan will eventually reach 115,000 in the subsequent nine-year conflict.

1980

I JAN

Ships of the *Ticonderoga* (DDG 47) class are reclassified as guided missile cruisers (CG) with same hull numbers to better reflect their capabilities and cost. These are the first warships fitted with the Aegis radar/weapons control system. Initially, they will be commanded by captains.

The NATO Airborne Early Warning (NAEW) force is established. This first NATO aviation force consists of 18 NATO-operated Boeing E-3A Sentry Airborne Early Warning And Control System (AWACS) aircraft and 7 E-3D variants of No. 8 AEW Squadron of the Royal Air Force. The NATO planes are based at Geilenkirchen, Germany, and the RAF planes at Waddington in Lincolnshire, England. The NATO planes are manned by integrated crews from 11 nations—Belgium, Canada, Denmark, Germany, Greece, Italy, the Netherlands, Norway, Portugal, Turkey, and the United States.

10 JAN

Ens. Roberta L. McIntyre, USN, the electrical and "E" division officer of the submarine tender *Dixon* (AS 37), becomes the Navy's first woman to be designated as a Surface Warfare Officer (SWO).

14 JAN

The US aircraft carrier *Nimitz* (CVN 68) enters the Indian Ocean after transiting around the Cape of Good Hope. Accompanied by the nuclear-propelled missile cruisers *California* (CGN 36) and *Texas* (CGN 39), the addition of the *Nimitz* brings the number of US carriers in the Indian Ocean to three, accompanied by 22 other combat and support ships. The carriers *Kitty Hawk* (CV 63) and *Midway* (CV 41) are already on station. This is the largest concentration of US naval ships ever assembled in the Indian Ocean. The *Nimitz* group will reach the Arabian Sea on 23 Jan, having steamed 11,500 n.miles (21,310 km) from Italian ports at an average speed of 25 knots.

19 JAN

Local fishermen again protesting the use of Vieques Island, Puerto Rico, for naval gunfire practice, stop a naval firing exercise for more a than an hour before the Coast Guard forces the fishermen out of the area.

28 JAN

The 180-foot (54.9-m) US Coast Guard buoy tender *Blackthorn* (WLB 391) collides with the tanker *Capricorn* in Tampa Bay, Fla. The *Blackthorn* sinks with the loss of 23 personnel.

12 FEB

The Baltimore Sun reports that the governments of Kenya, Oman, and Somalia have agreed to permit US air and naval forces to have access to bases in those countries.

25 FEB

The Navy announces plans to retire 20 Navy ships during FY 1981: three active ships, three auxiliary ships of the Military Sealift Command, and 14 from the Naval Reserve Force. The active ships include the ballistic missile submarines *Theodore Roosevelt* (SSBN 600) and *Abraham Lincoln* (SSBN 602), the first such submarines to be decommissioned (*see* 28 Feb 1981). Under the SALT I agreement, the completion of the Trident missile submarine *Ohio* (SSBN 726) in 1981 will require the retirement of the older SSBNs.

Some 6,000 Japanese protesters demonstrate at Yokosuka against the Japanese Maritime Self-Defense Force sending two destroyers and eight aircraft to participate in the multination naval exercise RimPac 80. The 20-day exercise will begin on 26 Feb involving the navies of five Pacific countries—Australia, Canada, Japan, New Zealand, and the United States. The exercise will include 41 ships and 20,000 personnel.

28 FEB

The Associate Press reports that Australia and New Zealand have agreed in discussions with the United States, under the terms of their alliance treaty, to expand their military role in the Indian Ocean. Australia agrees to send a carrier task group led by the carrier *Melbourne* into the Indian Ocean.

The US Army accepts its first two M1 Abrams main battle tanks. The M1 will become the principal tank of the US Army as well as the Marine Corps.

I MAR

The newly established Rapid Deployment Joint Task Force (RDJTF) headquarters is opened at MacDill

AFB in Florida. This headquarters will evolve into the US Central Command (*see* 1 Jan 1983).

The New York Times reports that Chief of Naval Operations Adm. Thomas B. Hayward, USN, has proposed to the Secretary of Defense that the four *Iowa* (BB 61)–class battleships be modernized and reactivated along with the mothballed carrier *Oriskany* (CV 34), and that the missile cruisers *Albany* (CG 10) and *Chicago* (CG 11) be retained in active service and not retired. Hayward's proposal is meant to expand near-term Navy strength to meet commitments in the Indian Ocean.

Exercise Team Spirit 80 begins with US and South Korean forces of all services participating.

3 MAR

The pioneer nuclear-propelled submarine *Nautilus* (SSN 571) is decommissioned. After being modified, she will be towed to Groton, Conn., in 1985 and formally transferred to private control on 6 July 1985 for use as a museum.

14 MAR

A US Marine amphibious unit of 1,800 land in Norway as part of exercise Anorak Express, coming ashore from the *Newport* (LST 1179), *Ponce* (LPD 15), and *Saipan* (LHA 2).

7 APR

The US government breaks diplomatic relations with Iran.

Secretary of Defense Harold Brown announces that the United States plans to deploy seven ships loaded with miliary equipment and supplies to the Indian Ocean for contingency use by the Rapid Deployment Joint Task Force (RDJTF). The ships would be "married" with troops flown into a secure port from the United States. This is the start of the Maritime Prepositioning Ship (MPS) concept.

12 APR

The Washington Post reports that the fleet oiler *Canisteo* (AO 99) was unable to get under way because of a shortage of skilled sailors. This was the first time since the mid-1960s that a Navy ship has been unable to sail because of a shortage of personnel.

The carrier *Nimitz* celebrates being at sea for 100 continuous days, a US Navy record in the post–World War II period. Non-watch-standing personnel aboard the carrier, steaming in the Indian Ocean, celebrate with a picnic that includes two cans of beer, the alco-holic treat being especially authorized by Secretary of the Navy Edward Hidalgo.

The US Navy announces that the eight Polaris-armed missile submarines that are based at Guam would be withdrawn between July 1980 and Sep 1981. These are the last submarines armed with the Polaris A-3 missile.

16 APR

A US Navy master chief petty officer, attached to a NATO logistics office, is ambushed and killed by Turkish terrorists in Istanbul.

24 APR

In a complex operation attempting to rescue the 53 American hostages held at the US Embassy in Tehran, six USAF C-130 Hercules aircraft launch from Egypt and eight Navy RH-35D Sea Stallion helicopters launch from the carrier *Nimitz* in the Arabian Sea. The C-130s carry a joint US commando team, which are to transfer to the helicopters at a remote Iranian location known as Desert One. However, a sand storm forces two of the helicopters to land short of the base and one of the remaining helicopters develops mechanical problems. The mission is canceled and, during a refueling at Desert One a C-130 and one of the RH-53Ds collided. Three Marines and five Air Force personnel are killed in the accident.

27 APR

A nine-ship US battle group led by the carrier *Constellation* (CV 64) enters the Indian Ocean. This brings to 34 the number of Navy ships in the Indian Ocean–Persian Gulf area. The "Connie" will relieve the *Coral Sea* (CV 43) battle group.

29 APR

A three-ship US battle group centered on the carrier *Dwight D. Eisenhower* (CVN 69) enters the Indian Ocean, bringing to 37 ships the strength of US naval forces in the Indian Ocean–Persian Gulf area. The "Ike" group will relieve the *Nimitz* battle group.

4 MAY

The US government withdraws its last diplomats in Libya; however, diplomatic relations with Libya are not broken.

6 MAY

The Poseidon-armed US submarine *Ulysses S. Grant* (SSBN 631) arrives at La Spezia, Italy, for a four-day visit. This is the first SSBN to visit an Italian port.

8 MAY

Exercise Solid Shield 80, scheduled to begin in the Atlantic and Caribbean Sea, is modified because of the large numbers of refugees fleeing Cuba by boat. The amphibious landing, planned for the US naval base at Guantanamo Bay, Cuba, is canceled and the five amphibious ships and six ocean minesweepers that were to participate in the landing are ordered to assist the Coast Guard in aiding the refugees.

9 MAY

The US carrier *Coral Sea* arrives at Subic Bay in the Philippines after an Indian Ocean deployment. The ship had been at sea for 102 consecutive days.

21 MAY

The US Coast Guard Academy graduates 156 new ensigns, including the first woman graduates, numbering 14.

22 MAY

The US carrier *Coral Sea* is ordered to steam toward the Korean peninsula in response to civil strife in South Korea.

26 MAY

President James E. Carter, Jr., embarks in the carrier *Nimitz* off the coast of Virginia to thank the men of the *Nimitz, California,* and *Texas* upon their return from a nine-month deployment to the Mediterranean and Indian Ocean. The deployment included the *Nimitz* spending 144 consecutive days at sea.

28 MAY

At Gaeta, Italy, Vice Adm. William N. Small, USN, Commander Sixth Fleet, shifts his flag from the guided missile cruiser *Albany* to the destroyer tender *Puget Sound* (AD 38). This marks the end of the use of large cruisers as flagships for the US Navy's numbered fleets. (*See* 4 Oct 1985.)

At graduation ceremonies at the US Naval Academy, 55 women officers are among the 770 new ensigns and Marine 2nd lieutenants who are commissioned.

29 MAY

The US Joint Chiefs of Staff, testifying before a congressional committee, claim that President Carter's FY 1981 defense budget is insufficient to keep pace with Soviet military advances.

3 JUNE

In the first embarkation of Chinese officials in an aircraft carrier, 24 officials of the People's Republic of China, led by Vice Premier Geng Biao, embark in the USS *Ranger* (CV 61) off the coast of San Diego. The event, which includes an aerial firepower demonstration, is in reciprocation of the Jan 1980 visit by Secretary of Defense Brown to Chinese fleet headquarters in Shanghai.

President Carter approves a six-week, involuntary callup of up to 900 Coast Guard reservists to supplement active duty personnel who are involved with the Cuban refugee operation.

5 JUNE

The US State Department announces that the United States and Oman have formally agreed to American use of air and naval bases in Oman in exchange for technical, economic, and military aid.

12 JUNE

The US Coast Guard–directed Cuban refugee operation begins to wind down after the assistance of 125,000 refugees moving by sea to the United States. The operation cost the US government $51 million and involved large numbers of Coast Guard and Navy ships, aircraft, and personnel.

21 JUNE

The Washington Post reports that eight women sailors accused of lesbian activity on board the missile test ship *Norton Sound* (AVM 1) were informed that they would be charged with homosexual misconduct. Eight other women sailors were cleared of possible homosexual charges by an investigation. There are 61 women assigned to the *Norton Sound*.

30 JUNE

Representative Paul Trible (R-Va.), a member of the House Armed Services Committee, charges that three Navy ships about to deploy to the Sixth Fleet are not ready for combat. According to Trible, the carrier *John F. Kennedy* (CV 67), the cruiser *Josephus Daniels* (CG 27), and destroyer *Coontz* (DDG 40) are so short of skilled enlisted men that they were placed in the C-4 (not ready for combat) readiness category.

1 JULY

In one of the largest rescues of Vietnamese refugees, the US naval tanker *Sealift Antarctic* (T-AOT 176) picks up 176 refugees and nine Indonesians from a disabled Indonesian craft in the South China Sea.

11 JULY

HMS *Invincible*, Britain's first new-construction VSTOL carrier, is placed in commission. The full-deck carrier, with a full-load displacement of 20,600 tons, carries 18 Harrier VSTOL aircraft and helicopters. Two sister ships are under construction. These ships were initially designated as "through-deck cruiser" and then "anti-submarine cruiser" to avoid the term aircraft carrier.

Iranian authorities release American hostage Richard Queen, the vice consul of the American Embassy in Tehran, because he is seriously ill.

14 JULY

The US Navy reveals that seven UH-1 Huey helicopters assigned to the Naval Reserve Helicopter Light Attack Squadron (HAL) 4 at NAS Norfolk, Va., had been sabotaged by the cutting of electrical cables.

15 JULY

The British government announces that Great Britain will procure the Trident submarine missile system to replace the Polaris A-3 missile as that nation's nuclear deterrent force.

21 JULY

United Press International reports that a congressional spot check in Feb 1980 found that more than half of the Atlantic Fleet's F-14 Tomcat fighters at NAS Oceana, Va., were unprepared for combat.

23 JULY

The first production-line HH-65A Dolphin short-range recovery helicopter makes its maiden flight. The Coast Guard helicopter is based on the French-designed SA 360 (the HH-65A being the SA 366G variant).

5 AUG

The US Department of Defense reports that the seven near-term Maritime Prepositioning Ships (MPSs), loaded with matériel for 12,000 troops, were all on station at Diego Garcia in the Indian Ocean. The ships are the SS *American Champion*, SS *American Courier*, USNS *Jupiter* (T-AKR 11), USNS *Mercury* (T-AKR 10), USNS *Meteor* (T-AKR 9), USNS *Sealift Pacific* (T-AOT 168), and SS *Zapata Patriot*.

The Associated Press reports that the US carrier *John F. Kennedy* had to "borrow" about 50 petty officers from other ships because of shortages of experienced personnel before departing Norfolk, Va., en route to the Mediterranean for a six-month deployment with the Sixth Fleet.

6 AUG

The Norfolk newspaper *Virginian Pilot* reports that the Navy would begin a "triad" selective manning ex-

periment as a means of dealing with personnel shortages. The experiment involved "borrowing" petty officers from two Norfolk-based frigates and assigning them to a third ship. Thus, one ship would be fully manned for deployment, one manned for coastal operations, and the third manned only to provide for security and pier-side maintenance and training. The ships are the *Ainsworth* (FF 1090), *Donald B. Beary* (FF 1085), and *Thomas C. Hart* (FF 1092).

18 AUG

A Navy administrative board rules that an 18-year-old woman fireman apprentice had engaged in homosexual activity aboard the *Norton Sound* and recommended her discharge from the Navy. On 21 Aug a board will rule that a 25-year-old woman fireman recruit also had engaged in homosexual activity aboard the *Norton Sound* and recommends her discharge from the Navy. Charges against other women on the ship are dropped while two others charged with misconduct are cleared.

21 AUG

A Soviet Echo II-class nuclear-propelled submarine catches fire and loses power some 90 n.miles (167 km) east of Okinawa. Nine crewmembers are killed and three injured in the accident. The submarine is taken in tow by a Soviet tug.

22 AUG

Secretary of Defense Brown announces that the United States has made a major technological advance in "stealth" technology that will enable aircraft to evade radars. The statement is in response to critics of the Carter Administration who demand production of the B-1 strategic bomber.

24 AUG

The former US light cruiser *St. Louis* (CL 49), a veteran of many World War II engagements, sinks in heavy seas off the coast of South America. The cruiser had been sold to Brazil in 1951; retired from that Navy, she was being towed to Taiwan for scrapping when lost.

26 AUG

United Press International reported that Navy officials said the number of unauthorized absentees in the Navy climbed to its highest level since World War II, reaching 38,200 in FY 1979, representing an 83.4 AWOL rate per 1,000 enlisted personnel, a five percent increase over the previous year.

28 AUG

The Japanese Self-Defense Agency announces an accelerated program including the construction of ten warships amounting to a record 21,480 tons, or more than double the current year's naval program.

4 SEP

The Iraq-Iran War begins, initiated by Iraq, whose dictator Saddam Hussein believes that the fundamentalist revolution in Iran and lack of US military logistics support has greatly weakened Iranian military forces. On 22 Sep Iraqi land and air forces will attack across the Shatt-al-Arab estuary that separates the two countries.

10 SEP

US Secretary of the Navy Hidalgo announces delays in the delivery of seven nuclear-propelled submarines under construction at the Electric Boat yard in Groton, Conn. The problems include a five-month delay in the delivery of the first Trident submarine, the *Ohio*. The delays for six *Los Angeles* (SSN 688)–class attack submarines range from three to 14 months.

The major NATO exercise Team Work 80 begins in the Atlantic. Eight nations are participating with 170 ships, 400 aircraft, and 60,000 personnel.

17 SEP

The US and Chinese governments sign major trade agreements to open the ports in both countries to each other's merchant ships for the first time since 1948.

29 SEP

The NATO exercise Display Determination 80 begins in the Mediterranean with forces from seven countries participating: Great Britain, Italy, the Netherlands, Portugal, Turkey, and the United States; France, although not part of NATO's integrated military structure, also had forces participating.

Swedish Defense Minister Erik Korenmark announces that the Swedish Navy will drop explosives close to an unidentified submarine lying off Stockholm to force her to surface. The submarine, assumed to belong to a Warsaw Pact navy, was believed to have been in Swedish waters for two weeks.

30 SEP

The US Department of Defense announces that four USAF E-3A Airborne Warning And Control System (AWACS) aircraft would be deployed to Saudi Arabia to provide early warning of possible Iranian air attacks against Saudi Arabia.

The US aircraft carrier *Saratoga* (CV 60) arrives at the Philadelphia Naval Shipyard to begin the first Service Life Extension Program (SLEP) overhaul of a carrier. The $526-million, 28-month effort will include rehabilitation of the ship's hull, propulsion, auxiliary machinery, and piping systems, with improved radars, communications equipment, and new aircraft launch and recovery systems. SLEP is intended to add about 15 years to a carrier's nominal 30-year service life.

All US naval districts except Naval District Washington (D.C.) are disestablished. The naval district functions are transferred to appropriate local or naval base commanders.

1 OCT

The Office of Anti-Submarine Warfare and Ocean Surveillance Programs (OP-095) in the Office of the Chief of Naval Operations, which dates from 1964, is renamed the Office of Naval Warfare. It is a far-reaching change as the Chief of Naval Operations, Adm. Hayward, seeks to address naval programs from a "warfare" as well as "platform" perspective. The first Director of Naval Warfare is Vice Adm. Kinnaird R. McKee, USN. (*See* 1 May 1964.)

5 OCT

The Washington Post reports that the Three Mile Island nuclear accident has aggravated a "crisis" in the Navy's nuclear submarine force as private utilities are hiring away experienced Navy nuclear-qualified specialists. The Vice Chief of Naval Operations, Adm. James D. Watkins, USN, is quoted saying, "I consider it [loss of Navy nuclear-power specialists] to be the most serious personnel readiness situation that I have seen in over 31 years in the Navy."

7 OCT

Iranian artillery sinks three foreign freighters and damage two others in the Iranian port of Khorramshar during an exchange of gunfire with advancing Iraqi forces. These are the first attacks on merchant ships in the Iraq-Iran conflict. (*See* 21 May 1981.)

11 OCT

Secretary of Defense Brown states that the guided missile cruiser *Leahy* (CG 16) has been ordered into the Persian Gulf to provide air defense for Saudi Arabia. It was also announced that two Air Force tanker aircraft were dispatched to Saudi Arabia to support the four USAF E-3A AWACS aircraft already in Saudi Arabia.

12 OCT

US Under Secretary of the Navy Robert J. Murray testifies before Congress that the shortage of submarine officers is particularly severe. Of the 700 new submarine officers needed in the current year, that Navy projected a 100-officer shortfall. While the Navy needs to retain 60 percent of its submarine officers after their initial five-year obligation, in 1979 only 42 percent were retained. The 1980 officer retention rate was expected to drop to 34 percent. Enlisted submarine retention was also critical; with a goal of keeping 60 percent of the second- and third-term submariners, only 45 percent are reenlisting.

17 OCT

The New York Times reports that more than 60 Australian, British, French, and US warships are operating in the Persian Gulf, Arabian Sea, and Indian Ocean to prevent interference with tanker traffic moving to and from the Persian Gulf.

18 OCT

The US nuclear-propelled guided missile cruiser *Arkansas* (CGN 41) is placed in commission at Newport News, Va., with Capt. Dennis S. Read, USN, in command. She is the ninth and last US nuclear-propelled surface combatant to be built. (Nuclear aircraft carrier construction will continue.)

20 OCT

The 16-day, Anglo-American naval exercise called Beacon Compass begins in the Indian Ocean with 25 ships, 170 aircraft, and 18,000 personnel taking part.

24 OCT

The 9th US Court of Appeals in San Francisco upholds a Navy regulation requiring personnel who are known to have engaged in homosexual conduct to be discharged from naval service.

27 OCT

The US naval tanker *Sealift Arctic* (T-AOT 175) rescues 300 Vietnamese refugees in the South China Sea.

28 OCT

French Navy officials announce the formation of a five-ship task force consisting of four minesweepers and a command and control ship to be placed on standby alert to steam into the Persian Gulf if mines are used to threaten tanker traffic in the Iraq-Iran conflict.

7 NOV

The US Department of Defense announces that Egypt has invited the United States to send a 1,400-man unit from the Rapid Deployment Joint Task Force (RDJTF) to Egypt to train with Egyptian air and ground forces in Nov 1980.

11 NOV

The US Navy confirms that the service is investigating possible arson on the carrier *Saratoga* (CV 60), undergoing a major overhaul at the Philadelphia Naval Shipyard, after four minor fires were reported between 22 and 26 Oct 1980.

14 NOV

Former President Richard M. Nixon embarks in the nuclear-propelled attack submarine *Cincinnati* (SSN 693) for a brief cruise.

19 NOV

A week-long combined American-Philippine exercise called Valiant Blitz begins on Mindoro Island in the Philippines. Participating are 5,000 US Marines and 16 ships plus aircraft from the US Seventh Fleet.

25 NOV

The New York Times reports that the US Navy's Trident submarine program is suffering from technical and managerial problems and that completion of the first Trident submarine, the *Ohio*, may be delayed until 1982. The Department of Defense states that the *Ohio* is "on track" for a 29 June 1981 delivery.

2 DEC

The Department of Defense reverses an earlier statement and says that there have been several slippages in work on the Trident submarine *Ohio*, making her delivery date uncertain. (*See* 25 Nov 1980.)

6 DEC

The New York Times reports that the Navy has signed a consent decree in federal court agreeing to spend between $2 and $5 million to clean up unexploded ordnance over one-third of Kahoolawe Island, Hawaii. The Navy maintained in the decree that it intended to keep the uninhabited island as its principal training area in the mid-Pacific.

8 DEC

A surprise random urinalyses test by the US Navy of San Diego and Norfolk sailors in pay grades E-1 through E-5 shows that 48.2 percent of the 1,050 San

Diego sailors tested and 48.6 percent of the 1,017 Norfolk sailors tested had positive signs of marijuana or hashish use. Confidence level in the test was 95 percent.

9 DEC
Four USAF E-3A Airborne Warning And Control System (AWACS) aircraft are deployed to a base in West Germany in response to Soviet troop buildups near Poland. US Navy E-2 Hawkeye aircraft from carrier Airborne Early Warning Squadron (VAW) 124 will be sent to Iceland to replace the Air Force planes. Subsequently, these E-2s will be replaced by Naval Air Reserve volunteers from squadrons VAW-18 and VAW-78.

11 DEC
In the continuing rescue of Vietnamese "boat people," the US destroyer *Robison* (DDG 12) picks up 250 in the Gulf of Thailand.

18 DEC
The US State Department announces that the US government has accepted $16 million from Israel as the final settlement on the US claim for compensation for damage to the US intelligence collection ship *Liberty* (AGTR 5) as a result of Israeli air and naval attacks on 8 June 1967. The government of Israel had already paid a claim of $6.7 million on behalf of the families of those who were killed and injured in the incident.

22 DEC
The US carrier battle group composed of the carrier *Dwight D. Eisenhower* and the cruisers *South Carolina* (CGN 37) and *Virginia* (CGN 38) returns to Norfolk, Va., after a 251-day deployment, the longest for US Navy ships since World War II. The "Ike" was under way for 152 continuous days.

23 DEC
President Carter signs into law the Military Pay and Allowances Benefit Act of 1980 that substantially increases sea and submarine special pay, making the latter a career incentive pay similar to aviation career pay.

30 DEC
The Soviet nuclear-propelled missile cruiser *Kirov* is placed in commission. The world's largest warship built since World War II except for aircraft carriers and amphibious helicopter carriers, the *Kirov* has a full-load displacement of 28,000 tons. Later renamed *Admiral Ushakov*, this is the first of four such cruisers that will be completed through 1996.

1981

5 JAN

Submarine Squadron 17 is established at Bangor, Wash., to direct the operations of *Ohio* (SSBN 726)–class Trident submarines in the Pacific.

7 JAN

Adm. Harry D. Train II, USN, Comander in Chief US Atlantic Fleet, reports that fleet retention is up in the wake of the Oct 1980 compensation increases passed by Congress. Citing Nov 1980 figures, Train states that first-term Atlantic Fleet reenlistments were up 25 percent, second-term reenlistments were up 21 perecnt, and career reenlistments were up 14 percent over the previous year.

15 JAN

The American tuna trawler *Rosa D* is seized by the Ecuadorian Navy 65 n.miles (120 km) off Ecuador's coast and charged with unauthorized passage through waters claimed as territorial by Ecuador and fishing without a license. The following day Rep. Bill Lowery (R-Calif.) announces plans to challenge the sale of the destroyer *Southerland* (DD 743) to Ecuador. Sale of the destroyer will be canceled.

20 JAN

Ronald Reagan is sworn in as the 40th President of the United States. Simultaneous with his taking office, Iran frees the 52 hostages taken at the American Embasssy on 4 Nov 1979. Among the hostages, freed on their 444th day of captivity are nine Marines and three Navy personnel. They will arrive in the United States on 25 Jan.

5 FEB

John F. Lehman, Jr., is sworn in as the 65th Secretary of the Navy and the same day testifies before the Senate Armed Services Committee. Lehman declares that the United States must reestablish maritime superiority. He calls for a fleet of 600 active ships, including 15 aircraft carriers.

At the same hearing, Chief of Naval Operations Adm. Thomas B. Hayward, USN, states "Our margin of comfort is gone. We are operating at the ragged edge of adequacy when it comes to our globally disposed naval forces."

At Camp Lejeune, N.C., a court martial finds Private 1st Class Robert R. Garwood, USMC, guilty of collaboration with the enemy while a prisoner of war in Vietnam.

Vice Adm. Bobby Ray Inman, USN, former Director of the National Security Agency (NSA), is confirmed by the Senate to be Deputy Director of Central Intelligence with promotion to the rank of admiral in that position. Inman is the first Navy intelligence specialist (1630 designator) to attain four-star rank.

NATO maritime exercise Test Gate 81 begins in the North Atlantic and western Mediterranean with air and naval forces from Belgium, Canada, West Germany, Great Britain, Italy, the Netherlands, Portugal, and the United States participating.

7 FEB

The Philadelphia Inquirer reports that the Thai Navy, with $2 million in US aid, has begun operation of an air-sea task force to halt the pirate raids on Vietnamese refugees in the Gulf of Thailand.

24 FEB

Exercise ReadEx 1-81 begins in the Atlantic and Caribbean with US Second Fleet ships and aircraft.

28 FEB

The US Polaris missile submarines *Theodore Roosevelt* (SSN 600) and *Abraham Lincoln* (SSBN 602) are decommissioned and stricken on this date. They are the first Polaris submarines to leave the fleet, marking the first time since 1967 that there have been less than 41 strategic missile submarines in commission in the US Navy.

4 MAR

US Secretary of Defense Caspar W. Weinberger announces details of the Reagan Administration's revised FY 1981 Supplemental and FY 1982 Defense Budget. The proposals provide $57.8 billion for the Navy Department in FY 1981 and $70.8 billion in FY 1982, increases of 11 precent and 15 percent, respectively, compared with Carter budget proposals. Among the Reagan changes are proposals to reactivate the aircraft carrier *Oriskany* (CV 34) and the battleships *Iowa* (BB 61) and *New Jersey* (BB 62), and to increase ship construction programs.

12 MAR

Vice Adm. Earl B. Fowler, USN, Commander of the Naval Sea Systems Command, testifies before the

House Armed Services Seapower Subcommittee about the problems at the Electric Boat yard in Groton, Conn. Fowler says that quality assurance problems had significantly delayed construction of both the *Ohio* and *Los Angeles* (SSN 688) submarines.

17 MAR

Three US Marines are injured when a bomb is thrown at an American Embassy van in San Jose, Costa Rica.

25 MAR

P. Takis Veliotis, General Manager of the Electric Boat Division of General Dynamics Corp., testifies before the House Armed Services Seapower Subcommittee and states that the yard has been unfairly criticized by the Navy for submarine delays. According to Veliotis, much of the blame for delays has been due to Navy-provided equipment and design changes.

1 APR

The US Navy announces that the option with the Electric Boat Division of General Dynamics Corp. to construct the ninth Trident submarine (SSBN 734), authorized in FY 1981, would not be exercised. The option expired on 31 Mar 1981 and the delay in contract award reflected the Navy's concern over slippages in the construction schedules for the eight *Ohio*-class submarines already under construction at Electric Boat.

9 APR

The US strategic missile submarine *George Washington* (SSBN 598), operating submerged in the East China Sea, collides with the 2,350-ton Japanese merchant ship *Nissho Maru*. The merchant ship sinks in the collision, about 110 n.miles (204 km) southwest of Sasebo, Japan; two Japanese are killed and 13 survived. There is only minor damage and no injuries on the "GW." On 20 Apr Secretary of the Navy Lehman will announce that the US Navy accepts full liability for the collision.

10 APR

The US Department of Defense announces that the Extremely Low Frequency (ELF) communications project near Clam Lake, Wisc., will be reactivated with a planned initial operational capability in the fall of 1981. ELF is a shore-to-submerged submarine communications system to permit signal reception while the submarine is at operational depths and speeds.

12 APR

First orbital flight of the US space shuttle *Columbia* (STS-1), which stands for Space Transportation System. First landing from orbit of a reusable spacecraft. Launched from Cape Canaveral and piloted by astronauts Capt. John W. Young, USN (Ret.), and Capt. Robert L. Crippen, USN. After a flight of 36 orbits, which takes 2 days, 6 hours, 20 minutes, the craft lands on 14 Apr at Edwards AFB, Calif.

The space shuttle alleviates the need for ocean recovery of manned spacecraft, which had been a fundamental requirement of the US Mercury, Gemini, and Apollo space programs.

19 APR

Four US Navy sailors from the amphibious ship *Raleigh* (LPD 1) are picked up by a Cuban patrol boat when their recreation boat strays into Cuban waters near the US naval base at Guantanamo Bay, Cuba. The follow day the Cuban government will release the sailors to foreign diplomats representing US interests in Havana.

24 APR

Secretary of Defense Weinberger announces that over a period of three to five years the Rapid Deployment Joint Task Force (RDJTF) should evolve into a separate unified command. The first action toward this goal is the assignment of the Army's XVIII Airborne Corps to the RDJTF.

1 MAY

The US Atlantic Command begins exercise Solid Shield 81 in the Atlantic with more than 27,000 soldiers, sailors, airmen, and Marines.

3 MAY

The Associated Press reports than the American-owned, British-manned seismographic research ship *Western Sea* was seized by Iranian officials in the Persian Gulf. The 141-foot (43-m) ship with a crew of 19 strayed into the Iran-Iraq declared war zone in the Persian Gulf while operating under a research contract with Kuwait.

4 MAY

The combined Australian–New Zealand–US exercise Beacon South 81-2 begins in the Indian Ocean off the western coast of Australia. The exercise involves 10 ships, 120 aircraft, and 8,000 men.

5 MAY

In testimony before Congress, Adm. H. G. Rickover,

USN (Ret.), head of the Navy's nuclear propulsion program, cites alleged inefficiencies in private shipyards building Navy ships. He states that the Navy should start building submarines and perhaps acquire private facilities such as the Electric Boat Division of General Dynamics Corp., and hire civilian managers to operate them.

6 MAY

The USS *America* (CV 66) becomes the first large-deck US aircraft carrier to pass through the Suez Canal in nearly 14 years. She is en route to the Indian Ocean. The last US carrier to transit the canal was the smaller *Intrepid* (CVS 11) on 1 June 1976.

11 MAY

The previous Australian–New Zealand–US naval exercise (*see* 4 May 1981) expands into the eastern Indian Ocean with 12 ships, 85, aircraft, and 10,000 personnel involved.

16 MAY

Japanese fishermen claim that US Seventh Fleet ships taking part in a combined Japanese-US exercise sliced through the nets of Japanese fishing craft off the northern Japanese island of Hokkaido. Subsequently, the Commander Seventh Fleet indicates that the Soviet missile cruiser *Petropavlovsk*, which was monitoring the exercise, probably inflicted the damage.

18 MAY

Former American ambassador to Japan Edwin O. Reischauer, a Harvard professor, states that Japan has permitted US warships to carry nuclear weapons into Japanese ports under a 21-year-old confidential agreement. According to Reischauer, who served in Japan from 1961 to 1966, the agreement permitted the United States to put nuclear weapons ashore in Japan as well as having them in ships within Japanese ports.

19 MAY

British Prime Minister Margaret Thatcher dismisses Navy Minister Keith Speed for his outspoken criticism of planned major cuts in the Royal Navy's budget.

21 MAY

Iraqi aircraft attack and slightly damage the Panamanian-flag bulk carrier *Louise I* just outside the northern Iranian port of Bandar Khomeini. This is the first specific attack against merchant shipping by Iranian and Iraqi forces during their conflict. (*See* 7

Oct 1980.)

25 MAY

Japanese Prime Minister Zenko Suzuki tells the Diet that he believes that US nuclear weapons had *not* been brought into Japan despite statements by former US officials. The Japanese government also rejects a demand by the opposition party that the US carrier *Midway* (CV 41) be banned from returning to her home port of Yokosuka.

26 MAY

The USS *John Marshall* (SSBN 611) begins the final offloading of Polaris A-3 missiles from a US submarine; the offload is completed on 20 June 1981, when the *Marshall* is reclassified as an attack submarine (SSN).

A Marine EA-6B Prowler aircraft crashes while attempting to land on the aircraft carrier *Nimitz* (CVN 68) some 60 n.miles (111 km) off the Atlantic coast of Florida. The aircraft skidded across the flight deck starting fires. Three in the EA-6B were killed as were 11 on the flight deck; another 48 *Nimitz* crewmen were injured. The fires were quickly extinguished and the carrier returned to Norfolk where repairs required two days.

In June 1981 Rep. Joseph P. Addabbo (D-N.Y.), Chairman of the Defense Subcommittee of the House Appropriations Committee, will charge that illegal drug usage on board the *Nimitz* may have contributed to the *Nimitz* crash. He states that autopsies revealed that a majority of the flight deck sailors and Marine fliers killed were found to have traces of drugs in their bodies. Secretary of the Navy Lehman labels Addabbo's information as inaccurate and categorically denies that drug use or abuse contributed to the accident.

No evidence of illegal drugs is found in the bodies of the two Marine fliers that were recovered. However, six of the 11 flight deck crewmen killed in the crash are found to have evidence of marijuana in their bodies. Navy witnesses say that drug use did not contribute to the accident.

1 JUNE

The US Supreme Court rejects a challenge to Navy regulations in a case in which a former Navyman had appealed his 1975 discharge for engaging in homosexual acts while in the service. The justices, without comment, let stand a lower court ruling.

Testing begins of the US Cargo Aircraft Minelayer (CAML) system to permit conventional cargo aircraft such as the C-5 Galaxy, C-141 Starlifter, and C-130 Hercules to lay naval mines. The system, developed by the Lockheed-Georgia Co., will be tested for 2½ months, with mine drops from altitudes of 1,000 feet (305 m) and 2,000 feet (610 m).

5 JUNE

After a three-month deployment, the US carrier *Midway* arrives at her home port of Yokosuka as thousands of anti-nuclear demonstrators protest near the Japanese naval base.

7 JUNE

Eight Israeli F-16 Falcon fighter-attack aircraft destroy Iraq's nuclear facility at Osiraq. The surprise attack—the first ever against a nuclear facility—is a success, destroying Iraq's ability to develop nuclear weapons. Although guided bombs were available to the Israelis, they used 12 2,000-pound (907-kg) unguided "iron bombs." One watchman is killed in the Sunday strike. Six F-15 Eagle fighters flew protective cover for the attack.

17 JUNE

In a report to the House Appropriations Committee, the US General Accounting Office (GAO) states that the Navy would find it hard to conduct even the most limited mining or mine countermeasures operations. The GAO report calls for a higher budget priority for Navy mine warfare programs.

26 JUNE

The US helicopter carrier *Nassau* (LHA 4) departs the Mediterranean after a successful two-month deployment with the Sixth Fleet in a "sea control" configuration, having successfully operated 19 Marine AV-8A Harrier VSTOL aircraft.

27 JUNE

The US strategic missile submarine *James K. Polk* (SSBN 645) carrying 16 Poseidon C-3 missiles returns to Charleston, S.C., marking completion of the 2,000th SSBN deterrent patrol since Nov 1960.

1 JULY

The US submarine base at Bangor, Wash., is activated to support *Ohio*-class Trident missile submarines.

A Center for Naval Warfare is established at the Naval War College in Newport, R.I., to serve as a focal point for Navy strategic planning.

7 JULY

Naval infantry (marines) from the Soviet Mediterranean Squadron land in Syria during a training exer-

cise. This is the first such amphibious operation known to have occurred in the eastern Mediterranean.

US Deputy Secretary of Defense Frank C. Carlucci announces that the Army and Navy will transfer the sealift cargo and passenger assignment functions from the Navy's Military Sealift Command (MSC) to the Army's Military Traffic Management Command (MTMC). The MSC will continue as the sealift operator and procurement agent, and as the principal Department of Defense intermediary with the US Merchant Marine and the Maritime Administration.

24 JULY

Cuban MiG-21 fighters are twice turned back by US Navy F-14 Tomcat fighters as the Cuban aircraft came within 60 n.miles (111 km) of the carrier *Independence* (CV 62), operating southeast of Florida. No guns or missiles are fired.

27 JULY

The US guided missile destroyer *Kidd* (DDG 993) is placed in commission, the first of four missile-armed variants of the *Spruance* (DD 963)–class destroyers originally ordered by Iran but taken over by the US Navy. The ship's first commanding officer is Comdr. William Flannagan, USN. The three other ships will enter service in 1981–1982.

The US battleship *New Jersey* departs the Puget Sound Naval Shipyard (Wash.), under tow, en route to the Long Beach Naval Shipyard (Calif.) for a 21-month modernization and reactivation. She will be the first of the four *Iowa*-class battleships reactivated under the Reagan-Lehman naval buildup.

28 JULY

A US Navy spokesman announces that disciplinary procedures had been initiated in the case of three officers of the carrier *Ranger* (CV 61), including the commanding officer, Capt. Dan A. Pedersen, USN, following an investigation into the death of Paul E. Trerice, USN, an airman recruit on the ship on 14 Apr 1981. Action is also begun against 17 Navy enlisted men and eight enlisted Marines. The following day Pedersen will be awarded a letter of censure by the Commander Naval Air Force Pacific Fleet.

1 AUG

The largest US maritime exercise in several years, Exercise Ocean Venture 81, begins in the South Atlantic to test Atlantic-wide conduct of a war-at-sea. Combining several previous exercise series, ships and aircraft from 14 nations will be involved, totalling 250 ships and 1,000 aircraft manned by 120,000 personnel. The exercise will conclude on 15 Oct 1981 after operations in the Atlantic, Caribbean, and Baltic areas.

6 AUG

President Reagan signs into law the authorization to transfer the Maritime Administration from the Department of Commerce to the Department of Transportation.

12 AUG

The Associated Press reports that the Iranian News Agency (PARS) has stated that the Danish ship *Else Cat* carrying military equipment and explosives to Iraq was seized by the Iranian naval units as she passed through the Strait of Hormuz. Danish officials said that the ship was carrying 177 tons of dynamite bound for Baghdad and another consignment of ammunition destined for the Arabian Gulf Emirate of Dubai.

19 AUG

Two US Navy F-14 Tomcat fighters from the carrier *Nimitz* shoot down two Libyan Su-22 Fitter fighters over the Mediterranean, about 60 n.miles (111 km) off the Libyan coast. The Su-22s make what the US Navy called an unprovoked attack on the F-14s, which then shoot down the Libyan aircraft with Sidewinder missiles.

20 AUG

President Reagan visits the US carrier *Constellation* (CV 64) off the coast of southern California and observes a firepower demonstration.

21 AUG

The US Navy awards a contract to Sea-Land Industries Inc. for the purchase of six of the firm's SL-7 high-speed container ships. Eventually eight of these ships, built in 1971–1973, will be acquired by the Navy for fast sealift. The 33-knots ships, built in the Netherlands and West Germany, are the fastest merchant ships ever to sail under the US flag.

26 AUG

A North Korean surface-to-air missile is fired at a USAF SR-71 Blackbird reconnaissance aircraft over the sea, near the demilitarized zone between North and South Korea. The SR-71 is not damaged.

30 AUG

Protesting Puerto Rican fishermen refuse to allow Rear Adm. Ralph Hedges, USN, Commander US Naval Forces Caribbean, to moor his barge at Vieques for a local ceremony. Hedges transfers to a police launch and is greeted on shore by a pro-Navy group that then gets into a fight with anti-Navy protesters. Several teenage Sea Cadets are injured in the melee.

31 AUG

Classes at the Vieques, Puerto Rico, high school are suspended when 75 students, members of the Sea Cadet Corps, demonstrated at the school and demanded the dismissal of three teachers who had taken part in the anti-Navy demonstrations the previous day.

1 SEP

A Soviet naval task group comprised of a Kara-class guided missile cruiser, two Krivak-class guided missile frigates, and a Dubna-class replenishment ship come to within 230 n.miles (426 km) of the Oregon coast.

16 SEP

The Navy announces that the Navy and the Electric Boat Division of General Dynamics have reached agreement on the delivery dates for the first eight Trident submarines of the *Ohio* class, the first of which is now scheduled for delivery to the Navy on 1 Oct 1981.

The US House Select Committee on Narcotics Abuse and Control releases its report on drug abuse in the military that includes results of a June–July 1981 survey of 1,906 military personnel in Europe. The Navy–Marine Corps sample was 548 Navy and 222 Marine personnel. According to the report, Navy samples reflected higher illegal drug use rates than any other service for all drug categories except heroin, which was the highest among Army respondents, and alcohol, which was highest among the Marine sample. Reported figures indicated 49.27 percent of the Navy sample and 17 percent of the Marine sample used drugs. More that 60 percent of the Navy E-1 through E-4 respondents surveyed on board the carrier *Forrestal* (CV 59) reported using drugs and/or alcohol while on duty at least once in the previous month.

18 SEP

Rep. Addabbo, Chairman of the Defense Subcommittee of the House Appropriations Committee, claims that 20 percent of the naval air crashes in 1979 resulted from alcohol abuse. A Navy spokesman will later say that only five of

128 major air crashes in 1979 were proven to be related to alcohol abuse. Alcohol could have been a factor in another 17 accidents, but was listed as marginal or doubtful as a probable cause.

29 SEP

President Reagan, after an agreement with the Haitian government, orders the Coast Guard to intercept and turn around ships and craft on the high seas suspected of attempting to bring illegal Haitian immigrants to the United States.

I OCT

The US strategic missile submarine *Robert E. Lee* (SSBN 601) completes the last US Polaris deterrent patrol. The Polaris A-3TK variant remains in service in four British submarines.

2 OCT

President Reagan announces his plan to revitalize US strategic deterrent forces to (1) improve communication and control systems; (2) modernize strategic bombers with production of 100 B-1 bombers and continued research and development of a "stealth" bomber aircraft; (3) continue construction of Trident submarines and develop the D-5 missile with a 1989 deployment as well as deployment of Tomahawk land-attack missiles with nuclear warheads; (4) deployment of 100 MX land-based missiles in hardened silos and continued research on long-term basing options; and (5) upgrades of strategic defenses including research on ballistic missile defenses, replacing of the F-106 Delta Dart interceptor with F-15 Eagle fighters, and other improvements in air defense.

6 OCT

Egyptian President Anwar Sadat is killed during a military review in Cairo by Egyptian soldiers. The Muslim fundamentalist movement is behind the assassination. Units of the US Sixth Fleet and Rapid Deployment Force (RDF) are put on alert in response to the murder.

8 OCT

The Department of Defense announces that President Reagan has approved a plan to proceed with an improved Extremely Low Frequency (ELF) shore-to-submarine communications system with transmitter sites in Michigan and Wisconsin.

9 OCT

The Associated Press reports that 19 sailors on board the US carrier *Midway* were under investigation in a marijuana selling conspiracy. During the investigation 18 pounds (8 kg) of marijuana were seized by Navy agents on a Subic Bay pier, about to be loaded aboard the carrier.

14 OCT

Rep. Addabbo reports that autopsy records reveal that the pilot of the Marine EA-6B Prowler aircraft that crashed aboard the carrier *Nimitz* on 26 May 1981 had an abnormally high dosage of a prescription drug in the antihistamine family of drugs. (*See* 26 May 1981 and 18 Sep 1981.)

27 OCT

The Soviet submarine *U-137* of the Whiskey class runs aground near the Swedish naval base of Karlskrona, 300 miles (483 km) south of Stockholm. The submarine is in Swedish territorial waters and within a restricted military area. A Swedish salvage team will refloat the submarine and she will be released on 6 Nov 1981. There are indications that the submarine had two nuclear torpedoes on board.

5 NOV

First flight of the Marine Corps AV-8B Harrier production aircraft. The British-developed aircraft is built in the United States by McDonnell Douglas.

11 NOV

The USS *Ohio*, the first Trident submarine of the class, is placed in commission at Groton, Conn. Capt. A. K. Thompson, USN, is CO of the Blue Crew and Capt. A. F. Campbell, USN, is CO of the Gold Crew. The original contract had called for delivery in Apr 1979.

12 NOV

Secretary of Defense Weinberger announces that Adm. Rickover, head of the Navy's nuclear propulsion program for more than three decades, will leave active duty on 31 Jan 1982.

19 NOV

President Reagan makes a "zero option" offer to cancel deployment of the Pershing II and Ground-Launched Cruise Missiles (GLCMs) in Europe if the Soviets dismantle their SS-20 Saber intermediate-range ballistic missiles.

The French Defense Ministry announces the French government's new forward nuclear defense policy: (1) new tactical nuclear missile, the Hades, under development to replace the Pluton; (2) the SX intermediate-range missile force to replace the Mirage IV bomber in 1993; (3) the seventh strategic missile submarine will be constructed; (4) a sixth such submarine will be operational in 1985 armed with 16 M4 missiles; and (5) five ballistic missile submarines in service will be converted to launch the M4 missile.

23 NOV

Secretary of Defense Weinberger announces that on 1 Dec 1981, the Caribbean Contingency Joint Task Force at Key West, Fla., will become the US Forces Caribbean Command, reporting to the Commander in Chief US Atlantic Command.

1982

17 JAN

The USS *Ohio* (SSBN 726) carries out her first Trident C-4 missile launch while operating submerged off the coast of Florida.

12 FEB

US East Coast Marine Amphibious Units (MAU) are redesignated in the 20-series, with the first digit reflecting the II Marine Amphibious Force (MAF). Under this scheme the 32nd, 34th, 36th, and 38th MAUs became the 22nd, 24th, 26th, and 28th MAUs, respectively. The I and III MAFs in the Pacific will follow this organizational concept.

11 MAR

British Prime Minister Margaret Thatcher, in a letter to President Ronald Reagan, formally requests that the United States provide Trident D-5 missiles, fire control systems, and related equipment to Britain in a manner similar to which US Polaris missiles were provided.

13 MAR

The US nuclear-propelled carrier *Carl Vinson* (CVN 70) is placed in commission, the third ship of the *Nimitz* (CVN 68) class. The ship's first CO is Capt. Richard L. Martin, USN.

15 MAR

Exercise Gallant Eagle 82, sponsored by the US Readiness Command, begins. During the month-long exercises, about 15,000 Army troops and 10,000 Marines and sailors of the 7th Marine Amphibious Brigade as well as 650 aircraft will participate with Military Sealift Command ships moving personnel and equipment between the US East and West Coasts. On 30 Mar there is a parachute drop of more than 2,000 soldiers of the 82nd Airborne Division as part of the exercise.

16 MAR

Soviet President Leonid Brezhnev announces a moratorium on the deployment of new Soviet theater missiles targeted against Western Europe. The halt would be conditional with the United States halting the deployment of Pershing II and GLCMs in Europe.

17 MAR

An attempt is made by dissident military forces of Guatemala to take over the government in that country. US Marines are placed on the alert inside the American Embassy compound. There are no American casualties.

22 MAR

RimPac 82 begins, an exercise involving Australian, Canadian, Japanese, New Zealand, and US ships.

29 MAR

The British nuclear-propelled fleet submarine *Spartan* is ordered to embark stores and torpedoes at Gibraltar for deployment to the South Atlantic in response to increasing tension between Argentina and Great Britain over the Falkland Islands. Subsequently the *Spartan* steams south, followed by the nuclear submarines *Splendid* and *Conqueror*.

2 APR

At 0300 the Argentine submarine *Santa Fe* lands 20 commandos near Port Stanley in the Falklands and the missile destroyer *Santissima Trinidad* lands another 80 to secure the Government House and establish a beachhead. Later that morning the landing ship *Cabo San Antonio* sends ashore the main force of Argentine marines in 20 amphibious tractors (LVTs) to secure the airport and harbor area. The carrier *Vienticinco de Mayo*, with 1,500 troops on board, and other ships stand offshore. (The *Santa Fe* is the former USS *Catfish* [SS 339], and the *Vienticinco de Mayo* the former Dutch *Karel Doorman* and ex-British *Venerable*.)

3 APR

Argentine troops land by helicopter on South Georgia Island, 780 n.miles (1,445 km) east of the Falklands. Defending British marines shoot down one of the helicopters and damage an Argentine gunboat (with an anti-tank missile) before they are forced to surrender.

5 APR

A British task force centered on the VSTOL carriers *Invincible* and *Hermes*, with 1,500 Royal Marines embarked, deploy from Portsmouth, England, for the Falklands area, a voyage of 7,100 n.miles (13,156 km). The distance is only 400 n.miles (741 km) from Argentina.

12 APR

The British government announces a 200-n.mile (370-km) Maritime Exclusion Zone (MEZ) around the

Falklands. The exclusion zone will initially be enforced by nuclear-propelled submarines, with four SSNs patrolling off Argentina to track surface ships and radar-equipped aircraft.

22 APR
British SAS (Special Air Service) commandos are brought ashore by helicopter from the British VSTOL carriers to reconnoiter South Georgia Island. Two of the helicopters crash in a blizzard but all personnel are subsequently rescued by other ship-based helicopters.

1 MAY
An RAF Vulcan bomber, flying from Ascension Island with several in-flight refuelings, attacks the airstrip at Port Stanley in the Falkland Islands. The strategic bomber releases 21 1,000-pound (454-kg) bombs, one of which strikes the main runway. This is the first of five Vulcan raids on the Falklands, three against the runway and two against radar installations; they are ineffective. The same day British carrier-based Harrier VSTOL aircraft begin attacking Port Stanley and Argentine Air Force and Navy planes begin attacks against British ships. British Harriers will fly 1,100 air defense sorties and 215 ground attack sorties during the war; Argentine aircraft will fly about 300 sorties against British ships and landing operations.

2 MAY
The British nuclear-propelled submarine *Conqueror* attacks the Argentine cruiser *General Belgrano* (formerly the USS *Phoenix* [CL 46]) with a salvo of three Mk VIII torpedoes, two of which strike the 44-year-old ship. The two destroyers accompanying the *Belgrano* flee and the cruiser sinks with the loss of 321 men. (This number is from Dr. Robert Scheina, a distinguished American naval historian with close ties to the Argentine Navy; other sources have cited up to 368 killed and missing.)

After this event Argentine surface forces, including an aircraft carrier, play no further role in the conflict.

4 MAY
The British guided missile destroyer *Sheffield* is attacked by two Argentine Super Etendard attack aircraft, each firing a single Exocet missile at the ship. One hits and although the warhead does not detonate, the fires ravage the ship and she is abandoned with the loss of 20 crewmen. The *Sheffield* will sink on 10 May while under tow. (Super Etendard aircraft will launch

five Exocets against British ships during the conflict, three from aircraft and two from land launchers.)

7 MAY
The British government announces that any Argentine warship or military aircraft located more than 12 n.miles (22.2 km) from Argentina's coast will be treated as hostile.

8 MAY
The US Coast Guard announces a research program to examine the feasibility of employing trained pigeons for locating people in the water. The birds, which can scan a far wider area than humans, can watch for a longer period and have excellent color vision.

9 MAY
British Harrier VSTOL aircraft attack and heavily damage the Argentine fishing trawler *Narwal*, being employed in the intelligence-collection role. One Argentine is killed and 25 taken prisoner by British surface ships before the craft sinks.

11 MAY
During a night action, the British frigate *Alacrity* attacks and sinks the Argentine naval cargo ship *Islas de los Estados* in Falkland Sound (between the two main islands of the Falkland group).

12 MAY
In heavy fog, Argentine A-4 Skyhawk attack planes strike the British destroyers *Brilliant* and *Glasgow* near the Falklands. Two A-4s are shot down and a third crashes into the sea trying to evade a surface-to-air missile. The *Glasgow* is damaged when a bomb passes through her hull without exploding.

The liner *Queen Elizabeth II* departs England for the Falklands carrying the 5th Infantry Brigade and other personnel for the Falklands operation totalling more than 3,000.

14 MAY
A 45-man British SAS team and naval gunfire spotters are landed by two Sea King helicopters from the carrier *Hermes* on Pebble Island in the Falklands. After a three-mile (4.8-km) trek, the commandos along with naval gunfire from warships lying offshore, destroy 11 Argentine aircraft on the ground, an ammunition dump, and a radar installation. The commandos are returned by helicopter to the *Hermes* seven hours after they departed, having suffered two injured.

17 MAY

During an extensive "cross-decking" of personnel and equipment in the British amphibious force steaming toward the Falkland Islands, a Sea King helicopter carrying SAS commandos crashes into the sea, killing 22.

20 MAY

UN Secretary Perez de Cuellar announces that Argentine-British negotiations over the Falklands have collapsed.

21 MAY

British troops land from amphibious ships and transports at four separate points around San Carlos in the Falkland Islands. The landings, which will eventually put more than 10,000 British troops ashore, begin in the pre-dawn darkness. Argentine aircraft counterattack in several waves. The British frigate *Ardent* is sunk by Argentine bombs and two other warships are hit by bombs that do not explode, having been released too low to arm. Two other ships are seriously damaged. Fifteen Argentine aircraft are reported to have been destroyed in this attack.

23 MAY

Argentine Mirage and A-4 Skyhawk aircraft attack British warships in the Falklands area. One frigate, HMS *Antelope*, is damaged while six Mirages and one A-4 are shot down. The *Antelope* blows up and sinks on the following day during an attempt to disarm an unexploded bomb that was lodged in the engine room.

24 MAY

Argentine aircraft continue to attack British ships with two tank landing ships being damaged. Eight Argentine aircraft are reportedly shot down.

25 MAY

Argentine aircraft continue to strike British ships in the Falklands area. The destroyer *Coventry* is struck by several bombs and rapidly capsizes; 19 are lost in her sinking. Two Super Etendards launch Exocet missiles against the container ship *Atlantic Conveyor*. The ship, carrying several helicopters and military supplies, is set on fire and sinks, killing 12 men. Lost with her will be three of the four heavy-lift Chinook helicopters being carried to the Falklands. Seven A-4s are shot down.

26 MAY

A small British task force stages an assault on South Georgia Island. After a naval gunfire barrage, British troops land and the Argentines on the island quickly surrender. The Argentine submarine *Santa Fe* is sighted nearby on the surface and attacked by British helicopters; damaged and unable to submerge, the submarine is beached at Grytviken Harbor. (She will later be towed out to deeper water and sunk.)

NATO exercise Display Determination 1-82 begins with ships and aircraft from the British, Greek, Italian, Turkish, and US navies taking part. The Greek destroyer *Themistocles* withdraws from the exercise on 27 May following the allegation of Turkish violation of Greek airspace in the Aegean Sea.

27 MAY

Amid continuing Argentine air attacks on British ships, British troops continue to make advances in the Falklands. Two A-4 Skyhawks are reportedly shot down.

28 MAY

British Army paratroops capture Goose Green and Darwin, East Falklands, after 12 hours of fighting.

30 MAY

Argentine Super Etendard and A-4 Skyhawk aircraft attack the main British carrier force off the Falklands, but inflict no damage. Three A-4s are reportedly shot down.

31 MAY

The British diesel-electric submarine *Onyx* arrives in San Carlos water, providing a platform for commando operations more suitable than nuclear-propelled submarines or surface ships.

2 JUNE

A naval exercise in the Atlantic begins under French direction—called Suroit 82—with two US frigates as well as British, Dutch, Portuguese, and a large number of French ships and aircraft taking part.

6 JUNE

Israeli troops cross into southern Lebanon in retaliation for Palestinian Liberation Army (PLO) attacks against settlements in northern Israel. The Israeli drive will reach eastern Beirut on 14 June, encircling the capital and imposing a blockade to destroy the power of the estimated 15,000 PLO combatants in the city. The US and other nations put military forces in the Mediterranean on alert.

7 JUNE

Royal Marine commandos capture Mount Low in the Falklands, overlooking the Stanley Airfield.

The US Embassy in Beirut, Lebanon, is attacked with rockets and machine guns. One Marine sentry is wounded by shrapnel.

8 JUNE

Argentine Mirage and A-4 Skyhawk aircraft attack two partially loaded British infantry landing ships at Fitzroy in the Falklands, the *Sir Galahad* and *Sir Tristram*. Both are set afire with the loss of 32 troops and 18 crew. Damage to the *Sir Galahad* is severe and she is scuttled. British helicopters and small craft valiantly brave the flames to rescue scores of other troops and seamen.

The British frigate *Plymouth* is seriously damaged by air attacks in Falkland Sound. Four Argentine aircraft are believed shot down.

12 JUNE

The British destroyer *Glamorgan* is hit by a land-launched Exocet missile while operating off the Falklands. She suffers moderate damage and the loss of 13. This is the last attack on British ships during the campaign.

13 JUNE

British troops begin assaults against the remaining Argentine positions in the Falklands.

14 JUNE

British forces reach the outskirts of Stanley, capital of the Falklands. With most of the high ground captured, there is a ceasefire and, that night, the Argentine forces formally surrender.

20 JUNE

The US Coast Guard cutter *Boutwell* (WHEC 719) seizes the sailboat *Orca* 1,500 n.miles (2,780 km) southwest of Kodiak, Alaska. The boat is found to be carrying 1½ tons of marijuana. Subsequently, three Coast Guardsmen will be charged with attempting to sabotage the *Boutwell* and seize the marijuana-laden sailboat. One Coast Guardsman drowns in the incident.

The Royal Australian Navy decommissions the light fleet carrier *Melbourne*, ending fixed-wing carrier operations in that navy. Australia had planned to purchase the British VSTOL carrier *Invincible*, but that plan died with the Falklands War.

23 JUNE

The initial evacuation of the American Embassy in Beirut begins because of fighting in the area between various Christian and Muslim groups. The building will be closed on 24 June, with remaining personnel, including a nine-man Marine security detachment, moving to the ambassador's residence in the nearby city of Yarze.

30 JUNE

US Navy Light Photographic Squadron (VFP) 63, flying the RF-8G Crusader, is disestablished. It was the last specialized carrier-based, photo-reconnaissance unit in the US Navy. (Some Marine RF-4B Phantom photo-reconnaissance aircraft will continue to fly from US carriers.)

Opening of the Strategic Arms Reduction Talks (START II) between the United States and Soviet Union in Geneva.

25 AUG

Some 800 US Marines of the 32nd Marine Amphibious Unit (MAU) go ashore at Beirut, Lebanon, from Sixth Fleet amphibious ships. The US troops along with 400 French and 800 Italian troops are to provide security during the withdrawal of some 12,000 members of the Palestine Liberation Organization (PLO) and their families. US warships escort the merchant ships carrying the PLO members. The Marines will reboard their amphibious ships on 10 Sep 1982.

9 SEP

Senior US Air Force and Navy leaders sign the "Memorandum of Agreement on Joint USN/USAF Efforts to Enhance USAF Contributions to Maritime Operations." The agreement will lead to increased Air Force participation in ocean surveillance, anti-ship, and minelaying operations.

10 SEP

The US Marines ashore in Beirut reembark in their amphibious ships.

20 SEP

Six days after the assassination of Lebanese President-elect Bashir Gemayel, President Reagan orders US Marines back into Lebanon to help preserve order.

29 SEP

The 1,200 US Marines of the 32nd Marine Amphibious Unit (MAU) again go ashore in Lebanon, joining 2,200 French and Italian troops already ashore. They establish a compound adjacent to the Beirut International Airport. The Americans will be relieved beginning on 29 Oct 1982 by the 24th MAU.

1 OCT

The Trident missile submarine *Ohio* departs Bangor, Wash., on her first deterrent patrol, armed with 24 C-4 missiles. She will return to Bangor on 10 Dec 1982.

4 NOV

US Marines of the 24th MAU extend their presence in Beirut to the eastern (Christian) section, patrolling the "Green Line" that divides the city into sectarian parts.

17 NOV

The US Coast Guard's surface effect ships *Sea Hawk* (WSES 2), and *Shearwater* (WSES 3) are placed in commission. The high-speed craft will operate in Florida waters to interdict drug smugglers. A third unit of this class, the *Petrel* (WSES 4), will be commissioned on 8 July 1983. (The WSES 1 was a US Navy craft—designated *SES-200* and *IX 515*—evaluated by the Coast Guard.)

23 NOV

The US guided missile cruiser *Mississippi* (CGN 40), with a Coast Guard boarding party embarked, becomes the first Navy ship to assist directly in the seizure of a drug-laden ship on the high seas.

13 DEC

A US Marine company in Lebanon begins training Lebanese soldiers in basic infantry skills at a camp near Beirut.

28 DEC

The battleship *New Jersey* (BB 62) is commissioned at Bremerton, Wash. She is the first of the four *Iowa* (BB 61)–class dreadnoughts to be recommissioned under the Reagan-Lehman 600-ship Navy program. This is the fourth time the ship has been placed in commission—1943, 1950, 1968, and 1982.

1983

1 JAN

Commander in Chief US Central Command (CINC-CENT) is established under Lt. Gen. Robert C. Kingston, USA. CINCCENT—with responsibilities for US military operations in east Africa and the Middle East region—evolved from the Rapid Deployment Joint Task Force (RDJTF) (*see* 1 Mar 1980). Central Command will normally not have forces assigned, but will draw them as required for exercises and operations, mainly from the US Atlantic and Pacific Commands. (Later ships of the naval component of Central Command, the Middle East Force, will be permanently assigned to CINCCENT as the Fifth Fleet.)

11 JAN

The US nuclear-propelled attack submarines *Aspro* (SSN 648) and *Tautog* (SSN 639) surface at the North Pole, the first two-submarine surfacing since 31 July 1962. The two submarines remain surfaced together at the geographic top of the world for 16 hours.

22 JAN

The USS *Ticonderoga* (CG 47) is placed in commission with Capt. Roland Guilbault, USN, in command. She is the first warship to be fitted with the Aegis radar/weapons control system. The *Ticonderoga* is the most flexible surface combatant afloat with major anti-air and anti-submarine capabilities. Twenty-seven ships of this class will be completed through 1994.

1 FEB

Exercise Ahuas Tara begins in Honduras as US and Honduran forces conduct counter-insurgency training. US Navy ships participate in the operation which included 520 Navy personnel, 450 Army troops, and about 175 support and communications personnel from different services.

2 FEB

Capt. Charles B. Johnson, USMC, personally confronts three Israeli tanks as they attempt to pass through his company checkpoint in Beirut. The Israelis back down in this serious incident.

4 FEB

The US Coast Guard cutter *Bear* (WMEC 901) is placed in commission, the first of 13 medium-endurance cutters to be completed. These are multi-purpose cutters; however, their lack of anti-submarine weapons and sensors make them unsuitable for employment in the ASW role without extensive modification. They will also be criticized for their slow speed and they ride poorly in heavy seas. The *Bear's* first CO is Capt. Robert G. Bates, USCG.

23 FEB

The first French nuclear-propelled attack submarine, the *Rubis*, is placed in service. She is completed 12 years after the first French nuclear-propelled strategic missile submarine entered service. The *Rubis* is a relatively small nuclear submarine, only slightly larger than the US *Tullibee* (SSN 597), the smallest US nuclear submarine.

12 MAR

More than 3,200 Marines from the US 4th Marine Aircraft Wing begin exercise Operation Skyhawk, the largest training operation yet held for Marine air reservists. Approximately 100 aircraft and personnel from 48 units take part, providing support for ground units of the 3rd Marine Amphibious Brigade. The exercise takes place in Nevada and California.

16 MAR

Five US Marines are wounded in the first direct attack on US peacekeeping troops in Lebanon. An Islamic fundamentalist group claims responsibility.

23 MAR

President Ronald Reagan addresses the nation, calling for support for the Strategic Defense Initiative (SDI), a high-technology defense against attacking strategic missiles. A New York newspaper promptly labels the SDI plan "Star Wars," for the science fiction movies of director George Lucas.

The battleship *New Jersey* (BB 62) becomes the first battleship to fire a guided missile, launching a Harpoon anti-ship missile during operations off southern California. Simultaneously a P-3C Orion patrol aircraft fires a Harpoon in the joint firing exercise.

18 APR

A terrorist bomb explodes in a car outside of the heavily fortified US Embassy in Beirut, collapsing one-third of the building. Sixty-one persons are killed in the blast, including 17 American citizens; more than 100 persons are injured. The casualties include one US Marine killed and eight wounded. The Islamic Jihad (Holy War) fundamentalist movement claims responsibility for the attack.

20 APR
Vice Adm. Robert L. Walters, USN, Deputy CNO (Surface Warfare), in his statement before the House Appropriations Committee, declares "No segment of Naval Warfare has been under funded for so many years as has the Mine Warfare community. Despite the large stockpiles of sophisticated modern mines possessed by the Soviets, we have only recently begun to respond to the threat."

10 MAY
The *New Jersey*, steaming off the coast of southern California, becomes the first surface ship to launch a land-attack version of the Tomahawk cruise missile.

9 JUNE
The battleship *New Jersey* departs her home port of Long Beach, Calif., for a three-month cruise to the western Pacific. (*See* 5 May 1984.)

23 JUNE
The Soviet nuclear-propelled submarine *K-429* of the Charlie II class sinks off Petropavlovsk (Kamchatka Peninsula) with the loss of 16 crewmen. The submarine will be salvaged and repaired, but subsequently will sink at dockside and become an immobilized training submarine.

25 JUNE
US Marines conduct the first combined patrols in Beirut with Lebanese Army troops.

26 JULY
A US carrier battle group centered on the Pacific Fleet carrier *Ranger* (CV 61) arrives off the pacific coast of Nicaragua in response to the flow of Soviet arms into the country.

1 AUG
A US Marine Corps OV-10A Bronco lands on the helicopter carrier *Nassau* (LHA 4). This is the first time a twin-engine Bronco, which has no arresting hook or catapult capability, has operated on board a carrier.

26 AUG
A Navy task group led by the battleship *New Jersey* arrives off Central America following an 11-day transit from Hawaii. After exercises off the Pacific coast of Central America, the dreadnought passes through the

Panama Canal on 12 Sep 1983 and then continues eastward at a speed of 25 knots, entering the Mediterranean on 20 Sep. (The ships that accompanied the *New Jersey* to Central America do not cross the Atlantic with her.)

29 AUG
Lebanese terrorist attacks against US Marines in Beirut escalate with an artillery bombardment of Marine positions near the Beirut Airport. Two Marines are killed and 14 wounded during the five-hour attack. The Marines return fire with 155-mm artillery and AH-1 Sea Cobra gunship strikes. The firing at Marine positions will continue, with two Marines being killed on 6 Sep 1983. French and Italian positions also come under fire.

31 AUG
The Department of Defense authorizes hostile fire pay of $65 per month for Marines and sailors of the 24th MAU serving in Lebanon.

1 SEP
Soviet air defense forces intercept a Korean Airlines Boeing 747 airliner (flight KAL 007) that strays over the Kamchatka Peninsula and Sakhalin Island. In the pre-dawn intercept an Su-15 Flagon fighter shoots down the airliner with two missiles, causing the death of all 269 persons on board (61 are American citizens, including Rep. Lawrence P. McDonald of Georgia). A US communications intercept station in Japan monitors the conversations between the Soviet fighter pilot and his ground controller.

The US and Japanese Navy and Coast Guard units as well as Soviet Navy and KGB Maritime Border Troops begin searching to the west of southern Sakhalin Island for debris from the KAL 007 flight. The Soviets recover the aircraft's flight recorders, but do not reveal the find. US naval forces will search the area for the recorder and debris until 5 Nov 1983.

First flight of the US Navy's MH-53E Sea Dragon Mine Countermeasures (MCM) helicopter. (A CH-53E Super Stallion in the MCM configuration first flew on 23 Dec 1981.)

7 SEP
US and French carrier-based aircraft begin overflights of the Beirut area. The US planes, from the carrier *Dwight D. Eisenhower* (CVN 69), include F-14 Tomcat fighters fitted with the Tactical Airborne Reconnaissance Pod System (TARPS).

8 SEP

In response to continued firing at US Marine positions in the Beirut area, the US frigate *Bowen* (FF 1079) fires at Muslim Druze artillery positions with her 5-inch (127-mm) gun. Other US ships will participate in gunfire missions later in the month.

21 SEP

After encountering light anti-aircraft fire, US F-14 reconnaissance aircraft overflying Lebanon are fired on by surface-to-air missiles. Missile launches are again reported on 23 Sep.

24 SEP

The battleship *New Jersey* arrives off the coast of Lebanon after a high-speed transit from Central American waters.

1 OCT

Secretary of the Navy John F. Lehman, Jr., announces formation of the Navy Space Command (NAV-SPACECOM), to consolidate existing naval activities and organizations that operate and support Navy-related space systems.

The US Navy's Strategic Systems Project Office (SSPO) begins full-scale engineering development of the Trident II/D-5 strategic missile.

The US Air Force achieves a limited operational capability for sea control operations when three B-52G Stratofortress bombers at Loring AFB, Maine, are declared operational carrying Harpoon anti-ship missiles. Plans call for two squadrons of B-52s to have Harpoon missiles by the end of the year.

19 OCT

Following a Marxist takeover of the island of Grenada in the Caribbean, Prime Minister Maurice Bishop and several other former officials are executed.

23 OCT

A terrorist truck laden with an estimated 12,000 pounds (5,443 kg) of explosives is driven into the Marine compound in Beirut and detonates, killing 241 American servicemen, mostly Marines; another 70 are injured. The Marine sentries at the compound had unloaded rifles. The Islamic Jihad terrorist movement takes credit for the attack.

Almost simultaneous with the attack on the US compound, Islamic fundamentalists attack the French military compound, killing 58.

US Air Force C-141 Starlifter transports begin flying replacement Marines into Beirut.

24 OCT

In response to the worsening situation on Grenada and possible danger to more than 600 American medical students and other foreign nationals on the island, Operation Urgent Fury begins to destroy the Communist government on the island. Marines of the 22nd Marine Amphibious Unit (MAU) land on the northern end of the island and easily capture the airport. Army Rangers parachute into Port Salines airstrip at the southern end of the island and encounter heavy resistance. A US Navy SEAL force comes ashore at the residence of the British representative to ensure his safety and accomplish its mission, albeit with some non-combat losses. Portions of the 22nd MAU re-embarked in amphibious ships and were brought around the island for a second landing in support of the Rangers. The joint task force is commanded by Vice Adm. Joseph Metcalf III, USN, with Maj. Gen. Norman Schwartzkopf, USA, as his deputy.

27 OCT

All US objectives on Grenada are secured. American casualties are 18 servicemen killed and 116 wounded. Twenty-five Cuban and several Grenadian military personnel were killed as are 24 civilians, all but three in a mental hospital bombed accidently in the belief that it was a military installation. US forces round up the survivors from the 784 Cubans who were on the island as well as 900 nationals of other Soviet Bloc countries. Massive amounts of weapons were found on the island, far more than defense requirements for Grenada's 110,000 population.

1 NOV

US Marines of the 22nd MAU land on the island of Carriacou, 15 n.miles (28 km) northeast of Grenada, where US intelligence located a small number of military troops and arms caches. The simultaneous helicopter and surface landing is a complete surprise and no resistance is encountered as the 17 Grenadan soldiers surrender and a large number of weapons are recovered.

2 NOV

The 22nd MAU re-embarks in amphibious ships and sails for the Mediterranean to relieve the 24th MAU in Beirut.

4 NOV

A suicide driver blows up the Israeli headquarters building at Tyre on the coast of Lebanon, killing 29 Israeli soldiers and 32 Muslim prisoners held in the building.

18 NOV

A landing by 1,200 US Marines of the 28th MAU and 500 Honduran soldiers near Puerto Castilla, Honduras, marks the highlight of exercise Big Pine II, which will run through Feb 1984.

19 NOV

Marines of the 22nd MAU, who had participated in the Grenada operation, come ashore in Beirut to relieve the battered 24th MAU.

22 NOV

US Secretary of Defense Caspar W. Weinberger states that the 23 Oct 1983 attack on Marines in Beirut was carried out by Iranians with the "sponsorship, knowledge, and authority of the Syrian government."

23 NOV

Deliveries of US Air Force Ground-Launched Cruise Missile (GLCM) components to Great Britain mark the beginning of NATO's deployment of Intermediate-range Nuclear Force (INF).

3 DEC

At least ten surface-to-air missiles are reported to be launched against US reconnaissance aircraft overflying Lebanon.

4 DEC

In retaliation for anti-aircraft fire against US reconnaissance aircraft, the US carriers *Independence* (CV 62) and *John F. Kennedy* (CV 67) launch a strike of 12 A-7E Corsair and 16 A-6E Intruder attack aircraft against gun and missile positions in the hills near Beirut. The pilots, flying into the sun, are fired on by "at least" 40 missiles as well as heavy anti-aircraft guns. One A-6E is shot down, its pilot, Lt. Mark A. Lange, USN, killed, and the bombardier/navigator, Lt. Robert O. Goodman, USN, taken prisoner. (He will be released on 3 Jan 1984 through the efforts of the Rev. Jesse Jackson meeting with Syrian President Hafez al-Assad.) An A-7E is also shot down, its pilot rescued, and another A-7E was damaged but returns to the "Indy."

The US Department of Defense states that the attack is "very successful," with one missile site demolished and at least 11 point targets struck. The Syrian government later states that two Syrians were killed, 10 wounded, and one vehicle and an ammunition dump destroyed.

The same day as the air strikes, a four-hour shelling of Beirut kills eight US Marines in a bunker near the airport. US destroyers fire counter-battery missions.

14 DEC

The US battleship *New Jersey* (BB 62) fires 11 rounds of 16-inch (406-mm) ammunition at artillery positions in Syrian-occupied Lebanon. This is the first time naval guns larger than 5 inch (127 mm) have been used in action since the end of the Vietnam War. The *New Jersey*, in commission for almost a year, has steamed about 30,000 n.miles (55,590 km).

An explosives-laden truck crashes into the US Embassy compound in Kuwait, the blast killing five Kuwaitis and injuring 37. There are no Americans among the casualties. The suicide attack is coordinated with raids on the French Embassy in Kuwait, the airport control tower, a power station, and the Raytheon Co. compound.

1984

2 JAN

Heavy fighting erupts in the suburbs of Beirut between the Lebanese Army and Shiite militiamen. The fighting soon spreads to most of the city.

20 JAN

The Italian contingent of the multinational force in Lebanon departs. British, French, and US troops remain.

25 JAN

The US aircraft carrier *Ranger* (CV 61) with embarked Carrier Air Wing 9 arrives at Subic Bay in the Philippines, having been at sea for 121 continuous days, of which 95 days were in the northern Arabian Sea. The *Ranger* is believed to have set a record for time at sea for a non-nuclear carrier.

7 FEB

President Ronald Reagan announces his decision to redeploy US Marines from the Beirut Airport area to amphibious ships offshore, leaving behind a force of about 100 Marines to protect the US Embassy and other American interests, and an 80-man Army training team.

8 FEB

The *New Jersey* (BB 62) fires 288 rounds of 16-inch (408-mm) ammunition at Syrian gun positions in the mountains near Beirut. The bombardment, highly publicized, is the heaviest of the Lebanon operation and will be controversial with regard to its effectiveness. The destroyers *Caron* (DD 970) and *Moosbrugger* (DD 980) fire 250 and 150 rounds of 5-inch (127-mm) gunfire, respectively, at targets in the hills east of Beirut.

The British contingent of the multinational force in Lebanon departs by helicopter for ships offshore.

10 FEB

A two-day helicopter evacuation begins of American civilians and other foreign nationals from Beirut to ships offshore.

21 FEB

US Marines of the 22nd Marine Amphibious Unit (MAU) begin embarking in offshore amphibious ships. The last Marines will go aboard ship on 26 Feb, ending the US ground force presence in Beirut. (About a dozen Marines remain as part of the American Embassy security force.) Only French troops of

the multinational force remain in the Beirut area in significant numbers, the last to depart on 31 Mar 1984, in the amphibious ship *Ouragan*. (*See* 31 July 1984.)

26 FEB

The battleship *New Jersey* fires her 16-inch (406-mm) guns at Syrian gun batteries for the last time.

7 MAR

The US Navy Strategic Systems Project Office (SSPO) is renamed the Strategic Systems Program Office to reflect wider responsibilities for sea-based strategic weapons development.

11 MAR

The 9th Marine Amphibious Brigade is part of a 60,000-man American force and 147,000 South Korean troops that begin Team Spirit 84, the ninth and largest US-ROK exercise of the Team Spirit series.

21 MAR

A Soviet Victor nuclear-propelled attack submarine collides with the US aircraft carrier *Kitty Hawk* (CV 63) in the Sea of Japan, about 150 n.miles (278 km) east of South Korea. The Victor SSN had surfaced ahead of the carrier; both ships are damaged. The damaged submarine then steams to the port of Vladivostok on the surface, escorted by a Soviet cruiser.

24 MAR

A US Marine CH-53 Sea Stallion helicopter crashes into a mountain near Pohang, South Korea, during the Team Spirit 84 exercise. Eighteen US Marines and 11 Korean Marines are killed. The CH-53 was one of six that took off for a night insertion operation, but were recalled because of deteriorating weather.

26 MAR

Technicians from the Israeli firm Tadiran fly a Mastiff Remotely Piloted Vehicle (RPV) from Israeli to the US helicopter carrier *Guam* (LPH 9), steaming off the coast, land the RPV and take it off without incident. The Mastiff will become the basis of the US Navy–Marine Corps RPV program. (*See* 24 Sep 1984.)

9 APR

The US ocean surveillance ship *Stewart* (T-AGOS 1) is placed in service with the Military Sealift Command (MSC). The *Stewart* is fitted with the Surveillance Towed Array Sensor System (SURTASS), a submarine detection system towed at slow speeds to supplement the seafloor Sound Surveillance System (SOSUS). The Navy will build 22 of these ships through the late 1990s.

28 APR
The US battleship *Iowa* (BB 61) is the second ship of her class to be recommissioned as part of the Reagan-Lehman 600-ship naval buildup. Following training operations, the *Iowa* will take part in the Unitas XXI exercise around South America from June to Oct 1984.

2 MAY
The first US Navy Landing Craft Air Cushioned (LCAC) is rolled out at the Bell Aerospace Textron shipyard in New Orleans, La. This is the first of 84 high-speed landing craft that will be procured for use with Navy-Marine amphibious forces.

5 MAY
The battleship *New Jersey* returns to her home port of Long Beach, Calif., having been deployed for 11 months. The dreadnought had departed Long Beach in June 1983 on what was to have been a three-month Western Pacific cruise. She had been under way for 322 days and had steamed 76,000 n.miles (140,830 km), nearly half while in the Mediterranean.

13 MAY
A series of explosions begin at the Soviet naval complex at Severmorsk on the Kola Peninsula, near Murmansk. The detonations and fires at weapons magazines will last until 18 May and destroy a reported one-quarter to one-third of the Northern Fleet's surface-to-air missile stockpile as well as other missiles and munitions.

23 MAY
Former Capt. James H. Webb, Jr., USMC, a decorated Vietnam veteran and novelist, is sworn in as the first Assistant Secretary of Defense for Reserve Affairs. He previously served as minority counsel to the House Committee on Veterans Affairs. (He will become Secretary of the Navy in 1987.)

29 JUNE
The Soviet government issues a statement proposing US–Soviet talks on preventing the "militarization" of outer space. The US government accepts the Soviet invitation.

2 JULY
Nearly 10,000 Thai and US troops begin exercise Cobra Gold 84, a major military exercise around the Gulf of Thailand and the largest in this annual series that began in 1981. Included in the exercise, which lasts until 10 Aug 1984, are minelaying and sweeping, special warfare operations, amphibious landings, and simulated air and sea combat.

9 JULY
A mine explodes under the Soviet-flag merchant ship *Knud Jesperson* in the Gulf of Suez and inflicts slight damage. Through 20 Sep 1984 another 18 ships will report seeing mines or experiencing nearby explosions in the Gulf of Suez and Red Sea. Some of the ships are damaged but none sunk.

31 JULY
A spokesman claiming that he speaks for the Islamic Jihad terrorist group calls several European press agencies to take credit for the explosions in the Gulf of Suez. He says that 190 mines have been laid.

4 AUG
The US Navy surveying ship *Harkness* (T-AGS 32) arrives in the Gulf of Suez to join the mine countermeasures force consisting of ships and aircraft from Egypt, Great Britain, Italy, France, the Netherlands, Soviet Union, and United States.

6 AUG
About midnight the first USAF C-5A Galaxy transport departs the United States carrying RH-53D Sea Stallion Mine Countermeasures (MCM) helicopters. The helicopters will be flown to Rota, Spain, where they will be reassembled and flown out to the amphibious ship *Shreveport* (LPD 12) on 9 Aug.

17 AUG
The *Shreveport* arrives in the Gulf of Suez with four RH-53D Sea Stallion MCM helicopters from Navy Mine Countermeasures Squadron (HM) 14; three other RH-35Ds will operate from Jidda. The squadron will conduct 22 days of consecutive MCM operations.

7 SEP
The US maritime prepositioning ship *Cpl. Louis J. Hauge Jr.* (T-AK 3000) is placed in service with the Military Sealift Command (MSC). The *Hauge* is the first of 13 specialized MPS ships that will be forward deployed in three squadrons, each carrying weapons and equipment for a Marine Amphibious Brigade.

12 SEP
A seafloor mine detected about 15 n.miles (28 km) south of the entrance to the Suez Canal is recovered

by the British minehunter *Gavinton*. The seafloor mine was of Soviet manufacture, dated [19]81. It was subsequently determined that the mines were laid by the Libyan roll-on/roll-off freighter *Ghat*, which transited the Suez Canal and Gulf of Suez in early July 1984.

18 SEP

A Soviet Victor nuclear-propelled attack submarine collides with the Soviet merchant ship *Bratstvo* in the Strait of Gibraltar as the submarine is making a night transit, exiting from the Mediterranean. Damage to the submarine is extensive; she will "limp" into Hammamet, Tunisia, for repairs performed by a Soviet support ship.

20 SEP

An explosives-filled van detonates at a US Embassy building in Beirut, killing 23 persons, including two US military personnel. The American ambassador and four Marine security guards are injured. The Islamic Jihad takes responsibility for the bombing.

The Saudi Arabian–flag cargo ship *Belkis I* is damaged by an underwater explosion some 20 n.miles (37 km) south of Suez City. This is the last ship to report an explosion in the Suez area, although Royal Navy divers will inspect the ship and state that the damage is *not* indicative of external explosion.

24 SEP

The US Marine Corps' 1st Remotely Piloted Vehicle (RPV) Platoon is activated at Camp Lejuene, N.C. The 42-man unit will operate four Israeli-designed Mastiff-3 RPVs for reconnaissance and artillery spotting.

5 NOV

A three-day exercise of US and Egyptian naval forces begins in the eastern Mediterranean to test the ability of Egyptian air, naval, and air defense forces to repel an attack. This is the first exercise of the kind between the two countries.

17 NOV

Two Dutch naval minesweepers depart the Gulf of Suez, the last of the multinational mine countermeasures forces that began arriving in the Gulf in early Aug 1984.

25 NOV

Assailants fire four 60-mm mortar rounds into the US Embassy compound in Lisbon, Portugal. There are no injuries. A leftist guerrilla group claims responsibility for the pre-dawn attack.

26 NOV

The United States and Iraq resume diplomatic relations. Iraq had broken off relations with the United States in June 1967 at the onset of the Arab-Israeli Six-Day War.

1985

7 FEB

A US Marine Corps selection board names the first woman Marine to be advanced to the rank of brigadier general, Col. Gail M. Reals, USMC.

9 APR

The US Naval Material Command is disestablished, eliminating a layer of management above the naval systems commands, which develop hardware and manage logistics and provide other support for the Navy.

The Navy establishes the Space and Naval Warfare Systems Command (SPAWAR), based in part on the former Naval Electronic Systems Command (NAVELEX). The other matériel commands are Air Systems, Sea Systems, Supply Systems, and Naval Facilities Engineering Command.

6 MAY

A US Marine CH-53D Sea Stallion helicopter crashes off the island of Yakushima in the Sea of Japan. All 17 Marines on board are lost. The helicopter was en route from the Marine air station at Iwakuni, Japan, to its home base on Okinawa.

20 MAY

Retired US Navy Chief Warrant Officer John A. Walker, Jr., is arrested by FBI agents in Rockville, Md., and charged with espionage. Walker, who retired in 1976, had begun spying for the Soviet Union in 1968 and was able to pass on vast amounts of information about US submarine and surface operations as well as key lists by which the Soviets could decipher classified US radio communications. He will plead guilty and be sentenced to life imprisonment. Walker had recruited his brother, son, and best friend, Jerry Whitworth, to spy for the Soviets, and his wife assisted him. This is the most significant espionage case involving US Navy personnel ever revealed.

14 JUNE

Steelworker 2nd Class Robert D. Stethem, USN, a Navy diver flying a commercial TWA flight, is killed by Arab terrorists. The hijackers had taken over the plane just after take-off from Athens and forced it to land at Beirut. Stethem was brutally beaten and then murdered on the plane, with his body thrown onto the tarmac. (A destroyer is later named in his honor, the DDG 63.) The aircraft, controlled by terrorists, flew to Algiers and then returned to Beirut. There 37 American hostages were taken off the plane and hid in Beirut; the last will be released on 30 June.

The Coast Guard commanders of the Atlantic and Pacific areas take command of the newly established Maritime Defense Zone Atlantic and Maritime Defense Zone Pacific, respectively. These zones have responsibility for planning and conducting wartime operations in and around US coasts and harbors, and protecting nearby sea lines of communication. (The area commanders are vice admirals.)

19 JUNE

Four off-duty Marines and two American businessmen are among 13 people slain when terrorist gunmen open fire on an outdoor cafe in San Salvador, El Salvador. The Marines, part of the embassy security guard, were wearing civilian clothes at the time.

3 JULY

In a White House meeting, Robert C. McFarlane, national security advisor to President Ronald Reagan, and David Kimche, an Israeli foreign ministry official, discuss the Iranian situation. This meeting is considered the starting point for the Iran-Contra affair, the worst political scandal of the Reagan Administration. Lt. Col. Oliver L. North, USMC, who did not attend the meeting, was an assistant to McFarlane and became the "action" officer for the project.

5 JULY

Operation Bright Star 85 begins in the Middle East, the largest US training exercise yet held in the area. Some 2,300 Marines are among 9,000 US servicemen who participate in amphibious, air, and live-fire exercises held mostly in Egypt, with some phases conducted in Jordan and Somalia. The exercise will end on 11 Aug 1985.

9 JULY

The fully loaded Turkish supertanker *M. Vatan* is attacked by Iraqi aircraft in the Persian Gulf. The ultra-large crude oil carrier, of 392,799 deadweight tons, is the largest ship yet damaged in the Iraq-Iran conflict and probably the largest marine casualty in history in terms of tonnage.

10 JULY

The converted trawler *Rainbow Warrior*, operated by the Greenpeace environmental and anti-nuclear test movement, is sunk by explosive charges in Auckland harbor, New Zealand. A Portuguese photographer is killed in the sinking. The ship was preparing to sail for the French nuclear test site at Mururoa Atoll. The charges, it will be determined, were set by two French intelligence agents, who will be arrested in New Zealand. The French government will later admit to sending agents to "watch" the *Rainbow Warrior*; as a result of the sinking, in Sep 1985 the French minister of defense is forced to retire and the chief of the General Directorate of External Security (DGSE) is dismissed.

30 JULY

Maritime Prepositioning Squadron 1 becomes operational. Its four cargo ships will be deployed in the Atlantic area carrying vehicles and equipment for a 16,500-man Marine Amphibious Brigade. Squadron 2 will deploy to the Indian Ocean and Squadron 3 to the Western Pacific.

21 AUG

The US strategic missile submarine *Sam Rayburn* (SSBN 635) begins offloading Poseidon C-3 missiles prior to being decommissioned and dismantled. This will be the first missile submarine to be retired in compliance with the SALT I agreements. Dismantling of the *Rayburn* will begin on 16 Sep 1985.

29 AUG

In the largest NATO exercise held to date, 157 ships, 70,000 personnel, and hundreds of aircraft take part in Ocean Safari 85. Ten nations are represented in the exercise, that will run until 20 Sep 1985.

30 AUG

The US 1st Marine Brigade at Kaneohe Bay, Hawaii, is redesignated as the 1st Marine Amphibious Brigade (MAB). The unit is renamed and reconfigured to conform with the maritime prepositioning structure.

23 SEP

Commander in Chief US Space Command (CINCSPACE) is established with responsibility for US military activities in space. Gen. Robert T. Herres, USAF, is named the first CINCSPACE.

4 OCT

The modified amphibious ship *Coronado* (AGF 11) replaces the destroyer tender *Puget Sound* (AD 38) as flagship of the US Sixth Fleet in the Mediterranean.

7 OCT

Four Palestinian terrorists seize control of the Italian-flag cruise ship *Achille Lauro* in the eastern Mediterranean. Armed with AK-47 assault rifles, hand guns, and grenades, the terrorists take control of the ship. The terrorists demand the release of 50 terrorists held in Israel. While holding the ship they murder a handicapped American Jew. (His body will later wash ashore; an autopsy will show that he had been shot at close range in the head and back.)

9 OCT

After intensive negotiations, the four terrorists leave the *Achille Lauro* off the coast of Egypt and the ship enters Port Said. The terrorists, under the terms of the agreement, remain in Egypt at the Al Maza military airfield. On the evening of 10 Oct the *Achille Lauro* terrorists take off from Egypt in an EgyptAir Boeing 737 airliner. The flight is intercepted at night by four F-14 Tomcat fighters from the US carrier *Saratoga* (CV 60) and forced to land at the Sigenolla air base on Sicily. On the ground, the 737 is surrounded by US troops and Italian police, with the latter taking control of the terrorists, who are charged with weapons violations, kidnapping, and murder. US and Israeli intelligence activities played a key role in cueing the *Saratoga*'s aircraft to the 737 intercept.

8 NOV

The one-star rank of commodore in the US Navy is changed to rear admiral (lower half).

21 NOV

Jonathan Jay Pollard, a US naval intelligence analyst who spied for Israel against the United States, is arrested in Washington, D.C. His wife, Anne Henderson-Pollard is arrested the next day and charged with unauthorized possession of classified documents. Both were well paid by the Israelis. Pollard will be sentenced to life imprisonment; his wife will be sentenced to five years, but she will be released early because of medical problems. Two Israeli officials implicated in dealing with Pollard leave the United States on 22 Nov, immediately after US officials ask to meet with them.

5 DEC

Adm. of the Fleet Vladimir N. Chernavin becomes CINC of the Soviet Navy and a Deputy Minister of Defense. He succeeds Adm. of the Fleet of the Soviet Union Sergei G. Gorshkov, who had served in that position for almost 30 years. Gorshkov's tenure had spanned that of 13 US Secretaries of the Navy and nine Chiefs of Naval Operations. Chernavin, a former nuclear submarine commander, had been First Deputy CINC of the Navy and Chief of the Main Naval Staff since early 1982.

1986

12 JAN

For the first time during the continuing Iran-Iraq War, a US-flag merchant ship, the SS *President Taylor* owned by the American President Lines, is stopped, boarded, and searched. The ship is boarded by armed Iranian sailors about 30 n.miles (55.6 km) south of the port of Fujaira, United Arab Emirates, the ship's destination. The ship was in international waters when the Iranians stopped her for about two hours.

24 JAN

US carrier battle groups centered on the *Coral Sea* (CV 43) and *Saratoga* (CV 60) begin Operation Attain Document in and near the Gulf of Sidra to demonstrate freedom of the seas to Libya. The exercise ends on 31 Jan and will be followed by a second (Attain Document II) from 10 to 15 Feb 1986.

28 JAN

In the first space shuttle mishap, the *Challenger* explodes during lift-off from Cape Canaveral, Fla., killing all seven astronauts on board. Several Navy and Coast Guard ships, including the nuclear-propelled submersible *NR-1* and the battery-powered *Alvin* (DSV 2), participate in the search for wreckage of the spacecraft.

21 FEB

The first US Coast Guard cutter of the *Island* class, the 110-foot (33.5-m) *Farallon* (WPB 1301), is commissioned.

21 MAR

US Marine fighter readiness training squadron VMFT-401 is established at Yuma, Ariz., to provide adversary training aircraft for active and reserve Marine squadrons. The squadron—nicknamed "Snipers" —initially will fly 13 F-21A Kfir fighters, leased from Israel Aircraft Industries, from June 1987 to Sep 1989.

22 MAR

The Trident missile submarine *Georgia* (SSBN 729) collides with the Navy tug *Secota* (YTM 415) after completing a personnel transfer off Midway Island in the mid-Pacific. The tug looses power alongside the submarine, strikes the larger craft's stern planes, and sinks. Ten members of the tug's contract-hire crew are rescued and two are lost. The *Georgia* is undamaged.

24 MAR

Libyan forces launch two SA-5 surface-to-air missiles at US aircraft flying offshore from the carrier *Coral Sea* (CV 43). The missiles, fired at extreme range, miss the aircraft as do up to four additional missiles fired during the day. The Libyan action is intended to prevent US warships and aircraft from operating in international waters off the Libyan coast.

In response to the missile firings and the approach of a Libyan Combattante II-class missile craft to the US task force, the craft is heavily damaged by two Harpoon missiles launched by A-6E Intruders from the carrier *America* (CV 66). That evening A-7E Corsairs from the carrier *Saratoga* (CV 60) fire high-speed anti-radiation missiles (HARMs) at radars supporting shore-based SA-5 missile launchers. Next, an A-6E attacks a Libyan Nanuchka-class missile ship with Rockeye cluster bombs; a second attack is thwarted when the patrol boat seeks refuge alongside a neutral merchant ship. The damaged Nanuchka returns to Benghazi under cover of darkness. There is another attack by two A-7Es with HARM missiles against a radar site at Surt. These actions are collectively called Operation Prairie Fire by US commanders.

25 MAR

At 0200 A-6E Intruders from the US carriers *Coral Sea* and *Saratoga* attack a Libyan Nanuchka-class missile ship as she enters international waters. The craft is observed dead in the water with life rafts nearby. Libyan forces cease hostile operations against US ships and aircraft operating offshore.

5 APR

Terrorists, apparently with Libyan sponsorship, bomb a West Berlin discotheque, killing a US soldier and a Turkish civilian and wounding 79 persons.

11 APR

Chief of Naval Operations Adm. James D. Watkins, USN, becomes the first US CNO to visit China. He is met upon arrival in Bejing by Adm. Liu Huaquing, Commander of the Navy of the Chinese People's Liberation Army. The visit will last through 16 Apr.

15 APR

Eighteen US Air Force F-111F strike aircraft, flying from bases in Britain, and 12 Navy and Marine A-6E carrier-based aircraft from the *America* and *Coral Sea* attack targets in Libya. Numerous other carrier-based aircraft provide air defense, electronic, and other support for the strike aircraft in Operation El Dorado Canyon. The pre-dawn strike against a variety of Libyan targets is made with the loss of only one US aircraft, an F-111 en route to the target with both crewmen lost. France and Spain deny permission for F-111 overflights, hence they fly a circuitous route over the Atlantic with several in-flight refuelings required, a total of 6,000 n.miles (11,120 km).

6 MAY

Three US nuclear-propelled attack submarines surface at the North Pole: the *Archerfish* (SSN 678), *Hawkbill* (SSN 666), and *Ray* (SSN 653). The operation—dubbed Icex 1-86—is the first time in history that three submarines are simultaneously at the top of the world.

10 MAY

The battleship *Missouri* (BB 63) is the third ship of the *Iowa* (BB 61) class to be recommissioned, in ceremonies at San Francisco, Calif., as part of the Reagan-Lehman 600-ship naval buildup.

14 MAY

The aviation logistic support ship *Wright* (T-AVB 3) is placed in naval service. The *Wright* and her sister ship *Curtiss* (T-AVB 4) were converted from roll-on/roll-off container ships to provide maintenance and logistic support for Marine aircraft in forward areas. (The AVB 1 and AVB 2 were converted tank landing ships [LST] configured to support land-based and flying boat patrol aircraft in the Mediterranean area.)

18 MAY

The *Sgt William R. Button* (T-AK 3012), the last of 13 Maritime Prepositioning Ships (MPS) to be loaded with Marine vehicles and equipment, is placed in service. The 13 ships (five new construction and eight converted cargo ships) are being deployed in three squadrons, each of the three carrying weapons and equipment for a Marine brigade.

20 MAY

The cruiser *Bunker Hill* (CG 52) becomes the first US ship, other than the missile test ship *Norton Sound* (AVM 1) and the *SES-100B* to launch a missile at sea from a vertical-launch cell. (*See* 18 Apr 1976.)

7 JULY

The guided missile cruiser *Belknap* (CG 26) becomes flagship of the US Sixth Fleet in the Mediterranean, replacing the *Coronado* (AGF 11) in that role.

12 AUG

The Iraq-Iran conflict escalates as Iraqi Mirage strike aircraft attack the floating tanker terminal at Sirri, Iran. The range of the strike, more than 600 miles (965 km) from the closest Iraqi airfield, means that the Iraqis had developed an in-flight refueling capability. While the raid does not seriously disrupt Sirri operations, it helps discourage commercial tankers from entering the Persian Gulf by contributing to a boost in insurance fees.

15 AUG

The US Navy issues a request for proposals on an "operational development model" for a fleet air defense airship. The first flight is specified to take place within 36 months of the contract award. Goodyear Aerospace Corp. and Westinghouse Airship Industries will submit proposals on 20 Oct 1986. The concept will not be pursued.

29 AUG

Eight US Marines are killed and 13 others injured when a CH-46 Sea Knight helicopter crashes shortly after taking off from the amphibious ship *Saipan* (LHA 2). The Marines are participating in Northern Wedding 86, a major NATO exercise in Norway.

10 SEP

The battleship *Missouri* departs Long Beach, Calif., on an around-the-world shakedown cruise. The 100-day cruise will end at Long Beach on 19 Dec, the ship having steamed approximately 24,000 n.miles (44,470 km).

20 SEP

The Aegis guided missile cruiser *Bunker Hill* (CG 52) is commissioned, the first US Navy warship to be armed with a vertical-launch system. The five previous cruisers of the *Ticonderoga* (CG 47) class have two Mk 26 twin missile launchers with a total of 88 weapons stowed in rotating magazines. The *Bunker Hill*, with two Mk 141 61-cell vertical-launch systems has a total of 122 weapons, with more launch flexibility than the Mk 26 system. Her first CO is Capt. Philip M. Quast, USN.

OCT

The US attack submarine *Augusta* (SSN 710) suffers an underwater collision with a Soviet Delta-class strategic missile submarine in the North Atlantic. At least one other Soviet submarine is in the area at the time. The *Augusta* was able to return to port, having suffered $2.7 million in damage. The Soviet submarine had only minor damage.

1 OCT

The Goldwater-Nichols Defense Reorganization Act of 1986 becomes law. Named for Sen. Barry Goldwater (R-Ariz.) and Rep. Bill Nichols (D-Ala.), the law places the Chairman of the Joint Chiefs of Staff (JCS) in the chain-of-command, between the Secretary of Defense and the unified commanders, adds the position of Vice Chairman of the JCS (at the four-star level), and makes other changes to the US defense structure including a strenthening of the role of the unified (area) commanders in chief.

6 OCT

The Yankee-class ballistic missile submarine *K-219* sinks some 600 n.miles (1,110 km) east of Bermuda. Three days earlier seawater had entered a missile tube of the submerged submarine, at the time on patrol with 15 SS-N-6 missiles with nuclear warheads. The casualty was followed by a missile propellant explosion, the escape of toxic gases, and fires. The submarine surfaced but despite damage control and an attempt to tow the craft, she sinks 40 hours after the explosion. Four of the 119 crewmen are killed in the explosions; two others die later from injuries. (One missile tube was not in use because of an earlier accident.)

15 OCT

A US Marine CH-46 Sea Knight helicopter crashes into Onslow Bay off North Carolina, killing 15 of the 19 servicemen on board. The helicopter had just taken off from the amphibious ship *Guadalcanal* (LPH 7). The fatalities were 14 Marines and one Navy chaplain.

25 OCT

The US nuclear-propelled carrier *Theodore Roosevelt* (CVN 71) is placed in commission. The first CO of this fourth ship of the *Nimitz* (CVN 68) class is Capt. Paul W. Parcells, USN.

5 NOV

In the first visit by US Navy ships to China since 1949, three US warships enter the port city of Qingdoi for a six-day visit: the cruiser *Reeves* (CG 24), destroyer *Oldendorf* (DD 972), and frigate *Rentz* (FFG 46). Adm. J. A. (Ace) Lyons, Jr., USN, Commander in Chief US Pacific Fleet, is embarked in the *Reeves*.

18 NOV

The battleship *Missouri* arrives at Istanbul, Turkey, to commemorate the ship's historic visit to the port 40 years earlier. The dreadnought is on a three-month, around-the-world cruise.

26 NOV

For the first time since World War II, the US Third Fleet becomes a sea-going command as Vice Adm. Diego E. Hernandez, USN, Commander Third Fleet, breaks his flag in the flagship *Coronado*. Previously the Third Fleet was based ashore at Pearl Harbor.

15 DEC

The US Navy hospital ship *Mercy* (T-AH 19) is placed in service. Converted from a tanker, the *Mercy* and her sister ship *Comfort* (T-AH 20), to be completed in 1987, are the world's largest hospital ships with a full-load displacement of 69,360 tons and an overall length of 894 feet (272.6 m).

1987

10 JAN

The US Marine Corps announces the arrest of Sgt. Clayton J. Lonetree, USMC, accused of betraying secrets for sex while serving as a guard at the American Embassy in Moscow between Sep 1984 and Mar 1986. Two other former Moscow security guards will be arrested but espionage charges against them will be dropped. Lonetree will be tried by court martial and, on 24 Aug 1987, found guilty on 13 counts of espionage.

15 JAN

The first flight test of a Trident D-5 missile from Cape Canaveral, Fla., is successful.

7 MAR

In response to the "tanker war" in the Persian Gulf, the Reagan Administration agrees to reflag 11 Kuwaiti oil tankers with the American flag and place the ships under US naval protection.

16 APR

Commander in Chief US Special Operations Command (CINCSOC) is established with Gen. James J. Lindsay, USA, the first CINCSOC. This is the first US unified command without a geographic area of responsibility. "SOCOM" is the "provider" for all Special Operations Forces (SOF)—Army, Navy, Air Force, and Marine Corps.

21 APR

The US frigate *Richard L. Page* (FFG 5) sinks the fishing boat *Chickadee* in a collision off the Virginia coast during a fog.

5 MAY

The House and Senate open nationally televised hearings into the Iran-Contra scandal, with a key player being Lt. Col. Oliver L. North, USMC, on the staff of the National Security Council. North, a Vietnam veteran, will lie to Congress and on 4 May 1989 will be found guilty of three felony counts: obstructing Congress, unlawfully mutilating government documents, and accepting an illegal gratuity. However, his conviction will be set aside because of prior promises of immunity.

14 MAY

An Iraqi Mirage F-1 aircraft approaches the destroyer *Coontz* (DDG 40) in the Persian Gulf. The US de-stroyer prepares for an engagement but the approaching aircraft keeps its radar in a surveillance rather than fire-control mode. The Mirage comes within ten n.miles (18.5 km) of the *Coontz* and subsequently attacks a tanker.

17 MAY

An Iraqi Mirage F-1 aircraft launches two Exocet missiles in a night attack on the US frigate *Stark* (FFG 31) in the center of the Persian Gulf. Both missiles, the first launched from a distance of 22.5 n.miles (41.7 km) and the second from 15.5 n.miles (28.7 km), strike the *Stark*, inflicting extensive damage and killing 37 sailors. The ship, unprepared to defend against an attack, survives because of the crew's outstanding damage-control performance.

25 MAY

For the first time the US Navy provides escort for a merchant ship in the Persian Gulf, that being a Kuwaiti-flagged freighter carrying US arms to Bahrain.

18 JUNE

At a Pentagon press briefing a Navy captain observes that the Iranians "have some potential capability to moor mines . . . but nothing that we would think of as minelaying capability in military terms and no modern mines. . . . So we would say that their mine warfare capability is limited."

1 JULY

Commander in Chief Forces Command (CINCFOR) is established as a US unified command with Gen. Joseph T. Palastra, Jr., USA, as the first commander in chief. Previously Forces Command was an all-Army specified command.

Commander in Chief US Transportation Command (CINCTRANS) is established to coordinate all US military transportation. Gen. Duane H. Cassidy, USAF, is the first CINCTRANS.

21 JULY

The first convoy of Kuwaiti tankers reflagged by the United States begins in the Persian Gulf. The convoy includes the reflagged, 401,382-deadweight-ton tanker *Bridgeton*, one of 11 Kuwaiti tankers that have been reflagged by the United States. The US Navy will escort 22 transits of the Persian Gulf.

24 JULY

The tanker *Bridgeton* strikes a Soviet-made floating mine about 20 n.miles (37 km) west of Farsi Island. The tanker is damaged, but not in danger of sinking.

24 AUG

The US destroyer *Kidd* (DDG 993) fires warning shots across the bows of two dhows when they approach a US-escorted convoy entering the Strait of Hormuz, departing the Persian Gulf. The same day an Iranian warship approaches a US-escorted convoy, but turns away when the frigate *Jarrett* (FFG 33) moves between the Iranian ship and the convoy.

21 SEP

US Army MH-6 Cayuse special operations helicopters attack and capture the *Iran Ajr*, an Iranian landing craft being used for covert minelaying about 50 n.miles (93 km) northeast of Bahrain. The helicopters flew from US Navy frigates.

22 SEP

A US Navy frigate fires warning ships across the bow of an Iranian hovercraft that approaches the US ship towing the *Iran Ajr*.

3 OCT

Saudi fighter aircraft and naval forces reportedly turn back a force of about 60 Iranian speedboats heading toward the Saudi offshore oilfield at Khafji. The Saudis were reportedly alerted to the speedboats by US forces.

8 OCT

US Army frigate-based MH-6 helicopters attack four Iranian speedboats about 15 n.miles (28 km) southwest of Farsi Island after one of the boats fired on a US helicopter. One boat is sunk and two are damaged and captured, with six Iranians being captured, two of whom die from wounds.

15 OCT

The American-owned, Liberian-flagged tanker *Sungari*, at anchor nine n.miles (16.7 km) off Kuwait's Mina al-Ahmadi terminal, is hit and damaged by a Silkworm missile fired by Iranian troops from the Fao Peninsula. The ship is damaged, but no one is killed or injured.

16 OCT

The reflagged Kuwaiti tanker *Sea Isle City*, about ten n.miles (18.5 km) off Mina al-Ahmadi, is hit and damaged by a Silkworm missile fired by Iranian forces from the Fao Peninsula. The ship is damaged with 18 injured.

19 OCT

In response to the 16 Oct attack, US destroyers shell and Navy SEALs blow up an Iranian oil platform east of Bahrain, and destroy electronic equipment on a second platform.

8 DEC

The Intermediate-range Nuclear Forces (INF) treaty —officially the Treaty Between the United States and the Soviet Union on the Elimination of Their Intermediate-Range and Shorter-Range Missiles—is signed in Washington, D.C., by President Ronald Reagan and President Mikhail S. Gorbachev. This is history's first treaty to eliminate a complete class of weapons, with the more than 7,600 INF weapons to be eliminated by 31 May 1991. The treaty also establishes unprecedented rights for the parties to conduct on-site inspections in the United States and Soviet Union.

The US Navy's Strategic Systems Program Office (SSPO) is renamed Strategic Systems Programs (SSP), reflecting new missions, functions, and tasks related to a still further broadening of its responsibilities.

12 DEC

Helicopters from the US destroyer *Chandler* (DDG 996) evacuate 11 people from the Cypriot-registered tanker *Pivot* after the ship is attacked by Iranian speedboats. A helicopter chartered by CBS News evacuates another 29.

22 DEC

French warships in the Persian Gulf deter an Iranian attack on a Liberian-flag merchant ship by steaming toward the approaching Iranian ship.

24 DEC

An Iranian speedboat fires shots at a US frigate-based helicopter as the helicopter investigates a Liberian-flagged tanker attacked by Iranian speedboats. (A total of six merchant ships are sunk in the Persian Gulf during 1987, compared to three in 1984, none in 1985, and two in 1986.)

1988

5 JAN

A Soviet nuclear-propelled, cruise missile submarine of the Charlie I class is transferred on lease to the Indian Navy. Renamed *Chakra*, the submarine will be returned to the Soviet Pacific Fleet in Jan 1991. This is the first time a nuclear-propelled submarine has been transferred to another nation.

16 JAN

French warships in the Persian Gulf deter an Iranian attack on a Liberian-flag merchant ship by steaming toward the approaching Iranian ship.

5 FEB

US Marine Corps renames the Marine Air-Ground Task Force (MAGTF) organizations: Marine Amphibious Force (MAF) became Marine Expeditionary Force (MEF), Marine Amphibious Brigade (MAB) became Marine Expeditionary Brigade (MEB), and Marine Amphibious Unit (MAU) became Marine Expeditionary Unit (MEU). Also, 15 permanent MAGTFs are established:

Expeditionary Forces	Expeditionary Brigades	Expeditionary Units
I MEF	5th, 7th MEB	11th, 13th, 15th MEU
II MEF	4th, 6th MEB	22nd, 24th, 26th MEU
III MEF	1st, 9th MEB	

12 FEB

The US guided missile cruiser *Yorktown* (CG 48) and destroyer *Caron* (DD 970) are bumped by a Soviet frigate and destroyer, respectively, in international waters off the Soviet Black Sea base of Sevastopol.

17 FEB

Lt. Col. William R. Higgins, USMC, head of a United Nations' truce supervision team monitoring the Israeli-Lebanon border, is kidnapped by Islamic terrorists while driving alone near the Lebanese port of Tyre. On 31 July 1989 a group believed to be part of the Muslim fundamentalist party Hizballah (Party of God) will release a videotape of Higgins being hanged.

22 FEB

Secretary of the Navy James H. Webb, Jr., resigns in protest of what he considers to be Secretary of Defense Frank C. Carlucci's lack of support for the 600-ship Navy. His decision is triggered by Carlucci's decision to discard 16 frigates from the fleet. However, Webb, in a recent speech before the National Press Club, stated that America's future ties should be primarily in the Pacific region. This statement creates problems for the Reagan Administration.

14 APR

The US frigate *Samuel B. Roberts* (FFG 58) strikes a mine in the Persian Gulf. The ship is heavily damaged and suffers extensive flooding; she is kept afloat with the assistance of other US ships in the area and the damage-control expertise of the *Roberts'* crew. Ten were injured; there were no fatalities.

The Soviet government agrees to withdraw its troops from Afghanistan, with the official withdrawal beginning on 18 May 1988.

16 APR

First flight of the US Navy T-45A Goshawk undergraduate jet training aircraft. It will be used to train Navy, Marine, and Coast Guard pilots.

18 APR

In retaliation for the mining of the frigate *Samuel B. Roberts*, aircraft from the US carrier *Enterprise* (CVN 65), steaming in the Gulf of Oman, and US warships in the Persian Gulf attack Iranian ships and installations. During Operation Praying Mantis, the Iranian frigates *Sabhand* and *Sabalan* are attacked, the former sunk and the latter heavily damaged but allowed to be towed back to port. The Iranian missile craft *Joshan* and a small Boghammer attack craft are also sunk and offshore platforms are attacked. Two Standard-ER SM-2 missiles fired by the US cruiser *Wainwright* (CG 28) apparently damages an Iranian F-4 Phantom flying in the area.

24 APR

The US submarine *Bonefish* (SS 582), one of the Navy's last diesel-electric submarines, is racked by a battery explosion and fires during exercises off Cape Canaveral, Fla. Three of her crew of 92 are killed. The submarine is abandoned, with crewmen taken aboard other US Navy ships. The submarine will be towed to Charleston, S.C., and decommissioned.

27 MAY

The US Coast Guard cutter *Bibb* (WHEC 31) is decommissioned after 52 years of service. She is the last of the six Secretary-class cutters built in 1936–1937 to be retired. All served in World War II; a seventh ship of the class, the *Alexander Hamilton* (WPG 34), was sunk by a German U-boat during the war.

28 JUNE

The US naval attaché to Greece, Capt. William E. Nordeen, USN, is killed by a bomb while driving to his office in an Athens suburb. A leftist group calling itself "November 17" claims credit for the murder.

30 JUNE

The General Dynamics/Electric Boat yard is shut down by striking union workers. The strike, which will continue to 12 Oct 1988, will further delay the completion of strategic missile submarines of the *Ohio* (SSBN 726) class.

3 JULY

In the midst of a series of engagements against Iranian speedboats, the US guided missile cruiser *Vincennes* (CG 49) launches two Standard SM-2 surface-to-air missiles against what is believed to be a descending Iranian aircraft. The target is actually a climbing Iran Air Airbus, which is destroyed with the loss of all 290 passengers and crew on board.

6 AUG

The US nuclear-propelled attack submarine *San Juan* (SSN 751) is commissioned with Comdr. Charles B. Young, USN, in command. She is the first submarine of the "Improved" *Los Angeles* (SSN 688) class, fitted with 12 vertical-launch tubes for Tomahawk missiles and other improvements.

20 AUG

A ceasefire is announced in the eight-year war between Iran and Iraq. Iraqi forces have attacked more than 320 merchant ships in the Persian Gulf and Iranian forces more than 221. In addition, the US frigate *Stark* (FFG 31) was severely damaged by Iraqi guided missiles and the *Samuel B. Roberts* almost sunk by a mine laid by Iranian forces.

22 OCT

The battleship *Wisconsin* (BB 64) is the fourth ship of her class to be recommissioned as part of the Reagan-Lehman 600-ship naval buildup. This marks the first time since 8 March 1958 that all four ships of the *Iowa* (BB 61) class were in commission.

7 DEC

President Mikhail S. Gorbachev announces a unilateral plan to reduce the Soviet armed forces by ten percent and to withdraw 50,000 troops from Eastern Europe. At the time the Soviet forces in Eastern Europe were estimated by Western intelligence agencies at approximately 500,000 ground troops in addition to aviation units.

31 DEC

The Soviet government announces that its remaining troops in Afghanistan will cease fire on 1 Jan 1989, and that the USSR will stop supplying weapons to the Kabul government.

1989

4 JAN

Two Libyan MiG-23 Flogger fighters are shot down by US Navy F-14 Tomcat fighters over international waters when the missile-armed MiG-23s approached the F-14s in a hostile manner. The F-14s, flying from the carrier *John F. Kennedy* (CV 67), fire Sidewinder and Sparrow missiles to down the MiGs.

20 JAN

George Bush is inaugurated as President of the United States. Former Vice President, Director of Central Intelligence, member of Congress, and oil industry executive, he is the sixth US president to have served in the Navy. During World War II he saw combat as pilot of a TBM Avenger torpedo plane. He was shot down by Japanese ground fire and rescued by a submarine in the western Pacific.

7 FEB

Igor A. Rogachev, a Soviet deputy foreign minister, announces at a Moscow news conference that "By February 15 not a single Soviet soldier will remain in Afghanistan." Also at the conference, another Soviet official revealed that up to 15,000 Soviet troops and airmen were killed in the nine-year conflict. However, the civil war in Afghanistan will continue into 1995.

19 MAR

First flight of Boeing-Bell V-22 tilt-rotor VSTOL aircraft (later named Osprey by the US Navy). The aircraft is intended for several combat and support roles in the Army, Navy, Air Force, and Marine Corps, with the last service being the largest user (to replace the CH-46 and CH-53A/D helicopters).

20 MAR

A Marine CH-53D Sea Stallion helicopter crashes near Pohang, South Korea, during exercise Team Spirit 89. Eighteen Marines and a Navy hospital corpsman are killed in the crash. (*See* 24 Mar 1984.)

21 MAR

The first submarine-launch of a Trident D-5 missile, from the USS *Tennessee* (SSBN 734), is a failure. The Navy had conducted 19 flight-pad test launches with only two minor failures. (The second submerged launch was successful, although the third again failed; changes were made in the nozzle system to correct

flaws.) The failures force a delay in the Trident D-5 becoming operational from Dec 1989 to Mar 1990, the first significant delay in the otherwise highly successful Trident program.

7 APR

The Soviet nuclear-propelled submarine *Komsomolets (K-278)* suffers a fire while running submerged and sinks 112 n.miles (207.5 km) southeast of Bear Island, off the Norwegian coast. The submarine, given the NATO code-name Mike, is an advanced combat submarine capable of operating at depths to 3,280 feet (1,000 m). The submarine is brought to the surface where most of the crew escape; five are ejected in an escape chamber as the submarine subsequently plunges to the ocean floor (with only one man surviving because of toxic gases in the chamber). Many will succumb to the cold before being rescued. A total of 42 die; 27 are rescued.

19 APR

The battleship *Iowa* (BB 61) suffers an explosion in her No. 2 16-inch (406-mm) gun turret while the ship is operating some 330 n.miles (612 km) off Puerto Rico. One officer and 46 enlisted men in the turret and below-deck projectile handling spaces are killed in the explosion and flash fire; 11 sailors in lower powder magazines escaped without harm with those spaces partially flooded to prevent a powder explosion, which most likely would have destroyed the ship. The damaged gun—center gun of No. 2 turret—is not repaired before the ship is mothballed in 1990.

30 MAY

A US Marine CH-46 Sea Knight helicopter crashes while taking off from the amphibious ship *Denver* (LPD 9) during night operations. The crash kills 13 Marines and a Navy hospital corpsman.

3 JUNE

The US Marine Corps begins a two-day operational stand-down for all Marine aviation units in reaction to seven aircraft mishaps and the loss of 45 Marines during the first five months of the year.

14 JUNE

The US nuclear-propelled submarine *Houston* (SSN 713) snags a submerged tow cable from the commercial tugboat *Barcelona* off the coast of southern California. The submarine pulls the tug underwater and a civilian crewman is lost. (Two other incidents on board the *Houston* will result in her commanding officer being relieved in Dec 1989.)

21 JULY

Three Soviet naval ships arrive in Norfolk, Va., for a five-day visit, the first to the United States since a 1975 visit to Boston (*see* 7 May 1975). Visiting Norfolk are the missile cruiser *Marshal Ustinov* flying the flag of Vice Adm. I. V. Kasatonov, the First Deputy Commander in Chief of the Northern Fleet. The cruiser is accompanied by the missile destroyer *Otlichny* and the replenishment oiler *Genrikh Gasanov*.

1 AUG

The US Marine Corps University is established to direct Marine educational activities, including the basic and amphibious warfare schools, three staff noncommissioned academies, 17 noncommissioned officers schools, the Marine Corps Institute, and the Professional Military Education (PME) Program.

4 AUG

The US missile cruiser *Thomas Gates* (CG 51) and the missile frigate *Kauffman* (FFG 59) visit the Soviet port of Sevastopol, headquarters of the Black Sea Fleet. The visit, in reciprocation for the Soviet task force visiting Norfolk in July, marks the beginning a series of port visits by US and Soviet warships.

5 AUG

The US frigate *Ingraham* (FFG 61) is placed in commission, the last of 51 ships of the *Oliver Hazard Perry* (FFG 7) class. The *Ingraham* will be the last US frigate authorized up to the time this book is published. The ship's first CO is Comdr. Charles S. Vogan, Jr., USN.

7 SEP

First flight of an the aerodynamic ES-3A conversion of an S-3A Viking ASW aircraft. The ES-3A will replace the long-serving EA-3B Skywarrior as a carrier-based electronic surveillance aircraft. (The second conversion is the first with a full electronics suite; first flight on 21 Jan 1992; 12 ES-3A aircraft will be converted.)

14 SEP

First full conversion flight of the tilt-rotor V-22 Osprey—from vertical mode to horizontal mode,

demonstrating the validity of the concept for a full-size aircraft. Produced by a Bell-Boeing consortium, the aircraft is intended for a variety of roles in all services, albeit principally as a Marine aircraft.

25 OCT

Construction begins at the Electric Boat yard in Groton, Conn., on the submarine *Seawolf* (SSN 21), the first unit of the post–*Los Angeles* (SSN 688) class. (The *Seawolf* will suffer several delays because of technical and material problems, not being completed until the spring of 1997.)

30 OCT

Five crewmen are slightly injured when a Navy F/A-18 Hornet aircraft accidently drops a 500-pound (227-kg) bomb on the guided missile cruiser *Reeves* (CG 24) during exercises in the Indian Ocean.

1 NOV

Honored Test Pilot of the USSR Viktor Pugachev makes the first conventional aircraft landing on a Soviet ship, flying an Su-27K Flanker aboard the carrier *Tbilisi* (later renamed *Admiral Flota Sovetskogo Soyuza Kuznetsov*). Subsequently MiG-29K Fulcrum and Su-25UTG Frogfoot aircraft as well as helicopters will operate from the ship.

9 NOV

This night East Germans begin passing through the Berlin Wall without interference from East German or Soviet guards. In the first four days after the wall is opened 4.3 million East Germans will cross over to West Berlin, most of whom will return to their homes after shopping and sightseeing.

11 NOV

The US nuclear-propelled aircraft carrier *Abraham Lincoln* (CVN 72) is placed in commission, the fifth ship of the *Nimitz* (CVN 68) class. The ship's first CO is Capt. William B. Hayden, USN.

14 NOV

Chief of Naval Operations Adm. Carlisle A. H. Trost, USN, orders a Navy-wide, 48-hour safety stand-down following a series of unrelated accidents over a period of several weeks. The order requires that every ship, aviation squadron, and shore training facility interrupt normal operations and review basic safety and operating procedures.

East German workmen begin dismantling the Berlin Wall, a project that will take until 21 Nov.

16 NOV

Adm. Trost reports to Congress that at 67 major mishaps for 1989, the Navy's accident rate for the year was still lower than the previous year's all-time low of 69 major mishaps. The Navy defines a major mishap as an accident that results in a fatality and/or damage exceeding $1 million.

2 DEC

The US missile cruiser *Belknap* (CG 26) and the Soviet missile cruiser *Slava* rendezvous in Marsaxlokk Bay, Malta, to support the two-day meeting of President Bush and President Mikhail S. Gorbachev. A storm, however, prevents the leaders from meeting on board the warships as originally planned and the Soviet liner *Maksim Gor'kiy*, alongside a pier, hosts the leaders. President Bush lives on board the *Belknap* during the meetings.

7 DEC

The US battleship *New Jersey* (BB 62) becomes the first dreadnought in modern times to enter the Persian Gulf. She will visit ports in Bahrain and the United Arab Emirates before departing through the Strait of Hormuz on 12 Dec.

16 DEC

Four unarmed US officers in civilian clothes, driving to a restaurant in Panama City, lose their way and are stopped at a roadblock by members of the Panamanian Defense Force. The threatening attitude of the sentries and the gathering of a crowd of civilians cause the Americans to speed away. Their car is fired on and 1st Lt. Robert Paz, USMC, is mortally wounded and another officer is hit. A US Navy lieutenant and his wife, stopped at the same roadblock, witness the incident. They are taken into custody and held for four hours with the lieutenant being beaten and his wife sexually threatened before being released.

17 DEC

The 12,000 US troops in the Panama Canal Zone are placed on alert. Additional US forces are flown into the area.

20 DEC

In a night attack, 24,000 US troops—half of them flown into the country—seize control of Panama in an effort to arrest Gen. Manuel Noriega, president of the country, who is wanted by the US government for drug trafficking. Operation Just Cause is a success, although Noriega escapes to the Vatican mission, but surrenders to US officials on 3 Jan 1990. The operation was simplified by having US troops already in-country and unlimited access through US-controlled airfields. The participating troops were mostly US Army with about 700 Marines committed. Despite US forces having total control of the skies over Panama, the Air Force uses two F-117A "stealth" attack planes to strike Panamanian targets; their guided bombs widely miss their intended targets.

1990

16 JAN

The USCGC *Mellon* (WHEC 717) becomes the first Coast Guard cutter to fire a guided missile, launching a Harpoon surface-to-surface missile.

12 FEB

Officials of NATO and the Warsaw Pact countries begin three days of meetings in Ottawa to develop the concept of "Open Skies" inspections of various countries with reconnaissance aircraft.

29 MAR

The US strategic missile submarine *Tennessee* (SSBN 734) departs on the first deterrent patrol carrying the Trident D-5 missile. She will complete that patrol, returning to Kings Bay, Ga., on 23 Apr 1990. (In Apr 1992 the *Tennessee* will complete the 3,000th fleet ballistic missile submarine patrol—31 years after the pioneer *George Washington* [SSBN 598] conducted the first such patrol. This number does not take into account the 41 patrols conducted by five Regulus-armed guided missile submarines from mid-1960 to mid-1964.)

2 APR

Iraqi President Saddam Hussein declares, "I categorically deny that we have atomic bombs but let [Iraq's critics] know here and now that we do possess binary chemical weapons which only the United States and the Soviet Union also have."

The Iraqi state radio announces: "Those who are threatening us with nuclear bombs, we warn them that we will hit them with these binary chemical weapons. I also say that if Israel dares to hit even one piece of steel on any industrial site we will make the fire consume half of Israel."

8 MAY

The US missile destroyer *Conyngham* (DDG 17) is crippled by fire while under way off the coast of North Carolina. The blaze, which started in a boiler room, swept through several decks, killing one officer; 18 crewmen were injured. The *Conyngham* will not be repaired and will be decommissioned later in the year.

27 MAY

A US Navy amphibious squadron carrying the 22nd Marine Expeditionary Unit (MEU) departs the port of Toulon in the Mediterranean for waters off Monrovia, Liberia, in response to unrest and threats to US citizens. The destroyer *Peterson* (DD 969) is directed to accompany the three ships of Amphibious Squadron 4 in an operation to be named Sharp Edge.

The US guided missile cruiser *Yarnell* (CG 17) and frigate *Kauffman* (FFG 59) begin a three-day visit to Gdansk, the first visit to Poland by US Navy ships in 45 years.

24 JULY

Iraq deploys a large ground force to the Kuwaiti border following accusations of Kuwait stealing Iraqi oil through illegal drilling practices. US warships in the Persian Gulf area are placed on alert.

2 AUG

Approximately 100,000 Iraqi troops, supported by tanks and aircraft, invade Kuwait beginning at 0200. The Emir of Kuwait flees to Saudi Arabia as his country is quickly overrun.

5 AUG

As the civil war escalates in Liberia, a US amphibious task force offshore begins evacuating US and foreign nationals by helicopter from the US Embassy compound in Monrovia. The evacuation from Liberia—Operation Sharp Edge—will continue into Nov 1990.

6 AUG

The UN Security Council passes Resolution 661, ordering a global embargo of trade with Iraq.

The Saudi government agrees to permit US and foreign troops on Saudi territory in response to the Iraqi invasion of Kuwait.

7 AUG

President George Bush orders US combat troops, aircraft, and warships to Saudi Arabia to protect that country from possible Iraqi attacks. This is the start of Operation Desert Shield. The Navy's Military Sealift Command begins directing sealift ships to appropriate ports and ordering the activation of ships from the ready reserve fleet.

A US carrier battle group centered on the *Dwight D. Eisenhower* (CVN 69) transits the Suez Canal into the Red Sea. The *Independence* (CV 62) battle group arrives in the Gulf of Oman. Their air wings are the first US combat-ready aircraft to enter the Persian Gulf area.

8 AUG

Iraq annexes Kuwait. In a broadcast over Baghdad radio, Saddam Hussein defends his takeover of Kuwait as "necessary" to redress the "flawed regional borders" drawn up by colonial powers that had left a "corrupt minority" in control of some of the Arab world's richest territory.

The first elements of the US Army's 82nd Airborne Division are flown into Saudi Arabia. Also arriving are the first US Air Force F-15 Eagle fighters and E-3A Airborne Warning And Control System (AWACS) aircraft.

Ships of Maritime Prepositioning Squadron 2 sail from Diego Garcia and Squadron 3 from Guam toward the Persian Gulf.

9 AUG

The UN Security Council passes Resolution 662, declaring Iraqi's annexation of Kuwait "null and void."

10 AUG

In Cairo, 12 of 21 members of the Arab League vote to honor the United Nations' embargo of Iraq, endorse the Saudi invitation to American troops, and agree to commit forces to an all-Arab military force to join in the defense of Saudi Arabia.

US Air Force F-16 Fighting Falcon fighters from bases in the United States begin arriving in Saudi Arabia.

12 AUG

Saddam Hussein announces a peace plan linking an Iraqi withdrawal from Kuwait to an Israeli withdrawal from occupied territories on the West Bank and Gaza, and Syrian withdrawal from Lebanon.

13 AUG

The first of eight fast converted SL-7 sealift ships, the *Altair* (T-AKR 291) and *Capella* (T-AKR 293), depart Savannah, Ga., for the Persian Gulf with heavy equipment for the Army's 24th Mechanized Infantry Division. The converted SL-7 ships will make the 8,700-n.mile (16,120-km) voyage to the Saudi port of Jubail at an average speed of 27 knots. (Seven of the ships will make multiple transits during Desert Shield with the *Antares* [T-AKR 294], which had suffered previous machinery problems, having an engine breakdown during her initial Atlantic crossing in Aug; she is towed into a Spanish port and her cargo is shifted to other sealift ships.)

14 AUG

Advanced elements of the US 1st Marine Expeditionary Force (MEF) and 7th Marine Expeditionary Brigade (MEB) arrive in Saudi Arabia by airlift.

15 AUG

Saddam Hussein agrees to all Iranian demands to end the Iran-Iraq conflict.

US maritime prepositioning ships from Diego Garcia begin arriving at Jubail to unload equipment and vehicles for Marines being flown into Saudi Arabia.

17 AUG

Iraq announces that Westerners in the country will be held at civil and military installations as human shields against attacks.

The first maritime interception of ships bound for Iraq takes place when the US frigate *John L. Hall* (FFG 32) stops the northbound Iraqi tanker *Al Fao* in the Red Sea. As the ship is empty, determined by the amount of freeboard visible, she is allowed to proceed. Four hours later the US cruiser *England* (CG 22) challenges two northbound Iraqi ships in the Persian Gulf, the *Al Abid* and *Al Byaa*.

The US battleship *Wisconsin* (BB 64) transits the Suez Canal en route to the Persian Gulf. She will enter the Gulf on 24 Aug.

18 AUG

The UN Security Council passes Resolution 664 demanding the immediate release of all foreigners being held in Iraq and Kuwait.

22 AUG

President Bush authorizes a callup of selected reserve personnel for support of Operation Desert Shield.

The *Saratoga* (CV 60) carrier battle group transits the Suez Canal en route to the Red Sea.

25 AUG

The UN Security Council passes Resolution 665 authorizing the use of force by Western navies to enforce economic sanctions against Iraq.

9 SEP

President Bush and Soviet President Mikhail S. Gorbachev meet in Helsinki, Finland, where they declare unconditional support for the United Nations' sanctions against Iraq.

12 SEP

Representatives of the US, Soviet, British, and French governments reach an accord known as the Two Plus

Four Treaty that will recognize the creation of a new, post–Cold War German state. (The "two" were the German Democratic Republic and the Federal Republic of Germany—East and West Germany, respectively.) On 3 Oct 1990 the Federal Republic of Germany becomes the sole German state, ending the 45-year division of Germany into western and eastern areas, a major manifestation of the Cold War.

25 SEP

The UN Security Council passes Resolution 670 extending the economic embargo of Iraq to include air traffic to and from Iraq and Kuwait, except for humanitarian purposes.

28 SEP

Desert Shield sealift reaches a peak with 90 ships at sea—69 en route to the Middle East from the United States and Europe, and 21 "empties" returning to the United States for more cargo. Had the ships been evenly spaced on the route from the US East Coast to the Persian Gulf, there would have been one ship every 100 n.miles (185 km). When the "phase II" of Desert Shield is undertaken in Nov 1990 to build up a US offensive force in the Persian Gulf, a peak of 172 ships at sea will be reached on 2 Jan 1991.

1 OCT

The US carrier *Independence* transits the Strait of Hormuz and enters the Persian Gulf, the first time an aircraft carrier has been in the Gulf since 1974 (*see* 25 Nov 1974). The "Indy" will conduct flight operations before departing the Gulf on 4 Oct.

The US diesel-electric attack submarine *Blueback* (SS 581) is decommissioned. She is the last non-nuclear combat submarine active in the US Navy. (The only other diesel-electric submarine in US service is the research craft *Dolphin* [AGSS 555].)

US military forces formally end their presence in West Berlin. More than 30 US military facilities in Berlin will be closed through Sep 1994.

11 OCT

First flight of the US X-31 Enhanced Fighter Maneuverability (EFM) demonstrator, an advanced research aircraft intended to examine whether it is possible to exploit the high-angle-of-attack flight regime to enable a fighter to achieve tighter, faster turns, and earlier weapon firing opportunities. Flight testing of two X-31A aircraft will be carried out by an international

test organization made up of representatives from NASA, Defense Research Projects Agency (DARPA), Navy, Air Force, Germany, and the firms of Rockwell International and Messerschmitt-Bolkow-Blöhm (MBB).

26 OCT

The battleship *Iowa* (BB 61) is decommissioned, marking the start of the mothballing of the four ships of that class.

8 NOV

Secretary of Defense Dick Cheney directs the deployment of additional US air, ground, and naval forces—totalling some 200,000—to the Persian Gulf area as a buildup to offensive operations against Iraq.

15 NOV

US and Saudi forces conduct a joint training exercise—named Imminent Thunder—inside Saudi Arabia, including a major amphibious exercise along the coast. The exercise will continue through 21 Nov.

29 NOV

The UN Security Council approves Resolution 678 authorizing the use of military force if Iraq does not vacate Kuwait by 15 Jan 1991.

30 NOV

Operation Sharp Edge—the evacuation from Liberia—ends with 2,609 persons, including 330 Americans, being taken aboard US Navy amphibious ships standing offshore.

6 DEC

Saddam Hussein announces the release of all foreign hostages.

14 DEC

Secretary of the Navy H. Lawrence Garrett III signs a memorandum reorganizing the Navy's research, development, test, and evacuation activities. In the streamlining effort, four warfare centers are established: Air, Surface, Undersea, and Command, Communications, and Ocean Surveillance. The Navy's laboratory structure is also realigned.

21 DEC

The Israeli-chartered ferry *Tuvia* shuttling crewmen of the US carrier *Saratoga* capsizes and sinks off the Israeli port of Haifa, drowning 21 American sailors.

1991

1 JAN

US troop strength in the Persian Gulf area totals more than 325,000 including 35,000 Navy personnel at sea, and 55,000 Marine personnel, mostly ashore. At the time the US Navy has 25 ships in the Persian Gulf, 20 in the North Arabian Sea/Gulf of Oman, and ten in the Red Sea.

The US battleship *Missouri* (BB 63) arrives in the Gulf of Oman. She will enter the Persian Gulf on 3 Jan.

3 JAN

The US ambassador in Mogadishu, Somalia, asks for immediate evacuation of the remaining embassy staff as the two-week-old civil war threatens all Westerners in the east African country. Armed looters are already within the embassy compound.

4 JAN

The US amphibious ships *Guam* (LPH 9) and *Trenton* (LPD 14) begin Operation Eastern Exit to evacuate US citizens caught in the civil war in Somalia. The evacuation begins at night when two Marine CH-53E helicopters make a night flight of 466 n.miles (864 km) from the *Guam* into Mogadishu with two in-flight refuelings by Marine KC-130 tanker aircraft. The helicopters land 51 Marines and a nine-man Navy SEAL team to secure the US Embassy compound. The CH-53 and CH-46 helicopters then evacuate 281 people, including 51 Americans, plus the 60-man evacuation team flown in, to the offshore amphibious ships. The evacuees will be unloaded in Miscat, Oman, on 11 Jan.

7 JAN

The Department of Defense cancels the Navy's planned A-12 Avenger carrier-based attack aircraft. The plane was intended to replace the A-6 Intruder on carrier decks and in Marine attack squadrons. Its cancellation marks the end of long-range strike aircraft in the Navy (which had begun with the AJ Savage in the late 1940s); the A-6 will be phased out of Marine squadrons in 1993 and Navy squadrons in late 1996.

12 JAN

The US Congress votes to allow President George Bush to use military forces if necessary to end the Gulf crisis. The vote is 52 to 47 in the Senate and 250 to 183 in the House of Representatives.

A carrier battle group led by the USS *Ranger* (CV 61) arrives in the North Arabian Sea.

The carrier *Midway* (CV 41) returns to the Persian Gulf. (She had operated briefly in the Persian Gulf in early Nov 1990.)

14 JAN

The US carrier *Theodore Roosevelt* (CVN 71) and accompanying ships transit the Suez Canal and enter the Red Sea.

15 JAN

The *America* (CV 66) and accompanying ships transit the Suez Canal and enter the Red Sea. There are now four US carriers operating in the Red Sea and two in the Persian Gulf. (The carrier *Dwight D. Eisenhower* [CVN 69] had earlier departed the Gulf area.)

Ship		Air Wing	Location
CV 41	*Midway*	Carrier Air Wing 5	Persian Gulf
CV 60	*Saratoga*	Carrier Air Wing 17	Red Sea
CV 61	*Ranger*	Carrier Air Wing 2	Persian Gulf
CV 66	*America*	Carrier Air Wing 1	Red Sea
CV 67	*John F. Kennedy*	Carrier Air Wing 3	Red Sea
CVN 71	*Theodore Roosevelt*	Carrier Air Wing 8	Red Sea

Also in the Persian Gulf are the battleships *Missouri* and *Wisconsin* (BB 64) as well as numerous other US and coalition warships.

16 JAN

B-52 Stratofortress bombers carrying Air-Launched Cruise Missiles (ALCM) take off from Barksdale AFB, La., at 1535—11 hours, 25 minutes before the conflict begins. After a direct flight involving in-flight refuelings, they will launch their missiles at Iraqi targets two hours after the conflict begins.

At 1900 in Washington, the White House announces "the liberation of Kuwait has begun!"

17 JAN

Operation Desert Storm begins as US and other coalition aircraft begin a month-long period of intensive air attacks against Iraq. The opening blows of the aerial assault begins at 0238 when eight US Army AH-64 Apache helicopters of the 101st Airmobile Division dart undetected across the far western border of Saudi Arabia and Iraq to use Hellfire laser-guided missiles, rockets, and cannon fire to destroy two Iraqi radar installations. Shortly afterward coalition strike aircraft pour through this hole in Iraqi radar defenses, with more than 1,000 attack sorties being flown during the first 24 hours of the aerial assault. F-117A "stealth" attack aircraft had passed over the targeted Iraqi radar sites.

The first weapons to strike major targets in Iraqi are US Navy ship-launched Tomahawk cruise missiles. Nine US Navy warships, led by the Aegis cruiser *Bunker Hill* (CG 52), began to launch Tomahawk land-attack missiles against Iraqi installations from positions in the Red Sea and Persian Gulf at 0130—90 minutes before striking their targets in Baghdad. (US Navy surface ships and submarines will fire 288 land-attack variants of the Tomahawk during Operation Desert Storm; of those, 106 are launched during the first 24 hours of the air war. Battleships, cruisers, and destroyers fire 276 of the missiles; submarines fire 12.) Tomahawks and F-117A "stealth" aircraft will be the only US weapons to strike targets in the Iraqi capital of Baghdad, the F-117As at night and the Tomahawks both day and night.

The first air-to-air kills of the Gulf War occur when US Navy F/A-18C Hornet strike-fighters from the carrier *Saratoga* shoot down a pair of Iraqi MiG-21 fighters using Sidewinder and Sparrow missiles. The F/A-18s are carrying bombs on a strike mission when radar surveillance aircraft vector them to the intercept; after downing the MiG-21s they continue their bombing mission.

(During the Gulf War USAF F-15 Eagle fighters will destroy 36 Iraqi fixed-wing aircraft and helicopters; one Iraqi aircraft will be forced to crash by a USAF EF-111A electronics aircraft; two Iraqi aircraft will be shot down by USN F/A-18C aircraft; one by a Navy F-14A Tomcat fighter; two Iraqi aircraft will be shot down by a single Saudi F-15C fighter; and two USAF A-10 Thunderbolt ground-attack aircraft shoot down two Iraqi helicopters. US aircraft combat losses will total 32 and other coalition countries nine during the war.)

The first Iraqi ballistic missiles fired during the war—al-Hussien (modified Soviet Scud-B)—missiles fall on Tel Aviv, Israeli, shortly after 0200, and a short time later in Saudi Arabia.

At the time the air offensive begins, the United States has 425,000 troops and aviation personnel in the Gulf area; the 28 other countries in the allied coalition bring the number to almost 700,000.

19 JAN

The US submarine *Louisville* (SSN 724), operating submerged in the Red Sea, launches the first of eight Tomahawk missiles she will fire against targets in Iraq. This is the first combat missile launch in history by a submarine. Subsequently, the submarine *Pittsburgh* (SSN 720) fires four Tomahawks from a position in the eastern Mediterranean.

21 JAN

The US carrier *Theodore Roosevelt* enters the Persian Gulf, bringing the number of carriers in the Gulf to three and the number in the Red Sea to three.

The carrier *Tbilisi* is commissioned into the Soviet Navy. Displacing 67,500 tons full load, the 1,000-foot (305-m) warship is the first full-deck carrier and the largest warship ever built in the Soviet Union. She can operate some 50 fixed-wing aircraft and helicopters. (The carrier will later be renamed *Admiral Flota Sovetskogo Soyuza Kuznetsov*; a sister ship, the unfinished *Riga*, later renamed *Varyag*, will be scrapped before completion.)

29 JAN

US Marines of the 13th Marine Expeditionary Unit (MEU) land by helicopter from the carrier *Okinawa* (LPH 3) and occupy the small Iraqi island of Umm al Maradim, 12 n.miles (22.2 km) off the Kuwaiti coast. The island had been recently abandoned by Iraqi troops.

31 JAN

In a late-night operation, Iraqi tanks roll into Khafji, six miles (9.6 km) within Saudi Arabia. The few US Marines in the town evade the Iraqis for 36 hours, some hiding in buildings occupied by Iraqi troops. In a violent fire fight including USAF AC-130 Spector gunships and Army AH-1 Cobra gunship helicopters support US, Saudi, and Qatari troops as they expel the invaders in a violent, 12-hour fire fight. Some 50 Saudis are killed as are 11 Marines, the first US combat deaths on the ground.

7 FEB

The US aircraft carrier *America* enters the Persian Gulf, bringing the number of carriers in the Gulf to four and the number in the Red Sea to two as the air campaign against Iraq continues.

18 FEB

The US Aegis missile cruiser *Princeton* (CG 59) and the helicopter carrier *Tripoli* (LPH 10) both strike mines in the Persian Gulf. The ships suffer minor damage with minor personnel injuries; there are no fatalities. The *Princeton*'s damage requires her to be towed to port, although at no time is the ship in danger of sinking and most of her combat systems remains operational. Repairs are made during a seven-week "availability" at Dubai in the United Arab Emirates followed by a two-month yard period in the United States. The *Tripoli*, operating minesweeping helicopters when mined, is repaired in a drydock in Bahrain, requiring one month to repair the damage.

22 FEB
President Bush denounces Saddam Hussein's "scorched-earth" policy against Kuwait and gives him an ultimatum: Get out of Kuwait, unconditionally, by Saturday noon, 23 Feb.

Late in the night two US Marine task forces cross the Saudi border into Kuwait to prepare paths through layered Iraqi defensive obstacle belts and minefields. Iraqi forces counterattack, but are defeated by the Marines, who retain positions up to 12½ miles (20 km) inside Kuwait.

24 FEB
The coalition ground offensive begins in the Persian Gulf at 0400. With intensive air and naval support, US and other coalition forces cross into Kuwait and Iraq in four major thrusts along a 250-mile (402-km) front stretching westward from the coast of the Persian Gulf.

By evening the coalition commander, Gen. Norman Schwartzkopf, USA, states that coalition casualties are "remarkably light" and more than 5,500 Iraqi prisoners had been taken. (The report of Iraqi prisoners was increased to almost 10,000 before Schwartzkopf's briefing was completed.)

25 FEB
A Silkworm surface-to-surface missile is fired from Iraqi territory toward the US battleship *Missouri*, operating offshore. A US Navy electronic surveillance aircraft detects the missile and provides warning to nearby naval forces. The British destroyer *Gloucester*, riding "shotgun" for the *Missouri*, fires two Sea Dart interceptor missiles that destroy the incoming missile. A second Silkworm is fired upon but falls into the sea. US naval aircraft attack the missile launching site.

An Iraqi Scud-type missile strikes a barracks in Dahahran, Saudi Ababia, killing 28 US soldiers and wounding almost 100 more. (US intelligence esti-

mates that the Iraqis fired 88 ballistic missiles during the conflict—42 toward Israel and 46 at Saudi Arabia and other Persian Gulf states.)

In his congressional testimony, Chief of Naval Operations Adm. Frank B. Kelso II announces that the Navy is launching a search for a less-expensive attack submarine to succeed the *Seawolf* (SSN 21) design. This successor submarine will initially be labeled Centurion and, subsequently, New Attack Submarine (NSSN).

27 FEB
By the end of the day US Marines and Arab forces have liberated Kuwait's airport and control the access routes to Kuwait City. US and Arab special forces enter the city and occupy the US Embassy building.

A Pioneer drone reconnaissance aircraft from a US battleship sights two small boats fleeing Faylaka Island off Kuwait City. US Navy attack planes destroy the craft, believed to be carrying Iraqi secret police. Subsequently the battleship *Missouri* bombards the island and hundreds of Iraqi soldiers on the island surrender to a Pioneer drone circling overhead.

In Washington, President Bush announces that effective "at midnight tonight, Eastern Standard Time, exactly 100 hours since ground operations commenced and six weeks since the start of Desert Storm, all US and coalition forces will suspend offensive combat operations. It is up to Iraq whether this suspension on the part of the coalition becomes a permanent cease-fire." (The suspension takes effect 0800 on 28 Feb in the Persian Gulf.)

6 MAY
The last US nuclear weapon to be eliminated under the Intermediate-range Nuclear Forces (INF) treaty, a Pershing II missile at Longhorn, Italy, is dismantled.

4 JULY
The guided missile destroyer *Arleigh Burke* (DDG 51) is commissioned, the second US Navy warship class fitted with the Aegis radar/weapons control system. While having a potent anti-air and anti-ship/land-attack Tomahawk weapons capability, the lack of a helicopter capability limits the ship's anti-submarine effectiveness. The *Burke*'s first CO is Comdr. John G. Morgan, Jr., USN.

18 AUG
At the vacation dacha of Soviet President Mikhail S. Gorbachev at Foros in the Crimea, on the Black Sea,

the Soviet leader is placed under house arrest by the KGB as a coup begins, led by Vice President Gennady Yanayev and other hard-liners. All communications between dacha and outside are cut.

At 2350 Vladimir Kryuchkov, head of the KGB, convenes a meeting of coup conspirators in the Kremlin to announce a state of emergency to the Soviet people.

19 AUG

Soviet Vice President Yanayev takes over the duties of president because of President Gorbachev's "inability" to perform his duties because of illness.

The leadership of the Russian Federation Supreme Soviet (parliament) meets and, under the leadership of Boris Yeltsin, adopts a statement of demands that include the release of Gorbachev.

Soviet troops and tanks are seen on Moscow streets and take up positions near the Parliament Building (White House) and, subsequently, clear Red Square. Armed citizens take up positions around the White House to defend members of parliament from supporters of the coup.

20 AUG

Massive demonstrations in Leningrad and other Soviet cities express opposition to the coup leaders and, in some instances, support for Yeltsin. Soviet tanks and troops move to within a mile of the White House, which is surrounded by a crowd of about 150,000, ostensibly against the coup leaders. Acting President Yanayev promises Yeltsin that troops will not attack the White House. However, many coup leaders, including Kryuchkov of the KGB, urge an attack on the Parliament Building but later decided against such action.

21 AUG

At about 0100 three civilians are killed when violence erupts between protesters and troops in Moscow.

Minister of Defense Marshal of the Soviet Union Dmitri T. Yazov meets with the Defense Board, which votes in favor of withdrawing all military troops from Moscow. The withdrawal begins at 1100.

Several coup leaders fly to the Crimea to meet with Gorbachev. Upon arrival at the dacha the plotters are placed under arrest by Gorbachev's bodyguards after which communications are restored to the dacha. Gorbachev then makes a telephone call to President Bush, stating that he is again in control as president of the Soviet Union. Subsequently, at 2350,

Gorbachev and his family depart the Belbek Airport in the Crimea on a flight back to Moscow. They will arrive in Moscow at 0215 on 22 Aug.

23 AUG

Yeltsin signs a decree suspending all activities of the Communist Party in the Soviet Union. Gorbachev dismisses acting Minister of Defense Mikhail Moiseyev as well as his foreign minister, and calls on the rest of the government to resign for failing to actively oppose the coup.

Col. Gen. of Aviation Yevgeni I. Shaposhnikov, who had become Commander in Chief of the Soviet Air Forces in 1990, is appointed Minister of Defense. He had strongly opposed the coup. A former fighter pilot with extensive service as a political worker, he is the first Air Forces officer to be appointed to the senior Soviet military post. He is promoted to the rank of Marshal of Aviation upon being named Minister of Defense. (He will serve as minister until May 1992.)

Marshal of the SU Sergei F. Akhromeyev commits suicide by hanging. He was appointed military advisor to President Gorbachev in early 1989 after having served as Chief of the General Staff and Deputy Minister of Defense from 1984–1989. (He was not implicated in the coup.)

24 AUG

President Gorbachev resigns as General Secretary of the Communist Party of the USSR and turns all property of the Communist Party over to the government. This is effectively the end of the 74-year reign of the Communist Party, which began in Oct 1917.

28 AUG

The Soviet prosecutor's office charges 13 with leading the abortive coup, including former Minister of Defense Yazov and Deputy Minister Valentine Varennikov. Another official will be charged on 5 Sep 1991.

29 AUG

The Soviet parliament votes to suspend all activities of the Communist Party.

2 SEP

The Soviet Congress of Peoples Deputies votes to dissolve the Soviet Union with President Gorbachev declaring that the nation is "on the brink of catastrophe."

8 SEP

The battleship *New Jersey* (BB 62) is decommissioned, having been in active service for almost nine years as part of the Reagan-Lehman naval buildup initiated in Jan 1981. Her sister ship *Wisconsin* will be decommissioned on 30 Sep, having served less than three years in active service. Only the *Missouri* will remain in commission, albeit briefly.

11 SEP

The US aircraft carrier *Independence* (CV 62) arrives at her new home port of Yokosuka, Japan. She replaces the *Midway* (CV 41) as the only US carrier based overseas; the *Midway* had been based in Japan since 1973. Carrier Air Wing 5 shifted from the *Midway* to the "Indy" at Pearl Harbor in Aug 1991.

President Gorbachev announces that the Soviet Union will negotiate with Cuba over the withdrawal of Soviet military forces that have been on the island since 1962.

27 SEP

President Bush announces a "sweeping package" of nuclear arms reduction. His proposals will bring about the most fundamental changes in nuclear weapons strategy, tactics, and inventory since nuclear weapons were first introduced in the US arsenal. Bush calls on the Soviet Union to do likewise.

6 OCT

Meeting in Cracow, Poland, the foreign ministers of Czechoslovakia, Hungary, and Poland state the wish for their countries to be associated with NATO.

President Gorbachev announces the abolition of Soviet short-range nuclear weapons and the removal of all tactical nuclear weapons from Soviet warships.

8 NOV

The last of the 24 World War II–built *Essex* (CV 9)–class aircraft carriers, the USS *Lexington* (AVT 16), is decommissioned. (Her official decommission date is 26 Nov 1991). Completed in 1943 as the CV 16, the "Lex" saw extensive combat in World War II; she served as a training carrier from 1963 to 1990. The last fully operational *Essex*-class carrier was the *Oriskany* (CV 34), which was decommissioned in 1976.

7 DEC

President Bush participates in memorial services at Pearl Harbor to mark the 50th anniversary of the Japanese surprise attack, including ceremonies on the battleship *Missouri*. The *Missouri* was the site of the Japanese surrender in Tokyo Bay on 2 Sep 1945, ending World War II.

21 DEC

The battleship *Missouri* steams into the Long Beach Naval Shipyard, Calif., for deactivation. She will be decommissioned there in 1992 (*see* Postscript).

25 DEC

President Gorbachev announces that he will shortly resign as head of the Soviet Union.

27 DEC

The Russian parliament votes to change the republic to the Russian Federation or simply "Russia." At 1935 the Soviet flag is lowered from the Kremlin and ten minutes later the white, blue, and red flag of Russia is raised in its place.

President Gorbachev turns over the control codes for Soviet nuclear weapons to officials of the Russian Federation, headed by Yeltsin.

30 DEC

President Gorbachev, with the presidents of Belarus and Ukraine, declare the Soviet Union to be extinct, being succeeded by several of the former Soviet republics joining the Commonwealth of Independent States (CIS). The leaders agree on a permanent unified command to control nuclear weapons of the CIS. Gorbachev then resigns.

The COLD WAR is over!

POSTSCRIPT

The world and the world's navies changed rapidly with the end of the Cold War. Significantly, a few remnants of World War II remained in the US Navy at the end of 1991—two warships, the battleship *Missouri* (BB 63) and the aircraft carrier *Midway* (CV 41), representative of the two largest US warship designs of World War II.

The *Missouri* steamed into the Long Beach Naval Shipyard, Calif., in Dec 1991 for deactivation. She was decommissioned there on 31 Mar 1992, and towed to the Bremerton Naval Shipyard, Wash. The *Missouri*, first commissioned in 1944, had been mothballed from 1955 to 1986. The *Missouri* and her three sister ships of the *Iowa* (BB 61) class were stricken from the Naval Vessel Register on 12 Jan 1994, ending the battleship as a ship type in the US Navy. The "Mighty Mo" will be retained as a memorial, at Pearl Harbor. However, the high cost of maintaining such ships as memorials/museums makes it unlikely that her sister ships *Iowa* (BB 61), *New Jersey* (BB 62), or *Wisconsin* (BB 64) can be preserved.

The *Midway* was decommissioned on 11 Apr 1992, at Naval Air Station North Island, in San Diego. The carrier had been in continuous service since she was commissioned in 1945 except for overhauls and modernizations—a 46-year career. The *Midway* remained on the Naval Vessel Register, in reserve for possible (albeit unlikely) future reactivation.

Of several auxiliary ships still in active US naval service when the Cold War ended, the oldest was the submarine tender *Proteus* (AS 19), first commissioned on 31 Jan 1944. She served in World War II and was later converted (and lengthened) to serve as the first tender for Polaris missile submarines. She was decommissioned on 30 Sep 1992 and stricken.

The post–Cold War US Navy will be smaller, much smaller than at any time since before the Korean War. In that period, 1945–1950, the US political leaders largely accepted the Air Force doctrine that manned strategic bombers, possibly carrying nuclear weapons, could be arbitrator of all future conflicts. The Navy's leadership fought this doctrine, both for parochial reasons as well as logic that a one-weapon strategy could lead to disaster as the United States would be hesitant to use the atomic bomb. The Korean War—and the Cold War—provided the validity of the Navy views.

The debates over force sizes, service roles and missions, and basic budget issues that dominate the defense debates in the last decade of the 20th century will undoubtedly result in a relatively small Navy. The lack of a major external threat to the United States coupled with the attitude that military forces must be "balanced" prevent objective decision-making about post–Cold War forces.

SOURCES

Multi-tier sources were used in compiling this chronology. The initial entries were derived largely by reviewing newspapers, especially *The New York Times, The Washington Post,* and *The Times* (London); the monthly magazine *Naval Aviation News;* and the Soviet military newspaper *Krasnye Zveda* (Red Star).

Subsequently, the authors reviewed existing naval chronologies, primarily the excellent *United States Naval Aviation,* published in several editions by the US Navy's aviation history office (now part of the Naval Historical Center); the US Air Force chronology *The Cold War and Beyond,* published by the Air Force History and Museum Program; *American Naval History,* published by the Naval Institute Press; and the chronologies of naval events published from 1962 to 1969 in the annual *Naval Review,* also published by the United States Naval In-stitute, and subsequently in the Naval Review (May) issue of the United States Naval Institute *Proceedings.*

Key dates and technical data on US and Soviet ships are derived from various editions of *Jane's Fighting Ships, The Ships and Aircraft of the U.S. Fleet, Guide to the Soviet Navy,* and *Combat Fleets of the World* (the latter books published by the Naval Institute Press).

Space dates are derived primarily from the outstanding *Space Log,* an annual publication of the TRW Space & Electronics Group.

Finally, a cross-check of key dates as well as names was made using the resources of the Naval Historical Center, especially the ships' histories managed by Mr. John C. Reilly, and the aviation files supervised by Messrs. Roy A. Grossnick and W. Todd Baker.

SHIP INDEX

PERSONALITY INDEX

ABOUT THE AUTHORS

Norman Polmar, an internationally known defense analyst and writer, is the author of more than 30 books on naval, aviation, and intelligence subjects, including the U.S. Naval Institute's reference books *Ships and Aircraft of the U.S. Fleet* and *Guide to the Soviet Navy*. He also writes a regular column for the Naval Institute's monthly magazine, *Proceedings*.

Mr. Polmar's interest in the education field includes serving on the advisory committee of the Elliott School of International Affairs of the George Washington University in Washington, D.C.

He is a graduate of American University in the nation's capital.

Eric Wertheim is a defense consultant and author who specializes in naval issues. He currently serves as a senior researcher and consultant to several best-selling authors. Previously, he held positions with the U.S. Naval Institute and with Jane's Information Group.

His column about historic U.S. ships, "Lest We Forget," has appeared in *Proceedings* magazine since 1994, and he was coauthor, with Messrs. Polmar and Mark Warren, of *Dictionary of Military Abbreviations* (Naval Institute Press, 1994).

Mr. Wertheim is a graduate of the American University.

Andrew Bahjat, a naval analyst, is currently the senior technical writer and a consultant for Johnston McLamb CASE Solutions, Inc., and a consultant to the director Air Warfare. His articles on aviation subjects have been published in the U.S. Naval Institute *Proceedings, Wings of Gold,* and *Navy Times*. He has also contributed to the Naval Institute Press's *Ships and Aircraft of the U.S. Fleet* and *Bluejackets' Manual*.

From 1993 to 1996 he was consultant to the director of Aircraft Carrier Programs, and Mr. Bahjat has done research and writing for the Naval Sea Systems Command's Aegis program office and surface ship hardening program.

Bruce Watson, a businessman, previously performed research for several of the military books authored by one or both of his late parents, Bruce and Susan Watson. Like Messrs. Wertheim and Bahjat, he also served as a summer intern at the U.S. Naval Institute.

He is a graduate of Virginia Tech in Blacksburg.